SAMS
Teach Yourself

Computer Basics

Jill T. Freeze

in 24 Hours

THIRD EDITION

SAMS   *201 West 103rd St., Indianapolis, Indiana, 46290 USA*

Sams Teach Yourself Computer Basics in 24 Hours

Copyright © 2002 by Sams Publishing

International Standard Book Number: 0-672-32301-X

Library of Congress Catalog Card Number: 2001094225

Printed in the United States of America

First Printing: October 2001

04   03   02   6   5   4

Trademarks

All terms mentioned in this book that are known to be trademarks or service marks have been appropriately capitalized. Sams Publishing cannot attest to the accuracy of this information. Use of a term in this book should not be regarded as affecting the validity of any trademark or service mark.

Warning and Disclaimer

Every effort has been made to make this book as complete and as accurate as possible, but no warranty or fitness is implied. The information provided is on an "as is" basis. The author and the publisher shall have neither liability nor responsibility to any person or entity with respect to any loss or damages arising from the information contained in this book.

ACQUISITIONS EDITOR
Betsy Brown

DEVELOPMENT EDITOR
Heather Goodell

MANAGING EDITOR
Charlotte Clapp

BOOK PACKAGER
Justak Literary Services

COPY EDITOR
Mamata N. Reddy

INDEXER
Johnna Dinse

PROOFREADER
Lara SerVaas

TECHNICAL EDITOR
Bob Temple

INTERIOR DESIGNER
Gary Adair

COVER DESIGNER
Alan Clements

PAGE LAYOUT
William J. Hartman

Contents at a Glance

Contents

HOUR 16 Sending and Receiving E-mail — **295**

About the Author

Jill T. Freeze is a freelance management consultant who has worked with such organizations as the John F. Kennedy Center for the Performing Arts, the National Endowment for the Arts, The Smithsonian Institute, and the White House. Having used computers extensively for more than a decade for work and play, Jill finally decided to put her experience to good use writing computer books. She has written 10 well-received titles that have garnered rave reviews from readers and reviewers worldwide, and have been translated into a number of languages. Recent books include *Sams Teach Yourself Computer Basics in 24 Hours, Third Edition* (Sams, 2001), *Microsoft MapPoint 2002 for Dummies* (Hungry Minds, 2001), *Savvy Online Shopping* (Microsoft Press, 2000), and *Peter Norton's Complete Guide to Microsoft Office 2000* (Sams, 1999). You'll also find her articles in *MS OfficePRO* magazine.

In addition, Jill is a top-rated beta tester for Microsoft, having won awards for her active participation in Internet Explorer, Office, MapPoint, and Windows beta programs.

Her formal education includes a bachelor's degree magna cum laude from the University of Massachusetts at Amherst (in Arts Administration and Writing) and a master's degree from George Washington University (in Nonprofit Administration).

For fun, Jill likes listening to music, playing with her four cats and Golden Retriever, writing fiction, quilting, reading a variety of fiction titles, volunteering at her children's school, watching NASCAR races, surfing the Net, playing her flute, and playing with her husband, Wayne (also a computer book author and columnist), and two children, Christopher and Samantha.

Jill can be reached at JFreeze@JustPC.com, or you can visit her on the Web at www.JustPC.com.

Dedication

Acknowledgments

Writing a computer book can be a real challenge, especially when you're putting it together while the software is still being tested! Of course, that's the only way a book can be in your hands the same day new software is released....

This type of book requires a special team of editors—a group of people who are speedy on their feet (and in their minds), who have a good eye for catching subtle changes in screen shots, and who are masters at putting words together into clear, understandable prose. The intense production schedule also requires a number of skilled people who massage the screenshots, and format and index the book. I've been fortunate to have worked with such a team on this project.

It started with Sams' acquisition editor Betsy Brown, who decided it was time to do a third edition of Computer Basics, and my agent, Laura Belt, who put the deal together. From there, the project extended to include the following professionals: Heather Goodell, Bob Temple, and Marta Justak. As time went on, the list kept growing to include Mamata Reddy, Bill Hartman, Lara SerVaas, Johnna Dinse, and anyone else who I may have forgotten. You are all very much appreciated!

Putting a book together quickly also takes its toll on the author's family. My husband, Wayne, held everything together when he should have been finishing up his own books. And my kids, Christopher James and Samantha Ashley, didn't see a whole lot of Mommy this summer. I am so fortunate to be surrounded by such loving, understanding, and supportive family members. I love you guys a whole bunch!

Tell Us What You Think!

As the reader of this book, *you* are our most important critic and commentator. We value your opinion and want to know what we're doing right, what we could do better, what areas you'd like to see us publish in, and any other words of wisdom you're willing to pass our way.

You can fax, email, or write me directly to let me know what you did or didn't like about this book—as well as what we can do to make our books stronger.

Please note that I cannot help you with technical problems related to the topic of this book, and that due to the high volume of mail I receive, I might not be able to reply to every message.

When you write, please be sure to include this book's title and author as well as your name and phone or fax number. I will carefully review your comments and share them with the author and editors who worked on the book.

Fax: 317-581-4770
Email: consumer@samspublishing.com
Mail: Mark Taber
         Sams Publishing
         201 West 103rd Street
         Indianapolis, IN 46290 USA

Introduction

Welcome to *Sams Teach Yourself Computer Basics, Third Edition*!

If someone asked you to guess how many PCs one of the leading manufacturers ships each year, what would you guess? A hundred thousand? A million? Believe it or not, the answer is really between five and ten million. I can't divulge who told me that (they would have to kill me if I did), but it's the truth, and that's just one PC manufacturer!

Each year, millions of people like you join the ranks of new PC users. Why? Maybe it's the desire to get online, or perhaps it was the irresistible offer of a $99 PC with a three-year Internet service contract. No matter the case, you are bound to want some guidance on this grand adventure, so this book is here to give you just that—friendly guidance pure and simple.

If you are feeling a bit uneasy about jumping into the world of computers, just remember that you are not alone. In fact, I was terrified of computers when I first started working with them. I was convinced that one wrong keystroke would bring the world of computing to a grinding halt. Not so. As you will see throughout this book, there is very little you can do to your PC that can't be fixed, as long as you don't panic and you know how to respond. I may not be able to calm you in the midst of crisis, but I can see to it that you are armed with everything you need to recover from potential mishaps.

We (meaning the team of editors at Sams and I) have put a lot of time and energy into this revision of the book. We wanted it to cover everything the new user would ever want or need to know. But as we developed the table of contents and read through the vast numbers of e-mails we received about previous editions of the book, one thing stood out: new computer users may still be intimidated by these brainy machines, but they no longer want to know how everything works in excruciating detail. Instead, they want to know how to do cool things with this new purchase. There is a big difference between the two!

In response to that, we have replaced long, meandering passages about how each piece of your PC works with things like how to make the most of digital photography with your digital camera or scanner, burn your own music

CDs containing a mix of your favorite tunes, chat with friends or family in real time using an instant messaging tool, optimize Windows to run your favorite computer games as smoothly as possible, build a Web page, safely shop online, make your own music videos, and other fun and useful things like these.

We sprinkled relevant bits about hardware throughout the book too, so that you will know everything you need to know to make your PC run well, without being bored to tears with rambling lectures about the nuts and bolts you could probably care less about. With so much neat stuff out there, it was tough melting it down to 24 lessons. We did our best to give you a practical but fun book, and I think we get closer and closer with each revision.

If we have fallen short of giving you the best all-in-one book we can, please e-mail us with your suggestions and ideas at JFreeze@JustPC.com. Your thoughts and opinions do count; however, please keep in mind that we have a broad audience to consider.

Likewise, if you found this book useful, please drop us a line at the same e-mail address and let us know that, too. Your kind words will help fuel us through the all-nighters it takes to create a book like this.

Now back to business....

Who Should Read This Book?

This book was written with the new computer user in mind. If you can answer *yes* to any of the following, then *Sams Teach Yourself Computer Basics in 24 Hours, Third Edition* is for you!

- Did you just acquire a PC and are wondering how to use it?
- Are you contemplating buying a computer but are afraid it may be too hard to learn how to use?
- Have you spent some time surfing on WebTV and now find yourself ready to make the jump to a PC?
- Are you looking for a single volume that covers hardware, software, and the Internet?

How This Book Is Organized

Inside the front cover of this book, you will find a tear card with spaces for you to fill out information about your computer. Fill in as much of it as you can right now (you will learn how to complete the remaining blanks throughout the book). This information will come in handy if you need to call the technical support of your PCs manufacturer for help.

This book is organized into four parts that lead you smoothly and logically through the PC learning process.

- **Part I: PC Basics.** When you set up your PC and turn it on, you are looking at the Windows desktop. Your journey begins by getting acquainted with the "brain" of your PC so that you can tell *it* what to do, rather than the reverse! A working knowledge of Windows will also help you install and configure a printer and those cool computer toys discussed in Part IV.

- **Part II: Making Things Happen with Software.** Learn about the many types of software available to you and unleash the power of Microsoft Word 2002 and Excel 2002 to get organized and to create professional-looking documents.

- **Part III: Logging onto the Internet.** Get the scoop on setting up your Internet connection, finding Web sites, sending e-mail, shopping online, participating in newsgroups, building your own Web page, and other fun activities on the Internet. You will even learn how to download shareware and free Clip Art and then install it on your computer!

- **Part IV: "The Multimedia PC."** Discover how to upgrade parts of your computer, watch DVDs and listen to music on your PC, manage electronic photographs, and create music videos. You will learn all sorts of tips and tricks designed to bring sights and sounds to your computer.

Finally, I added three appendixes for your convenience. Appendix A, Optimizing Game Performance, is devoted to optimizing Windows XP for computer game performance. (Believe me, it's a bit trickier than it sounds!) Appendix B, So You Want to Purchase a Computer..., is written especially for those of you who have yet to purchase your computer. I present a list of things to think about before you make the big purchase. Finally, Appendix C, Getting Your New Computer Ready for Action, offers valuable tips for unpacking and setting up your new PC.

About the Sams Teach Yourself in 24 Hours Series

Each Sams Teach Yourself in 24 Hours title is divided into 24 one-hour lessons designed to explore a specific topic in detail. At the beginning of the hour, you will see a bulleted list of items covered in that lesson. Then, throughout the hour, you will be guided through the steps needed to accomplish the goals set forth at the beginning of the hour. A smattering of tips, tricks, and new term definitions inject further depth into the topic at hand.

At the end of each hour, we help you put your newfound knowledge to the test. You will take a multiple-choice quiz to test what you have learned. Don't feel pressured; the quizzes are pretty easy, and in many cases, they have significant entertainment value too! A recommended activity follows, and although it is not a major project by any stretch, it does require you to start up your computer and go through the steps outlined in the hour. There is no better way to learn than by actually doing.

A Friendly Warning...

If you have read any of my books in the past, then you are fully prepared for what follows; but for those who haven't, you should be forewarned about my quirky sense of humor.

Learning needn't be stuffy and boring. In fact, literally hundreds of readers have e-mailed me, expressing their appreciation for my lighthearted style. One woman even went so far as to say after reading one of my books, she felt like she had known me for years! (What can I say, humor is my favorite coping strategy. As Simba in Disney's *The Lion King* said, "I laugh in the face of danger!") I know that learning something new can be stressful enough without having to wade through page after page of pompous candor.

Lighten up and have fun getting to know your new computer! After you get up and running on the Internet, visit my Web site at http://www.JustPC.com and say "hi!"

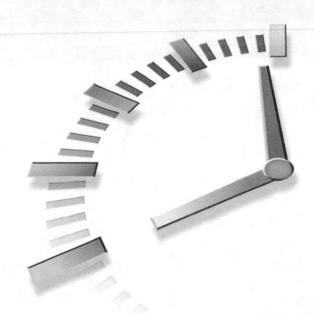

PART I
PC Basics

Hour

HOUR 1

Beyond the On Switch...

This is the moment you've been waiting for. You've lugged the boxes into your home or office and have managed to piece together all the cables, cords, and system components. At last, it's time to start playing with your new toy.

Go ahead—flip the switch, press the button, or do whatever your computer's manufacturer tells you to do to get the thing up and running.

Are you ready to move on? Great! We have a lot of territory to cover. In this first hour alone you'll learn the following:

- Unlock the universe of personal computing with the Start button.
- Become comfortable with your pointing device.
- Learn about the shortcuts that reside on your desktop.
- Discover how the taskbar works as well as what it does.

Did you hear that? That sound was Windows revving into action. If you bought your computer in late October 2001 or later, the tones you heard were most likely those of Microsoft Windows XP, Home Edition (the operating system we'll focus on in this book).

But whether you're using Windows XP, Windows ME, or even Windows 98, you'll notice some striking similarities between what's discussed on these pages and what you'll see when you stare into your monitor.

What in the World Is an Operating System?

Now that you've joined the ranks of proud computer owners everywhere, you'll need to adjust your definition of windows. Rather than being a mere clear pane of glass that separates you from rain, snow, bitter cold, and sweltering heat, it also now is Windows with a capital *W*.

Even if you're entering the world of computers for the first time, you've undoubtedly heard about Microsoft Windows on the news. It's that revolutionary, controversial operating system that caused such a stir over its inclusion of the Microsoft Internet Explorer web browser. Court battles went on for ages until eventually Microsoft allowed computer manufacturers like Gateway and Dell to remove Internet Explorer or include non-Microsoft software.

Whoa, back up a minute! Operating system? Web browser? Okay, first things first. We all know how air traffic controllers monitor airport comings and goings to make sure everything runs smoothly, right? Well that's basically what an operating system does on your computer. It tells various pieces of software what to do when. I often refer to it as the brain of the PC because it has to do all the thinking. Windows helps your PC prioritize its workload in much the same way corporate managers need to prioritize and re-prioritize depending on the projects or crises at hand.

A PC without an operating system is like a flashlight without batteries—pretty much useless. Given that, the operating system is the first piece of software to get installed on your machine. In virtually every case, the operating system is preinstalled on your new computer so that when you hook up the machine and turn it on for the first time, you'll be greeted by what's known as the Windows desktop (see Figure 1.1).

Uh, that's not what I want when I boot MY PC! Microsoft ships Windows XP Home Edition with the Bliss background seen in Figure 1.1. The manufacturer of your PC, however, may opt to customize it. For example Gateway might put cow spots all over the screen. You may also see a lot more icons on the desktop as a result of software pre-installed on your new machine.

FIGURE 1.1

The new, modernized look of the Windows XP Home Edition Desktop is the first thing you'll see once your computer finishes booting.

Once an operating system has been successfully installed however, you can do all sorts of neat things with your new investment. You can install a word processor to generate a professional-looking resume. You can get a spreadsheet application and perform all kinds of complex calculations. You can play the hottest computer games. And with Windows XP, you can effortlessly publish family photos to the Web, "burn" a music CD containing all your favorite tunes, and even create a funky music video. And these ideas only scratch the surface of what you can do with your PC!

So What's Behind the Name "Windows"?

Windows is much more than just a product name. In fact, it represents a whole new way of computing (that is, it's "new" when you compare it to how things were done in the early years of personal computing). Way back in the old days of personal computing, machines were run by an operating system called *DOS*. With DOS, you could do only one thing at a time. If you were writing a letter and needed to reference a specific number in a spreadsheet, for example, you would have to shut down the word processing program, open the spreadsheet application to get the information you needed, shut down the spreadsheet program, and finally reopen the word processor to continue drafting your letter—a major hassle to say the least.

After much research and development time (and a whole lotta cash), the folks at Microsoft came up with an operating system that let users do two things at once (known as *multitasking*). That operating system was known as *Microsoft Windows* because it literally created a separate window for each application or task you had running. That enabled you to easily hop from your word processor to the spreadsheet and back again with a few simple mouse clicks—a major improvement over the cumbersome, text-based DOS.

Windows offered other advantages besides multitasking, however. At the time Windows was created, Macintosh computers were reputedly the most user-friendly because they relied heavily on graphics rather than esoteric keyboard commands in order to complete various tasks. For example, to print a document, you would click on a picture of a printer rather than typing in the Print command, pressing Ctrl P, etc. With Windows, you can still use those shortcuts, but new users also have a more foolproof method of learning how to use their PCs—pictures (also known as *icons*). You know what they say about pictures being worth a thousand words….

Those gooey graphics… When a program depends on the user clicking icons in order to run, the collection of graphics and resulting commands are referred to as a graphical user interface (or GUI, as in "My daughter Samantha just loves chewy, gooey brownies, fresh from the oven.") This is far from being a must-know term, but boy would it make impressive cocktail chatter the next time you're hanging out with your more nerdy acquaintances!

Microsoft tried to emulate Mac's ease of use in Windows. It took a few revisions of the software to produce a viable product (and some will argue that Windows is still far from being stable), but it has evolved and improved over time to become the operating system you have on your computer today: Windows XP, Home Edition.

Trivia buffs, might be interested to know… The incredible popularity of game shows like *Who Wants to be a Millionaire?* and *Weakest Link* proves that people love trivia. I can't guarantee knowing this stuff will win you a million bucks, but you never know!

Here is a brief rundown of critical Microsoft Windows release dates: Windows 1.0 on November 20, 1985; Windows 3.1 on April 6, 1992; Windows 95 on August 24, 1995; Windows 98 on June 25, 1998; Windows 98, Second Edition on May 5, 1999; Windows Millennium Edition on September 14, 2000; and finally Windows XP, Home Edition on October 25, 2001. Of course, there were many other incremental release dates; however, these are the most relevant to home PC users.

How Can I Tell If I Have Windows XP?

Many of the leading computer manufacturers, such as Gateway, Dell, and so on, started shipping their systems with Windows XP, Home Edition in late October, 2001. The same goes for machines sold in stores across the country.

If the version of Windows you have isn't clearly identified in the printed documentation included with your computer, then turn on your machine and watch it boot (start up).

When Windows is ready to launch, you'll see the logo for the operating system you have installed on your machine. If you miss it in passing, the default grassland wallpaper (which is actually referred to as Bliss in some more advanced Windows options) and bright green Start button in the lower-left corner of the screen is a dead giveaway that you're running Microsoft Windows XP, Home Edition.

Even if you don't have the latest and greatest release, you'll still be able to learn a great deal from this book. In fact, the differences between various versions of Windows are minimal in many ways with the exception of a few new bells and whistles, which I'll share in a few minutes. (I'll even show you how to make your Windows XP machine look like a Windows 98 machine in the next hour.)

And these differences typically appear in subtle things, such as in changes in the graphics as opposed to more radical variations of how tasks are done. After you've spent some time behind the keyboard with Windows XP, everything you may have learned or experienced in an earlier version of Windows will come rushing back to you. And if it doesn't, don't sweat it; you've got me here to help you!

The New and Improved Windows XP

Okay, so what's the big deal about Windows XP anyway? Actually there's a lot to cheer about if you're among those who own Windows XP. Here's just a sampling of how your operating system differs from others (we'll dive into the details of some of these features in the hours to come):

- **Easy PC sharing**—If you like your icons big, and your spouse likes them small, you're both in luck! Windows XP lets you save your personal preferences into separate accounts that you can now move to and from with ease.

- **New Task-Focused design**—Rather than presenting users with an often esoteric assortment of words and phrases from which to choose an option, Windows now "asks" you what you'd like to do based on your current activity on the machine. For example, opening the My Documents folder from the Start menu will present you with the following possibilities: Make a new folder, and Publish this folder to the Web. It may not sound like much now, but compared with the old maze of menus, it is truly a big deal.

- **See it to believe it**—When browsing your folders full of documents, Windows XP will show you a thumbnail picture of the selected document. That way you can verify you have the material you want before you launch the necessary program and open the wrong file.

- **Photo-friendly**—Connecting a digital camera to your PC is easier than even with Windows XP, and once the photos are on your hard drive, you can effortlessly create a slide show, print them, publish them to the Web, e-mail them to a friend, or even order professional quality prints from one of Microsoft's Internet partners.

- **Gamer's delight**—With XP's new Compatibility Mode, running those "oldie but goodie" computer games is a snap. No more fretting over whether your favorite game will run on the new operating system.

- **Get remote assistance**—Everywhere we go, my husband and I are forever getting coaxed into fixing people's computer woes. A casual get-together quickly turns into a disk reformatting, file backup, virus removal party! I have great news for those who don't have an in-house computer expert: it's called *Remote Assistance*. That's right, you can now e-mail your favorite computer nerd an invitation to come and fix your computer, and best of all, you don't even have to serve him or her coffee or a soda; that person can take control of your machine from another location entirely!

- **Makin' movies like a pro**—If you've ever fantasized about being the next Britney Spears, Madonna, Michael Jackson (or fill in the name of your favorite musical artist), then you're in for a treat. Microsoft has spruced up the movie-making tools introduced in Windows ME to bring you a simpler, more powerful moviemaker in Windows XP. It's easier than ever to send videos via e-mail, publish them to the Web, make music videos, and add special effects and voiceovers to your movies.

Some operating system version releases are little more than bug fixes, but Windows XP's major overhaul and facelift may very well sport enough funky new features to make upgrading worthwhile to current computer owners.

What's What on the Windows Desktop

As I mentioned earlier, after your computer finishes booting, you'll see a screen similar to the one shown back in Figure 1.1. This view is known as the Windows Desktop. In Figure 1.2, I'll show you what each of the desktop elements are, then I'll go on to tell you a bit more about each of them.

FIGURE 1.2
These are the crucial parts of the Windows Desktop.

Desktop ———

Start button ———

Task/Window button   Taskbar   Shortcut icon   Notification area

This desktop is meant to resemble your desk at work or in your den in that it keeps the most regularly used items close at hand. In the case of Windows, however, those items include shortcut icons and task buttons rather than pens, note paper, scissors, and tape.

Wait a minute, you said this was going to be easy! Throughout this lesson, I occasionally use terms that may be unfamiliar to you. Don't panic! I'm not assuming you know them; rather, I'm helping you feel at ease with the lingo without bombarding you with a plethora of boring definitions. The more time you spend on your computer, the more the technical terms will become second nature to you. When you think about it, many of the terms are pretty self-explanatory anyway.

The Windows Desktop: Just Another Pretty Face

Like your desktop at work, the Windows desktop is the surface you can actually see when the desktop is clean of application windows (in other words, the word processor, e-mail program, Web browser, and so on are all closed). Instead of wood grain Formica however, the Windows desktop is adorned with a colorful image of grassland that you can easily change, as you will learn in the next hour.

The sole purpose of the Windows desktop is to hold all those important program buttons and icons. Believe it or not, it can get just as cluttered as your desk if you're not careful!

Taking Shortcuts

The little pictures you see dotting your Windows desktop are called *icons*. Microsoft ships Windows with a lone Recycle Bin icon in the lower right corner of the screen, but chances are your PC manufacturer loaded your desktop with goodies when they pre-installed all that free software for you.

Each icon is a graphical representative of your word processing program, your Internet connection, or some other application. When you double-click an icon, the corresponding program (or document or Web site) launches.

Don't fret over how to double-click the icons properly; I'll bring you up to speed on working with your mouse in a moment.

You also should be aware that you could put your own shortcuts on the desktop. This gives you immediate access to the resources you use most. I'll show you how to create your own shortcuts in the next lesson.

Getting a Good Start in Computing

As you'll quickly discover, the Windows Start button is where it all begins. By clicking it, you open lists of everything on your computer. These lists are called menus because you can make a selection from the items presented to you. (Sorry, Windows XP cannot substitute onion rings for French fries.)

Try clicking the bright green Start button. If you've ever "done" Windows before, you'll notice a striking difference—the Start menu has become larger, more colorful, and customizable.

The menu appears in two columns. The white part on the left is where Windows displays your most frequently used applications. (I'll show you how to modify this number in our next lesson.) The blue part on the right is reserved for shortcuts to predefined Windows folders, the Control Panel, and the Search and Help tools.

Dealing with the Tasks at Hand

At the bottom of your screen is a narrow, bright blue band known as the taskbar. This is where you'll find a button for each application you have running (or, as is the case with Microsoft Word 2002 and Excel 2002, each document you have open). Simply click the desired button, and the corresponding item appears at the front of your display.

FIGURE 1.3
Windows XP, Home Edition keeps your most frequently used programs close at hand.

The Windows taskbar is without a doubt the simplest way to move from one task to another. And in Windows XP, it's become a lot less cluttered. In previous versions of Windows, there would be a task button for each Word document open. Now Word has a single button, which, when clicked, displays a list of all open Word documents from which you can choose (see Figure 1.4). You'll learn a lot more about using Word in lessons 8 and 9.

FIGURE 1.4
Consolidated taskbar buttons keep clutter under control.

Presenting the Windows Notification Area

As was illustrated back in Figure 1.2, the Notification Area is in the lower right corner of the Windows desktop. At bare minimum, it holds the system's clock and icons for MSN Messenger Service status as well as alerts for available Windows updates.

Other tools you may find there, depending on the software you have installed and the type of machine you're using, might include an icon to access your antivirus program;

your RealPlayer program that plays sounds and movies on the Web; and, in the case of laptops, an icon showing whether the computer is powered by electricity or its battery.

We'll revisit some of these tools in greater depth as you progress through the lessons in this book.

Making (Mouse) Tracks

Working with Windows requires using a mouse—that corded two-button thing that sits next to your keyboard (see Figure 1.5), or some other pointing device such as a touch pad or trackball.

FIGURE 1.5

This little rodent will help you get all your work done in a snap.

Of mice and men... Mice can be a flaky lot. Their parts can get clogged with dust and lint, making them more frustrating than useful. Likewise, trackballs can tired your wrists or fingers. To spare you the agony, I'd like to tell you about one of my favorite PC gadgets—an optical wheel mouse. This little bugger is awesome! It's comfortable on the hand; navigation by light eliminates the skipping and jumpiness commonly associated with standard mice; the wheel makes scrolling up and down Web pages and Word documents trivial; and the two side buttons act as Back and Forward buttons on your Web browser. With special software installed, you can do even more with these mice. I have Microsoft's Optical IntelliMouse, but other brands have since entered the market.

To make getting used to your mouse easier, I'll walk you through a fun and educational exercise that will help you get used to moving the pointer where you want it.

Enough of all the talk; let's take the book over to the PC and get started!

> **When a mouse isn't a mouse...** If you have a laptop, you may be using a touch pad instead of a mouse. Or maybe you tried a trackball at your friend's house and decided to use one of those rather than a mouse. In any case, you can still follow the steps below even if you're not working with a mouse. Rather than dragging the mouse in the direction indicated, touch pad users will move their index finger in the same direction across the touch pad. Likewise, trackball users will roll the little ball as indicated. No matter what type of pointing device you use, it's imperative that you grow comfortable with it.

Learning All the Moves

Perform the following steps to start getting acquainted with your pointing device of choice:

1. If you've not already done so, turn on your computer.

2. After you see a screen similar to the one shown back in Figure 1.1, jiggle your mouse around to help you find the pointer. You're looking for a small, white arrow.

3. When the arrow is in sight, try to drag it in the direction of the Start button.

4. With the arrow resting over the top of the Start button, press the left mouse button. You'll see a Start menu similar to the one shown in Figure 1.6.

FIGURE 1.6

The Start menu is the first step in locating what has been installed on your computer.

5. Hover the mouse pointer over the green More Programs arrow. An expanded Programs menu pops out. A black arrow to the right of a word means another menu will appear if that option is selected.

6. From the resulting menu, point to Games and then click Solitaire. The window shown in Figure 1.7 appears.

FIGURE 1.7

*Solitaire is a fun way
to learn how to control
your mouse.*

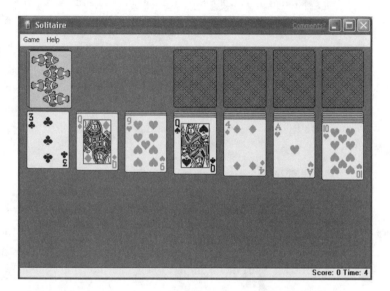

8. That's right, I'm actually using a game to help you practice your mouse-eye coordination! Look at the cards that are face up and see if there are any valid moves.

Not sure what you're doing? For those of you who aren't familiar with the rules of Solitaire, here's an oversimplification. The object is to get all the aces up top and build them up, one-by-one, according to suit. You reveal additional cards by arranging them in descending order, alternating red and black suits as you go. Don't knock yourself out trying to become a Solitaire pro; the point here is to get comfortable using Windows. I must warn you, however, Solitaire can be very addicting; it may be hard to stop playing once you start!

9. If there are any aces at the front of any of the lines of cards, simply double-click them (press the left mouse button twice in rapid succession), and they will automatically move up to one of the four slots at the top of the screen.

10. To move a card from one row to another, click on it and, with the button still pressed, drag the card to the desired location and release the button to drop it. This maneuver is referred to as drag-and-drop. (Big surprise, huh?)

11. After you make all possible moves, click the pile of cards on the upper left to draw a card and place it like you did the others. If it doesn't fit anywhere, draw again.

12. Keep playing until you've made all possible moves and have run out of cards in the draw pile.

13. Hooked and want to play again? See the word "Game" at the left end of the gray bar at the top of the Solitaire window? Click it to reveal a menu. Choose Deal to play another round, or Exit to end the game and close the window.

The more you play, the more at ease you should feel working with Windows and your mouse. Hey, who said learning couldn't be fun?

That's All, Folks!

Okay, our hour's about up so let's make sure you know how to safely shut the computer down. No, don't just flip the switch; that could stress your machine and make the next start up a long, agonizing process as Windows attempts to repair itself.

To make life more pleasant for you and your computer, do the following when you're ready to shut down the machine for the day:

1. Click the bright green Start button.

2. Click the red Turn Off Computer button. The Turn Off Computer screen shown in Figure 1.8 appears.

3. Click Turn Off, and the PC will safely power down on its own.

FIGURE 1.8

From here, you can put your PC on standby, turn it off, reboot it, or cancel the entire process.

Summary

In this hour, you learned how to find your way around the Windows desktop. As you'll continue to discover in subsequent lessons, comfort with Windows is vital to your success with PCs.

By now, you also should feel a lot better about using a mouse. From this point on, it only gets easier! I find the progress of a lot of new computer users is hampered by the ability to use a mouse effectively. The old adage, "Practice makes perfect," applies to mouse use as well. After a few hands of Solitaire, however, you'll be a pro!

In the next hour, *Windows Your Way,* I'll show you how to make your desktop look the way you want it to.

Workshop

Now it's time to see just how much you learned in this lesson. I'll give you a short, multiple-choice quiz to test what you learned, followed by a suggested activity designed to enhance the skills you acquired during the hour.

Quiz

Select the best answer to the questions from the choices provided and then check your answers in the "Answers" section.

Questions

1. Which element is *not* found on the Windows desktop?
   a. Notification Area
   b. Taskbar
   c. Snack bar

2. Choose the correct name of a pointing device from the following list:
   a. Rat
   b. Touch Ball
   c. Track Ball

3. What do you call it when you click on an object, drag it to a new location, and drop it into place?
   a. Drag-and-Drop
   b. Push-and-Plop
   c. Dump-and-Go

Answers

1. C is the correct choice, although you may wish it weren't during late night work sessions at the computer!

2. Again, C is the correct answer. A track ball is an alternative to a mouse—sort of like a mouse lying on its back.

3. The correct answer is A, although I guess you could argue that the others work just as well .

Activity

Grab your mouse and cruise on over to the Start button. Click it and select Programs from the menu. Finally, work your way through each of the selections to see what kind of software has been installed on your computer. Remember, the black arrows at the end of a word mean there is yet another menu to uncover. Don't open any of the programs for now; this is just an exercise.

This activity not only refines your mouse skills, but it introduces you to many of the goodies that may be tucked away on your machine as well.

HOUR 2

Windows Your Way

No two people are alike, so why should your Windows desktop look (and sound) like everyone else's? Whether you're a Golden Retriever nut and want your PC to reflect that, or you simply can't stand the thought of staring at that blissful grassy knoll background another day, you'll be happy to know all that and more can be changed.

Here are some of the topics you have to look forward to in this hour's lesson:

- Learn how to rearrange your desktop icons and make them larger.
- Make your taskbar disappear until you need it.
- Change the look of your desktop in a few quick mouse clicks
- Configure the Start menu to display your favorite items in an easy-to-locate spot.

Altering the appearance of your Windows desktop may seem like a frivolous waste of time at first glance, but there are times a change may be legitimately warranted.

I'm visually impaired, for example, and I'm here to tell you there are times when those larger desktop icons come in handy! Or perhaps you're colorblind and could greatly benefit from a color scheme with more contrast.

Whether the changes you want to make are a necessity or just for fun, I'll show you how to get them done in the remainder of this hour.

Rearranging the Desktop Icons

If you want to move a certain shortcut from one location to another, simply click it and drag it into position, just as you dragged the Solitaire cards in the last hour.

For more global changes in the icon layout, right-click on a clean spot of the desktop (any part of the grasslands picture) and select Arrange Icons By from the resulting shortcut menu (see Figure 2.1). This produces a menu of choices for arranging the icons including by Name, Type, Size, or Date Modified. Just click the desired option to rearrange your desktop in the specified order. By default, the icons are auto arranged, which means Windows automatically places them in the most space efficient, aesthetically appealing layout.

FIGURE 2.1

Rearrange your desktop icons using this shortcut menu.

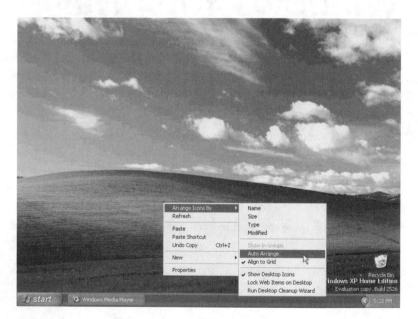

> **The quickest way to clean your desk(top)...** When you're working on a dozen windows at once, it can seem like you'll never uncover the desktop. Oh sure, you can do it all right, but it could take an eternity to individually minimize each window. To minimize all application windows at one time, simply right-click the taskbar and click Show the Desktop from the menu. That clears the desktop in seconds, leaving the respective task buttons available on the taskbar so you can get back to work in an instant. If only cleaning off my desk were that easy....

2

Making It Big: Enlarging Your Desktop Icons

Small detailed icons can be a bear to see. Luckily, Windows makes it easy to enlarge them without affecting the way your programs run.

Not sure the larger size will help much? Take a look at Figures 2.2 and 2.3 to see just how big a difference the change makes. Even I can see the details on those icons!

FIGURE 2.2

Regular sized desktop icons.

FIGURE 2.3
*Enlarged desktop
icons.*

To make your desktop icons larger, just follow these steps:

1. If you can't see a piece of your Windows desktop, right-click the taskbar and click Show the Desktop from the resulting shortcut menu.

2. Right-click over the desktop to reveal the same shortcut menu you accessed to arrange your icons (see Figure 2.1).

3. Select the Properties item from the menu to open the Display Properties dialog box.

"Talk to me," said the dialog box... Although the term dialog box may sound a bit intimidating, the concept is quite simple. A dialog box basically is a window that opens and prompts you to provide information or answer a question.

4. The Display Properties dialog box contains a series of tabs that you can open to change various settings. Access the Appearance tab and then click the Effects button to see the options in Figure 2.4.

5. Next, click the Use Large Icons check box.

6. Click the OK button to exit the dialog box and click OK again to clear the Display Properties dialog box. In a few moments, the icons will look similar in size to the ones shown in Figure 2.3.

FIGURE 2.4

The Effects dialog box.

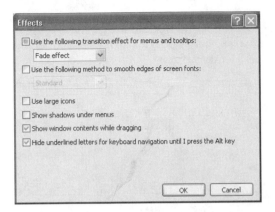

To return the icons to their normal size, just repeat the preceding steps. The option check boxes are like toggle buttons—clicking it turns the option to the opposite state you found it in (that is, clicking an enabled option turns it off; clicking it a second time turns it on again, and so on).

Maximize Screen Size by Hiding the Taskbar

Depending on your work style, the taskbar can occasionally take up valuable real estate onscreen that could be better allocated to your work.

If this situation describes you, then you may want to consider hiding your taskbar. When hidden, the taskbar stays out of sight until you hover the mouse pointer over the taskbar area. At that point it pops up, letting you work with it as usual.

While it increases the amount of viewing area onscreen, it has the drawback of being a royal pain when working on the bottom portion of a program window. That may not seem like a problem at first glance, but when you consider the fact that many popular word processors have buttons in that area you need to get to on a regular basis, it can potentially drive you batty. You may be trying to use the scroll bars to navigate your document and find the taskbar popping up at seemingly random intervals.

A variation on the theme... If the hiding taskbar gets in the way of your work, there's another possibility that may let you have your cake and eat it too, so to speak. Consider moving the taskbar to one side of the screen. That way you can gain the onscreen real estate without making yourself crazy. To move the taskbar, you'll first have to unlock it. To do this, just right-click the taskbar and click the Lock the Taskbar option to remove the

checkmark. Then just click the taskbar and drag it toward the desired edge
of the screen while holding the left mouse button down. An outline of the
taskbar's footprint appears in the specified location. If you like what you
see, release the button to drop the taskbar into place.

To make your taskbar disappear until you need it again, simply do the following:

1. Make sure part of your taskbar is empty. This is crucial to getting the menu you'll
   need.
2. Right-click over the taskbar to open its corresponding shortcut menu.
3. Select the Properties item to launch the Taskbar Properties dialog box.
4. Select the Taskbar tab of the Taskbar and Start Menu Properties dialog box as
   shown in Figure 2.5.
5. Click the Auto-hide the taskbar check box to enable the option, and then click OK
   to exit the dialog box.

Here again, you can repeat the process to restore the taskbar to its previous state.

FIGURE 2.5

*The Taskbar tab of the
Taskbar Properties
dialog box is where
you'll find the setting
to hide your taskbar.*

Banishing the Desktop Blues

Now for the fun part—changing your desktop's appearance. As I mentioned earlier, whether the change is a necessity or simply for fun, you'll want to know how to do it. I'll take you step-by-step through several ways to give your desktop a much-needed facelift.

Changing the Background Texture Using Files Provided

The simplest way to make a switch is to change the display's background using one of the files provided by Microsoft with Windows.

To do this, you'll need to perform the following steps:

1. Right-click over an uncovered portion of the desktop to open the now-familiar shortcut menu.
2. Choose the Properties item to launch the Display Properties dialog box.
3. Select the Desktop tab shown in Figure 2.6.

FIGURE 2.6

Microsoft gives you a host of background textures from which to choose.

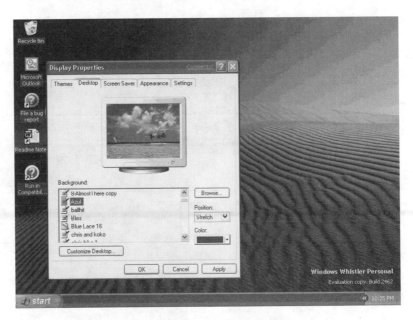

4. In the Background section of the tab, select the name of the file you want to use by clicking it. You'll see a preview of what it will look like in the monitor at the top of the tab.

5. If you like what you see, click OK to apply the design to your desktop. If it doesn't quite suit you, keep choosing from the designs available until you hit on the right one. You can also use the Color drop-down box (the arrow button) to select a solid color background for your desktop.

A neat-o, nifty desktop trick. If you get a scanner or digital camera someday, you might be interested to know that you can even use those images for your background. Just follow the preceding steps, except rather than choosing the name of a background file, click the Browse button and surf over to the desired file. The only gotcha' is the file needs to be in .bmp or .jpg format. Not only can you use a personal image, but you can click the black arrow next to the Display options box in the Background tab to choose an effect for the image. As the following figures illustrate, you can stretch, center, or tile the image.

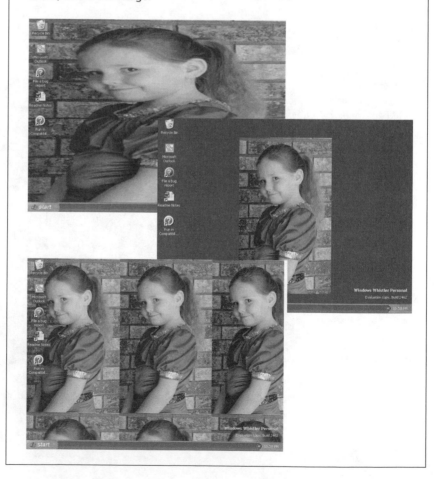

Coming Up with a New Scheme

Microsoft has taken the facelift thing even further by enabling you to choose a totally new color scheme for Windows as a whole. Not only can you change the desktop color, but you also can change the colors of other Windows elements, such as dialog boxes.

To apply a new color scheme, just follow these simple steps:

1. Find a clear area of your desktop and right-click it to access the shortcut menu.

2. Click the Properties menu item to open the familiar Display Properties dialog box.

3. Click the Themes tab and use the drop-down box (click the arrow button) to choose a new theme for your desktop.

4. After you click the name of the chosen color scheme, you can preview it at the bottom of the tab, as shown in Figure 2.7.

5. Click OK to apply your selected color scheme and exit the dialog box.

FIGURE 2.7
There aren't many color schemes available at first, but just wait....

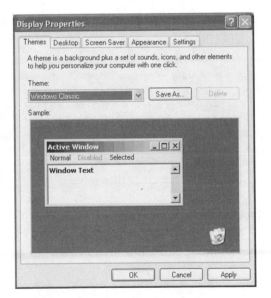

The Best of Desktop Decorating

If all the things you can do to change the appearance of your desktop impressed you so far, then you better sit down before I continue.

Okay, are you ready? Not only can you add special images to your desktop, but you can install entire desktop themes containing a wide range of sounds and animations as well.

That's right, you can turn your PC into a virtual jungle complete with monkey noises, among other possibilities! Some desktop themes even include customized animated mouse pointers that change, depending on where the mouse is hovering!

While you may not have many themes at your disposal now (you have to admit it would take a bit more than a Windows Classic theme to cause a stir), just wait until you become skilled with using the Internet! If you surf over to www.themeworld.com, you will find hundreds of desktop themes devoted to TV shows, cars, rock stars, cartoons, you name it. When I checked last, there was a Porsche theme for my husband, a few James Bond themes for my son, and several Britney Spears themes for my daughter.

Web sites with their own themes available for free download will have their own downloading and installation instructions, so be sure to read them thoroughly before you attempt to download and install them. If you're not careful, you could end up stuck with honking geese for new e-mail alert sounds and car crashes for Windows shutdown sounds permanently!

> **Hold it right there!** I'll remind you of this again in Hour 4, but just in case you get overly enthusiastic and start downloading things before you even get there... please, please, please be sure to run a virus scan on any software you download from the Internet before you install it. In the vast majority of cases, the program is clean, but it's not worth the risk. Check your PC to see whether Norton AntiVirus or McAfee AntiVirus is installed. Many computer manufacturers preinstall virus protection software on their systems, but you have to keep them updated in order for them to do their job effectively.

Imitation: The Highest Form of Flattery

If you're feeling nostalgic and would like to resurrect the classic Windows look and feel, here's what you'll need to do:

1. First, let's recapture the look and feel of a Windows Classic desktop. To begin doing this, right-click over an exposed part of the desktop to launch the familiar shortcut menu.

2. Choose Properties from the menu and then open the Themes tab on the Display Properties dialog box.

3. Next, use the drop-down box to select the Windows Classic theme and then click OK. Voila, the desktop looks just like many of its predecessors!

4. Now it's on to the Start menu. Right-click over the Start button and choose Properties from the shortcut menu.

5. The Taskbar and Start Menu Properties dialog box appears. Select the Start Menu tab and then click the Classic Start menu button.

6. Click OK; then you're done! At least on the surface, the results look and feel like the old Windows (see Figure 2.8).

FIGURE 2.8

With a few tweaks, you can step back in time and turn this cutting edge operating system into a clone of its past.

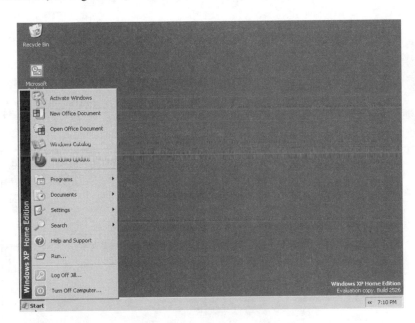

Defining Your Own Desktop Shortcuts

The best way to define a shortcut for easy access depends on the type of file you're dealing with. If the item is a document or Web page, you can simply click on its icon and drag it to a clear space on your desktop.

When you attempt to drag-and-drop an icon, one of two things will happen. Either it appears on your desktop on the spot, or Windows launches a dialog box saying it can't move the selected item in that manner. If Windows is unable to create the shortcut on the spot, it asks you if you really intended to make a shortcut. Click the Yes button, and Windows does what it needs to build the shortcut.

So where do you find a file's icon? Click the Start button followed by the My Computer link and then click your way to the desired file. This will make more sense to you after you've completed the next lesson, "Getting Organized with Windows." In the case of Web pages, surf to the Web page

you want; then drag its icon from the Internet Explorer Address Bar to your
desktop. (The location of the Address Bar will be covered in Hour 12, *One
Way or Another: Navigating the Information Superhighway*.)

If the shortcut is intended to launch a program rather than a specific file, you'll want to
complete the following steps for the best results:

1. Find a clear surface on your desktop and right-click to open the shortcut menu.

2. Choose New and then Shortcut from the menu to reveal the dialog box shown in
   Figure 2.9.

FIGURE 2.9

*This dialog box is your
key to accessing your
favorite applications
quickly.*

3. To make your life easier, click the Browse button.

4. Now comes the tricky part. You will need to double-click your way to the file you
   want. Please note that you will find the core programs (your word processor and
   such) in the Program Files folder. When you find the appropriate program, double-
   click it. You will return to the dialog box shown in Figure 2.9, except this time, the
   file's address appears in the Command box.

5. Click the Next button to continue. The first thing you will need to do is give the
   shortcut a name. Note that a shorter name is more suitable for a shortcut since
   Windows may only display a few characters of the chosen name at once. (In some
   cases, a name may be suggested. This especially is true for Microsoft applications.)

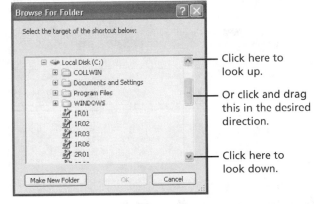

Hey, I can't see the Program File folder! You'll find this group of folders hiding out under My Computer, local disk (C:). To move through the list of files displayed, use the scroll bar tools as described in the figure below. Use the arrow buttons to move short distances, and the scroll box to move longer distances quickly.

Click here to look up.

Or click and drag this in the desired direction.

Click here to look down.

6. If the selected program doesn't have a special icon associated with it, you will be given the opportunity to choose one from several provided with Windows.

7. After you complete steps 5 and 6 as necessary, click the Finish button to save the shortcut to your desktop.

Customizing the Windows XP Start Menu

One of the draws of Windows XP is its ability to offer customized Start menus. You can tell Windows what you do and don't want it to display, you can tell it how you want the information displayed, or you can even have it serve up frequently opened documents or spreadsheets.

Changing the Look of Your Start Menu

Windows XP not only lets you change the size of the icons displayed on your Start menu, but you can also tell it how many of your most recently used applications you want it to show at any given time.

To make these adjustments, just follow these steps:

1. Right-click the Start button and select Properties from the menu. (Gee, you've done that a time or two before, haven't you?)

2. Open the Start Menu tab of the Taskbar and Start Menu dialog box.

3. Next, click the Customize button. The Customize Start Menu dialog box shown in Figure 2.10 pops up with the General tab displayed by default.

FIGURE 2.10

The power of customized Start menus starts here.

4. In the first section of the dialog box, you can choose whether you want the Start menu icons to be large or small by clicking the respective button. (Large icons are displayed by default.)

5. The middle section of the dialog box is where you will specify how many recently used programs you want Windows to give you instant access to. The default number is 6; however, you can adjust this number as desired by clicking the arrow button and clicking the number you want. Your choices range from a low of zero, to a high of nine.

> **Uh, I take that back...** In time, you may find your Start menu cluttered with all kinds of programs you may not want or need anymore. You can clear this list of program shortcuts by clicking the Clear List button. Of course, this doesn't remove the programs from your machine; it simply clears the list of most recently used programs so only the most heavily used (your default Internet and e-mail programs in Microsoft's opinion) remain.

6. Finally, in the bottom section of the dialog box, you can decide whether or not you want Windows to include your Internet or e-mail programs on the list. Just check the option (or options) you want; then use the arrow buttons to select the specific Internet and e-mail program you want it to display. Typically, Internet Explorer and Outlook Express will appear by default.

7. When the settings meet with your approval, click OK to dismiss the Customize Start Menu dialog box. You'll need to click OK again to close the Taskbar and Start Menu dialog box.

Power Tweaking the Start Menu

Okay, so maybe you're not a power user in the technical sense of the word yet, but that doesn't mean you shouldn't get everything you want when it comes to customizing your Start menu.

We're about to start working with Advanced Start menu options, but don't let the term *advanced* intimidate you. When it comes to computers, sometimes advanced simply means more of the same. You certainly don't need these adjustments in order to function behind the keyboard, but boy can they make your life easier.

Now follow these steps to put the finishing touches on your personal Start menu:

1. Again, right-click the Start button and select Properties from the shortcut menu.

2. Open the Start Menu tab of the Taskbar and Start Menu Properties dialog box.

3. Click the Customize button and then choose the Advanced tab. The resulting dialog box will look like the one shown in Figure 2.11.

FIGURE 2.11

The Advanced tab is where you can tell Windows how certain programs should appear on the Start menu.

4. The first section of the Advanced tab lets you make additional modifications to the Start menu's behavior. By checking the appropriate check box, you can open submenus when you pause your mouse over them (enabled by default) and highlight newly installed applications (also enabled by default).

Ah, there you are! The more software you install on your PC, the trickier it can be to find that new program on your Start menu for the first time. Windows XP has the perfect solution—it will highlight newly installed software in yellow as shown in the figure below. All my Office XP applications are highlighted since the suite was just installed.

Activate Windows
Windows Catalog
Windows Update
New Office Document
Open Office Document

Accessories ►
Games ►
Startup ►

Internet
Internet Explorer

E-mail
Microsoft Outlook

Internet Explorer
MSN Explorer
Outlook Express
Remote Assistance

Windows Media Player

Windows Media Player
Windows Movie Maker
Windows Messenger
Collage Complete ►

Tour Windows XP
Microsoft Office Tools ►
Microsoft Access

MSN Explorer
Microsoft Excel
Microsoft FrontPage

Screen Capture
Microsoft Outlook
Microsoft PowerPoint

Files and Settings Transfer Wizard

All Programs
Microsoft Word

5. The second section is where you will do some heavy-duty configuration. Windows lists each main element and gives you the option to have it displayed one of three ways. Those three ways (which you choose simply by clicking the appropriate button) include the following:

- **Display as a link**—This option displays the selected item as a hyperlink, which you click to work further with the element.

- **Display as a menu**—A black arrow will display behind the chosen item letting you know there are additional menu items from which you can choose. By default, hovering your mouse pointer over such an item pops out a submenu.

- **Don't Display This Item**—No matter how often or how recently the specified directory was accessed, it will never appear on the Start menu. You can always find it, however, by using one of the methods I'll teach you in the next lesson.

6. In the Advanced tab's last section, you can tell Windows to display the most recently opened documents on the Start menu. All you need to do is check the Show most recently used documents check box, and you're on your way. And you can always return to this spot and clear the list by clicking the Clear List button.

7. When you're finished, simply keep clicking OK buttons until all of the dialog boxes have closed.

Flying Toilets and Swirling Colors (Screen Savers)

A long time ago (boy, am I ever starting to date myself!), computer monitors used to suffer from a problem called *burn-in*. Burn-in occurred when the same image was displayed on the monitor for long periods of time. Eventually, the image became etched on the phosphorus of the screen, and you would see a ghosted image of that screen on your monitor forever no matter what you did.

To prevent burn-in, screen savers were created, the primary purpose of which was to display a constantly changing picture on the monitor. A screen saver would start any time the computer had not been used for a few minutes and would automatically stop anytime the user pressed a key on the keyboard or moved the mouse.

Since screen savers were first introduced, they have become an art form with many different styles and patterns available. That's where the flying toilets part of this section's title comes in. A commercially designed and marketed collection of novelty screen savers, called After Dark, fueled the trend toward bizarre screen savers like toasters with wings, flying toilets, and the like. Even today you will find a host of funky screen savers in clearance bins at computer stores nationwide. And, of course, there are plenty just waiting to be downloaded from the Internet.

Windows XP, Home Edition includes a number of different screen savers that you can select and configure by using the Screen Savers tab of the Display Properties dialog box (see Figure 2.12). To get there, right-click on the desktop, click Properties and then open the Screensavers tab.

FIGURE 2.12
The Screen Saver tab helps you express yourself.

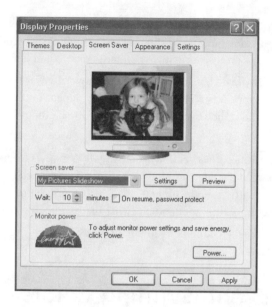

You can choose a screen saver from the Screen Saver drop-down list box. After you choose one, the monitor area of the window will show you a small preview of the screen saver. You can see a full screen preview of the screen saver by clicking the Preview button. Pressing any key on the keyboard or moving the mouse will return you to the Display Properties dialog box.

Most screen savers have a series of settings that allow you to refine how they work. These options often control values such as the object displayed, the speed with which the object moves, and the color of the object. In the case of 3D Text and Marquee screen savers, you can even enter the text you wish to have appear onscreen.

Hey, check this out! Windows XP lets you create a screen saver from your very own electronic images. Just place the images you want to use in your screen saver in the My Pictures folder, and select My Pictures Slideshow from the screen saver list. Clicking the Settings button lets you select the length of time each slide is viewed. What a terrific way to show off pictures of the new baby, new home, wedding, or any other special event!

These settings are specific to each screen saver, so I'm not going to cover them here; however, they are easy to change. Press the Settings button to display the dialog box with the screen saver's settings.

After changing the settings, you can test them by closing the Settings dialog box and clicking the Preview button. Moving the mouse or pressing any key will stop the screen saver and take you back to your regular desktop.

You may also wish to change the wait time for your screen saver. By default, Windows XP will wait for 10 minutes of keyboard/mouse inactivity to fire off the screen saver. Depending on your work habits or personal preferences, you may want to adjust the time. You can do this by clicking the up or down arrow buttons as necessary.

2

Summary

In this hour, I introduced you to dozens of ways to personalize your Windows desktop. From reorganizing the icons to modifying the background's appearance and creating your own special shortcuts, it's all here. In many cases, tinkering with these settings is as much a necessity as it is fun. Visually impaired individuals can benefit immensely from larger icons or high contrast desktop color schemes. It can even enhance your productivity by keeping frequently used programs and documents close at hand.

In the next hour, *Getting Organized with Windows,* I'll help you come up with the optimal scheme for organizing your computer files, teach you how to find a file on your computer no matter how little you know about it, and give you some other tips designed to keep you sane during the time you spend behind your PC.

Workshop

Now it's time to see just how much you learned in this lesson. I'll give you a short multiple-choice quiz to test what you learned, followed by a suggested activity designed to enhance the skills you acquired during the hour.

Quiz

Select the best answer to the questions from the choices provided, and then check your answers in the following section.

Questions

1. Which method *cannot* be used to adjust the placement of desktop icons?
    a. Drag-and-drop
    b. The Microsoft Telepathic Interface
    c. The Arrange Icons item on the desktop shortcut menu

2. You can use any image on your computer for a desktop background.

    a. Yes, without a doubt.

    b. Images can't be used in that way.

    c. Yes, but only if the images are in .bmp or .jpg file format.

3. What's the difference between a shortcut on your desktop and one located on your Start menu?

    a. You have to double-click the shortcut on the desktop, but only need to single click the Start menu.

    b. They are accessed the exact same way; the only difference is you can see Start menu shortcuts from the Start menu no matter how many windows are open.

    c. There is no difference. Why did you waste all this book space talking about it?

Answers

1. B may sound convincing because of its fancy name, but unfortunately, Microsoft has yet to develop such a tool. If only….

2. If you chose C, you're absolutely right. Unfortunately, Windows does have some limitations on the types of images that can be used for desktop backgrounds.

3. A was the appropriate answer here. If you read the lesson thoroughly, the last two options should have been ruled out almost instantly.

Activity

Take this book over to your computer and give yourself time to experiment with the various desktop facelift possibilities.

Getting a new desktop is almost like buying a new piece of clothing you absolutely adore—it can perk you up on an otherwise crummy day. Have fun!

Hour **3**

Getting Organized with Windows

Have you ever had the opportunity to work with or see a substantial collection of paper files up close? I'm not talking about the two lateral file cabinets you might have at work; I'm talking about the banks of ceiling-high cabinets you may find behind the counter of many doctors' offices. There literally are thousands of files crammed in there! And the file dividers go way beyond the simple A, B, and C structure. They have to, or the people who need to access them in a hurry could be there for days flipping through the folders, one-by-one! Situations like these often warrant extra subdividers, so rather than A, B, and C, you might see A, An, Ar, B, Be, Br, C, Cl, Cr, and so on.

Your computer files are no different. Right now, you may not be able to imagine the number of files on your PC becoming uncontrollable, but trust me, it happens quicker than you think. And when it does happen, you end up wasting valuable time plowing through dozens, if not hundreds, of files, trying to find what you want.

In this lesson, I will show you how to get and keep your files under control. Here are some other topics to be covered in this hour:

- Discover why luck is already on your side when it comes to file management.
- Learn how to plan the document filing system that is right for you.
- Find out how to create your own set of folders in which to store your files.
- Use the Windows XP Search Companion to locate a specific file.

Thinking About Getting Organized

Think of the folders you will be creating on your PC as the electronic equivalent of the *B* drawer at the doctor's office. The more you compartmentalize, the easier it should be to find what you want, when you want it. Folders can also have subfolders.

Consider this example: if I shared a PC with my family, there may be separate folders for each family member (Wayne, Jill, Christopher, and Samantha). Each person could then have his or her own group of folders. I tend to divide my Jill folder into subfolders such as Books, Fiction, Proposals, and so on. Then my Books folder may be further broken out by creating a folder for each title I write. Within that, I have folders for material submitted, author review documents, screenshot files, and so on. Each person's network of folders forms a pyramid, or hierarchy, of sorts.

Obviously, the complexity of your network of folders will vary, depending on the frequency with which you use your computer. If you use it once a month to write Aunt Linda a letter, that's one thing; but if you produce document after document for various projects at work or school, then you may benefit greatly from a highly organized system.

> **You've got mail!** Diligent file management is also a good idea for your e-mail correspondence. It not only enables you to find specific notes quickly, but it can also be a great way to document the progress of a project or proposal.

Think about your computer use and ask yourself the following questions. Your answers should give you some valuable clues as to which type of file organization may help you most.

- **Is your machine primarily for business, personal use, or a combination of both?** Business or combined use generally would suggest use of a more complex filing scheme. Educational or personal use may warrant a more methodical approach.

- **In your business use of the computer, do you tend to think of items in terms of type of tasks (such as a budget, proposals, and so on), or do you plan to work on a variety of document types for various clients?** As you might guess, your answer provides tips for potential folder names. Your top-level folders may be budgets, proposals, and reports (with documents named after each company you work with), or they may be JustPC, WalTech, or The Serendipity Shoppe (with documents under each named budget, annual report, and so on).

- **Will you use the PC a lot or just occasionally?** If you rarely save files on your computer, having a complex folder hierarchy actually might make it more time consuming to find the information you are seeking.

- **Think the way you work.** This concept is closely linked to choosing appropriate filenames because it is extremely useful to have a meaningful naming scheme. For example, I design the newsletters for my daughter's nursery school, Calverton-Beltsville Community Nursery School (CBCNS). Rather than name each related file something outrageously long like cbcnsjan2000 (the school's initials, followed by the publication date of this particular newsletter), I create a special CBCNS folder (or even a CBCNS Newsletters folder for other work done for the school) and give the files simpler names such as jan00. That way, I can find the file you need in a snap.

- **Who will be using the new computer?** If the new toy is to be shared, then you will want to get the high-level family member folders in place as soon as possible (such as the Wayne, Jill, Christopher, and Samantha folders). That way, everyone's business is kept separate, and you won't be facing a hideously long file-moving session later. (Another option might be to create separate Windows XP user accounts for each person using the machine. I will explain how this is done later in this hour.)

Now that you have answered some critical questions, it is time to sit down with a pen and paper and jot down a filing scheme that adequately meets your needs. I strongly urge you to take this assignment seriously and give it the time it deserves. The time you invest now will be time saved in the future.

Getting to Know Windows Explorer's Filing Headquarters

Although there are multiple ways to create new folders on your system, I'm going to introduce you to a way that remains the same, regardless of what other software you have installed on your machine.

3

By using the Windows utility called *Windows Explorer,* you get a bird's eye view of the files on your computer. As you can see in Figure 3.1, Windows Explorer literally enables you to visualize how your folders are structured, and it is easy to do just about anything with the folders you see onscreen.

To begin working with Windows Explorer, click the Start button, point to All Programs, Accessories, and then click Windows Explorer.

FIGURE 3.1

Click the plus sign next to a folder to reveal the folders nested underneath (also known as subfolders).

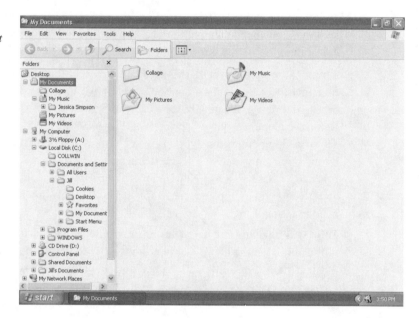

The Windows XP Windows Explorer screen is divided into three parts. On the far left is the Folders pane, reminiscent of earlier versions of the operating system. By clicking the plus signs, you can reveal subfolders and drill your way down to the most focused folders on your machine. Likewise, clicking minus signs will compress the folder hierarchy.

In the middle of the screen is the Windows XP Folders pane. This is where you will find many of Windows XP's user-friendly links to specific tasks, other locations on your computer, and so on. The area on the far right of the screen displays the contents of the selected folder.

There is much more you can do with Windows Explorer, as you will see in the remainder of this hour. From this utility, you can create new folders and subfolders, move files from one folder to another, or even copy a few select files that really fit into two or more folders equally well.

Creating a New Folder

Perform the following steps to create high-level folders (also known as *parent folders*). Family member names are a good example of a type of parent folder you might want to create on your hard drive.

1. Launch Windows Explorer by clicking the Start button, hovering the mouse over the bright green Programs arrow, and then selecting Accessories, Windows Explorer. Doing this launches a window similar to the one shown in Figure 3.1.

2. Click the icon corresponding to your hard drive. (You may need to start with My Computer and drill your way down.) You will find it near the top of the Folders pane; it is typically labeled (C:).

3. From the Windows Explorer menu bar, click File and then point to New, Folder. A New Folder icon and label highlighted in dark blue appears in the main viewing window (that is, the window pane to the far right of the screen).

4. Type in the name you want for your new folder in the highlighted area.

5. After you finish, press Enter to save the folder.

Adding a Subfolder to the Hierarchy

The steps needed to create a subfolder mirror the steps you followed to create a parent folder but with one small exception. Rather than clicking the hard drive icon like you did in step 2, you click the folder under which you want to place the new folder.

To follow up with the example I have referred to throughout this hour, you would click on the Jill folder and then continue with the preceding outlined steps to create a sub-folder called *Computer Basics* to hold the files related to this book.

Renaming a Folder on Your Computer

If your filing needs change or you simply think of a better name for some of the folders later on, you will want to know how to rename them.

Renaming a folder is as simple as following these brief steps:

1. Launch Windows Explorer as you normally do.

2. Right-click the icon of the folder you want to rename. The shortcut menu shown in Figure 3.2 appears.

3. Choose Rename from the shortcut menu. The selected folder's name will appear highlighted in dark blue.

4. Simply type in the new name for the folder.

5. Press Enter to save your edit.

3

FIGURE 3.2
You and this Windows Explorer shortcut menu will become old friends.

Deleting a Folder from Your System

There may come a day when you decide to delete a folder from your computer. Perhaps you finish your master's degree and want to archive the documents rather than take up space on your hard drive, or maybe one of your clients moves on. Either way, you will want to know how to delete a folder. Just follow these steps to perform the deletion:

1. Start the Windows Explorer utility, as directed earlier.

2. Right-click the icon of the folder you want to remove from your computer and select Delete from the shortcut menu.

3. A dialog box like the one shown in Figure 3.3 opens, asking you to verify the fact that you really want to delete the selected folder and all of its contents. Click Yes or No as appropriate.

Look before you delete! Remember that the Delete command will not only erase the selected folder, but also all the files within it. As a result, I *strongly* suggest that you click the folder to examine the files before you perform the deletion.

FIGURE 3.3
Look closely at the name of the folder about to be deleted before you make a final selection.

> **Stay alive, archive!** In the next hour, *Health Care for PCs*, I will show you how to back up files on a floppy disk or CD; that way, you can perform a little spring cleaning on your PC without having to worry about losing anything important.
>
> And once the files are safely stored in another location, you can go ahead with any necessary deletions. I would, however, verify that the documents on your disk are not corrupt or otherwise damaged first. To do this, launch the application in which the document(s) was created and choose File, Open. Next, click your way to your floppy drive and try to open the file(s) stored there.

Good File Naming Techniques: Another Organizational Aid

With a network of well-defined folders in place, your filenames can now become shorter and more descriptive themselves.

As you create a document, whether it is a spreadsheet or a word processing document, think about a name for it that fully and accurately describes its contents. Use the following tips as a guide for coming up with that all-important document name:

- Want to be able to uncover a file just by glancing through the appropriate folder? A good filename can make a world of difference. Make the name short but descriptive.

- Let's go back to my CBCNS newsletter example. If I included the school's name in every filename, as well as the document's title (such as a spreadsheet named *CBCNS Budget,* a Word document named *CBCNS Grant Application,* and so on), it would be much harder to find the file I want because they would all begin with CBCNS. A better filing strategy would be to create a special CBCNS folder; that way, I can simply call the documents *Budget* or *Grant App.* Of course, if I only use the computer for school volunteer work, there may not be a need for the school's name to be on the document or folder at all.

- Consider using a date or year somewhere in the filename if it's relevant. Documents with names such as Budget, New Budget, and Projected Budget, for example, are not as comprehensive as Fall 02 Budget or 2003 Projected Budget.

- Name the way you work. If your work involves creating many types of documents for a single entity (such as budgets, newsletters, and grant applications for the school alone), then you will want to emphasize the document's contents in its filename. If, however, you create a quarterly newsletter for multiple entities (the nursery school, the Parent-Teacher Association, a local animal rescue organization, and so on), you will want the entity's name to appear prominently in the file's name. Why not create a separate folder for each entity? Four documents a year doesn't really warrant a separate folder, so you may want to consider archiving the newsletters into folders dedicated to a specific year instead.

Some of these tips may seem to clash with one another at first glance. For example, how can you have a short, descriptive filename when you are trying to incorporate a date, an organization's name, and the type of document? The answer is simpler than you may think. For starters, try combining the folder and file naming strategies discussed previously. The two naming strategies are not mutually exclusive. In fact, they should, and do, work hand-in-hand to get the job done.

Remember, the goal here is to keep the number of entries in a given folder or directory to a minimum. Given that, it is extremely helpful if you take a long, hard look at the way you intend to use your new computer. Every little detail, from the total number of documents you create over the span of a year to the types of documents, influences how you name your folders and files. Although sophisticated file searching tools make finding things a lot easier than it used to be, nothing beats good file organization from the get-go!

Once You Create It, Know Where to Store It

I will discuss how to save files in various applications in the specific lessons dedicated to them later on. Knowing where to place a document when you do save it, however, is a great addition to the file management issues covered in this lesson.

The proper placement of a file in your computer's network of folders goes hand-in-hand with the document's name when it comes to enhancing the capability to find the file again when you need it.

Consider the following as you decide where to store a newly created document in the computer's filing system:

- Don't just let all your Microsoft Office documents accumulate in the My Documents folder (the folder Office XP saves everything in it unless you tell it otherwise). That's just begging for trouble! It's like throwing all of your household garbage into one can and then having to sift through it all again to separate the recyclables from the regular trash.

- Do you tend to include your organization's name in a filename, as well as the document's title, instead of putting things into descriptive folders (such as a spreadsheet named *CBCNS Budget*)? Consider creating a folder for the school (in which case, the document could simply be called *Budget*). If that's still too broad, then make a subfolder under the organization's folder called *Finances* that could then store the Budget document. Having large numbers of documents with similar names like CBCNS Budget, CBCNS Newsletter, or CBCNS Reg Form can make finding what you need much harder than it needs to be.

- If you know up front the types of documents you will be generating, it may be worth your while to sit down and sketch out a list of appropriate folder names on paper before you sit down with Windows Explorer. With a little forethought, you can avoid having grossly unbalanced folders where some contain a handful of files and others contain dozens.

- Microsoft has always made it easy to create new folders on-the-fly, and as you saw earlier in the hour, it's especially easy for Windows XP users. If you don't see a category that fits a document when you go to save it, don't hesitate to create a new folder on the spot. Doing so as you save the document eliminates the hassle of having to go through scads of entries later on and manually move them to more logical locations. I will show you how to do this from within a Microsoft Office XP application in Hour 20, *Jumpstart Word Processing*.

- Don't overdo it! Just because you see the logic in creating multiple folders doesn't mean it's the right thing for you. If you produce very few documents, having them stored in multiple locations can actually cost you more time than it saves.

Although I would love to give you the definitive method to organizing your files, attempting to do so would be inappropriate; everybody's situation is just too different.

You deserve the truth and as wishy-washy as it sounds, "it depends" really is the best answer here. As long as you try to follow the preceding guidelines, however, you will be in great shape or at least in better shape than you would have been without them!

Relocating Files on Your Machine

We have all had to do a little spring cleaning around the house every year. Well, sometimes your computer needs a little spring cleaning too!

You delete a file in the same way you delete a folder: open Windows Explorer, right-click on the file you want to remove, select Delete from the shortcut menu, and respond Yes to the question posed to you.

Moving or copying files to a second location, however, opens up a whole world of new techniques. For example, you can click a file you want to move; then while holding the mouse button down, drag it to its new folder.

Alternatively, you can right-click a file and select the appropriate option from the short-cut menu. You can then move to the new folder and insert it.

And, of course, with Windows XP, you can always click the folder to select it and then use the links in the middle of the screen to accomplish your task.

Because these processes are a bit trickier than they may seem on the surface, I'm going to guide you step-by-step through each method.

Dragging and Dropping a File to a New Location

You may be thinking you have the drag-and-drop feature mastered, but when it comes to using this technique in Windows Explorer, it can get a bit hairy.

> **Movin' can get confusin'!** Dragging and dropping folders or files from one location to another can be a bit tricky. If you attempt to drag and drop a folder or file from one place on the same disk drive to another, the folder will be moved. If you drag and drop a folder on your hard drive to your floppy drive, then the item will be copied to the second location.

To be on the safe side, here are the steps you will need to follow from within Windows Explorer to drag and drop a file from one folder to another:

1. Click on the folder containing the file you want to move and then use the scroll bars in the main Windows Explorer viewing window to bring the desired file into view.

2. Now turn your attention back to the Folders pane and use the scroll bars to locate the destination folder. But whatever you do, do *not* click the destination folder! If you do, you will lose sight of the file you intended to move. If the destination folder is a subfolder, click the appropriate plus (+) sign to make the folder appear onscreen.

3. Finally, click the file you want to move, drag it to the destination folder, and drop it into place (see Figure 3.4).

FIGURE 3.4

It's fairly easy to see just where the selected file is being dragged.

When there's more than one file to be moved... Sure, you can go back and repeat the preceding steps to move additional folders, but wouldn't it be more efficient to move more than one file at a time? Well, you can, assuming that the files reside in the same folder. Keep these tricks in mind because you can also use them for the next file copying/moving technique I'm about to present.

To move multiple files scattered throughout a folder's listing, click the first file to be moved, press and hold down the Ctrl key (there are two Ctrl buttons on your keyboard, one on the lower left side and one on the lower right side), and then click additional files you want to move. If the files happen to be listed in sequence, you can click the top file you want to move on the list, press and hold down the Shift key, and then click the last file on the list you want to move. All the files between the two you clicked on will be highlighted. Drag and drop as usual.

Using the Right-Click Method to Copy Files

Although many people prefer the drag-and-drop technique to move files, you will need to be familiar with right-clicking to copy files. Please note that you can also use these steps to move files, but it's a bit more cumbersome than dragging and dropping. I suggest you go this route for copying files only.

You will need to do the following from within Windows Explorer to copy files to additional folders on your machine:

1. Select the files you want to copy (using the tricks presented in the previous section if necessary).

2. Right-click over any of the highlighted files and choose Copy from the shortcut menu. (If you are moving the files, you should choose Cut instead.) Remember that you can also use the links in the middle of the screen if you're using Windows XP.

3. Next, use the Folders pane to click your way to the folder to which you want to copy (or move) the selected files.

4. Right-click over the newly selected folder and then select Paste from the shortcut menu. The highlighted files will be copied (or moved) to the specified folder.

Using the Search Companion to Find Files on Your Computer

Searching for a file on your computer has never been easier thanks to the Windows Search Companion. A cute little animated dog guides you through the entire search, asking you relevant questions to help him retrieve the desired file as quickly as possible.

To begin working with the Search Companion, click the Start button and then click Search. The Search Companion window shown in Figure 3.5 opens.

Consult the sections below to learn how to find specific types of files.

FIGURE 3.5

Your search begins by telling the Search Companion what kind of file you're looking for.

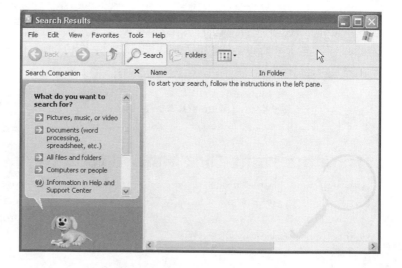

Locating a Multimedia File

Given the popularity of and ease in working with digital photos, music, and videos in Windows XP, Home Edition, it's only natural to assume that you'll eventually end up with a large number of these files on your machine.

Should you ever lose track of any of the files, however, the Search Companion is there to help. To find a multimedia file on your machine, launch the Search Companion as described previously and then follow these steps:

1. First, click the Pictures, music, or video link. The Search Companion presents you with a new set of options.

2. You are then asked to specify the exact type of multimedia file you're looking for: Pictures and Photos, Music, or Videos. Check the appropriate option.

3. Near the bottom of the Search Assistant, you'll see a text box. In it, you are asked to supply the name (or partial name) of the file you're trying to find. Type it in and then click the Search button.

4. The Search Companion returns a list of possibilities in the right pane (see Figure 3.6). Right-click the file you want to work with to take action on it (move it, delete it, rename it, and so on).

FIGURE 3.6

When searching for images, you actually see the files, not just meaningless filenames.

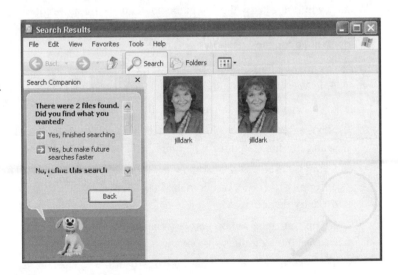

Searching for Documents

The Search Companion is also highly effective at helping users locate word processing documents, spreadsheets, or other types of Microsoft Office documents.

To find such a document, simply launch Search Companion and follow these steps:

1. Click the Documents (word processing, spreadsheet, etc.) link to uncover the next set of search options.

2. Next, to narrow the field of possibilities, the Search Companion asks you when you last modified the document you're looking for. By default all documents will be considered, but if you remember a timeframe that could speed things up a bunch. Click the appropriate option and then scroll down the Search Companion pane a bit.

3. If you know the name of the document or even part of it, type it in the text box provided and then click the Search button.

Again, the results of the search appear in the right pane. To open the document, all you need to do is double-click it.

Finding Files of Any Type

What if you don't know the file name but can remember unique words or phrases used in the document? No sweat; the Search Companion can help! In fact, these are the steps to follow for the toughest searches out there:

1. On the opening screen of the Search Companion, click the All files and folders link. You'll find a number of neat search parameters you haven't seen before.

2. If you can recall even part of the file name, enter it in the text box provided.

3. Next, enter a word or phrase you feel was unique with regard to the document you're searching for. (Obviously pictures, videos, and music files don't have words, but....)

4. Using the Look in dropdown box, you can instruct the Search Companion to search a floppy drive, CD, or alternate disk drive. (The search will be performed on the C: drive by default.)

5. If you remember when you last opened the document, click the When was it modified? button, and then choose the appropriate option.

6. The rest of the options aren't terribly useful to a casual user. (I mean, there aren't very many of us who can eyeball a document, shake our head in admiration, and exclaim, "Wow, that's the best 100KB of text I've ever seen!") But seriously, if you entered all the other information (or even a fair chunk of it), clicking Search should bring you the file you're looking for.

Summary

In this hour, you were introduced to the concept of electronic file management. You took a look at some invaluable organizational tips and even learned how to find the files you need when you need them.

In the next hour, *Healthcare for PCs*, you will be introduced to a number of tools you can use to keep your computer in tip-top shape.

Workshop

Now it's time to see just how much you learned in this lesson. I'll give you a short multiple-choice quiz to test what you learned, followed by a suggested activity designed to enhance the skills you acquired during the hour.

3

Quiz

Select the best answer to the questions from the choices provided and then check your answers in the following section.

Questions

1. When is the best time to plan and define your computer's folder hierarchy?

    a. Do it only when you have a gigabyte worth of data files on your hard drive.

    b. Wait until you have used your computer for a year or two so that you know what types of folders you will need.

    c. As soon as possible; sound file management practices are much easier to maintain if you start early.

2. Which of the following is the best file naming advice?

    a. Give files short, descriptive names and store them in well-labeled folders whenever possible.

    b. Use the longest filenames possible; that way a file search is more likely to pull up the files you really want.

    c. You don't need filenames; Windows does it for you.

3. What is the Windows tool used to locate files?

    a. Fetch!

    b. Retriever

    c. Search Companion

Answers

1. C is the proper answer. The longer you wait to get organized, the bigger the mess you will have on your hands.

2. A is the answer to this one. Long filenames accomplish little. When you allow Windows to name your files, it can make up filenames for you, but they would more than likely be useless. After all, how much does a filename like Document 3 tell you, besides the fact that it was the third document you created?

3. All the words may have similar meaning, but only C, Search Companion, is a real Windows tool. (Hey, the other two options would have been great candidates too since there's a little dog onscreen to sniff out elusive files!)

Activity

Come up with a list of five potential folder names that would be of use to you.

1. _____

2. _____

3. _____

4. _____

5. _____

If you are really serious about keeping all the files on your machine under control, you also should take the time to write down the types of documents you think will go into each folder. That will help you solidify the purpose of each folder you define so that when it comes time to save a document, you will immediately know the best place to store it.

HOUR **4**

Health Care for PCs

You wouldn't dream of running your car thousands and thousands of miles without a periodic checkup or, at the very least, an oil change, would you? Well, the same holds true for your computer. The more software you install or uninstall and the more files you add or delete, the more pertinent it becomes to perform maintenance on your system.

In this lesson, I'll show you how to keep your investment in tip-top shape with the help of free utilities included with Windows XP, Home Edition. It should be noted that most of these utilities came with Windows ME and Windows 98 as well.

You will also find out more about the following topics:

- Which files should you save when you back up your hard drive?
- Defrag the hard drive? That's supposed to be a good thing?
- How can I protect myself against computer viruses?
- I installed a game demo on my computer and my machine hasn't been the same since. What can I do?

Archiving Your Files

To protect your valuable data, it's best to make an extra copy of it. The easiest way to do so is to back up your files onto a diskette, recordable CD, or a Zip drive cartridge. Then, if something happens to the original file (or worse yet, to your hard drive), you can restore the backup copy onto your hard drive.

> **So you think archiving is boring?** Well, guess what? Thanks to all the neat new gadgets and PC components, you can now burn CDs of your favorite photographs to protect them for years to come (no fading or tearing here); you can transfer home videos to CD to keep them from wearing out (or to keep a hungry VCR from eating them); and finally, you can record your very own music CDs, picking and choosing each track yourself. Oh, the possibilities! I'll show you how to do all of this later in the book.

Choosing Your Backup Media

As mentioned above, with today's computers, data are typically backed up onto diskette, CD, or Zip drive. Owners of older PCs also had the option of using Jaz drive media and tape backup units, but the limited storage capability, high price of storage media, and lack of market share made these options all but disappear in the light of affordable CD recording capabilities.

With all these options, deciding what to use when may get a bit confusing. There are basically three factors that should be considered in making your decision: (1) what devices you have available to you, (2) what type of data you want to back up, and (3) your intended use of the backup media.

Do You Have Drive?

I realize this first factor is obvious; after all, it's a little difficult to burn a CD when your computer doesn't have a CD recordable/read writable drive. However, it is an issue nonetheless. The same goes for Zip drive backups. Almost every machine has a floppy drive, but other devices or drives are often optional. Obviously, the type of backup method you use will depend on your computer's components. If you have a recordable/read writable CD drive and/or a Zip drive, you will also need to take the following factor into account when making your decision.

Yeah, I've got one of those thingies! Now would be a great time to take stock of your computer and all its components. Use the handy-dandy tear card in the front of this book to keep track of everything. To learn everything under the sun about your PC, click the Start button and then choose All Programs, Accessories, System Information. A few mouse clicks will tell you everything you need to know and then some!

So *That's* What You Want to Put on That Disk!

If your goal is to back up word processing documents or spreadsheets, just about any of the backup media options will do. However, when it comes to graphic-intensive documents, photographs, and audio and video files, you will need to take into account the storage capacity of each type of media. Table 4.1 shows you just how much material you can fit onto each type of storage media.

TABLE 4.1 Storage capacity of various types of media

Media	Data capacity
High-density diskette	1.44MB
Zip disk	100MB or 250MB
CD-ROM	650MB

4

Now that's BIG! Did you realize a CD-ROM can store the same amount of data as 450 diskettes? If you think that's a lot, consider this: you can fit more than 300,000 pages of text on a single CD-ROM. That's more than 600 copies of this book on one CD, excluding graphics)!

With that in mind, it should come as no real surprise that in order to deal with the cool stuff (photographs, video files, or music files), you will need to work with CD-ROMs or Zip disks.

Here's just one example: a photo taken with my 3.3 megapixel Sony CyberShot camera with the best quality settings available took up 1,441KB of space on my hard drive. That's more than 1MB of space—too close for comfort to put on a diskette without editing or compressing it. (You will learn more about working with photographs in Hour 22, *Digitally Yours: Working with Electronic Images.*)

I gotta get me one of those! Recordable/read writable CD drives keep coming down in price. If you didn't get one with your computer, you can buy one for under $100 at your local computer store. (Of course, getting it installed will add to the price unless you have a computer savvy buddy who can help you out in exchange for a pizza!)

Music files can also get big in a hurry. A standard 3- to 4-minute song can easily reach 3MB when converted to the popular MP3 format. We can do a lot to trim the size down a bit, as you will see in Hour 20, *Getting Sights and Sounds on Your Computer;* however, the file size will never reduce to where diskettes can be your best option.

CD-Rs versus CD-RWs. When you go shopping for blank CDs, you will notice that there are two flavors: CD-R (recordable) and CD-RW (read writable). The newest drives will record on either, but check your documentation just in case. Some older drives will take only one type.

There's a big difference between CD-Rs and CD-RWs. CD-Rs can only be written to once. You can always add data to the unused parts of the disk with the right software, but you can't overwrite the data recorded on the disk; once it's there, it's there for good. This makes it a fine alternative for creating music CDs and virtual photo albums but perhaps a waste for data backup, since you would probably want to overwrite your data backups periodically to reflect any changes.

CD-RWs are sort of like overgrown diskettes; you can write over them again and again, making them good data backup candidates. However, CD-RWs can only be read by other CD-RW drives. If the plan is to make a CD to play in your car or at a friend's party, you will definitely need to go with CD-Rs.

What Are Your Plans for the Disk?

Admittedly, this falls under the "of course" category too, but you will be surprised at how easy it is to forget all of this! When deciding which type of backup media to use, make sure that the intended recipient can work with it. Also, think back to the earlier caution about the differences in blank CDs.

Defragmenting Your Hard Drive

When a file is stored to a hard drive, it is broken into tiny chunks, and each piece is stored in the first available sector of the hard drive. After the drive starts getting full and files are deleted (creating certain random sectors available here and there on the hard drive), file parts are no longer saved in adjacent sectors.

Thus a file may be scattered (or fragmented) all over the drive, which can slow down its retrieval. To improve the speed of your PC, you should defragment your hard drive. Defragmenting reorganizes the parts of each file so that they are once again adjacent to each other on the hard drive, eliminating excess search time.

To help you visualize this, let me share a personal story. My mother-in-law is famous for being able to cram huge amounts of food into her refrigerator. And she's got it down to a science—so much so that no one else can even help put anything away! Like your computer's hard drive, food in her refrigerator is nested and stacked in such a way as to maximize space. All the fruits and vegetables may not be in the same location, but they are all in there, much like the files on your hard drive. When food is taken out, consumed, or replaced, the refrigerator's contents need to be repacked again to make sure everything fits. Likewise, as files come and go on your hard drive, you will need to defragment it to fill in some of those "holes" on your hard drive.

Analyze Before You Defragment

Defragmenting a drive can take seemingly ages, especially with the huge hard drives installed in new computers these days. Windows XP gives you the opportunity to analyze the hard drive before committing to a full defragmentation. The analysis takes almost no time at all, and it will tell you whether a full defragmentation is warranted.

Follow these steps to see whether it is time to defrag your hard drive:

1. Click the Start button; then point to All Programs, Accessories, System Tools, and click the Disk Fragmenter option. The Disk Fragmenter program window opens (see Figure 4.1).

2. By default, your primary hard drive should already be highlighted. Verify that this is the case and then click the Analyze button on the lower left part of the window.

3. After the Disk Fragmenter has finished its analysis, you will see a report like the one shown in Figure 4.2. You are given three options: View Report, Defragment, and Close. If the utility recommends that you defrag your hard drive and you have the time, go ahead and click the Defragment button. Otherwise, click Close and return to the task later. If the drive appears to be in good shape, simply click Close.

4. Close Disk Defragmenter by clicking the red X button in the upper right corner of the window.

4

FIGURE **4.1**
Any hard drives you have installed in your computer will appear in the Volume display window.

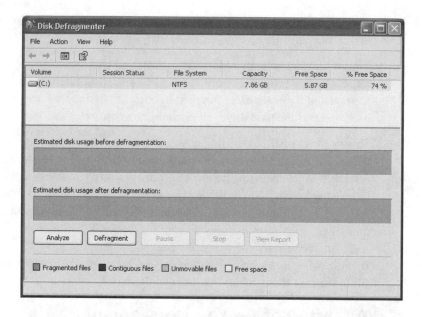

FIGURE **4.2**
A simple report lets you know exactly where you stand.

> **What colorful results!** If you look in the Analysis display in the center of the screen, you see a color-keyed representation of the state of your hard drive. *Red* marks space containing fragmented files, *blue* marks space occupied by files in a single location, *green* marks space housing files that cannot be moved, and finally *white* denotes free disk space. The more white and blue you see, the better it is. A lot of red means a disk defragmentation is definitely in order.

Running the Defragmenter

If you opted to run Disk Defragmenter at a later date, simply launch the program as you did previously, only this time, click the Defragment button instead of the Analyze button. The utility will work its way through the hard drive, making any repairs it can.

Generally, defragging a cluttered, fragmented hard drive helps Windows run a bit more smoothly.

Cleaning Your Disk

4

Another tool that can help you recover chewed-up space on your hard drive is the Disk Cleanup utility. It analyzes the specified disk, comes back with a list of "safe" files to delete, and lets you select which ones you want removed.

The amount of space you can recover using this tool varies from a fraction of a megabyte to tens of megabytes, so the results will vary, depending on the way you use your machine (or perhaps the way you have used your machine in the past).

Here are the steps you will want to take to reclaim some of your disk space:

1. To begin the Disk Cleanup process, click Start and then choose All Programs, Accessories, System Tools, and click Disk Cleanup.
2. After a bit of behind-the-scenes work, the Disk Cleanup tab shown in Figure 4.3 opens, showing you which files you can safely delete and how much disk space you would regain by making the selected deletions.
3. Click a file type's name to see a description of what it is and how deleting it would affect your system. Place a checkmark in the checkboxes of file types you want to remove from your system. Should you change your mind about deleting a file type, simply click the checkbox a second time to remove the check.

FIGURE 4.3
You might be surprised by just how much space you can get back!

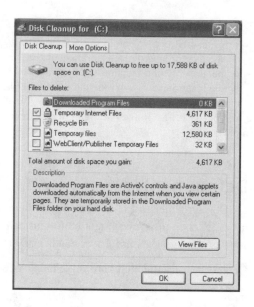

4. When you are ready to start deleting the files, click OK. The utility will ask you if you are sure about the deletion. Click Yes or No as appropriate.

   A status bar appears, displaying the progress of the job. When the files have been successfully deleted, the application shuts itself down.

Protecting Yourself Against Computer Viruses

Much like humans can catch a bug from unsuspecting carriers, computers can catch a virus. With a thorough understanding of viruses, how they are transmitted, what their symptoms are, and how you can protect yourself, your PC can lead a long, healthy life.

Antivirus Programs: Vitamin C for Your PC

The best bet for safe computing is getting, installing, running, and most importantly, *updating*, a good antivirus program. The two most popular antivirus manufacturers are Norton and McAfee.

There is a good chance your computer's manufacturer may have preinstalled one on your system before you bought it. It would be worth your while to poke around your computer's files a bit to see if such a treasure exists. If it does, spend a few minutes getting acquainted with the program. Learn how to turn it on and off, register it for regular updates, and even give it a test run on your hard drive in order to get comfortable with it.

From that moment on, keep the program running in the background so that it scans every file you come in contact with. If that drags down your system's performance too much, scan for viruses manually by following these steps:

1. Click the Start button and then click My Computer.

2. Next, click the name of the hard drive, floppy drive, or removable device you want to scan for viruses.

3. In the Tasks pane on the left side of the screen, you will see a Scan for viruses command (if an antivirus program is installed on your PC). Click that link to initiate the scan. The length of time required to complete the scan will depend on how large (or how small) the item is you're scanning.

4. Check your antivirus program's documentation for further instructions.

When Bad Things Happen to Good Systems: Using System Restore

"I downloaded a screensaver from the Internet and installed it on my computer. My PC hasn't been the same since!"

You would be amazed at how often I get an e-mail like that! Believe it or not, something as simple as installing a computer game can alter files on your system and unintentionally create all kinds of problems for you. Sadly, in the past the only solution seemed to be to reformat the machine's hard drive and reinstall everything from scratch, a major pain in the neck to say the least!

With Windows XP's new System Restore feature, you can literally take your computer back in time to when it worked its best, and most importantly, all your data files will remain perfectly intact. For those who have used a computer for any amount of time at all, it's just short of a miracle!

To restore your system to a previous working state, follow these steps:

1. Launch System Restore by clicking the Start button; then choose All Programs, Accessories, System Tools, System Restore. The System Restore welcome screen appears (see Figure 4.4).

2. Next, click the Restore my computer to an earlier time button and press the Next button.

3. A calendar like the one shown in Figure 4.5 opens, asking you to click a date and time to which you'd like to restore your computer.

FIGURE 4.4

A brief explanation of what System Restore does appears on the left side of the screen.

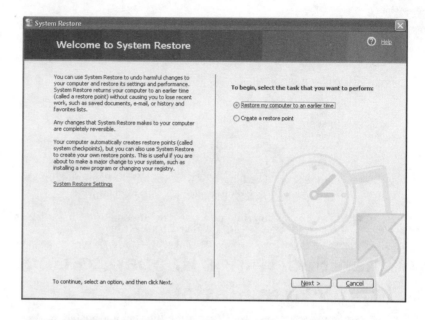

FIGURE 4.5

Pick your day to go back in time.

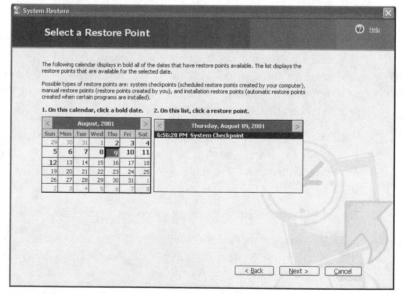

4. After you have chosen a date and time that you recall the PC working its best, click the Next button.

5. You are then asked to verify the date and time you chose. System Restore then urges you to save and close all other documents and applications because Windows will need to reboot your system to make the desired changes. If everything appears correct onscreen, click Next.

6. Windows restores your files and settings and then reboots itself so that all of the modifications can be made.

Summary

By now, you should be familiar with all the tools to help keep your computer in shape for years to come. Not only do you know how to call on the utilities when you need them, but you also learned how to protect yourself against nasty computer viruses.

Now that you are practically a PC doctor, it's time to shift your attention to getting additional help when needed. In the next lesson, Hour 5, *Sending Out an S.O.S.,* you will not only learn how to get help in the Windows help files and on the Web, but you will find out how you can use Remote Assistance to turn your "problem child" over to the capable individuals such as a professional technical support person or a friend who is knowledgeable about computers.

Workshop

Now it's time to see just how much you learned in this lesson. I'll give you a short multiple-choice quiz to test what you learned, followed by a suggested activity designed to enhance the skills you acquired during the hour.

Quiz

Select the best answer to the questions from the choices provided, and then check your answers.

Questions

1. Which tool helps get rid of unwanted files on your machine?

    a. ScanDisk

    b. Disk Cleanup

    c. Disk Backup

2. What is System Restore?

    a. A utility that fixes disk drive errors and rearranges files to optimize system performance

    b. A new vitanutrient that restores your colon to optimal condition

    c. A tool that lets you roll back your PC to a preproblematic state

3. Which backup media is best for recording music CDs to play in your car?

    a. CD-RW

    b. CD-R

    c. Diskette

Answers

1. B is undoubtedly the only tool listed for this task.

2. The only acceptable answer here is C. The first answer was meant to trick you, and the second was meant to make you laugh!

3. Your answer should have been B. A can't be read by many audio CD players, and C is too small to be of much use.

Activity

Let's see what kind of shape your hard drive is in. Launch Disk Defragmenter and run an analysis report. What color is more evident? Go ahead and run the defrag job itself if necessary; you deserve a rest after this intense lesson!

Hour 5

Sending Out an S.O.S.

Everybody needs help and advice from time to time. Whether you are trying to accomplish a more advanced task that may not have been covered in this book or you are trying to figure out why your computer is acting up, you will find the troubleshooting tips and tricks in this lesson helpful.

More specifically, we will take a look at the following issues:

- My computer is on, but why is my monitor pitch black?
- Is it possible to search for help rather than skim the index?
- These help files have been around forever. Where can I get updated help'?
- Can I really have a buddy fix my computer over the Internet?

Just when you think you have the hang of controlling this hunk of machinery, the unexpected happens. Maybe your monitor doesn't flicker into action when you boot your machine, or perhaps your computer doesn't seem to recognize the new CD you just put into the CD drive.

This chapter includes some of the more commonly encountered problems, along with some possible solutions. Looking here may solve your problem first, before you spend hours on hold waiting for technical support.

If you don't see your specific problem right away, stay tuned for the remainder of the lesson. I can show you how to get help no matter what!

Computer Chaos

In this section, I am presenting the most common problems encountered with a computer as a whole. Some solutions may seem overly obvious, but they are things you should always double-check. With children, pets, and other distractions, you may miss the warning signs of a computer acting up.

Likewise, you should understand that this lesson is meant to be a reference you can flip back to at a later date. Perhaps some of the topics should have been reserved for later when you've had the chance to get fully up and running on your new computer, but we want to give you the ammunition you need to solve any problems that may come up early on. That way you're ready for anything and know where to turn from the get-go.

My Computer Won't Turn On!

Before you panic, a number of things can remedy the problem. Ask yourself any of the following first:

1. Are all other electronics in the area working? If not, you could have a blown fuse, or you may have a general power failure on your hands.

2. Are the monitor and the console (the big box with the power switch and disk drives in it) plugged in and turned on? They both have power switches, so it is possible the console is spinning up; you just can't tell because the monitor may be turned off.

3. Is your power strip in the ON position? A pet can easily switch them off, as can a falling object from your desk, so it is worth a peek.

4. Is the power to your PC driven by a light switch? If so, verify that it is in the ON position.

5. Still nothing? Then double-check to make sure all of the cables are securely in place.

6. If you still get no response, try unplugging the computer and plugging something else into the power strip. If the other item works, you can assume the power strip is fine, but there may be a problem with the PC's power supply. That warrants a call to your PC's technical support because a blown power supply isn't repairable by an untrained person.

My Computer Froze! What Now?

Nothing's more unnerving than your computer freezing on you. No matter what you do, nothing happens; even Ctrl+Alt+Del (the keyboard shortcut to restart your computer) may fail. Before you start inventing new curse words as you yell at your PC, try the following:

1. If at all humanly possible, try to get into any open word processing documents or spreadsheets to save your work. The next steps you take may result in data loss if you don't. Of course, if your system is entirely frozen, you may not be able to get anywhere. (You did back up your hard drive recently, didn't you?)

2. Next try pressing Ctrl+Alt+Del, but do it only once! (If you do it twice, the system resets without giving you the chance to save anything.) The Windows Task Manager dialog box shown in Figure 5.1 appears, listing all open applications. If an open application is causing the problem, you will see the words Not Responding next to the application's name. Click the name of the problem application and then click the End Task button.

FIGURE 5.1

The Status column lets you see where the problem lies.

5

Here today; gone forever. Hopefully, the problem application wasn't one containing unsaved data. (Usually, it is a Web browser with a memory leak or some other innocuous problem.) If it was an application like your word processor or spreadsheet program, there may be no way to recover your work. Office XP programs boast an AutoRecover feature which should, in theory, attempt to recover the active document during the crash when you relaunch the application in question. I wouldn't count on this too heavily, though, since it seems to fail as often as it works. I will show you the best ways to protect your Microsoft Office documents when I present Microsoft Word (Hour 8, "Jumpstart Word Processing") and Excel 2002 basics (Hour 10, "The Numbers Game")in the next section of this book.

3. If there is still a problem, repeat step 2 to see whether a second application is not responding.

4. Still frozen? Rebooting may be the only answer. On the Windows Task Manager toolbar, click Shutdown, Restart. Hopefully, Windows will shut itself down smoothly. If it doesn't, you will have to turn the PC off, wait a few minutes, and then turn it on again. In cases like this, the system restart may take a bit longer than normal as Windows tries to repair itself.

5. If you get repeated system lockups with a certain application, check the Internet to see if a patch or update to the program is available that may solve the problem. An update or upgrade can often cure what ails your computer.

6. Have you checked for computer viruses, as directed in the last lesson?

7. When repeated system lockups occur and you can't trace them to a specific application, there may be an underlying hardware problem. It may be worth a call to your PC's technical support department to see whether they can offer additional guidance.

Disk and Drive Dilemmas

Nothing lasts forever, and that includes disk drives. That's why people are paranoid about backing up files. Disk drive failures don't happen often, but when they do, they can be catastrophic if you are not prepared. Likewise, you may be deceived into thinking your disk drive has failed when there is really a simple solution to the problem.

The Floppy That Won't Fit

Here again, there are several things you can try in order to isolate the problem. Please don't be offended by some of the more obvious suggestions; I know that I, for one, have made some pretty basic mistakes while working late at night.

1. Verify that the disk you are trying to insert is the same size as the drive into which you are trying to insert it. An ancient 5.25-inch disk stands no chance of fitting into today's standard floppy drive, and diskettes can't fit into a CD drive (something about square pegs in round holes…).

2. Is the disk in the right position? A disk that is upside down or sideways will not fit into the drive. In the case of CDs, even if an upside-down disk fits, it can't run using the wrong side of the CD.

3. Make sure you are really trying to insert the disk into a disk drive. I remember when I first started using a computer, I actually stuck one of the old 5.25-inch floppies into one of the vents in front of the console!

4. Examine the disk for any abnormalities such as warping, sticky spots, and other things because any of these could potentially cause a problem for you.

5. If there is still a problem, you may want to have a qualified person check out the drive itself. Under no circumstances should you ever stick an object other than a disk into the disk drive, especially when the machine is plugged in.

The Unrecognizable CD

CD-ROMs can be very finicky, depending on the sensitivity of your drive. If you run into a glitch, try the following:

1. Open the CD drive, take out the disk, and blow any dust off of it. Blow any dust out of the drive too. Examine the disk for any scratches, since they can also cause problems. Replace the CD and see if the computer recognizes it now.

2. Trouble still? A more thorough cleaning may be in order. Cleaning methods vary depending on whom you ask. There are plenty of commercial cleaning products on the market from which to choose. However, if you want to try cleaning a CD using things around the house, start by finding a soft cotton rag. I use an old cloth diaper that was used during infant feedings. It has been washed a million times and is softer than just about anything else around. Next, take out the CD and breathe hot air onto the bottom of the disk. Finally, wipe the CD gently from the inside of the disk to the outside in a straight line and retry it in the drive.

3. If that doesn't cure the problem, try putting another CD in the drive. If everything goes smoothly, you can attribute the problem to the CD itself. If it still doesn't work, you might want to try a third CD (perhaps a music CD, if the problem CD was a data CD, or vice versa) before calling technical support.

5

Monitor Messes

A computer is pretty much useless without a monitor or display. It is completely understandable to panic when the monitor starts acting funky!

All Powered Up and Nothing to See

If your computer is on but there is nothing to see, don't write off the monitor yet. Try the following things first:

1. If the monitor was on when it "died," check to see whether it is in Power Saver mode by moving your mouse or pressing a key. If it comes to life, you may want to consider either disabling or at least adjusting the Power Saver setting. Do this by clicking the Start button on the Windows taskbar and then clicking Control Panel. Click the Performance and Maintenance link near the bottom of the screen. On the bottom right corner of the Performance and Maintenance screen, you will see a link to Power Options; click that. The Power Schemes tab of the Power Options Properties dialog box shown in Figure 5.2 opens. Use the drop-down arrow buttons to make any desired changes and then click OK to save your settings.

FIGURE 5.2

Using the Power Schemes drop-down box, you can optimize your computer's power for use as a laptop or home PC.

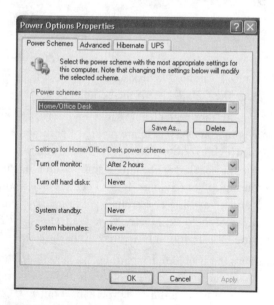

2. Verify that the monitor was not shut off manually, as opposed to with the rest of the computer via the power strip. (You may not have shut it off that way, but on more than one occasion, my well-meaning son has turned it off to save "'tricity," as he put it.)

3. If that doesn't do it, check the monitor's connection to the console and make sure that the monitor is plugged in.

4. Still in the dark? If the monitor's LED power light is on, you might want to try tweaking the brightness and contrast on your monitor. Because the location of these controls can vary depending on your monitor's manufacturer, consult the documentation that came with your system.

5. If it is still dead, it may be time to call your friendly technical support people. Be sure you have any warranty information with you when you call, along with the information you wrote on the tear card at the front of this book.

Printing Problems

It usually happens when you are more pressed for time than normal. You send a document to the printer, go over to pick it up, and find nothing. What can you do?

Assuming that your printer has been properly installed with the necessary drivers, there are tons of other quirky things that can happen to make life with your printer miserable. Here's a bit of guidance to help keep you sane.

Where's My Document?

When you send a document to the printer and nothing comes out, consider the following:

1. Is the printer turned on and plugged in? Furthermore, is the printer securely attached to your PC?

2. Make sure that the printer has enough paper to complete the job. This is especially true in the case of shared printers, since you may not know who has printed what when.

3. Is the printer online? Printers may unexpectedly go offline, which requires you to press the Online/Offline button on the printer to generate output. (Consult your printer's documentation for the exact location of this button.)

4. Check the printer's LED screen to see if it's given you a specific error message. You'll most likely need to consult the documentation or the printer manufacturer's Web site for an interpretation of anything but the most basic problems.

5. If the print request is routed through a server, as may be the case with a computer attached to a network, contact the server's administrator (or the house nerd in the case of a home network) to verify that the request actually made it. If it didn't, there could be a loose network connection.

6. If there is output, although blotchy, disfigured, or completely black, it may be time to change the toner/ink cartridge.

5

> **I'm all shook up!** If time is of the essence, chances are you can temporarily revive the printer by removing the toner/ink cartridges and shaking them up a bit. It works great for my old laser printer, but inkjet printer documentation should be read first to make sure you don't end up with a faceful of colored ink!

7. If everything listed here fails to remedy the problem, it is time to call a professional. Keep in mind that unless you purchased the printer from the company that manufactured and/or sold your PC, you will most likely need to call a different technical support number.

Partial Printing

Sometimes print jobs are not complete. This typically happens due to one of the following reasons:

1. Obviously, if your printer runs out of paper halfway through the print job, you will end up with an unfinished product.

2. Go into the application's Print dialog box and make sure that the All Pages option is checked. (You will find this by clicking File, Print in most any Windows application.)

3. Did you exit the application before the entire document could be downloaded to the printer's memory? Some older applications will abort a print job in this situation.

4. If the document was a frame-based Web page, you may not have gotten the frame you intended to print. Go into the Web browser's Print dialog box, select the applicable frame, and then resubmit the job.

5. Could there have been a power surge that interfered with the process? If so, simply resubmitting the job may be all you need to do.

Internet Irks

With something as massive as the Internet, complications can occur at any number of points. In fact, it may take significant amounts of time to isolate an Internet-related problem for that very reason. If you've worked your way through Hour 12, "Connecting to the Internet" and still have a problem, this is the place to turn.

Slow Connections

If your Internet connection is crawling at a snail's pace, several things could be going on, including any of the following:

1. If you are surfing during the day and find Web pages loading at an excruciatingly slow pace, chances are, the Internet is bogged down with traffic. Given the time differences across the United States, along with the millions of leisure surfers who log on from home, the Internet may very well be clogged at all hours of the day. The only thing you can do is surf at odd hours, invest in a high-speed Internet connection for your home, or simply tolerate the sluggishness.

2. For those of you who have the opportunity to take advantage of cable modem service, go for it. You get super speed, and you don't even have to tie up a telephone line! If you plan to do much surfing and there is anything less than a 56K modem in your computer, then you should seriously consider upgrading.

3. If things are crawling along into the wee hours of the night, there may be a cut cable somewhere along the line. Unfortunately, there is nothing you can do about it, since it is more than likely halfway across the country. In such a situation, you will certainly feel the effects of masses of rerouted Internet traffic.

4. Perhaps your connections are continually hit or miss. It could mean your Internet service provider (ISP) doesn't have a high-speed link to the Internet. If they don't plan on upgrading soon, you may want to shop around for better service.

Dropped Connections

If you keep getting those pesky "Do you want to reconnect?" messages, look into the following:

1. Pick up your phone and listen to the dial tone. Is it crisp and clear, or do you hear crackles and static? A bad phone line can often kill a connection. If the weather is stormy and windy, check the lines again when things settle down. If you have always had problems with your phone lines, there may not be much anyone can do about it until the phone company decides to upgrade or service its underground cables.

2. I have found that my older Windows 98 machine is almost hypersensitive to incoming calls. I don't have call waiting, but I do have voicemail through the phone company. Therefore, if the phone rings and the line is busy or goes unanswered, the call is forwarded to a mailbox at a phone company substation. Interestingly, when a call came in and was forwarded to voicemail, I would often get booted off the Internet. The hassle may not be worth giving up voicemail, but such a situation can occur. Luckily, Windows XP seems a bit better behaved in that regard.

3. Check your modem's configuration. Many machines are set up to drop an Internet connection if it remains idle for a given amount of time. To learn whether this is the case for you, click the Start button on the Windows taskbar and then click the

5

Control Panel. Click the Network and Internet Connections link and then click Phone and Modem Options in the See Also pane at the upper left part of the page. Open the Modems tab and look for an option under Call preferences that reads: "Disconnect a call if idle for more than ___ min." If this option is checked, you can either disable it by clicking it or adjust the time as desired by clicking inside the text box and entering a new number.

4. If the disconnects persist even in the absence of either situation mentioned previously, check with your ISP to see whether others have reported a similar problem. A flaky modem at its end can cause plenty of grief on your end. After you have the answer to this question, you should have a pretty good idea of whether the problem potentially lies with your modem or your ISP.

Busy Internet Connections

If you keep getting busy signals when you try to connect, here are some suggestions.

1. Get additional dial-up numbers from your ISP to try in a pinch. A high number of customers dialing in at once can clog lines in no time.

2. If that doesn't remedy the problem, call your ISP and inquire about the user-to-modem ratio. Someone once told me 7-to-1 is ideal, so if it is significantly higher than that, you may want to explore alternatives or pressure them to add more modems.

3. For the night owls among us, surfing in the middle of the night may be all that is needed.

4. Here again, cable, DSL, or ISDN access from home will eliminate the problem entirely. Certainly, it will cost you, but for those who need the Internet to work, there is nothing better, especially when you factor in the benefit of increased file transfer speed as well.

Help Is Right There in Front of You!

If you did not see your biggest computer annoyance in the sections above, don't worry; there is plenty of help right inside your computer. I will show you not only how to make the best of it, but also how to bring in outside help when the "big guns" are needed.

Help Is Just a Click Away with Windows Help and Support Services

No book can promise to cover every single computer glitch out there. Much like cars, computers have all kinds of things that can go wrong with them. That is why there is lots of information buried in the Windows XP help files. It is right there, ready and waiting for you to come to it whenever you need it.

You will learn about several ways to seek help in this hour, but the most simple of them involves clicking your way through Windows Help and Support Services links.

To begin your quest for help, click the Start button and then click Help and Support. The Help and Support Services windows shown in Figure 5.3 opens.

FIGURE 5.3

Help and Support Services: your starting point for the information you need most.

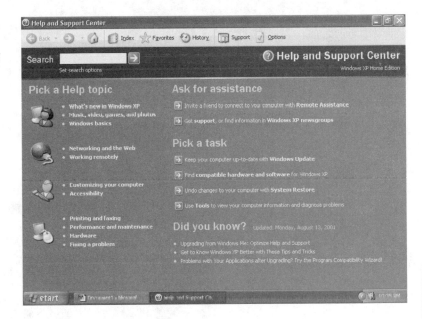

On the left side of the screen, you will see a set of links labeled Pick a Help topic. Simply click the link that best describes your problem or issue. The screen then divides in two with the left side devoted to various topics and the right side for selected content.

Plus and minus signs can be clicked to expand and collapse topics respectively, but let's take a closer look at this Help and Support Services window. There are several options available that you may not have noticed right away. I have pointed them out in Figure 5.4.

Table 5.1 explains where all these buttons take you and how they work.

This may seem like an overwhelming number of options for finding assistance, but we have only just begun. The methods and tools you see here are intended to appeal to a wide audience because not everyone likes to learn or gather information in the exact same manner.

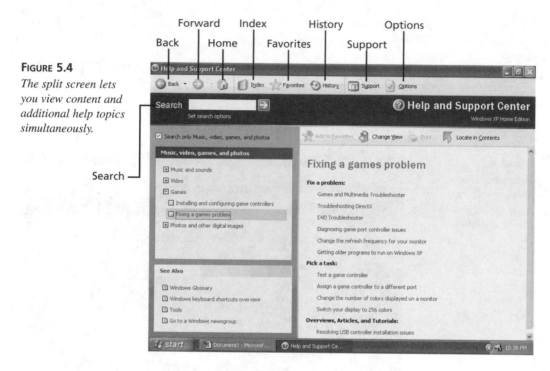

FIGURE 5.4
The split screen lets you view content and additional help topics simultaneously.

Table 5.1 Help and Support Services controls

Clicking this button...	...does this
Back	This takes you back to the previously viewed page in Help and Support Services. It acts much like a VCR's rewind button or a Web browser's Back button.
Forward	This moves you ahead to a previously viewed page in Help and Support Services. Think of it as a fast-forward button on a VCR.
Home	This puts you right back at the start of the Help and Support Services area so that you can head in an entirely different direction if needed.
Index	Rather than task-based links, the index lets you browse topics covered in the Help files, much like you would skim the index of this book to find something specific.
Favorites	Do you have a Windows task that causes problems every time? When the applicable help topic is displayed, click the Add to Favorites button. That way, you can quickly return to the page as needed by finding it on the Favorites menu shown in Figure 5.5.
History	If you have viewed a relevant page in recent history, clicking the History button will help you find it again, quickly and easily.

Clicking this button...	...does this
Support	Clicking this link will take you to the gateway to Windows-based Help that is not included on your PC (such as discussion groups, Web pages, software updates, and links to the Remote Assistant, as well, which we will discuss later.
Options	This button lets you customize Windows Help and Support Services itself.
Search	This text box lets you enter any term you want to search, rather than making you browse through the index or task- based links.

If you don't find what you need using any of these methods, believe it or not, there are still plenty of options for you.

Make a Date with a Windows Update

As time goes on, Microsoft and millions of Windows XP users are bound to stumble onto some things that need fixing or changing. Perhaps a bug keeps a popular new computer game from running smoothly or maybe an exotic security leak is what stops you! The fact remains that Windows XP makes installing a program update easier than you can possibly imagine. In just a few simple mouse clicks, you can have the absolute latest and greatest operating system on your machine. You should note, however, that a connection to the Internet must be configured and established in order to take advantage of this feature. (You will learn how to set this up in Hour 12, *Connecting to the Internet*.)

> **Tiny icons in the notification area.** A small icon will appear in the notification area of the Windows taskbar when an automatic Windows update is available for download.

5

To install a Windows update, just follow these steps:

1. From the Start menu, click Help and Support.
2. Under the Pick a Task section, click the Windows Update link. Windows XP will attempt to connect to the Windows Update Web site.
3. Once the page is displayed, click the Scan for update link.
4. After a few moments to evaluate your system, Windows comes back with a report of how many updates are available to you. Click the Review and install updates link to see a final report like the one shown in Figure 5.5.

FIGURE 5.5

The updates available to you are listed in a shopping basket with a complete description of their function.

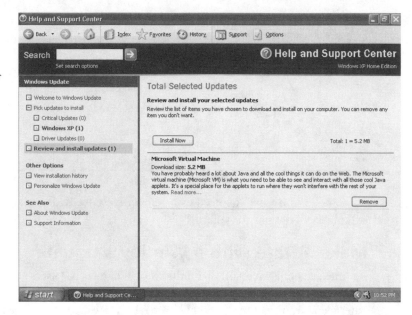

5. After reading the update descriptions and noting the file download size, click the Remove button of any updates you wish to skip for the time being.

6. Once you are happy with the contents of your virtual shopping basket, click Install Now to have Windows download and install the selected updates. In a few moments, you will have your computer back in tip-top form.

Seeking Help Online

It is possible that given how quickly the industry moves, updates to help files in Windows XP will be needed over time. What better place to get it than on Microsoft's Windows newsgroups?

Not again! Before posting your own question to a newsgroup, make sure you have sought out any FAQs that may have been published somewhere, either on the newsgroup itself or on an affiliated Web site. If you post something that has been repeatedly asked, people on the newsgroup can get a little uptight. Therefore, it is best to do your homework first. If you have, then newsgroups can be one of the most current and beneficial help tools out there!

From anywhere within the Windows XP Help and Support Services tool, you can click the Support button at the top of the screen. This takes you to the Support section where you can tap into Windows newsgroups and MSN communities and even seek help from Microsoft directly.

These newsgroups/communities are made up of people who post questions and others who answer them, comment on them, and so on. With regard to scope, it's almost like sending e-mail to tens of thousands of people at a time, and best of all, you can address your unique situation, not some general help file situation that kind of sounds similar. It gives users of all levels of experience the opportunity to seek help from and bounce ideas off of others around the world.

Simply click the desired resource and you are on your way. We will look at Microsoft Remote Assistance in greater detail in the following section, since it represents a revolutionary new way to address computer problems.

Putting Your Computer's Fate in Someone Else's Hands

If, after all of this, you are still stumped by a computer problem, it is time to call in reinforcements using the Windows XP Remote Assistant. As I mentioned earlier, these reinforcements can be professional technical support people, or they can be a computer-savvy family member or friend. In any case, it is absolutely imperative that you trust them, since they will have complete access to the files on your machine.

> **Get connected!** You must have a configured and active Internet connection in place, as described in Hour 12, in order to begin using Remote Assistant.

Before we get into the nitty-gritty of how to seek remote assistance, allow me to tell you a bit about how the utility works.

The first thing you do is send your remote assistant an invitation to help you. The thought of sending someone an invitation to help you may seem a little awkward, I know; it's as if the person at the receiving end should feel privileged that you have chosen them to save the day! Regardless, it is through this invitation that you basically give the recipient permission to take control of your machine over the Internet.

> **Be prepared.** In order for you to take advantage of Microsoft's Remote Assistance feature, both you and your "helper" will need to be running Windows XP on your machines.

Once contact has been made at the agreed-on time, both you and your assistant will be able to view your screen. This way, he or she can watch as you attempt to replicate the error, problem key sequence, or other issue at hand. You will also have access to a real-time chat screen where you can instantly compare notes about the situation. As you can imagine, this is a tremendous new feature for those who are apprehensive about using or fixing a computer.

Okay, let's get to it! To start working with Remote Assistance, you will need to follow these steps:

1. From anywhere within the Help and Support Services area, click the Support button.

2. Under Support Options, you will see a link called Ask a friend to help; click it. On the right side of the screen, a blurb about using Remote Assistance appears (see Figure 5.6).

3. Click the Invite someone to help you link.

FIGURE 5.6

Get a taste of what lies ahead when using Remote Assistance.

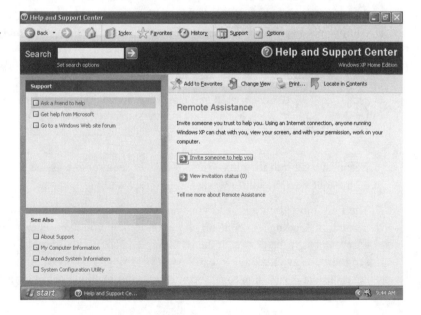

4. Next, you will get to choose how you would like to send an invitation, Windows Messenger (which you'll learn more about in Hour 22) or e-mail (covered in Hour 16). I recommend e-mailing it the first time. Enter an e-mail address for your friend (or click the Address Book link to select one from there once you get your address book all set up). After the information is entered, click the Invite this person link underneath the e-mail address text box.

5. You will then be asked to fill out the invitation shown in Figure 5.7. Information required includes the recipient's name and a message of your choice. (You will learn how to retrieve the recipient's e-mail address from your address book when we get done setting it up in Hour 17). When you are done, click the Continue button.

FIGURE 5.7

You have plenty of space in the invitation form to explain your situation.

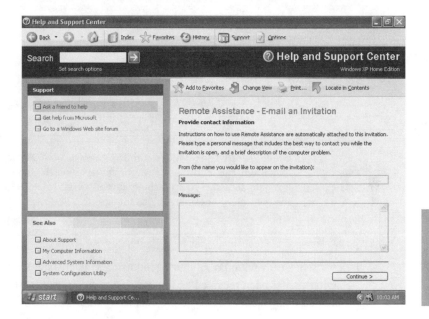

6. Using the drop down arrow buttons provided (see Figure 5.8), you can set the length of time for which the invitation is valid. You should also set up a password for your helper to use; that way, your system is less vulnerable to strangers. You will be asked to type this password twice to make sure it is correct. When everything is ready, click the Send Invitation button.

FIGURE 5.8

You will set the dura-
tion invitation to help
in this screen.

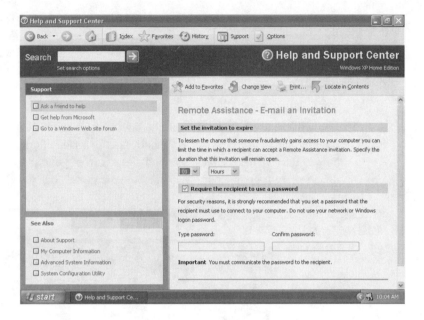

Oh, for safety's sake! Make sure the password is NOT included with your invitation. This is so that unauthorized eyes viewing the e-mailed invite cannot gain access to your machine. It is also wise to pick a unique password for the invitation, not one you use to log into Windows or any retail Web sites you may use.

Windows sends the invitation to your friend using your installed e-mail program. After your invitation has been received and opened, your fate (or at least your *computer's* fate) is in that person's hands once he or she decides to help.

As a new user, you don't really need to know much more about Remote Assistance—leave all that to the technologically advantaged folks. But please keep in mind that the person you have tapped to help you will need your help and cooperation, too. Try to explain your problem as thoroughly as possible, and be prepared to try certain things your helper suggests with your PC on your end, too. After all, that's why they call it Remote Assistance, not Remote Repair!

But seriously, as a team you should be able to get to the root of the problem in short order.

Summary

Okay, do you feel totally armed to handle anything now? Well, maybe not *everything*! You are certainly far more prepared than most new users, and with tools like Remote Assistance available to you, you will be all set!

As we draw this section of the book to a close, we are going to look at one last aspect of Windows: *Sharing Your PC with Others*. You will discover how to keep Windows just the way you like it, no matter how many people you have share your computer!

Workshop

Now it's time to see just how much you learned in this lesson. I'll give you a short multiple choice quiz to test what you learned, followed by a suggested activity designed to enhance the skills you acquired during the hour.

Quiz

Select the best answer to the questions from the choices provided and then check your answers.

Questions

1. What is the Windows XP help utility called?

    a. Sanity Central

    b. Help and Support Services

    c. ShatteredWindows.com

2. If the Internet is running slowly, what is the most likely cause?

    a. Oops, you forgot to pay the Internet service bill again!

    b. The Internet is supposed to be slow, silly!

    c. With the explosive growth of the Internet, sometimes too many people are online for things to run swiftly.

3. Which of the following statements is true with regard to Remote Assistance security?

    a. Send the password along with your invitation to make it more convenient for the recipient.

    b. Always set a password and deliver it to your helper separate from the invitation.

    c. Post the password to a newsgroup your helper-to-be frequents so that he or she can pick it up anytime they are ready.

5

Answers

1. B is undoubtedly the correct answer.

2. Of course, the only acceptable answer here is C. For starters, if you didn't pay the bill, there would be no Internet service at all!

3. Your answer should have been B. From a security standpoint, the others are down-right dangerous!

Activity

Even though your PC is fairly new, go ahead and run a check for Windows updates. Are there many available for download? Are there some that don't seem worth it to you? Once you have made your selections, run the download and installation and call it a day!

HOUR 6

Sharing Your PC with Others

What if every member of your family had his or her own PC? You wouldn't have to look at your daughter's Britney Spears desktop theme, and your desktop wouldn't be cluttered with icons for your husband's golf games or your wife's annoying screensaver. Also gone from your configuration would be your toddler's JumpStart educational programs! Computers have gotten less expensive, but unfortunately, they are not *so* cheap that you can buy one for each person in your family!

In this lesson, I will show you how to configure your computer for use by multiple people. You will also read more about the following topics:

- Where do I begin configuring the user options?
- What parts of the Windows environment can be customized for each user?
- How do users log into their customized desktop?
- Can other users see what software I have installed while in my personalized desktop?

So what exactly will having separate user accounts enable you to do? Here is just a sampling of the possibilities:

- Customize the way the Windows desktop looks for each user. In other words, you get to flaunt your passion!

- When you surf the Web, Internet Explorer lets you keep a list of favorite Web sites. It also keeps track of where you have been so you can literally go back in time to find a Web page you forgot to save. With separate user accounts, each person has his or her own Favorites and History lists. Everyone knows that favorites lists can get cluttered enough without having to share them!

- If you like your icons big, prefer to view files as thumbnail images instead of text listings, or need to enable one of Microsoft's accessibility enhancements, it's a snap to have it your way without affecting everyone else.

- Remember how I told you not to keep putting stuff into the default My Documents folder? This way, even if you do stuff some documents in there, no one else will ever know it because they will have their own My Documents folders.

Before I show you how to use the multiple user capabilities of Windows XP, you will need to enable it. And as usual, Microsoft provides a handy wizard to guide you every step of the way.

Modifying the Primary User's Account

When you accessed the Start menu earlier in this book, you may have noticed a picture of some chess pawns and the word *Owner* in the upper left corner of the panel. This means that you are currently working in the default Owner account that was created when Windows was installed. Two accounts were actually created on installation: Owner and Guest.

 That's not what MY Start menu says! If you installed or upgraded Windows yourself, it will have asked for your name as part of the installation process. In those cases, your name appears instead of the generic Owner account.

Both of these accounts can be modified to reflect the needs and tastes of the respective users rather than creating a whole new account right off the bat. (I will show you how to create a new account later in the hour, though, since you may need it if you have three or more people sharing the machine.)

Follow these quick steps to begin taking full advantage of the Windows XP multiple user accounts feature:

1. From the Start menu, click the Control Panel link.

2. Click the User Accounts link on the right side of the screen. This takes you to the User Accounts window shown in Figure 6.1.

FIGURE 6.1

Since this computer was upgraded to Windows XP, my name appears in place of the Owner account.

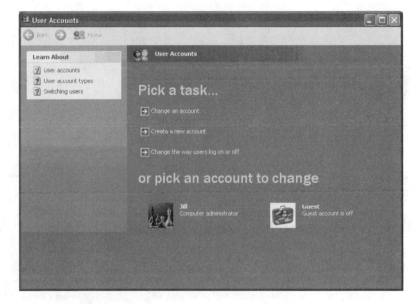

3. Click the Owner account button (or the button with the primary user's name on it in the case of self-installed or upgraded machines) near the bottom of the screen to begin making modifications to the account. You will be presented with a list of items you can edit for the selected account.

4. Let's start by finding a name for the account. If *Owner* sounds rather pompous and possessive to you, click the Change my name link and then type in the name desired. When you are finished, click the Change Name button to make the modification official. You will be kicked back to the User Accounts window shown in Figure 6.1.

5. You may also find that the default owner account image just isn't doing do it for you. Just click the Change my picture link to look for a replacement. Microsoft gives you 23 more to choose from (see Figure 6.2). Click the one you want and then click the Change Picture button. The screen in Figure 6.1 reappears, but this time, it has your newly selected picture in place instead of the airplane.

6

FIGURE 6.2
From airplanes to fish, many icon choices await you.

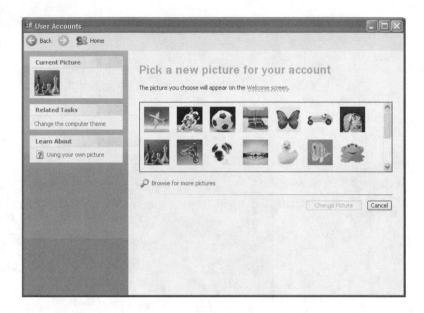

Hey, that's me on the Start menu! You can put your family's pictures in place of the standard icons provided with Windows XP. (It is another innovative way to use those digital photographs and photo scans you will be working with in Hour 23, Digitally Yours: Working with Electronic Images.) To do this, simply click on Browse for More Pictures underneath the choices Microsoft gives you. Click your way to the photo or image you want to use. Double-click it to select it and then hit the Change Picture button. Your gang is all present and accounted for on this machine!

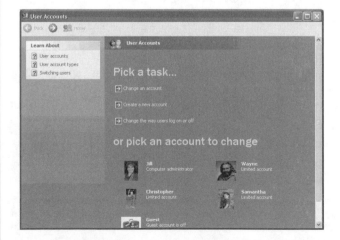

6. Since the primary user's account is already preconfigured to be the Computer Administrator (this is the only person who can see all the machine's files and make critical changes in security and system access), we don't need to modify the account type this time. However, setting a password to maintain security would be wise. Then, only you can make critical changes to each person's profile. Set a password by clicking the Create a Password link. That takes you to the screen shown in Figure 6.3.

FIGURE 6.3

Notice that there is a set of links along the left side of the screen that you can easily consult if you need additional help.

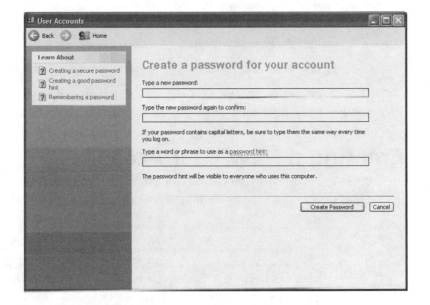

7. You will be asked to type the password in twice to be certain it is correct. You will also need to type in a password hint. Make sure it is a phrase that will help you remember the password the instant you see it. Once you have verified that everything you keyed in is correct, click on Create Password. Again, you will return to the main User Accounts screen shown in Figure 6.1.

Get a little mysterious. Since others may be able to access this hint, try to make it at least somewhat mysterious. Remember, if other users get access to the Computer Administrator's account, they can go in and remove any account limitations and security.

8. Finally, if you are afraid you might still forget the password, it might be a good idea to create a password reset disk. If you forget your password when prompted for it on the Windows welcome screen, you can insert this disk to change your password on the spot. To build such a disk (which, by the way, should be kept tucked safely away), you must log on to the computer administrator's account, and then click the Prevent a forgotten password link in the Related Tasks pane on the left side of the screen. This launches the Forgotten Password Wizard.

9. After reading the warnings provided onscreen, click the Next button to continue.

10. Insert a diskette into your floppy drive and then click the Next button. Follow an additional onscreen prompts until the process is complete.

Once the disk is written, you should be ready for anything.

These steps can also be used to modify non–Computer Administrator accounts; however, you may want to put some limitations on secondary accounts as described later on.

Creating a New User Account

When you go to configure your PC for a third user, you will need to step through a wizard of sorts to make sure everything is properly set up.

> **Wizards aren't just for science-fiction books anymore!** The word *wizard* may conjure up images of a man with long gray hair, an equally long flowing robe, and mysterious powers. In the world of computers though, it carries a bit different meaning.
>
> In computing, a wizard is generally a set of guided steps that a user can follow to accomplish a more advanced task. Not only are they easy to follow and ensure that you don't forget anything, but they give you all kinds of helpful pointers where needed.

To configure a user account from scratch, you will need to do the following:

1. Select Control Panel on the Start menu and then click the User Accounts link.

2. Click the Create a new account link to be taken to the wizard.

3. Predictably, the first step is to select a name for the account. Type in the name you want the account to carry and then click the Next button.

4. With regard to the account type, there are only two options: Computer Administrator and Limited. Choose Limited for all secondary accounts, especially those of new or inexperienced users, to eliminate stepping on one another's feet when it comes to setting systemwide options.

What does *limited account access* mean? Users with limited access cannot install their own software. This can be cumbersome if you, as the Computer Administrator, must then install every game your kids want on the computer. However, if other users in the household are young and inexperienced, it may be easier to install the software yourself than try to troubleshoot any botched attempts. Only you can make the best call, given the other users' preferences and capabilities.

5. Press the Create Account button to set it up. The user can now go in and change his or her picture if desired as described above.

Switching from One Account to Another

All you have to do to move from one account to another is shut down the programs in use, click the Log Off button on the Start menu, and verify that you want to log off by clicking the Log Off button (see Figure 6.4). Then, when the Welcome screen opens, click the name of the account onto which you want to log. It really is that simple!

By the way, the Welcome screen also appears when you boot the computer. Simply click the appropriate account to get started.

FIGURE 6.4
Logging off is a mouse click away.

Using Fast User Switching

Microsoft implemented multiple user accounts in previous versions of Windows, but to switch users, you had to shut down all active programs. This is not the case with Windows XP. If your son is surfing the Internet in search of rumors about the next James Bond film and you need to print out a copy of a photo you scanned for a relative, you can quickly hop onto the system, do your thing, and get off without so much as disturbing a single Web page.

6

Fast User Switching not working as anticipated? Perhaps it got disabled. You can enable it again by choosing Control Panel from the Start menu, selecting User Accounts, and then clicking the Change the way users log on or off option. Once there, you have two options you can toggle on or off: (1) Use the Welcome screen (on by default), which lets you choose the account you want to log onto by clicking the account's name or icon instead of having to manually key in the account name; and (2) Use Fast User Switching option, which lets you hop from one account to another without having to disturb a thing.

To execute a Fast User Switch, simply click the Log off button on the Start menu. Within seconds, you will be staring at a fresh Welcome screen from which you can choose the account you need to log in to.

Deleting an Account

When you get tired of sharing your PC and become a multiple PC household, you will want to know how you can delete any old user accounts. Just follow these steps to perform the deletion:

1. Access the Control Panel from the Start menu and then click the User Accounts link.

2. Click on the account you want to remove.

3. When asked what changes you want to make to the selected account, choose the final item on the list, the Delete the account item.

4. You will then be asked whether you want to keep or delete the account's files (see Figure 6.5). Make your choice by either clicking the Keep Files button or the Delete Files button. If you decide not to remove the account at this time, you can always bail out by clicking the Cancel button.

 Be careful what you wish for.... Only documents like Word and Excel files and such can be preserved in this manner. If you delete the account, e-mail and Internet files will be lost forever.

If you opt to keep the files, they will be placed in a special folder on the Desktop that is named after the deleted account member. This gives you access to the files from anywhere on the machine.

FIGURE 6.5

Removing the account doesn't mean the files have to go too.

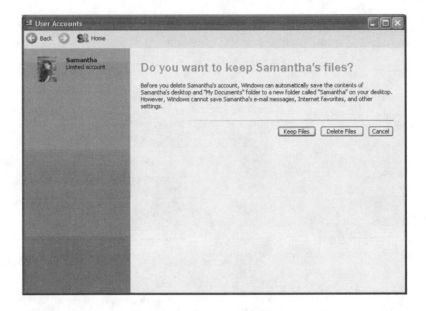

Gone in 60 Nanoseconds. Before deleting the files from the account about to be removed, take the time to verify that the material has been saved elsewhere, because once it's deleted here, it's gone for good. At a bare minimum, if you aren't sure of the status of the files, you may want to go ahead and back them up just to be safe.

Just Waiting: An Annoyance or Safety Feature?

Remember how I said screensavers would reflect each user's preference? Well, by default, when the screensaver kicks in and you "wake" the PC up by pressing a key or jiggling the mouse, you will be thrown back to the Windows XP Welcome screen. If you are working alone at the time, it can be annoying to have to log in each and every time.

Conversely, if you are sharing a PC with a child or co-worker, the action can be a blessing in disguise. Your child won't be able to circumvent any Internet access restrictions you may have set up for his account, or that co-worker cannot inadvertently have full access to all your files.

If you would rather just have Windows dump you back in the place you were working, you can do so by following these simple steps:

6

1. Right-click over an exposed part of the Windows XP desktop and select Properties from the resulting shortcut menu.

2. Access the Screen Saver tab as shown in Figure 6.6.

FIGURE 6.6
*One click toggles the
Return to the Welcome
screen on and off.*

CLICK here to
control the
Return to Welcome
screen option.

3. Right underneath the Screen Saver drop-down menu, you will see a check box labeled On resume, display Welcome screen. By default, this item is checked. To disable the option, simply click it again to remove the check mark.

Summary

With this chapter behind you, you will get as close to being a multi–PC household as possible without having to shell out some major dough. You also discovered it can be more than a matter of preference; it can also be a matter of security.

The next section of the book focuses attention on running software on your PC. In the next lesson, *It's All About the Software,* you will not only learn what kinds of software are on the market today, but you'll learn why it's a good idea to register software as well as how to decide when to upgrade or not.

Workshop

Now it's time to see just how much you learned in this lesson. I'll give you a short multiple-choice quiz to test what you learned, followed by a suggested activity designed to enhance the skills you acquired during the hour.

Quiz

Select the best answer to the questions from the choices provided, and then check your answers.

Questions

1. How many user accounts are set up by default?

    a. 0

    b. 1

    c. 2

2. Can you use your own pictures for user account icons?

    a. You bet!

    b. No, you can only choose from the nine Microsoft gives you.

    c. Yes, but they add 20 pounds to your normal weight.

3. What is the biggest advantage to enabling Fast User Switching?

    a. How can there be an advantage when there is no such thing?

    b. You can move from one person's account to another without having to close all of the programs.

    c. The default settings are far superior.

Answers

1. C. Windows sets up an Owner and a Guest account for you, which you can modify as needed.

2. A. Flip back to the earlier pages of this chapter to see how.

3. The correct answer is B.

Activity

Think about the people with whom you might have to share a PC. How many different accounts would you need to set up? Do you think setting passwords would be useful, or are separate user accounts mostly a matter of aesthetics and file organization? If you know others who could benefit from having access to your new PC, take a few moments to set up accounts for them now. That way you won't have to worry about it later on.

PART II
Making Things Happen with Software

Hour

HOUR 7

It's All About the Software

Windows acts as the brain for your computer, so the other types of software on your PC form what could almost be considered its personality.

Okay, so maybe that sounds a little weird, but think about it for a second. A computer loaded with plenty of productivity software suggests that someone who gets down to business and stays on task uses that machine. At the other extreme is the system with a screaming video card, sound system complete with subwoofer, a big monitor, and a sizeable hard drive, chockfull of the latest and greatest games. If that computer doesn't belong to a kid, it most certainly belongs to a kid at heart!

In this lesson, I will introduce you to the various types of software. I will also help you get comfortable with moving and resizing program windows. In addition, you will read more about the following topics:

- What is "edutainment" software anyway?
- How do I get all the various types of software?

- Should I register my software?
- When is it time to upgrade my software?

We have already taken an in-depth look at your computer's operating system; let's now shift our focus to other kinds of software you might find tucked away on your machine. I will also give you some names of popular programs that fit into each category, not so much as an endorsement of their quality but as a way of helping you further distinguish the various types of software from one another.

Software Defined

To perform a certain type of task using your computer, such as typing a letter, you need an application or program for that task. When you purchase a new PC, you might receive some applications as part of the purchase. In fact, many of the most reasonably priced systems today are shipped with some flavor of Microsoft Office XP (or at the very least, Microsoft Word 2002, which I will show you in the next couple of lessons). Likewise, Windows is, hands down, the operating system of choice for computers sold worldwide. As you may have noticed while exploring your new machine, Windows also includes some miniapplications such as a paint program, a calculator, and the ever-popular Solitaire card game.

The applications preinstalled on your computer should be more than enough to get you started. In fact, I strongly suggest you hold off buying any new software for your computer until you have spent significant time at the keyboard. However, if Windows is the only software loaded on your machine, you may want to consider some additional purchases. That is hardly likely though, since companies are getting more cutthroat as they compete to win people over to their part of the PC market share through the inclusion of comprehensive software packages.

As time passes, you will form your own preferences for the types of software you want to use. Software can get expensive, which is why I encourage spending time with an application before you sink loads of money into it. As you will see later in the hour, as well as in Hour 18, *Downloading Goodies from the Internet,* demonstrations, or demos, are a great way to "try before you buy" because they are typically free and give you the opportunity to experience how something works ahead of time.

After you get comfortable using your new system, you will want to purchase additional applications. Software generally falls into one of the categories described in the following sections.

Why can't I just borrow my buddy's disks to try a program out? It might seem simpler to borrow a friend's disks rather than wait for a lengthy download over the Internet, but as long as your buddy has registered the software and is still using it on his computer, doing so is breaking the law. The practice of installing the single-licensed software on multiple computers at once is referred to as *software piracy.* It is really no different than stealing a piece of jewelry from your local department store. The same copyright laws that protect books, music, and other works are also applicable to software.

What's in a Word? You will hear the terms *program, application,* or some combination thereof used interchangeably. They all mean basically the same thing.

Word Processors

The most common type of application is word processing software. You can use this type of program to create documents such as letters, memos, reports, resumes, manuscripts, and so on. If there is something you would have once done on a typewriter, you can now use a word processing program for the task. (Well, maybe not *everything.* Using word processing programs to fill out forms can be a real pain in the neck.)

Word processing programs are much more than just a fancy typewriter. They offer many editing and formatting features so that you have a great deal of control over the content and look of your document. Here is a quick list of some of the things you can do with this type of program:

- **Easily edit text.** You can move text from one page to another and even from one document to another. You can also copy or delete text with just a few keystrokes or mouse clicks.
- **Format text.** Formatting means changing the appearance of text. You can make text bold, change the font, use a different color, and so on. In Hour 8, *Jumpstart Word Processing,* you will learn how to make some formatting changes.
- **Format paragraphs and pages.** In addition to simple text changes, you can also format paragraphs (indent, add bullets, or add a border) and pages (change the margins, add page numbers, or insert a header).
- **Check accuracy.** Most programs include a spell-check tool for checking the spelling. Some programs also include a miniapplication, or applet, for checking grammar.

7

Word processing programs can differ in terms of what features they offer. If your needs are simple, you might do just fine with the simple word processing program included with Windows. This program, called *WordPad,* includes basic editing and formatting features.

If you plan to create a lot of documents and want a stunning professional appearance, you may want to purchase a more robust program. One of the most popular programs is Microsoft Word 2002, shown in Figure 7.1. You will learn a lot about this powerful tool in the next couple of hours. This program includes all the preceding features, as well as desktop publishing features for setting up columns, inserting tables, adding graphics, and so on. Word 2002 also includes features for sending faxes, creating Web documents, and much more. Although I can't introduce you to all of these powerful features in this book, I promise that you will have a good, solid foundation of word processing basics on which you can build.

FIGURE 7.1

Microsoft Word 2002, a part of the Microsoft Office XP suite, is the most popular word processing program.

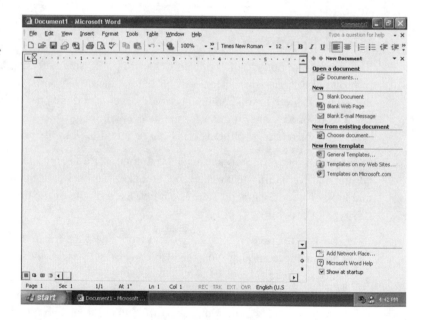

Other word processing programs you will see on store shelves include Corel WordPerfect and Lotus WordPro.

To produce the highest quality newsletters, brochures, catalogs, and other items, you may want a desktop publishing program. These programs provide even more control of the layout of the page. Microsoft Publisher 2002, which is technically part of the Office XP family but no longer included in the various suite packages, is a fairly simple desktop publishing program, yet it provides oodles of templates to achieve quick, professional-looking results. Adobe PageMaker is a more powerful package; however, it may take more time to master the subtleties, not to mention the fistful of cash you will need to purchase it!

Spreadsheets

If numbers are your game, you will most likely work with a spreadsheet application. This type of program enables you to enter and manipulate all kinds of financial information such as budgets, sales statistics, income, expenses, and so on. You enter these figures into a grid of columns and rows known as a *worksheet* or *spreadsheet* (see Figure 7.2). The intersection of a row and column is called a *cell,* and you enter text, numbers, or formulas into the cells to create a worksheet.

FIGURE 7.2

Use a spreadsheet program for any type of numerical data you want to calculate or track.

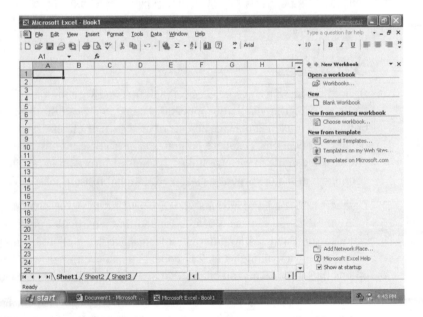

The benefit of a spreadsheet program is that you have so many options for working with the data you enter. You can do any of the following:

- **Perform simple-to-complex calculations.** You can total a column of numbers, calculate a percentage, figure the amortization of a loan, and more.
- **Format the data.** You can make changes to how text and numbers appear in the worksheet. You can also adjust the column width, add borders, change the alignment of entries, and more.

7

- **Chart the data.** You can create different types of charts to visually represent the data. For example, you can add a line chart to a report to illustrate a sales trend.
- **Manage data lists.** Most spreadsheets also include features for managing simple data lists. You can enter, sort, and query simple data lists using the grid structure of a worksheet.

Microsoft Excel 2002, Lotus 1-2-3, and Corel Quattro Pro are all popular spreadsheet programs. I will tell you more about the widely distributed Microsoft Excel 2002 in Hour 10, *The Numbers Game,* and Hour 11, *When Only a Database Will Do.*

In addition to spreadsheet programs, you can also use other types of financial programs. For example, you can purchase a program to keep track of your check register. Some of the most popular check management programs are Quicken and Microsoft Money. You can also find programs for calculating your income tax (TurboTax), managing your small business (QuickBooks), handling major accounting tasks (PeachTree Accounting), and others.

Databases

If word processing and spreadsheets rank first and second in application popularity, databases and other productivity applications come in a close third. You can use a database program to track and manage any set of data such as clients, inventory, orders, events, or personal collections. Database programs vary from simple list managers to complex programs you can use to manage linked systems of information residing on huge mainframe computers at major corporations and educational institutions.

Databases offer a lot of advantages when you are working with large amounts of information. First, you can easily search for and find a particular piece of information. You can also sort the data into different orders as needed, a client list alphabetically for a phone list, or a mailing list by ZIP code. You can even work with subsets of the data: all clients in South Dakota, all clients that ordered more than $1,000 worth of products, Beanie Babies purchased for more than $10, and so on.

Some popular database programs include Microsoft Access 2002, and Corel Paradox. As you saw in the spreadsheet section, you can even experiment with lightweight databases by modifying a spreadsheet application. I will even show you how to do it in Hour 11.

Graphics and Presentation Programs

Even if you aren't artistic, you can use your PC and the right software program to create graphics. Depending on your needs and skills, you can consider any of the three types of programs in this category:

- **Simple drawing programs.** You can use a simple drawing program, such as Paint, which is included with Windows, to create simple illustrations. In addition, larger applications like Word 2002 include applets like WordArt and AutoShapes that let you dabble in the visual arts, regardless of whether you have artistic talent or not.

- **Complex drawing programs.** You can also find more sophisticated programs for drawing and working with images. Adobe Illustrator and Adobe Photoshop are two such packages. For more technical renderings, you might consider Visio, a fairly recent acquisition of Microsoft. This product will undoubtedly go through some major revisions and enhanced Microsoft Office integration in the near future, but even older versions of Visio can easily be imported into Word 2002 documents.

- **Presentation programs.** If you ever have to give a presentation, you might want to use a program designed just for creating presentations. You can use this program to create slides, handouts, and notes—a great tool for educators, executives, or sales people. Microsoft PowerPoint 2002 (see Figure 7.3), Corel Presentations, and Freelance Graphics are popular presentation programs.

FIGURE 7.3

PowerPoint 2002's TriPane interface makes it simple to create colorful presentations.

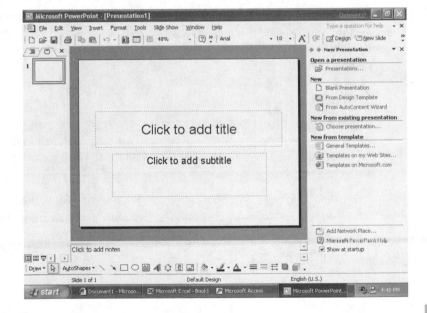

7

Suites or Bundles

Software manufacturers often create a package or suite of the most popular programs and sell them together. For example, Microsoft offers several versions of its Office suite of applications. One is a lower cost Standard Edition, another contains extra tools for software developers, and a third is designed for professional power users. You'll even find free office suites like OpenOffice (the free counterpart to StarOffice) if you want the power without the expense.

Corel and Lotus offer similar suites that include their most popular word processing, spreadsheet, database, and presentation programs. Microsoft Works Suite 2001 contains a word processor (an earlier version of Word, Word 2000), encyclopedia, greeting card designer, trip-planning program, and more.

Personal Information Managers

Most people have several things to track: people, events, appointments, places, and so on. Personal information managers (PIMs) store names and addresses, maintain your schedule, keep notes, and perform many other tasks. You can think of this type of program as an electronic planner. Microsoft Outlook 2002 (not to be confused with its little brother, Outlook Express, which comes free with Internet Explorer) acts as a PIM in addition to being an email program.

Games

When you go into a store that sells computer software, you will probably see more games than anything else. Within this broad category, you will find several classifications of the programs. Take a look at the following list to see what titles you might find in each category:

- **Puzzle/Arcade**: Just about anything you ever played in an arcade in college can be found on store shelves. Centipede, Pac-Man, and many other favorites, along with a slew of pinball machine programs can be found. You will even find familiar board games like Boggle and Clue. Even electronic versions of your favorite televised game shows are represented, such as *Who Wants to be a Millionaire?, The Weakest Link,* and *Wheel of Fortune,* are among them.

- **Strategy**: Among the classic games making up this category are Battleship, Mastermind, Scrabble, the best selling SimCity series, Microsoft's Ages of Empire series, Sid Meier's Alpha Centauri, The Sims, SimThemePark Word, and Railroad Tycoon II. Newer popular releases in this category include Black & White, Startopia, Zoo Tycoon, and Tropico.

- **Action**: If you like action-packed games, you might enjoy some of these titles: Duke Nuke'em 3D, Quake, Earthworm Jim, the Half-Life series, Descent 3, Tom Clancy's Rainbow Six, and Delta Force. Beware that many of these are gory primary shooter games that are not suitable for young players.

- **Adventure**: Harry Potter and the Sorcerer's Stone, Tomb Raider, Final Fantasy, Star Trek, and Star Wars, as well as series like Alone in the Dark, Myst, and King's Quest, fall into this category. In addition, for those with a sick sense of humor, the womanizing, but admittedly funny, Leisure Suit Larry series can perk things up.

- **Driving**: Whether you want to be behind the wheel of an exotic sports car, a motorcycle, or even a pod racer, you are bound to find something that strikes your fancy among these titles: eRacer; Star Wars Episode I Racer; NASCAR Racing 4; the Test Drive and Need for Speed series; Viper Racing; Lego Racer; Grand Theft Auto 2; Carmageddon and Carmageddon 2 (for those with a strong stomach); Destruction Derby 2; Moto Racer 2; and one of my favorites, Microsoft's Midtown Madness I and II.

- **Simulations**: Simulations are a lot of fun. You can fly an old warplane, drive a tank on the frontlines, pilot a helicopter over a city you built in SimCity, even run a hospital or theme park. Simulations you might want to take a peek at include Microsoft Flight Simulator 2002, Microsoft Train Simulator, Comanche 4, SimCopter, X-Wing Vs. Tie Fighter, Theme Hospital, and Independence War.

- **Sports**: No matter what sport you prefer, you will find a game that makes you want to be a part of the team. Some of the more popular sports titles include FIFA 2001 Major League Soccer, Madden NFL 2002, Tony Hawk's Pro Skater 2, NHL 2002, NBA Live 2001, Links 2001, Dave Mirra Freestyle BMX, and Cycling Manager.

- **Reference/Educational**: Titles found in this category include Compton's Encyclopedia, Microsoft Encarta, Mavis Beacon Typing, home designing software, family tree makers, as well as a wide range of college test preparation software and programs to help you learn a new language.

- **Edutainment**: Geared toward kids, this hybrid of educational and entertainment software is designed to help kids have fun at learning. Popular programs in this category include the JumpStart series, Reader Rabbit titles, and the Magic School Bus offerings. These programs really do give kids a head start. My own children are reading three grade levels ahead of their age thanks to a great school and a terrific collection of edutainment CDs at home.

- **Miscellaneous**: This includes everything that fits nowhere else! You will find titles like The Electric Quilt and Quilt Pro (for quilt designing), Microsoft Streets Plus

7

for trip planning, and collectibles cataloging software like Beanie Baby Collector. You can even find pregnancy and wedding planning software, astronomy programs, greeting card makers, photo editors, and other highly specialized titles.

Get the full scoop. Before buying a game, you may want to visit http://www.gamespot.com. From there, you can view descriptions, previews, and reviews of computer games before you invest in them. In many cases, you can even see screen shots of the game in action, watch videos, or download playable demos. In addition, if you get addicted to any popular games, you can even download free game guides instead of purchasing a strategy guide!

Internet Programs

If you want to use your computer to hook up to the Internet, you need a Web browser. The two most popular are Netscape and Microsoft's Internet Explorer, which I will cover in more detail later on in this book. These programs are actually suites of smaller Internet applications as well. For example, Internet Explorer also contains Outlook Express as an e-mail client, and Netscape has Netscape Mail.

Other Internet programs you might come across in your travels are Eudora (e-mail), Opera (comparable to Netscape and Internet Explorer), and AOL's Internet access software. There is also an ever-growing assortment of instant messaging applications like MSN Messenger, AOL's Instant Messenger, and others.

Utility Programs

When you want to fine-tune your computer, you may want to investigate some of the utility programs available. These programs add capabilities to your system such as virus checking or file backup. Norton Utilities is an example of this type of application. Other utilities include WinZip, which handles file compression; Partition Magic, which helps you subdivide your hard drive; and Norton and McAfee antivirus programs.

Purchasing a New Program

Although your computer more than likely came with a number of preinstalled applications, you may eventually want to make some changes. You may want to upgrade an existing program to the newest version or purchase an entirely new program.

You can find software in some retail stores, at online stores and auctions, in computer stores, and through mail-order outlets. Scan through any computer magazine to get an idea of what programs are available and how much they cost. You can also use the Internet as a resource for researching and finding programs. For example, ZDNet at `http://www.zdnet.com` nearly always has reviews posted for both software and hardware.

> **Finders Keepers**. You can find freeware and shareware at many Internet sites. Freeware programs are provided free to you. Shareware programs are provided for you to try without cost. If you like the program, you can pay a small fee to register and continue using the program. `http://www.share-ware.com` is one of my favorite places to shop for shareware online. Some developers even produce "postcardware," where you simply send the developer a postcard from your hometown in turn for registration, or "fabricware," which is one yard of 100% cotton fabric as a form of payment for quilting shareware. I'm sure you will stumble on variations of this over time.

When you are looking for new programs to purchase, be sure that you can run that program on your system. Each program has a set of system requirements—that is, the type of microprocessor, amount of memory, hard disk space, video card, and any other required equipment needed to run the software. You can usually find these requirements printed on the side of the software box. Check the requirements before purchasing anything to be sure your PC is capable of running the software. It might even be a good idea to test a demo of the software on your machine when one is available. You can find many of demos at `http://www.download.com` and `http://www.gamespot.com`. I will show you how to download them in *Hour 18, Downloading Goodies from the Internet.*

> **The fine print.** You may often see a reference to *minimum system requirements* on a box of software. Although the application can technically function with those specifications, it could be painfully slow. The reduced performance might not be noticeable in a word processor, but in a driving game, your vehicle might be nearly uncontrollable because of the jerky system performance. Just keep in mind that minimum system requirements are just that—the minimum. If you want stellar performance, you might want to shop around a bit before purchasing the software or consider upgrading your system in the near future.

7

Be sure that you get the right program for your system. If you have Windows XP, get programs designed for use under Windows XP. You can also purchase and run DOS, as well as programs designed for use on earlier versions of Windows, although they may require a bit more "babying" than most people are willing to do.

Hey, I could use a little help here. When it comes to computer game performance and optimization techniques, I can help! See Appendix A in the back of this book for where to find lists of Windows XP compatible software and how to run Windows in Compatibility Mode to get around some common problems.

The most popular software out there will be compatible with Windows XP. (After all, that's part of what Microsoft wants us beta testers to do—to help find incompatibilities before a product is released to the public.) Many popular programs may even come in several flavors to accommodate various operating systems, so be sure to read the boxes carefully.

As a final precaution, check to see if the software is distributed on diskettes, a CD-ROM, or a DVD-ROM. If you have both a floppy drive and DVD-ROM drive, you are safe, but if you don't have a DVD-ROM drive, be sure to get the version on standard CD or diskettes. CD-ROMs have become the most popular and least expensive method for distributing programs, especially large programs, so you might not even be able to find a version on diskette anymore.

Where to Buy Software

If you are in no hurry, some of the best prices can be had from online stores where competition is fierce. Although you must often pay postage, the absence of sales tax, along with a lower retail price, still make it worthwhile to buy online. Always research shipping costs and terms before you commit to buy. Many online retailers offer low prices but pad shipping costs to make up for the discount.

Be careful out there! Finding a reputable online retailer can be a challenge if you are not familiar with online shopping. Before buying anything online, be sure to read Hour 13, *The Savvy Netsurfer.* You can also pick up a copy of my book, *Savvy Online Shopping*, in the reference section of most major bookstores. The title is also available at many libraries in the United States.

If you are in a hurry, you can seldom beat Wal-Mart, your local wholesale clubs, or the Sunday circulars for good prices. Most popular computer games and productivity applications are pretty easy to find, but if you can't find what you want in those places, it's time to visit your local Best Buy, CompUSA, or Computer MicroCenter.

Now that we have dealt with the issues of urgency and price, I would like to present my personal list of software shopping strategies:

- **Be a scavenger.** When you enter your local software retailer, head straight for the bargain bins. You can often stumble onto some great finds. For example, on a recent trip to CompUSA, I picked up copies of SimPark, SimFarm, and Slingo, an addictive cross between Bingo and slot machines, for $1.84 each! SimFarm was originally released for between $30 and $40, but Slingo can still be found in many stores for $19.95. They may not be the newest versions out there, but they have provided me more entertainment than the Sunday paper, which costs just as much!

- **Good things come to those who wait.** When a new computer game is released, you can typically expect to pay full retail price the first week it is available. (That is often the price you pay to be the first on your block to have it.) However, waiting until the Sunday circulars boast a new release sale, usually some weeks after the software has hit the shelves, can help you secure a better price.

- **Pay what you want to for it.** You can often buy software for less than half the price in stores by watching Web sites like eBay (`http://www.ebay.com`). For example, one Christmas, my son requested the Star Wars: The Phantom Menace game. Somewhat reluctant to shell out $45 or more when it was first released, I managed to get a factory- sealed copy from eBay delivered to my home for less than $22! However, there are precautions you must take when dealing with auction sites. First, deal only with sellers who have been given an all-positive feedback rating by other buyers. Second, avoid used software like the plague. It may be cheap, but you can never be certain if a seller left the registration in her name or removed it from his machine. You would then be committing software piracy. In addition, stay away from software that was bundled with a computer system purchase; such software is marked *not for resale* and should not be sold separately. When you plan to make an auction purchase, look for descriptions like "in factory sealed box" or "new in box." You certainly don't want to end up with a copy of a hot game that someone illegally copied onto a blank CD!

7

Registering Your Software

When you purchase a piece of software, you will often find a postcard in the box requesting your name, address, e-mail address, location where the software was purchased, when it was purchased, and other points. This registration card enables software manufacturers to contact you if a bug fix becomes available over the Internet or when they simply want to inform you that an updated version of your purchase is now available.

Typically, manufacturers allow you to register their products online. When you install the program, it will ask you if you want to go online now and register the software or do it later; the choice is yours.

So, if you are wondering if you should bother registering software, yes, you should! Not only does registering it keep you up-to-date on the latest news about a given program, but it also leads to money-saving offers for program upgrades or add-ons. That alone could be worth dealing with the occasional junk mail.

Along a similar line, Microsoft now requires you to activate many of its products online before you use them for any length of time. It may be a royal pain in the neck, but it can potentially lead to extra support and a few good offers down the road.

Upgrading Software

When should you upgrade your software? (My answer may surprise you, since I make my living writing computer books!) Software is expensive to be continually purchasing newer versions, especially when you may not really need it. Much like with hardware upgrades, it is important to think about whether the computer or software does what you want and need it to do. If it does, then don't waste your money. You should wait until the need or a real desire for it is there.

This is especially true for productivity software like Word 2002, Excel 2002, and others. Enhancements are often targeted toward corporate or power users, offering no real value to the average consumer. Of course, an upgrade is warranted if there are file compatibility issues between your home and work machines, but even many of those can be resolved without costly software upgrades.

Games are a different matter, however. Technological advances, the desire to have new levels or playing arenas, and optimized performance might very well make upgrading a game desirable, especially if you really liked the game the first time around. Again, though, use extreme caution to make sure your machine can drive the latest and greatest offering.

Installing New Windows Programs

At some point down the road, you will undoubtedly want to put some new software on your machine. Most applications today come with their own installation programs, so installing software is a fairly simple process. Before you start, however, you should check the following items:

- Make sure you exit any programs you might be running. Because most installation programs make changes to your system files, exiting your programs prevents any conflicts from occurring. You may also need to restart your computer during the installation process, so exiting your programs prevents any possible loss of data.

- If you are upgrading your software to a newer version, be sure to make copies of all your existing data, in case something happens to it during the upgrade process. Also, be aware that some programs require you to uninstall the previous version before upgrading. Most, however, allow you to install the upgrade on top of the existing software. Read the installation manual before proceeding to avoid potential headaches.

To install a program, follow these basic steps:

1. Insert the first installation diskette or CD-ROM into its drive. CDs typically launch a special installation program, called a *wizard*, to guide you through the process step-by-step. If the wizard doesn't appear, move on to Step 2.

2. Click the Start button and select Run.

3. Type the path and the filename of the installation program and click OK. For example, to install a program from drive A, the floppy drive, you can type something like A:SETUP or A:INSTALL. (Check with the installation manual for the exact command you need to type.) The easiest method, however, is to click the Browse button and locate the setup file yourself.

Downloading a program from the Internet. Hour 18, *Downloading Goodies from the Internet,* is devoted to finding programs of interest on the Internet. After you download them and check them for viruses, however, you will be glad to know that installing them is no different than installing programs from CD or diskette. The only difference is that you will browse to a file on your machine instead of a disk to launch the program's installation/setup program.

7

4. At this point, the installation program will prompt you to make whatever selections are needed. For example, you may be asked to select the drive and folder into which you want the program installed. If you are upgrading a previous version, make sure you select the directory in which it was originally installed. Continue to follow the onscreen prompts until the program installation is complete.

Many applications offer a choice as to the type of installation you can select. For example, you may be offered the choices Compact, Typical, and Custom. Compact, in this case, would offer you a slimmed-down version of the program (a good choice if you are short on hard disk space), whereas Typical installs all the basic options. Custom enables you to pick and choose the options you want.

> **You may save disk space but not time.** Keep in mind that you may need to have the CD in your machine to run the more watered down installations. Although that may not seem like a big inconvenience, you should be aware that programs run from the CD may run more slowly than a fully installed counterpart. The difference in speed may not be noticeable for most productivity software, but for some games, it can be almost fatal. Games, such as flight and racing simulators, rely on speed. Without speed, the games are difficult to play.

The installation program automatically creates whatever folders are needed on your system. After checking to make sure there is enough space, it then copies the contents of the installation diskettes or CD-ROM to your hard drive. It also adds a command for starting the program to your Start menu, as well as an icon to your desktop that you can double-click to launch the application.

Uninstalling Software

If you have decided that you no longer need a particular program, you should remove it from your hard drive to make room for programs you do use. To do this, perform the following steps:

1. Click the Start button and then select Control Panel.
2. Next, click the Add or Remove Programs link. The Add or Remove Programs dialog box appears, as shown in Figure 7.4.

FIGURE 7.4

When you first get your PC, this dialog box will look sparsely populated. It can fill up in no time though.

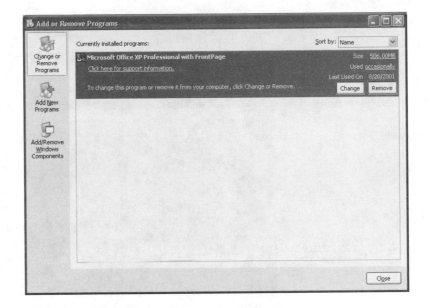

3. You will notice that each application has a detailed entry listing how much disk space it uses, when you last accessed the program, how frequently it is used, and additional information. Select the program you want to delete and then click the Change/Remove button.

4. You may be prompted to insert the installation diskette or CD-ROM for the program you are removing. Do so only if necessary and then click OK.

5. Your application's uninstall program starts. Follow the onscreen prompts to remove the program from your hard disk.

Some Unfinished Business

Earlier in the book, you were introduced to the elements of the Windows desktop, along with menus, toolbars, and dialog boxes. However, there are a few more odds and ends you should know before we move on to more advanced topics.

As you look at each program installed on your computer, you will notice they all have a similar look and feel. In Figure 7.5, you will see the names of these commonly found screen elements, along with their placement onscreen.

Table 7.1 presents the definition and purpose of each element illustrated in the preceding figure. Although some of them may seem self-explanatory, some occasional subtleties may seem less obvious.

7

FIGURE 7.5

The now familiar Solitaire screen models these common Windows program elements.

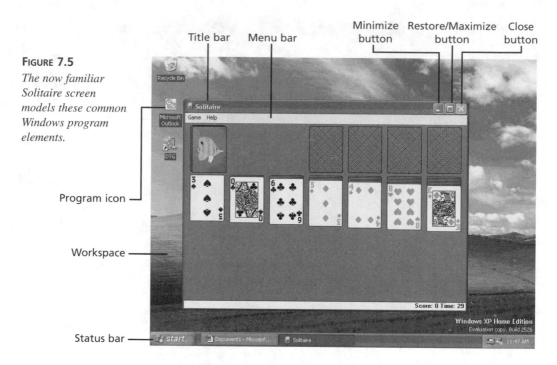

Title bar   Menu bar   Minimize button   Restore/Maximize button   Close button

Program icon

Workspace

Status bar

Table 7.1   Common Windows program elements and their functions

Element	Definition/purpose
Title bar	This bar, which is bright blue, unless you have applied your own desktop theme, is across the top of your program windows and displays the software's name, dialog box, and/or open file, if applicable. This is the same information you will see on the corresponding Windows taskbar button if the window is hidden.
Program icon	Residing at the far-left end of the title bar, the Program icon mirrors the icon shown on your Windows desktop (if you have created a shortcut for it). It is also the icon you will see on the Windows taskbar when the program is running. Double-clicking the Program icon also exits the program.
Menu bar	This portion of the application holds a list of command types under which you will find an assortment of items from which to choose. Under the File menu, for example, you should find items such as Open, Save, and others. When you move your mouse over a selection, it turns into a button you can click.

Element	Definition/purpose
Minimize button	The third button from the right end of the Title bar (the button with a single horizontal line on it) is the Minimize button. Click it to temporarily make the program window disappear. You can reopen it by clicking the corresponding button on the Windows taskbar.
Restore/Maximize button	Each Windows application has a predefined window size. That size often occupies only part of your workspace. Clicking the middle button on the right end of the title bar either enlarges the program window to full screen size or restores it to the size it was originally intended to be.
Close button	Click this button on the far right of the title bar to close the application in which you are currently working.
Workspace	The largest part of the program window, the workspace, is the area in which words are typed (as with a word processor) or cards are moved (as with Solitaire).
Status bar	You will find this element at the bottom of a program window. Typically, gray like a standard menu bar, the Status bar, gives you information about where you are in a program, such as the page number or number of inches down the page with a word processor, or the game's score (as with Solitaire). It also may contain other valuable data such as whether a certain program feature is active, error messages, and other information.

Resizing and Relocating Program Windows

In the preceding table, you saw how to make some basic changes to a program window's size, but you have a lot more options at your disposal. You can, for example, move windows around and narrow them so that you can see two documents at once. This may not seem like a big deal now, but it will become one as you get more comfortable working with your PC's various applications.

Moving a Program Window

When you launch a program, its window is often plopped in a seemingly random location on your screen. To move the window to a more convenient spot, simply drag and drop the program's title bar into place. You remember the old drag-and-drop maneuver, right? In this case, you click the bright blue title bar and, while keeping the left mouse button down, drag it into place and then release the button to drop it. It's that easy!

7

Resizing a Program Window

Tweaking a window to the desired size is equally simple; it, too, makes use of the now familiar drag-and-drop procedure.

To adjust a window's width, move your mouse pointer over the program's left or right borderline, the thin dark line that outlines the entire application window, until it turns into a double-headed east-west arrow (see Figure 7.6). Click on the line and then drag and drop it to the desired width. You can do this with both borders to achieve the exact results you want.

FIGURE 7.6

The Resize mouse pointer lets you know you are in the right spot to begin moving the borders.

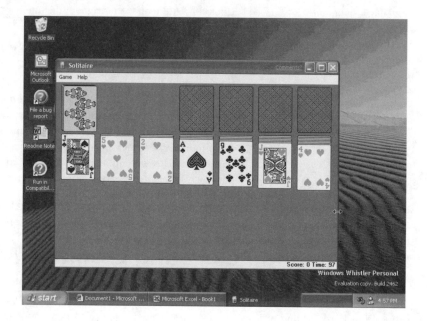

You can resize the top and bottom borders in the same manner; only this time, the mouse pointer appears as a north-south arrow when you are in the appropriate spot.

If you resize a window smaller than its original size, scroll bars might be added to the window (see Figure 7.7). These scroll bars enable you to see parts of the screen no longer in view due to the smaller window size.

Click the arrow buttons on the ends of the scroll bars to move in the desired direction in small increments. For larger jumps, click the scroll box and drag it in the appropriate direction until you see the item or text you are trying to find.

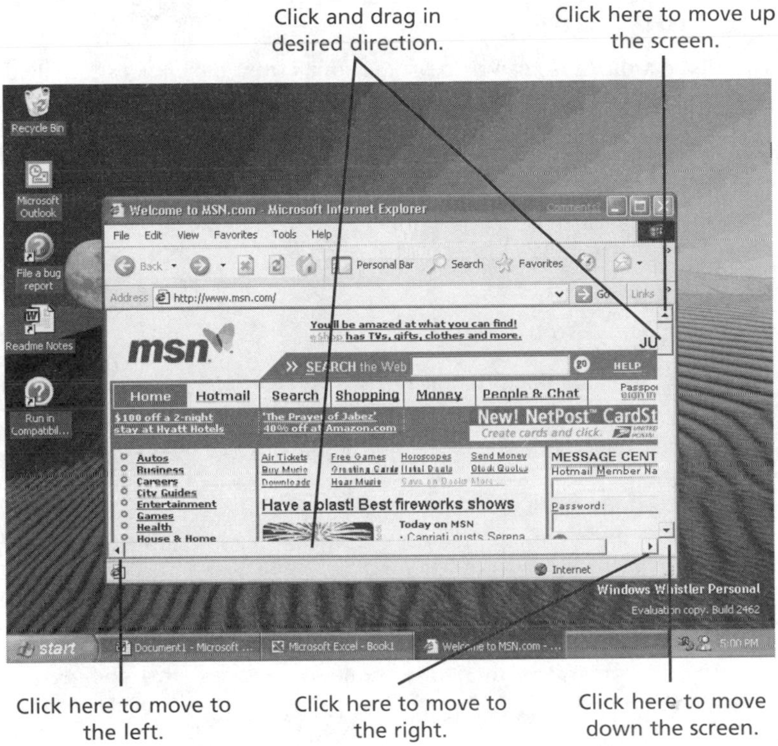

FIGURE 7.7
These scroll bar tools help you see what you are missing.

Click and drag in desired direction.

Click here to move up the screen.

Click here to move to the left.

Click here to move to the right.

Click here to move down the screen.

Summary

There you have it—everything you ever wanted to know about the types of software you can get, along with some guidelines for purchasing and upgrading your chosen software. You even got a feel for what kinds of titles you can find in each category of software.

In the next hour, I will help you get comfortable using Microsoft Word 2002, the most commonly installed word processing program on new computer systems.

Workshop

Now it's time to see just how much you learned in this lesson. I'll give you a short multiple-choice quiz to test what you learned, followed by a suggested activity designed to enhance the skills you acquired during the hour.

7

Quiz

Select the best answer to the questions from the choices provided, and then check your answers.

Questions

1. Which of the following is *not* a word processing program?

    a. PowerPoint

    b. Ami Pro

    c. Word 2002

2. What is the difference between Outlook 2000 and Outlook Express?

    a. They are the same; it is just that one comes with Office 2000, and the other does not.

    b. Outlook Express sends e-mail faster than Outlook 2000.

    c. Outlook Express is a smaller, less functional version of Outlook 2000 that is packaged with the Internet Explorer suite of applications.

3. When should you consider upgrading your software?

    a. When your software no longer does what you need or want it to.

    b. Upgrading is only for hardware.

    c. Whenever something new comes out, grab it; having the latest and greatest software on your machine is a real status symbol.

Answers

1. A is actually a presentation program designed to create professional-looking presentations; it is not, by any means, a word processing program.

2. The best answer, not to mention the only correct one, is C.

3. B is incorrect, and C is a waste of money; therefore, A is the only correct answer.

Activity

Go to your computer and look through the icons on your Windows desktop and the files listed on your Programs menu. Is there anything else you would like to do with your computer that you don't already have the software to handle? What about games? Did any of the ones I mentioned catch your fancy? List the types of tasks and games you want to consider here:

1. _____
2. _____
3. _____
4. _____
5. _____

Now go out and pick up a copy of the Sunday paper, if you don't already get it delivered to your home, and skim the ads for software. Don't forget that places like Target and K-Mart sell software, too.

In looking through the ads, try to find at least one application for each task you have listed. For example, if you listed letter writing as one of your tasks, you might want Word 2002. In the space below, list the application that fits each task or game mentioned above:

1. _____
2. _____
3. _____
4. _____
5. _____

This little exercise should help familiarize you with the types of software you will want to take a closer look at either via online demos and reviews, or by visiting a local computer store.

7

HOUR 8

Jumpstart Word Processing

Technically, Microsoft Word 2002 is considered a word processor. Although it does a superior job at that, it is really so much more than a word processor. Word can create Web pages loaded with hyperlinks, and it can produce newsletters that would push the capabilities of many small desktop publishing programs.

Word 2002 has many enhancements and improvements over its previous version. Unfortunately, busy work schedules and personal lives leave few people with time to play with these new features, let alone time to master them. In the next two lessons, I will provide simple, no-nonsense steps to help guide you through the basics.

Here are some other topics to be covered in this hour:

- Find out the various ways you can move through Word 2002 documents.
- Learn how to select blocks of text.
- Make your documents look unique by applying special formatting.
- Discover how to print the parts of a document you want.

To begin this lesson, launch Microsoft Word by clicking the Start button on the Windows taskbar and then choosing All Programs, Microsoft Word. A large screen with toolbars at the top will greet you. For the sake of this lesson, click the New Document button on the Formatting toolbar. It is the button at the far-left end of the toolbar that looks like a piece of paper with a dog-eared corner.

When you create a new document in this manner, Word applies a predefined set of attributes to it. Although these settings can be modified, as you will see later in the hour, the defaults are listed in Table 8.1.

Table 8.1 Word 2002 document defaults

Setting	Value
Font	Times New Roman
Text Size	12 point
Left/Right Margins	1.25 inches
Top/Bottom Margins	1 inch
Tab Stops	Every 0.5 inch
Page Orientation	Portrait

Anatomy of the Word 2002 Work Space

Knowing Word 2002's screen elements will go a long way toward helping you unleash its power. Figure 8.1 points out all the critical elements.

What do each of these elements do? In addition to the following list, many of these functions will be explored in greater detail throughout this lesson.

- **Title bar.** Contains the names of the program and document, as well as the Maximize/minimize, Restore, and Close buttons.
- **Language bar.** Lets you set the desired language for text, speech, and handwriting input. You can close it by right-clicking over it and then clicking the Close Language bar menu item.
- **Menu bar.** Allows you to select from a variety of pull-down menus needed to execute commands in Word 2002.
- **Standard toolbar.** Holds shortcut buttons to quickly execute common tasks such as printing, opening a new document, and so on. This toolbar can be modified to meet your specific needs.

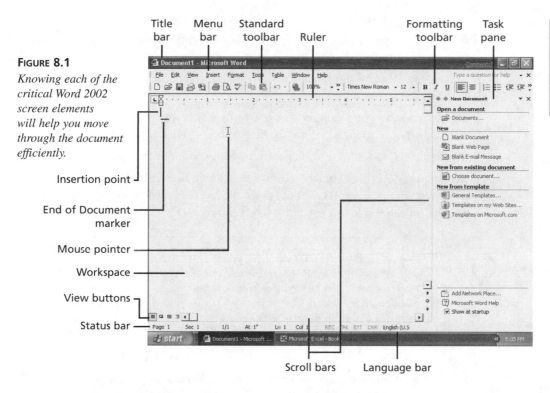

FIGURE 8.1

Knowing each of the critical Word 2002 screen elements will help you move through the document efficiently.

- **Formatting toolbar.** Presents buttons to quickly format text as you work. Selections include font style, font size, text alignment, and text traits (bold, underline, or italic).

- **Ruler.** Provides a quick and easy way to guide the setting of tabs and indents in your documents.

- **Task pane.** For the average user, the task pane may simply be a screen hog, but when it comes to doing more advanced functions such as inserting clip art, performing a mail merge, and other tasks, it can keep helpful to have menu options close at hand.

- **Insertion point.** Shows you where the text or graphics will be placed. In other programs, it may be referred to as a cursor.

- **End of Document marker.** Indicates the end of a document with a short, horizontal line. You cannot move past this point.

- **Mouse pointer.** Moves onscreen as you move the mouse to assist you in accessing menus and clicking buttons.

- **View button.** Enables you to adjust your view of a document. Choose from the following options located left to right on your screen: Normal, Web Layout, Print Layout, and Outline..
- **Status bar.** Displays information about your document including page count, line number, and other information.
- **Taskbar.** Allows you to toggle back and forth between applications already open or to launch new applications via the Start button.
- **Workspace.** Consists of a blank page on which you insert text and graphics.
- **Scroll bar.** Moves you quickly around a document. Either slide them with your mouse (point to the scroll box, hold down the left button of your mouse, and drag) or click on either side of the box for larger jumps.

Remember this! Keep these menus and toolbars fixed in your mind because you *will* see them again. Microsoft has worked hard at creating a common interface for its Office family of products. This makes it much easier to learn additional applications in the Office XP family, since you already know how to find the most frequently used commands.

NEW TERM

Inter-what? The term *interface* refers to the way a program looks and the way commands are executed within it. Thus, a common Office XP interface not only makes applications look very similar, but it helps users overcome the fear and intimidation of learning to use lesser known members of the popular office productivity suite.

Common Menus and Menu Options

Menus organize a number of commands and options into logical categories for easy reference. Just click the name of the menu to open its pull-down menu. In addition to the names of the options, Word 2002 displays the appropriate icon where available and lists the keystroke combination needed to execute the same option. Figure 8.2 illustrates a typical pull-down menu in Word.

As you access these menus, you will discover that for a few seconds, they display the most commonly used options. If you continue to hover your mouse pointer over the menu, a button at the bottom of the menu will turn blue. If you click it, it will expand the menu to reveal the entire list of commands for the selected menu. These are known as "smart" menus because they "learn" which commands you perform most and display them first in the list of commands.

FIGURE 8.2

The new Word 2002 "smart" menus make it easier to find the commands you use most.

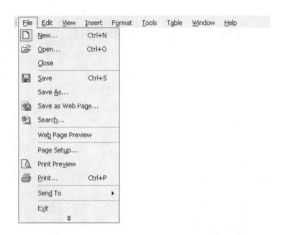

8

There are a number of menus shared by the Office XP family of applications:

- **File menu.** Gives users access to such commands as opening, saving, and renaming a document; setting print properties and launching the printing process; specifying file properties; and exiting the application. This is the first item on Word 2002's menu bar.

- **Edit menu.** Holds commands for cutting, copying, and pasting, as well as the Find and Replace commands. Options not available in a given circumstance are grayed out. For example, unless a block of text is selected, the Copy option will be grayed out. Look here first if you need to make a change in a document.

- **View menu.** Presents options needed to alter the screen's appearance. You can add toolbars, turn them off, create document headers and footers, and view your document in Outline mode to name a few. You can also zoom the page in and out to increase print size or reduce it to fit more onscreen.

- **Insert menu.** Allows you to add objects such as Clip Art into a file.

- **Format menu.** This menu allows you to format text or other objects like Clip Art or tables. If you want to change the way your text looks, add a list to your document, or add a border to your work, look here first.

- **Tools menu.** If there is anything you want to customize, the Tools menu is the place to start. Neat gadgets like Spelling and Grammar, Word Count, and AutoCorrect reside here.

- **Window menu.** Although the top half of this menu may change from application to application, the bottom half allows you to switch back and forth between open documents within an application (where available). To access a document listed, simply click its filename.

- **Help menu.** Leads you to a variety of Word help tools.

The Shared Standard Toolbar

Just as there are similarities between Office XP menus, there is a Standard toolbar shared by all the applications that has numerous buttons and icons you will see regardless of which application you are working with (see Figure 8.3).

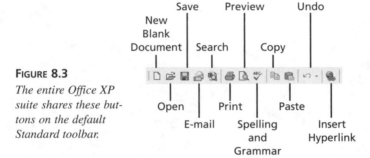

FIGURE 8.3
The entire Office XP suite shares these buttons on the default Standard toolbar.

These buttons are more than just shortcuts to the same option within a menu. In fact, in many cases, they have radically different results than their menu-driven counterparts, even though they essentially accomplish the same thing in the end.

For example, take the New document command in Word 2002. You can create a new document by choosing File, New to select a document type from Word 2002's library of templates and wizards. You can also create a new document by using a shortcut (clicking the New button on the Standard Toolbar or pressing Ctrl+N). Using shortcuts will, in this case, choose the default Word template—a blank page referred to as the *Normal* template.

> **Now I'm *really* confused!** With so many different ways to execute commands, it can be hard to settle on one method. A good rule of thumb is if you want to choose options when executing a command (like base a new document on a resume template or print only the first page of a 20-page document), follow the menu sequence. If the default (a blank page for a new document, one copy of the entire document to be printed, and so on) is acceptable, use the method most comfortable to you: the menus, the Standard toolbar button, or the applicable keystrokes. There is no right or wrong way; it is all a matter of personal preference.

Tweaking the Toolbars

Everybody uses Office applications differently. As a result, some of the buttons you use most may be missing on the toolbars. Likewise, other buttons you never use may take up valuable space.

To add a button to a toolbar, follow these steps:

1. Make sure the toolbar you want to modify is in view.
2. Choose Tools, Customize and select the Commands tab.
3. In the Categories box, click on the category of the button you want to add. The command names and icons, if available, are shown in the Commands box.
4. Click on the desired icon or command and then drag it into position on the toolbar.
5. Release the mouse button to set the button in place.

To delete a button from a toolbar, simply do the following:

1. Make sure the toolbar you want to modify is in view.
2. Choose Tools, Customize and select the Commands tab.
3. If necessary, drag the Customize dialog box to another location (click on the title bar and drag it) until the button you want to delete is visible.
4. Click on the button you want to delete and then drag it off the toolbar.
5. Release the mouse button to complete the deletion.

Keystrokes: Another Way to Get the Job Done

In addition to menus and toolbars, Office XP offers a host of shortcuts to access commands using the keyboard. Table 8.2 highlights some of the more common functions.

Table 8.2 Office 2000 keyboard shortcuts

Function/Command	Shortcut
New	Ctrl+N
Open	Ctrl+O
Save	Ctrl+S
Print	Ctrl+P
Cut	Ctrl+X
Paste	Ctrl+V
Copy	Ctrl+C

It should also be noted that these commands function identically in all Office applications, so they'll come in handy in Excel, PowerPoint, or whatever Microsoft Office application you may be working with.

Selecting Text

Many commands and operations in Office applications require you to select text first before you can make changes to it. For example, to change the font of text or move a block of text, you first have to select it. Selected text will appear highlighted, so you will easily be able to see what part of the document you have chosen to manipulate in some way.

Although there are a variety of ways to select items in Office XP, these steps introduce you to the most commonly used way.

1. Place the mouse pointer at the beginning of the desired text.
2. Click the left mouse button and hold it down while dragging it to highlight a block of text (see Figure 8.4).
3. After the desired area is highlighted, perform your chosen operation on the data as described in the next few sections.

FIGURE 8.4

It is clear which part of the document is about to be modified.

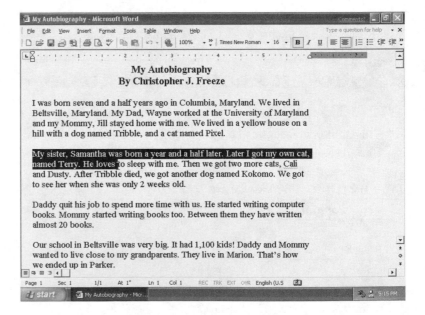

> **Oops, I didn't get the whole thing!** If you find you need to adjust the selected text area after you have released the mouse button, there is no need to start from scratch. You can hold down the Shift key and use the arrow keys to highlight the exact area you want, starting from where you click to where you let go of the mouse button.

Selecting Text with the Mouse

As usual, Microsoft gives you a plethora of ways to select text with your mouse, but in this case, you may actually grow to like some of the methods presented in Table 8.3.

Table 8.3 Additional Ways to Select Text with Your Mouse

To select this...	...Do this
Word	Double-click inside the word.
Sentence	Ctrl+click inside the sentence.
Paragraph	Triple-click inside the paragraph.
Graphic or image	Click the graphic or image.
Entire document	Move mouse pointer to the left of the text until it turns into a left upward-pointing arrow and then triple-click.
Vertical text block	Hold down the Alt key and drag the mouse pointer over the text.
Entire lines of text	Move the mouse pointer to the left of the text until it becomes an arrow; then click the left mouse button and drag the mouse until the desired block of text is highlighted.

Selecting Text Blocks with the Keyboard

For some reason, there are people who prefer to work with the keyboard rather than fiddle with the mouse. If you are one of those people, you will be interested in Table 8.4, the listing of shortcut keys for selecting blocks of text.

Table 8.4 Keyboard shortcuts for selecting text

To select this...	...Do this
One character at a time to the left of the insertion point	Press Shift+left arrow key and repeat until the desired number of characters is highlighted.
One character at a time to the right arrow of the insertion point	Press Shift+right arrow key and repeat until the desired number of characters is highlighted.

continues

Table 8.4 continued

To select this...	...Do this
The beginning of the word to the left of the insertion point	Press Shift+Ctrl+left arrow key and keep pressing the arrow key to select additional words.
The beginning of the word to the right of the insertion point	Press Shift+Ctrl+right arrow key and keep pressing the arrow key to select additional words.
The insertion point to the same position in the previous line	Press Shift+up arrow key
The insertion point to the same position in the next line	Press Shift+down arrow key
The insertion point to the beginning of the current paragraph.	Press Shift+Ctrl+up arrow key
The insertion point to the beginning of of the next paragraph	Press Shift+Ctrl+down arrow key
The insertion point to the beginning of the document	Press Shift+Ctrl+Home
The insertion point to the end of the the document	Press Shift+Ctrl+End

Manipulating Text

Back when I was in college, typewriters were the norm. In fact, on more than one occasion, I opted to leave a term paper disorganized rather than go back and retype the thing to get it the way I really wanted it. With computers, life is much simpler.

Moving a block of text from one location to another is an easy process; just follow these steps:

1. Select the text you want to move as described in the previous section, "Selecting Text."

2. Cut the text from its current location using one of the following ways: click the Cut button on the toolbar; use Ctrl+X; or choose Edit, Cut from the Menu bar. The text will disappear as it is copied to the Clipboard for future use.

It's gotta be here someplace! When you cut or copy Microsoft Office text, the material is kept in an electronic clipboard. This keeps it close at hand so you can locate it and place it wherever you want whenever you want it. Think of it as a manila folder sitting on top of your desk that holds all kinds of important scraps of paper.

3. Move the mouse pointer to the desired location in the document and single-click to set the insertion point in place.

4. To paste the block of text into the new location, click the Paste button on the toolbar; use Ctrl+V; or choose Edit, Paste from the Menu bar.

Copying Selected Text

Copying a block of text to another location can save vast amounts of time even if you have to make minor edits. For example, if you need to write a dozen thank-you letters to companies where you recently interviewed, instead of typing each letter, you may want to consider copying the text of the first letter and pasting it into subsequent pages to construct the rest of the letters. Then all you have to do is rekey the personalized parts like the greeting, company name, and so on. It may not be proper social etiquette, but it is *much* faster than typing each one!

To take advantage of this time-saving technique, just do the following:

1. Select the text you want to move, as described earlier in the hour.

2. Copy the text using one the following ways: click the Copy icon on the toolbar; press Ctrl+C; or choose Edit, Copy from the Menu bar.

3. Guide the mouse pointer to the desired location in the document and single-click to set the insertion point in place.

4. To paste the block of text into the new location, click the Paste icon on the toolbar; press Ctrl+V; or choose Edit, Paste from the Menu bar.

> **Paste it again, Sam!** If you want to place the copied text in more than one location (as in the example of multiple thank-you letters), simply execute steps 3 and 4 as many times as needed. There is no need to reselect the text.

Changing the Text Font

Perhaps the best way to enhance the appearance of your documents is to choose a distinctive font that fits the message. Whether it is script for the body of a formal invitation or a more playful style for a fundraiser handout, you can find the font for the job.

You can select a font one of two ways: by choosing it before you begin typing the text or selecting the text and then applying the change to the selection.

To select a font when there is no existing text to modify, click the arrow next to the Font window of the Formatting toolbar to open the drop-down list box. Each font available on your PC will appear "in character" by name. Choose from the fonts listed by clicking the one you want.

Notice that by using this drop-down list, you can instantly see what a certain font looks like before you apply it.

Adding Bold, Italic, Color, Underline, and Other Text Attributes

Whether you want to make a word bold for emphasis, or you simply want to italicize the title of a book, you need to know how to alter the attributes of your text. The Font tab of the Font dialog box (see Figure 8.5) gives you numerous ways to change the appearance of your text. Start by following these steps:

1. Choose Format, Font from the Menu bar to call up the Font dialog box.
2. Select the Font tab (see Figure 8.5) to choose a style or special effect for your text and see it in the Preview window before applying it.
3. Click OK to apply the selected type attributes.

You can incorporate any of these attributes into your text by selecting them from the beginning or following the steps for selecting a complex font, as described above.

FIGURE 8.5

Click the arrow next to each box to see a menu of choices or place a check mark in the box to apply the effect.

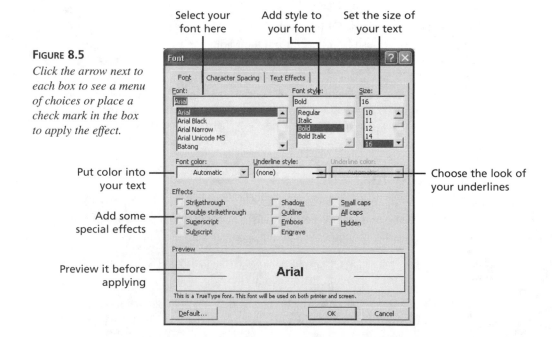

Becoming a Quick Change Artist

The fastest way to change text attributes is to select the block of text you want to change and then click the applicable button on the Formatting toolbar. See Figure 8.6 for a diagram of which toolbar buttons do what.

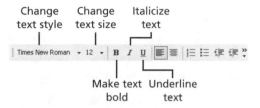

FIGURE 8.6

The Formatting toolbar is the fastest way to alter text.

Changing the Size of the Text

One way to emphasize certain parts of your document is to change the type size. Again, you can either specify the size before you start typing or select existing text and change its size. To change type size:

1. Click the arrow next to the Font window of the Formatting toolbar to open the drop-down list box.

2. Choose from the sizes listed or enter your own number. For those not familiar with point sizes—the larger the number, the bigger the text.

Inserting Text

To insert text into an existing Word document, move the pointer to the desired location, click once to set the insertion point, and then simply begin typing. If you want to over-write the document's text, however, click press the Insert button on your keyboard and begin typing. The text you enter will appear over the top of existing text.

Deleting Text

You may delete text in Word 2002 in any of these ways.

- Use the Delete key to delete characters to the right of the insertion point.
- Use the Backspace key to delete characters to the left of the insertion point.
- Select a block of text and then press Delete.

Are you sure you want to get rid of it altogether? If you are about to delete a large block of text that you may want to use later, consider using the Cut function instead of delete to temporarily copy the information to the

Clipboard. This way the deletion isn't permanent until you exit Word. With Office XP's multiple Clipboard feature, subsequent "cuts" will be added to the Clipboard entries until they are specifically added to a document.

Undoing Changes

If there is one set of keystrokes to memorize in Word, it is Ctrl+Z. Knowing how to undo something in a flash can save hours of reformatting, typing, and other tasks. Undo can also be accessed by clicking the Undo button on the toolbar.

Since Word has a multiple level Undo feature, you can click the arrow next to the Undo button to see a list of operations you can undo. If you undo an item far down on the list, all the items above it will be undone too. In this case, rekeying or reapplying the formatting may save you more time than using Undo. If you change your mind after undoing a change, you can always redo it by clicking the Redo button on the Formatting toolbar.

Aligning Text

After you get the words down on paper, you may want to spruce them up a bit. One way to do this is to modify the alignment of the text.

Text in Word can be aligned in four different ways: flush left, as in this book; centered; flush right; and justified, or stretched out to make both margins even. To align your text any of these ways, select the block of text and click the appropriate button on the toolbar, as shown in Figure 8.7.

If you know how you want the document to look before you begin, you can also choose the alignment beforehand and then enter the text to achieve the desired look.

Viewing Your Documents

Word 2002 offers a variety of document views that simplify document editing and formatting and, in some cases, even enhance navigation within your document. These views are easily changed by clicking the icons pictured here. To return to Word's normal view at any time, simply click the Normal view button at the left end of the row of View buttons.

FIGURE 8.7

Click any of the alignment buttons to instantly realign your selected block of text to produce the results shown here.

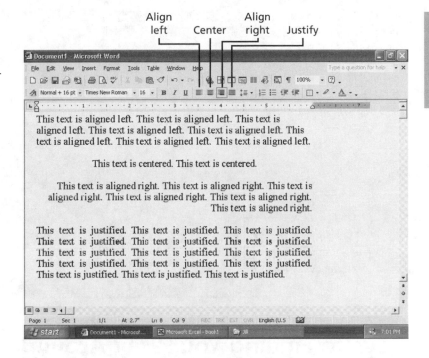

Available views from left to right include the following:

- **Normal view.** Word's default document view, the Normal view, is the standard view used for document editing and formatting. Although it shows document layout pretty much as it will appear on the printed page, the workspace remains uncluttered for quick and easy editing.

- **Web Layout view.** This is how a document would look if it were turned into a Web page.

- **Print Layout view.** In this view, you can see how a document will look before it is printed. This is a great way to evaluate a document's margins, headers and footers, and other printer qualifications.

- **Outline view.** The Outline view makes it easy to move or copy entire sections of text because it gives you customizable views of your document. You can see the relative importance of each section title, but only if you apply style codes or build the outline from scratch.

Figure 8.8 shows you exactly where to locate these buttons on your Word window.

FIGURE 8.8

Choose one of four views available to you.

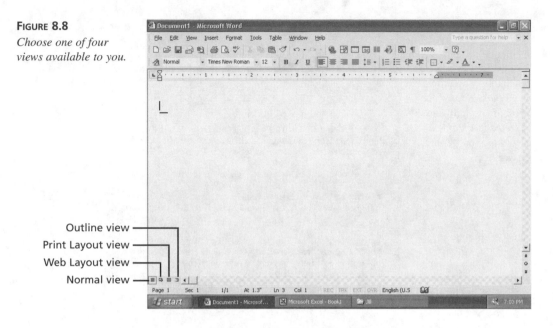

Outline view ──────
Print Layout view ──────
Web Layout view ──────
Normal view ──────

Keys to Finding Your Way Around a Document

Word 2002 gives you a number of shortcut keys to move swiftly from one location to another in a document. See Table 8.5 for a list of these.

Table 8.5 Word navigation shortcut keys

To move here...	Press...
One character to the right	Right Arrow
One character to the left	Left Arrow
To the end of a word	Ctrl+Shift+Right Arrow
To the beginning of a word	Ctrl+Shift+Left Arrow
To the end of a line	End
To the beginning of a line	Home
One line down	Down Arrow
One line up	Up Arrow
To the end of a paragraph	Ctrl+Shift+Down Arrow
To the beginning of a paragraph	Ctrl+Shift+Up Arrow

To move here...	Press...
One screen down	Page Down
One screen up	Page Up
To the end of a window	Alt+Ctrl+Page Down
To the beginning of a document	Ctrl+Shift+Home
To include the entire document	Ctrl+A

8

Creating Bulleted and Numbered Lists

The two kinds of lists you can use to draw the attention of the reader are bulleted and numbered lists. Bulleted lists use small icons, or bullets, to indicate each item in the list. Word 2002 even gives you the opportunity to use graphics bullets where the bullets are tiny pictures instead of the usual dots. Numbered lists use a numbering system for the items. Both types of lists can be modified to use different bullet and numbering styles.

Entering New Text Formatted as a List

To create either type of list before you start typing, follow these steps:

1. Type the text leading up to the list.
2. When you are ready to enter items on the list, place the insertion point at the location where you want the list to appear.
3. Click the Numbering or Bullets button on the Formatting toolbar.
4. Type each section of text and press the Enter key to set up subsequent bullets or numbered sections.
5. When the list is complete, press Enter and then click the Numbering or Bullets button again to turn off the formatting. (Samples of the resulting lists are illustrated in Figure 8.9.)

Generating a List from Existing Text

Select the text to be turned into a list and then click the desired list button on the Formatting toolbar. Keep in mind that each list entry must be followed by a hard return (pressing the Enter key); otherwise, the items will all be placed on a single list entry. This may require you to insert returns after you have formatted the list.

FIGURE 8.9
*This figure shows
simple numbered and
bulleted lists.*

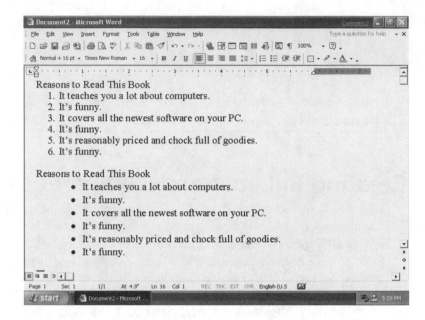

Changing the Bullet or Numbering Style

If standard bullets or numbers don't catch your fancy, you can apply something a bit more distinctive. Choose Format, Bullets and Numbering and then select either the Bulleted or Numbered tab as appropriate. The Bulleted tab gives you access to little black boxes, check marks, and other bullet styles. The Numbered tab can turn standard numbers into letters or even Roman numerals. Simply choose the style you want; then click OK to apply it.

Checking Spelling and Grammar

Nothing is more embarrassing than sending out an important letter with a typo that could have easily been avoided. Save yourself the headaches by accepting the help of Word 2002's spelling and grammar checker.

Word's spell-check feature can go crazy when it encounters acronyms, Internet addresses, and other unfamiliar text. The good news is you can save time dealing with these elements by telling Word to ignore them.

Choose Tools, Options and then select the Spelling and Grammar tab. From here, you can enable or disable spell-check by clicking the check box next to the Check spelling as you type option near the top of the tab. You can also tell Word to ignore words in uppercase, words with numbers in them, or filenames and Internet addresses. This will save you time when running through your document to correct potential errors.

I ain't got no problem with proper grammar, but if I did, this tool would sure help! It is great for helping you rewrite passive voice into active voice, but it is not infallible. There are definitely times (like the first sentence of this paragraph) when you will need a second opinion, but the benefits make it worth trying anyway.

To set grammar-checking options in Word 2002, follow these steps:

1. From within any Word document, choose Tools, Options and then select the Spelling and Grammar tab (see Figure 8.10).

FIGURE 8.10

The grammar options selected in this figure tell Word to keep grammatical errors in view in the current document and to check grammar the same time spelling is checked.

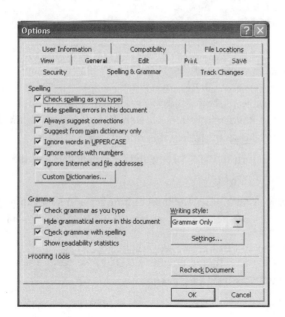

2. In the Grammar section of the tab, you can specify whether Word should check grammar as you type or whether you want any grammatical errors to be hidden. You may also check grammar the same time you check spelling by placing a check mark next to that option.

3. To have Word check for more specific errors, click the Settings button to bring up the Grammar Settings dialog box (see Figure 8.11).

4. Scroll down the Grammar and Style Options list box to select the elements you want Word to check for. Options include checking for improper capitalization, use of double negatives, and passive voice.

FIGURE 8.11

Select the elements you want Word to check in the Grammar and style options box, or request Word to double-check up to three usage requirements in the Require section of the Grammar setting dialog box.

5. In the Require section, choose any of the three usage requirements (comma place-ment, use of quotation marks, and the number of spaces between sentences) and define their usage in the drop-down lists next to each one. For example, you can specify that sentences must have one space between them and Word will tell you if it finds one that doesn't follow this rule.

6. Click OK to return to the Spelling and Grammar tab and then press OK to apply your newly defined options.

Word 2002 gives you the ability to correct grammar and spelling as you work, or you can perform a single pass of spelling and grammar checking when your document is finished.

I prefer to address issues as they are detected because my mind is still in the proper context to know what I really intended to say. If I take care of it at the end, I may have forgotten the point I was trying to make.

To address problems as you work, simply right-click over a word or phrase with a green (spelling) or red (grammar) squiggly underline. For spelling errors, the resulting shortcut menu will often present you with a number of possible choices for the word you had intended to type. To select a suggested word, simply double-click it. The menu also gives you the opportunity to ignore words, or add them to your personal spell-checking dictionary. For grammatical errors, Word will tell you what type of problem it found and will occasionally even rewrite the sentence for you. Again, you can double-click the suggested fix to apply it.

If you have additional editing to do and opt to leave all your fix-up work for the end, just press the F7 key to launch the spelling and grammar–checking tool. A dialog box will appear with the incorrect word or sentence displayed. Just click the applicable button to take action on the problem.

Saving Your Documents

I remember the day like it was yesterday. It was 4 a.m., and I was finishing up the last of an Excel chapter for my *Using Office 97* book. Then for some bizarre reason, my laptop froze. When I booted my system again, they were gone—14 precious pages of manuscript! I know I had saved them, but I made the mistake of relying on Word's AutoSave feature alone.

To prevent the same thing from happening to you, you should click the Save button on the Standard toolbar every few minutes for insurance, especially when you are working on something important.

The first time you click Save in a new document, you will see the Save As dialog box shown in Figure 8.12. Just click inside the File Name text box and type in the desired filename. Of course, before you enter a filename, it would be even smarter to click your way to a descriptive folder that will enable you to find the document again in a snap. If you don't, every document you ever create will be stored in the nondescript My Documents folder. After you have entered a name for the file, click the Save button in the lower-right corner to close the dialog box.

FIGURE 8.12

The Save As dialog box also lets you see what other documents are stored in the selected folder.

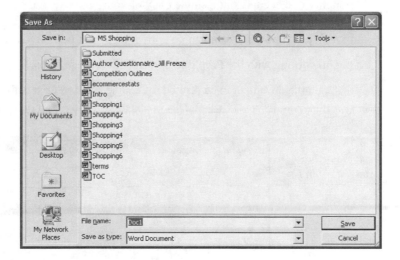

Opening an Existing Word Document

Many longer documents require more than one work session to complete them. When you need to reaccess a document that you worked on before, just launch Word 2002 as usual and then use one of these methods to locate and open the document you want:

- If you recently worked with the document you want to open, click the File menu and then look at the bottom of the drop-down menu. You will see a list of the last four documents you worked with in Word 2002.

- If the document is not on that list, click File, Open to access the Open dialog box. You will notice that it is nearly identical to the Save As dialog box pictured in Figure 8.11. Double-click your way to the appropriate folder and then double-click the name of the document you want to open.

I can't see the right folder! If the necessary folder does not appear on screen, you may need to click the Up One Level button (the yellow folder button with the upward pointing arrow) until you get to a location you recognize.

Printing a Word Document

What good is the most eloquently written document if nobody ever sees it? You will want to understand the subtleties of printing documents in Word 2002.

Although you can crank out a single copy of your whole document by simply clicking the Print button, I suggest you take the time to get to know the Print dialog box so that you know just how much you can do with a document before you send it to the printer.

To begin working with the Print dialog box, follow these steps:

1. Open the document to be printed (of course, if it isn't open already) and then choose File, Print, or press Ctrl+P. This opens the Print dialog box (see Figure 8.13).

FIGURE 8.13

The Print dialog box gives you full control of your output.

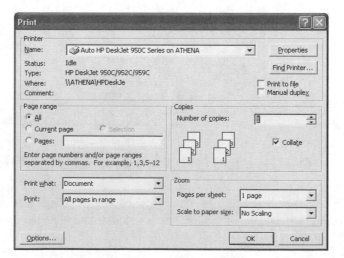

2. Once in the dialog box, confirm that the correct printer is defined. If it isn't, click the drop-down arrow next to the Name box to see the list of available choices. Click on the desired printer. Most typical users will have only one printer, so most likely you won't need to make any adjustments.

3. Specify the pages to be printed in the Page Range window (use 1–5 to print pages one through five and 1,5 for pages one and five) and then enter the number of copies to be printed in the Copies window.

4. Select the Collate check box if you want multiple copies of a document to be printed in order, or leave it unchecked if you want all of your Page Ones printed first, then all of the Page Twos, and so on. Of course, you need only bother with this option if you are printing more than one copy of the document.

5. After you have all of the correct options selected, click OK to print.

Summary

Wow, wasn't this lesson living proof that we could all use more time in our days? I didn't want to shortchange you in your introduction to word processing, so we covered a whole lot more than a single hour's worth of material here. If you feel a little lost, go ahead and read it over again.

In this lesson, I gave you enough information to create a simple document. You were shown the parts of the Word 2002 workspace, how to select blocks of text, and even how to generate a printed copy of your document. However, this only scratches the surface of what you can do in Word 2002.

Hour 9, *Polishing Those Documents,* whets your appetite for the more advanced functions available in Word such as inserting Tables and Clip Art, building a complex document with the help of a wizard, and other tasks.

Workshop

Now it's time to see just how much you learned in this lesson. I'll give you a short multiple-choice quiz to test what you learned, followed by a suggested activity designed to enhance the skills you acquired during the hour.

Quiz

Select the best answer to the questions from the choices provided and then check your answers.

Questions

1. Which of the following is a part of the Word 2002 workspace?

    a. Scroll bar

    b. Status bar

    c. Cocktail bar

2. What is the keystroke sequence to perform the Cut command?

    a. Ctrl+CUT

    b. Alt+X

    c. Ctrl+X

3. Which of the following options cannot be set in the Print dialog box?

    a. The color in which the text should be printed

    b. The specific pages of the document you want printed

    c. How many copies you want printed

Answers

1. I'm sorry to say there is no cocktail bar in Word 2002; A and B are both correct, though.

2. This one was a bit tricky, but C was the proper choice.

3. A is the correct answer. The text color is specified in the document itself, but not in the Print dialog box. Of course, selecting colors for your document is only useful if you have a color printer or plan to convert the document to a Web page.

Activity

Here is a simple but fun exercise for experimenting with many of the basic features in Word 2002:

1. Launch Word and create a new blank document.

2. On the first line, type your full name; on the second line, enter your street address; and on the third line, insert your city, state, and ZIP code.

3. Press Enter to place the End of Document marker beneath your text.

4. Now select your name only, using one of the techniques you learned in this lesson.

5. Using the drop-down arrows on the Formatting toolbar, select a font that matches your personality. While you are at it, make your name 16 points in size and bold to give it the proper emphasis it deserves.

6. Just for fun, click Format, Font and select a funky text color from the resulting dialog box. Remember to click OK to exit the dialog box.

7. Select all three lines of text and center them by using the Center button on the Formatting toolbar.

I'll bet you never thought word processing could be so much fun! (Okay, maybe calling it "fun" is stretching it a bit....)

8

HOUR 9

Polish Those Documents

This may shock you, but using the more advanced features of Word 2002 may cut your work time in half and improve the appearance of your documents a hundred times over. And the amazing part is I'm not exaggerating a bit when I say that.

In this lesson, I show you how to give your documents that final professional polish. Here are some additional topics I will cover this hour:

- Discover how to create great looking documents in a flash with the help of templates and wizards.
- Find out how to add headers and footers to your documents.
- Learn how to program Word to do some typing for you—really!
- Eliminate documents where a couple of lines spill over onto a second page using the handy Shrink to Fit feature.

Templates and Wizards: An Overview

Templates and wizards can go a long way toward helping you create professional-looking documents, regardless of whether you are a manager for a major corporation, a high school student wanting to submit high-quality college application materials, or a grassroots nonprofit organization seeking funding.

So what are these things, and how do they work?

Templates are documents or worksheets that contain the text, graphics, macros, customized toolbars, and formulas needed to create standardized documents.

Wizards are interactive help utilities that guide you step-by-step through an operation, offering explanations and tips along the way. Wizards will also ask you questions to help customize the output.

Achieving Professional Results Using Word 2002 Templates

Word 2002 gives you a variety of templates from which you can generate professional-looking letters, memos, and resumes by using preselected formatting, fonts, and occasionally even suggested text.

To access this library of templates from within Word 2002, click File, New. The New Document task pane appears on the right side of the screen, with an assortment of helpful links. For this part of the lesson, we are going to concern ourselves primarily with the New from Template section of the task pane. More specifically, we'll look at the General templates link.

Once the Templates dialog box opens (see Figure 9.1), you will notice categorized tabs make finding what you want a whole lot easier.

FIGURE 9.1

Distinctive icons make it easy to tell which items are templates and which items are wizards.

Word template ——

Word Wizard ——

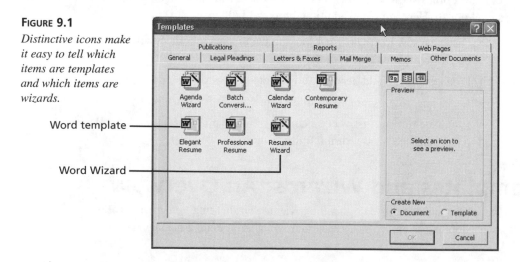

To begin working with a template, simply double-click the appropriate icon, and a new document based on the selected template will appear. If you aren't certain which template you may want to use, click an icon and see the preview of the template before you make a commitment to using it.

More, more, more! If you can't find an appropriate template or just want to have more choices at your disposal, establish a connection to the Internet and then click the Templates on the Microsoft.com link at the bottom of the task pane. This will take you to Microsoft's Web site, from which you can often download new templates and wizards. There are some awesome possibilities here to download sample press releases, letters of complaint, and billing and invoicing documents among others. Don't let downloading them intimidate you; Microsoft will guide you every step of the way.

Working with a Template

If you know the basic Word 2002 editing techniques (see Hour 8, *Jumpstart Word Processing,* for reference), you are one step ahead. Take the Professional Resume Template (found on the Other Documents tab of the Templates tab of the Templates dialog box) as an example. Creating a professional-looking resume is as easy as entering and deleting text. No need to worry about formatting or font selection; it's all done for you! Just click in the area in which you would like to work and then begin typing.

Templates can save you infinite amounts of time, enabling you to focus on content instead of formatting issues.

Switching Templates On-the-Fly

Suppose that you spent hours inserting text into a template, only to find that at the end, you are not as happy with it as you could have been. You may want to consider switching templates to see if the results are any better. I call this "switching templates on-the-fly" because you already have a document to which you can apply the template.

Great templates think alike! If you want to experiment with the look of a template-based document, be sure to apply a similar type of template, or you might get some pretty unusual results. So if you are working with a resume, use another resume template, not a legal briefing template. If you don't, that resume you worked so hard to create could turn into a garbled mess of text.

To apply a new template to a document using a similar template, do this:

1. Open the document in which you want to change the template.

2. Click Tools, Templates and Add-Ins to open the Templates and Add Ins dialog box shown in Figure 9.2.

FIGURE 9.2

The Templates and Add-Ins dialog box allows you to dramatically alter the appearance of a document in a few short steps.

3. Click the Add button to open the Add Template dialog box.

4. Browse through the folders to find the desired template and then click it to select it. You'll want to browse to C:/Program Files/Microsoft Office/Templates/1033 to find the installed assortment of templates.

5. Click OK to return to the Templates and Add-Ins dialog box.

6. Confirm that the file you selected is currently loaded. It will appear in the Global Templates and Add-Ins box.

7. Click the Attach button to open the Attach Template dialog box.

8. Select the desired template again and then click Open to return to the Templates and Add-Ins dialog box.

9. The path to the template you just selected should appear in the Document Template text box.

10. Check the Automatically update document styles check box to change the styles displayed by the current template.

11. Click OK to attach the new template to the active document.

By performing these steps, you can turn a professional resume (see Figure 9.3) into something noticeably different (see Figure 9.4).

FIGURE 9.3
A resume draft using Word's Professional Resume.dot template...

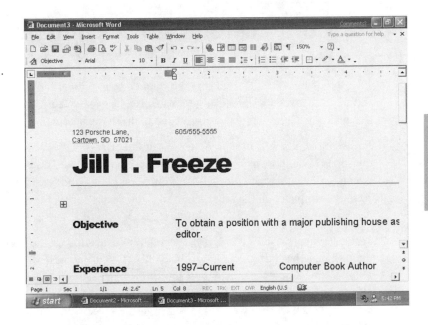

FIGURE 9.4
...can quickly be changed to this by following the steps provided.

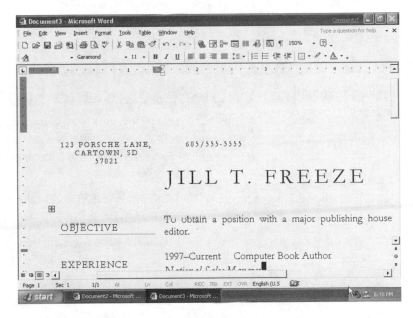

For a More Customized Document, Use a Wizard

Like templates, wizards result in high-quality, professional-looking output. The main difference between wizards and templates is that wizards help you create a customized document, whereas templates create standardized documents.

For example, you can use the Letter Wizard to create a letter. The wizard will ask you questions about how many letters you want to write, what date you want to appear on the document, whether the letter will be printed on plain paper or preprinted letterhead, and so on. A template, on the other hand, will simply produce a form letter into which you can insert text.

To locate these wizards, click the General Templates link on the Word 2002 task pane. (If the task pane has become hidden, click View, Task Pane on the Word menu bar.) You will see the same Templates dialog box shown back in Figure 9.1. Just double-click the icon corresponding to the wizard you want to work with, and you are on your way! The wizard will launch, asking you all kinds of relevant questions. Follow the onscreen prompts to help the wizard build the desired documents, and then begin editing the document just as you would have done with a template.

Adding Page Numbers, Titles, and Other Information with Headers and Footers

Headers and footers allow you to print page numbers, document titles, and other repeating information at the top or bottom of the page. Using headers and footers can add an air of professionalism to documents, and applying page numbers can help keep unbound documents in order.

To begin working with headers and footers, choose View, Header and Footer to open the Header and Footer toolbar shown in Figure 9.5.

The following list describes what each of the buttons on the Header and Footer toolbar does:

- **Insert AutoText.** Click this button to select a predefined header or footer from the AutoText list. For example, you can select the Author, Page #, Date option to have Word automatically insert your name flush left, a centered page number, and the date flush right.

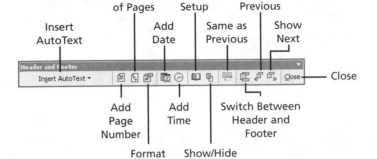

Insert Number   Page   Show
of Pages   Setup   Previous
Insert   Add   Same as   Show
AutoText   Date   Previous   Next

FIGURE 9.5
Header and Footer toolbar items make creating headers and footers a breeze.

Add   Add   Switch Between
Page   Time   Header and
Number   Footer

Format   Show/Hide
Page   Document
Number   Text

Close

> **Hey, that's not my name!** If you want to edit the name that appears in the Author field, choose Tools, Options and then select the User Information tab. Enter the name as desired in the Name text box and then click OK.

- **Insert Page Number.** Set the insertion point in the desired location in the header (press Tab once to center the element or twice to place it flush right) and then click this button to add the page number to your document header or footer.

- **Insert Number of Pages.** Use this button to create a "Page ___ of ___" format in the desired location.

- **Format Page Number.** With this button, you can select the format of the page numbers, and you can even tell Word where to begin numbering—an invaluable tool when you want to omit printing the page number on the first or title page of a document.

- **Add Date.** Set the insertion point using the Tab key if desired and then click this button to add the current date to the document's header or footer.

- **Add Time.** Works the same way as adding a date; of course, it adds the time instead of the date.

- **Page Setup.** This button enables you to define page margins and instruct Word to use a different header/footer for the document's first page.

- **Show/Hide Document Text.** Use this button to show/hide the document's text as you work on the header or footer.

- **Same as Previous.** Make the current header/footer the same as the previous one.

- **Switch Between Header and Footer.** Move between the header and footer on a given page by clicking this button.

- **Show Previous.** Show the previous page's header/footer.
- **Show Next.** Show the next page's header/footer.
- **Close.** Click this button to exit the header/footer view.

After you have defined a header or footer for your document, you can go in and edit it by clicking the Print Layout View button near the bottom left of the Word workspace and then click the element you want to modify.

Creating Tables in Word

Tables are an exceptional way to summarize large amounts of data in relatively little space. Even if you don't work with numbers a lot, you can put tables to good use for aligning columns of text.

There are essentially two ways to incorporate tables into your Word document:

- By formatting the table in Word itself
- By using an Excel worksheet

Obviously, if the information is already formatted in Excel and requires the use of defined formulas, it may be easiest to incorporate the Excel worksheet into your document rather than use a Word table. (We will discuss this option in more detail in the next lesson.) However, if it is a simple table you need to create, Word may very well be up to the task.

By selecting Table, Insert Table from the menu, you can build a table with up to 63 columns and an infinite number of rows. In addition, the table can be formatted with Table AutoFormat to give it a professional appearance with minimal effort.

To build a table using Word, you will need to do the following:

1. Position the insertion point in the desired location.
2. Choose Table, Insert Table from the Standard toolbar to open the Insert Table dialog box pictured in Figure 9.6.
3. In the Number of Columns spin box and the Number of Rows spin box, select the desired number of columns and rows by either typing the number directly or using the arrow buttons next to each box.
4. In the Fixed Column Width spin box, select the desired cell size using the arrow buttons or by selecting AutoFit to have Word determine the size of the columns. AutoFit to contents means the columns will be adjusted to accommodate the column's data, but the resulting table will not span the entire width of the page. It will

be aligned just as you have defined neighboring text alignment. AutoFit to window means the columns will be stretched to span the whole width of the page.

5. You can apply AutoFormat at this point by clicking the AutoFormat button. Choose a format for your table in the Table AutoFormat dialog box (see Figure 9.7) by clicking it. A preview will appear near the bottom of the box. When you find something you like, click OK to apply it.

6. Click OK to create the table and close the Insert Table dialog box.

FIGURE 9.6

Use the Insert Table dialog box to create tables up to 63 columns wide.

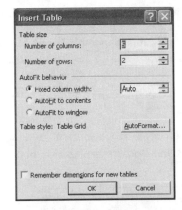

FIGURE 9.7

More than two dozen table formats await you in the Table AutoFormat dialog box.

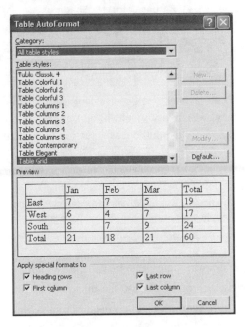

Emphasizing Content with Borders and Shading

When used judiciously, borders and shading can be extremely effective at drawing attention to selected text. You can use borders to add class to a fundraising handout or use the shading option to draw attention to a quote in a newsletter.

> **Don't leave me out here all alone!** Shading is seldom used alone, which is why I have included shading and borders in a single sequence of steps. Typically, a shaded box is outlined in a thin border at the very least.

Making use of these features is easier than you may think. To take advantage of them, perform the following steps:

1. Right-click on any visible toolbar to open a shortcut menu. Select Tables and Borders to display the Tables and Borders toolbar (see Figure 9.8).

FIGURE 9.8

Use the Tables and Borders toolbar to create dynamic borders and shading effects.

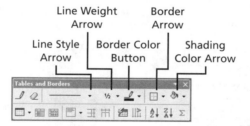

2. Select the text around which you would like to place a border (or the section of text you want to shade) by using the text selection techniques described in the previous hour.

> **Just so you know...** If no text has been selected, Word will find the insertion point and apply the formatting to that paragraph.

3. Click the arrow next to the Line Style box to choose a line style for the border.
4. Click the Line Weight arrow to choose the thickness of your border.
5. Click the Border Color button to add color to online documents or color printer output.

6. Click the arrow next to the Border icon to open a palette of available border styles. Although the desired option is most frequently Outside Border, you have a number of options to choose from.

7. Click the Shading Color arrow to see a pop-up shading palette from which you can make your selection.

8. To close the toolbar to maximize your workspace, click on the Close (X) button at the top-right corner of the toolbar.

You gotta have options. Want more border and shading options than the toolbar gives you? Select the text you want to add shading or a border to and then click Format, Borders and Shading to display the Borders and Shading dialog box. From there, you can access a large number of choices.

Working with Columns in Word

If you need to produce a newsletter for your son's nursery school, a brochure for your new business, or a magazine mock-up, you will want to know how to work with columns in Word. To set up columns:

1. Set the insertion point where you would like the columns to begin, or select the text you would like to format in columns.

Stylistically speaking. If you want a large headline to span the width of multiple columns, put the headline in place before formatting the columns.

2. Click Format, Columns to open the Columns dialog box pictured in Figure 9.9.

3. Choose the desired format of your columns in the Presets area. You can also specify a number of columns in the Number of Columns spin box or select the Equal Column Widths box.

4. To place lines in between columns, check the Line Between check box. You can preview the options you chose in the Preview area.

5. Column layouts can be applied to selected text, the entire document, or from a designated point within a document. You can set this option in the Apply To drop-down list box.

6. Click OK to confirm your selections.

FIGURE 9.9

The Columns dialog box gives you incredible flexibility when it comes to formatting multicolumn documents.

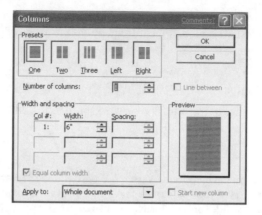

Using Shrink to Fit

Nothing is more frustrating than a letter with two lines spilling over onto the second page. Word has a feature to save paper (and your sanity) called Shrink to Fit. To access this feature, follow these steps:

1. Click the Print Preview button on the Standard toolbar. This will display your document as it would appear on paper (see Figure 9.10).

FIGURE 9.10

Click the Print Preview button on the Standard toolbar to see just how much of your text falls over to the next page.

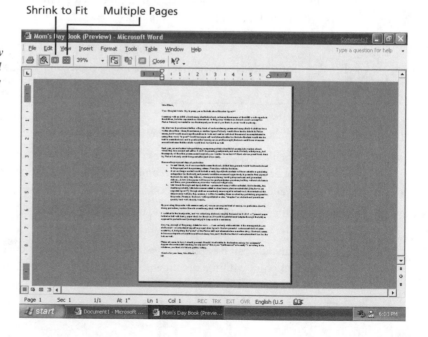

2. Click the Multiple Pages button so that you can see just how much text hangs over onto the second or final page.

3. To squeeze stray lines onto a single page, click the Shrink to Fit button. The results will be shown on the same Print Preview screen.

4. Close Print Preview by clicking the Close button and then proceed as usual with printing the document.

Organizing Your Thoughts by Building an Outline

Remember in high school when your English teacher used to make you turn in an outline for your term papers? It was always such a hassle to type it because I would inevitable find something I wanted to change but was too lazy to fix! Well, thanks to computers, not only is creating an outline easy, but it's also a snap to reorganize information contained in it!

To start building your outline, create a new blank document and enter Word's Outline view by clicking the Outline View button (fourth one from the left) on the horizontal scroll bar. From this view, you can assign varying levels of importance to your topics or heading titles. Table 9.1 shows you how to use the Outline toolbar.

Table 9.1 Outline Toolbar Buttons and Functions

Button	Button Name	Function
⬅	Promote to Heading 1	Increases the level of a heading to Heading 1
⬅	Promote	Pushes the selected heading(s) up one level in the outline
Level 3 ▾	Outline Level Selection Box	Use the dropdown arrow to select an outline level for the text you're about to type.
➡	Demote	Moves the text down one level.
⮕	Demote to Body Text	Use this button to enter body text while in Outline view

To continue creating your outline, simply enter text as you would normally do in Word. Then use the arrow buttons illustrated in Table 9.1 to assign the appropriate level of importance to your headings. The resulting outline format is shown in Figure 9.11.

FIGURE 9.11

Word's Outline view lets you see the organization of your large document at a glance.

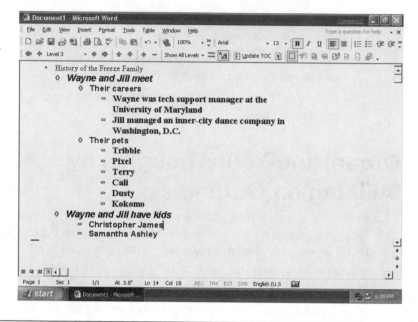

An outline quick trick. You can also use the Tab key to decrease the header's level of importance or Shift+Tab to increase its level of importance.

Editing an Outline

Don't like the placement of a particular topic? Moving it in Word's Outline view is a snap, using the following steps:

1. Place the document in Outline view by clicking the Outline View button on the horizontal scroll bar.

2. Collapse the outline so that only its headers are showing.

The case of the missing text. Failing to collapse the outline before moving headers could result in inadvertently leaving text fragments behind. Because body text moves with its parent header, selecting it while fully collapsed is the best way to ensure that everything gets moved safely.

3. Set the insertion point in the location to which you would like to move text.

4. To select outline text to be moved, click on the + or - at the beginning of the heading you want to move. Note that clicking + takes with it all subheaders and body text up to the next + at the same level as the header to be moved.

5. Confirm that the highlighted text is the text you want to move.

6. Click on the highlighted text, hold down the left mouse button (you will see a box appear at the base of the mouse pointer's arrow), and drag the text to its new location.

7. Release the button to place the text in its new position.

Oops! Did text show up in the wrong location? Never fear; just press Ctrl+Z on your keyboard and start the process again from the beginning.

9

Viewing the Outline While You Write

You can switch into Outline view within seconds, but Word has another option, Document Map, for letting you see the outline of your document as you write. This feature displays a map of your document's headers on the left side of your screen. See Figure 9.12 to see how this feature works.

Document Map Button

FIGURE 9.12

Word's Document Map feature allows you to see your outline as you write.

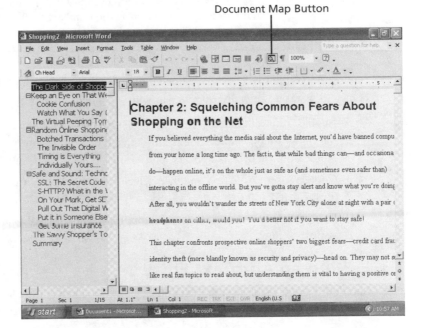

To enable the Document Map option, click the Document Map button on the Standard toolbar, or if it does not appear on your toolbar, click View, Document Map. Now you can see the outline on the left side of your screen as you write.

Using AutoText to Lighten Your Workload

We've all spent hours crafting paragraphs that pack a punch, so why not recycle our ingenuity? Word 2002's AutoText feature allows you to store frequently used phrases, sentences, even paragraphs so that they can be retrieved effortlessly, without the hassles of trying to find the phrase amidst hundreds of files or any copying and pasting.

Before you can have Word type for you, you will need to do a little bit of programming. Follow these steps to program your own AutoText entry:

1. Select the text or graphic you want to store as an AutoText entry.

2. Choose Insert, AutoText, New.

3. Word proposes a name for the AutoText entry that you can accept, or you can type a new one.

4. Click OK to save your entry and exit the dialog.

> **Getting ready for action!** If you plan to create, insert, or modify lots of AutoText entries, you may want to use the AutoText toolbar instead of following the steps above. To display the AutoText toolbar, right-click on any visible toolbar and then place a check mark next to AutoText.

So how do you tell Word when and what to type? You have multiple options when it comes to inserting an AutoText entry in your document, including the following:

- Enable AutoComplete by clicking Tools, AutoCorrect Options and then clicking the Show AutoComplete suggestions check box on the AutoText tab. When the AutoComplete tip box appears, press Enter to accept the AutoText entry.

- Choose Insert, AutoText and then select the desired entry from one of the categories listed.

- From the AutoText toolbar (see Figure 9.13), click the All Entries button and make your selection.

Editing an AutoText Entry

Should the contents of an AutoText entry change, you can edit the entry by doing the following:

1. Insert the AutoText entry into the document as described in the previous steps.

2. Edit the entry as desired.

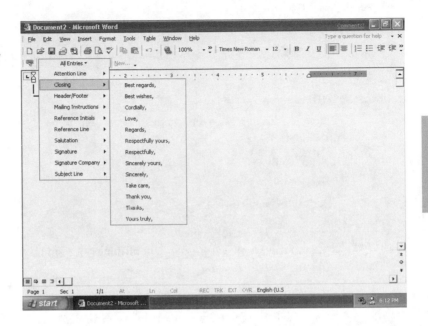

FIGURE 9.13
The AutoText toolbar simplifies creating and inserting multiple AutoText entries.

9

3. Select the revised AutoText entry text.

4. Choose Insert, AutoText, New and then type the original name of the AutoText entry.

See? I told you Word could literally do your typing for you!

Summary

In this lesson, you were introduced to a number of Word 2002 features designed to enhance both your image and productivity. You learned the ins and outs of creating headers, footers, and tables, and you became comfortable working with shading, borders, and outlines. Lastly, I proved my claim that Word 2002 can literally do your typing for you. As you may imagine, there is much more to learn about Word 2002, with plenty of thousand-page books on the market available if you need to know more.

In Hour 10, *The Numbers Game,* I will help you grow comfortable with the world of spreadsheets.

Workshop

Now it's time to see just how much you learned in this lesson. I'll give you a short multiple-choice quiz to test what you learned, followed by a suggested activity designed to enhance the skills you acquired during the hour.

Quiz

Select the best answer to the questions from the choices provided and then check your
answers.

Questions

1. Which tool/feature asks you a series of questions to help you create a custom
   document?

   a. Wizard

   b. Template

   c. AutoComplete

2. Can you format a Word document into columns?

   a. No way, you need a desktop publishing program for that!

   b. Yes

   c. Only documents that exceed one full page of text

3. What do you call the feature that helps you squeeze overflow text onto the last
   page of a document?

   a. The Amazing Ginsu Letter Formatter

   b. Honey, I Shrunk the Letter!

   c. Shrink to Fit

Answers

1. The answer is A. Templates are essentially standardized documents used as a basis
   for your document; AutoComplete has nothing to do with document creation.

2. B wins this one. See the section entitled, "Working with Columns in Word."

3. I'm just having a little fun with the answer choices here, but obviously the correct
   answer was C, Shrink to Fit.

Activity

The best way to discover some of the hidden gems in a program is to take the time to
explore its menus. To encourage you to do this, I'm going to give you a list of Auto features in Word 2002. It is up to you to scour the menus to tell me which are real features,
and which are not.

Circle the Auto features you find in your travels and cross out the "fake" ones.

AutoFormat	AutoSummarize	AutoFit
AutoComplete	AutoIndex	AutoText
AutoCorrect	AutoTab	AutoSave
AutoCaption	AutoReturn	AutoControl

Four of the features listed here are not legitimate. Some are probably more obvious than others. To check your work, type any of the features you see here into Word 2002. If the feature does not exist, a red squiggly line will appear underneath it.

9

HOUR 10

The Numbers Game

Have you ever wished you could track personal holiday spending or play around with various tax scenarios before filling out the papers? If so, you will gain a whole lot from this introductory spreadsheet chapter.

For some reason, many people are intimidated by spreadsheets. Maybe all of the spreadsheet-specific terms or the simple fear of spreadsheets make you math-phobic, like me. Whether you are terrified to start working with numbers or you can't wait to jump right in, this lesson will be easy to follow.

This hour introduces you to Microsoft Excel 2002 and spreadsheet terms and functions in general. Following are some other topics I will cover in the course of this lesson:

- Learn the proper names for spreadsheet elements.
- Discover how to navigate your way around Excel worksheets.
- Find out how to add a group of numbers in an instant using AutoSum.
- Apply descriptive headers and footers to your worksheet before you print it.

Learning the Spreadsheet Lingo

Knowing the proper terms for what you want to accomplish in Excel makes learning to use the program that much easier. The general Excel definitions you want to know include those in the following bulleted list. Obviously, dozens more are sprinkled throughout the lesson as you explore each function.

- **Spreadsheet**: A matrix of data cells arranged in columns and rows.

- **Worksheet**: Excel's term for an electronic spreadsheet.

- **Cell Address**: As you will see in Figure 10.1, Excel cells are "containers" that are capable of holding data. They are arranged in a series of lettered and numbered columns and rows. For example, the active cell in Figure 10.1 is A1 because the cell in the first column, A, and first row, 1, is highlighted. The cell address also is displayed in the Name box at the left end of the Formula bar.

- **Workbook**: Because you may want to create multiple related worksheets, Excel enables you to store them all together in a workbook.

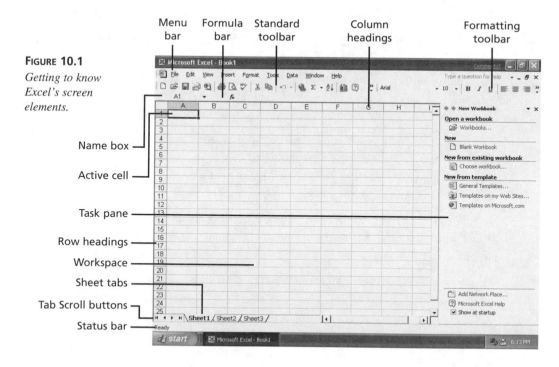

FIGURE 10.1

Getting to know Excel's screen elements.

- **Range**: In Excel, you are often asked to select or perform an operation on a range. A range is simply Excel's counterpart to Word's block of text; it is a group of cells chosen at one time that you can manipulate any number of ways, as you will see throughout the next couple of lessons.

Anatomy of the Excel 2002 Workspace

To get the most out of Excel, you want to be familiar with its critical screen elements because these elements often hold the key to timesaving shortcuts. Figure 10.1 presents all these elements, which are explained in detail later in the hour.

Although many of these elements are the same as those found in Word, following are some new ones.

- **Active cell**: A cell with a dark border (called a *cell selector*) around it. The active cell is the one you have selected to enter or edit data.

- **Column heading**: The lettered boxes across the top of Excel's workspace. Clicking one selects an entire column of cells, which you can format or move as a whole.

- **Row heading**: The numbered boxes down the side of Excel's workspace. Clicking one selects an entire row of cells, which you can format or move as a whole.

- **Sheet tabs**: Click these to move from one worksheet in a workbook to another.

- **Tab Scroll buttons**: If you can't see all the sheet tabs in your workbook, use these buttons to scroll to the ones that are hidden offscreen.

- **Formula bar**: This bar has two parts: a name box that displays the name given to the selected cell (or the cell's address if no name has been given) and a box displaying the selected cell's contents.

- **Formatting toolbar**: Excel's Formatting toolbar is nearly identical to Word's, except that it includes five useful buttons for formatting numbers: Currency Style, Percent Style, Comma Style, Increase Decimal Decrease Decimal.

- **Standard toolbar**: Excel replaces a few Word-specific buttons with AutoSum, a Paste dropdown box full of options, Sort Ascending, and Sort Descending buttons. This toolbar also gives you instant access to Excel's powerful ChartWizard and mapping function.

- **Name box**: This box at the far-left end of the Formula bar holds the address of the cell or cell range currently selected in Excel.

- **Menu bar**: In Excel, a Data pull-down menu replaces Word's Table menu.

10

- **Task pane**: Excel's task pane mirrors the one found in Word, although the tasks with which it assists you are logically spreadsheet related instead of being word processor specific.
- **Status bar**: The left side of Excel's status bar tells you which mode Excel is in: Ready, Enter, or Edit. The other parts contain information about commands being executed, whether Caps Lock is on, and so on.

Moving Around in Excel

To make a cell active, place the mouse pointer in the desired location and click. The cell selector, a thick dark border, appears around the cell you choose. If the cell is offscreen, you may need to use the vertical and horizontal scroll bars to find it. These scroll bars look and work just like those found in Word. Click the arrow buttons for small moves or drag the scroll box in the appropriate direction for larger moves.

You will find a number of shortcut keys invaluable for working with larger worksheets and workbooks. Table 10.1 lists the most common ones.

Table 10.1 Keystrokes for Navigating through Excel

Press This/These	To Move Like This
Name box, enter the Cell address, and then press Enter	Jumps to the cell specified
F5	Displays the Go To box; simply enter the desired cell address and click OK to move directly to that cell.
Arrow keys	One cell in the direction of the arrow
Tab	One cell to the right
Shift+Tab	One cell to the left
Enter	One row down
Page Up/Down	One full screen up or down
Ctrl+Home	To the beginning of the worksheet (usually cell A1)
Ctrl+End	To the last cell of the worksheet

Moving Between Sheets

Much like Word documents can have multiple pages, an Excel worksheet can have multiple worksheets that collectively make up what's referred to as a workbook. Let me give you an example. You're putting together a budget for your school's parent organization.

The expenses fall into several categories including education/workshops, carnival, advertising, and so on.

Rather than putting multiple categories one after the other on a single worksheet, it might make more sense to divide them into several worksheets. That way you can easily switch from one category to another to find what you're looking for.

The fastest way to get to another sheet in the active workbook is to click the appropriate sheet tab at the bottom of Excel's workspace. If the tab you want is out of view, use the tab scroll buttons next to the sheet tabs to find it. From left to right, these buttons perform the following actions:

- Moves to the first sheet in the workbook
- Moves to the previous sheet, using the current sheet as a guide
- Moves to the next sheet, also using the current sheet as a guide
- Moves to the last sheet in the workbook

Entering Worksheet Labels

One of the first things you want to do when creating a worksheet is to enter labels for the various columns and rows. These title labels show you where to insert the various data types and calculations. To enter these labels, perform the following steps:

1. To begin labeling the columns across the top of the screen, select the first cell you want to label.

2. Enter the title you want for the first column of your worksheet. To do this, simply begin typing the text as you would in Word.

3. Press Tab to label the next column to the right or press Enter to move to the next line, and begin labeling the rows.

4. Press Enter after you type each row title.

Trying to fit in. If some of your labels extend beyond the edge of a cell, see the section "Resizing Cells with AutoFit" in the next lesson.

Entering Numbers into Excel

The next step when creating a worksheet is to fill in your labeled columns and rows with appropriate numbers. Simply activate the cell into which you want to place data by clicking it; then enter the appropriate number. You can use the keystrokes presented in Table 10.1 to move from one cell to another.

Selecting Cells

You select a cell by clicking it. To select a range of Excel cells, however, choose from the following options:

- To select a large range of onscreen cells, click the first cell, hold down the mouse button, and drag it until all the desired cells are highlighted (see Figure 10.2). This is perhaps the fastest way to select a large range of onscreen cells.

- To select a large range of cells that extends off the screen, click the first cell, use the scroll bars to find the last cell in the range, and press and hold the Shift key while you click the last cell.

- You also may use the keyboard to select cell ranges. Click the first cell to activate it, press and hold the Shift key; then use the arrow keys to highlight the area you want to select.

- Selecting nonadjacent cells involves clicking the first cell, holding down the Ctrl key, and then clicking additional cells.

- Select all the cells in a worksheet by clicking the Select All button, which is a blank button located above the row numbers and to the left of the column letter headers (see Figure 10.2).

- To select an entire row or column of cells, click the heading for the row or column you want. In other words, click the A column button to highlight that entire column or 1 to select that entire row.

FIGURE 10.2
Click the first cell you want to select and then drag it until the entire range you want to select is highlighted.

Select All button

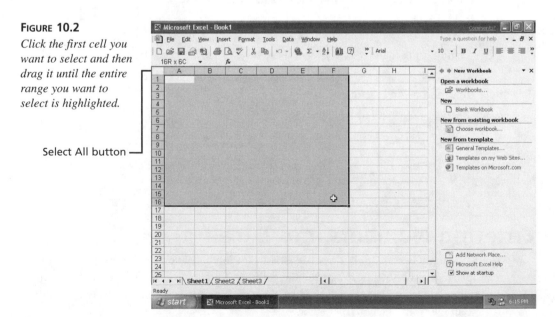

Editing Cell Contents

As they say, the only thing constant is change. You will undoubtedly find yourself making changes to your spreadsheets as well.

As you look through the following steps, you will notice how closely they parallel steps executed in Word. That was Microsoft's whole goal with Office XP and even with previous versions of the suite of applications—to make everything similar. Given that, you already know how to change font size and color in Excel, so you should find other commands similar too.

To edit the contents of an Excel cell, follow these simple steps:

1. Select the cell you want to edit.

2. Enter Edit mode by double-clicking the cell to start at the beginning of the cell, pressing F2 to move to the end of the cell, or clicking the formula box to place the insertion point in the Formula Bar.

3. The keys on your keyboard work differently in Edit mode. The left and right arrow keys move through the cell one character at a time, for example, rather than shifting you over an entire cell. Likewise, Home and End take you to the beginning and end of the cell respectively.

4. Insert or delete characters as you would in Word 2002.

5. After you complete your edit, click the Enter button (check mark) next to the formula bar or press the Enter key.

6. To abort the edit, press Esc or click the Cancel button next to the formula bar.

7. Finally, Excel returns to Ready mode, enabling you to continue with data entry or formatting.

Copying, Cutting, and Pasting Excel Data

Excel's Copy, Cut, and Paste functions are very similar to those found in Word. To copy or move a range of cells, perform the following steps:

1. Select the cell or range of cells you want to copy or move.

Not so fast, buddy! For now, you should use these techniques only to move data, not formulas. Of course, because you don't know how to enter formulas yet, this shouldn't be a big deal. Although you can use these methods with formulas, you might encounter significant consequences. Read the section entitled "Moving and Copying Cells Containing Formulas" later in the hour before trying these steps on formulas.

2. To copy the data, choose Edit, Copy. To move the cell(s), choose Edit, Cut. A moving dashed line, called a *marquee*, appears around the selected range.

4. Click the destination cell.

5. Press Enter to copy or paste the cell(s) in the new location. This returns Excel to the Ready mode.

6. If you want to copy the range of cells repeatedly, simply click the destination cell and choose Edit, Paste rather than pressing Enter. This keeps you in Move Data mode until you press Esc after the last copy or move.

Moving or Copying Cells Using Drag-and-Drop

Drag-and-drop is perhaps the fastest and easiest method to manipulate data within a screen view. You can drag and drop data to a new location in Excel by performing the following steps:

1. Select the cell or cell range you want to move or copy.

2. Place the mouse pointer on the thick border of the selected data. This turns the pointer's cross into an arrow.

3. To move the highlighted cells, click the border and drag the cell or selection to the new destination.

4. To copy the selected cell(s), press and hold the Ctrl key while dragging the selection to its new destination.

Moving and Copying Cells Containing Formulas

I haven't shown you how to make use of formulas yet, but this should come first anyway. If you attempt to copy or move a block of cells containing a formula, the results could be quite unpredictable or just plain wrong. Therefore, I want to take you through these important steps before addressing formulas in detail.

You need to keep in mind some special considerations when copying or moving cells with formulas. Following are two of the most important:

- When you copy a formula cell, Excel has a feature that enables a formula to change relative to the location to which the formula is copied. For example, if you copy the cell containing the formula for adding the numbers in your first column to the bottom of the second column, it totals the new numbers in the second column, not the original numbers in the first column.

- If you move a cell containing a formula, however, the cell references do not change. Therefore, if you move the formula cell for adding the numbers in your first column to the second column, the cell still displays the sum of the first column, regardless of the changes you make to the numbers above it.

Saving Your Worksheets

Flip back through Hour 8, *Jumpstart Word Processing,* which discusses how to save a document. You can save documents in Excel the same way you do in Word. It really is that simple!

Inserting and Deleting Rows and Columns

As time goes on, you will need to modify the size of your worksheet. You do this by inserting or deleting rows or columns in your spreadsheet.

To insert or delete a row or column in your worksheet, perform the following steps:

1. Select an entire row by clicking 1, 2, 3, or whichever number corresponds to the row above where you want to add a new row (Excel will add the new row above the selected row). Insert a column by clicking A, B, C, and so on (Excel will add it to the left of the one you selected). You can also select multiple rows or columns to add the same number of rows or columns to your worksheet. For example, if you select three rows, they will be inserted on top of the first row in the selected range.

2. Right-click the selection to open the shortcut menu shown in Figure 10.3.

3. Choose Insert or Delete.

FIGURE 10.3

Use Excel's shortcut menu to insert or delete elements of your worksheet.

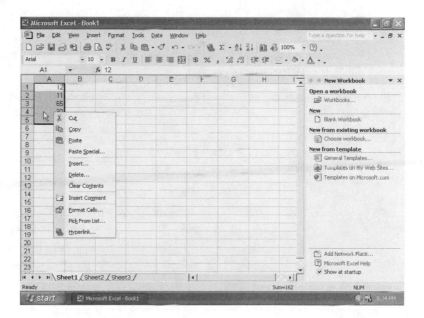

Inserting a Single Cell

You want to add a single cell to a worksheet without adding an entire row or column. Excel will add the new cell or cells above or to the left of the cell you selected for the insert function.

However, I suggest you use this technique sparingly because it can get pretty confusing, especially when formulas are involved. If you do decide to perform this task, all you have to do is follow these steps:

1. Select the cell location where you want to insert the new blank cell(s). You can insert multiple blank cells by selecting the same number of cells as you want to insert.

2. Choose Insert, Cells from the Menu bar.

3. Click Shift cells right or Shift cells down, as appropriate.

Adding and Deleting Worksheets

You can add a single worksheet to the open workbook by choosing Insert, Worksheet from the Menu bar. The new worksheet will be inserted before the current worksheet. If you want to add multiple worksheets, hold down the Shift key and then click the number of worksheet tabs you want to add in the open workbook. After you make your selection, choose Insert, Worksheet. The new worksheets are added to the front of the workbook.

Deleting a worksheet from your workbook also is a simple task. To select the worksheets you want to delete, see Table 10.2.

After you select the sheets, you can delete them by choosing Edit, Delete Sheet from the Menu bar.

Table 10.2 Selecting a Worksheet in Excel

To Select This	Do This
A single sheet	Click the sheet tab
Two or more adjacent sheets	Click the tab for the first sheet and then hold down the Shift key; then click the tab for the last sheet.
Two or more nonadjacent sheets	Click the tab for the first sheet; then hold down the Ctrl key and click the tabs for the other sheets.
All sheets in a workbook menu	Right-click a sheet tab and then click Select All Sheets on the resulting shortcut

Copying and Moving Worksheets

As your workbook begins to take shape, you might want to do some rearranging. You might even decide to put some worksheets into a separate workbook. To move or copy worksheets between workbooks, perform the following steps:

1. To move or copy sheets to another existing workbook, open the workbook that will receive the sheets.

2. Move to the workbook that contains the sheets you want to move or copy and then select the sheets as shown in Table 10.2.

3. Choose Edit, Move, or Copy Sheet.

4. In the To book box, choose the workbook into which you want to move or copy the sheets. You can move or copy the selected sheets to a new workbook by clicking New book.

5. In the Before sheet box, choose the sheet before which you want to insert the moved or copied sheets.

6. To copy the sheets rather than move them, choose the Create a copy check box, and then click OK.

> **I hope you know what you are getting into....**Use extreme caution when you move or copy sheets. Calculations or charts based on data on a worksheet might become inaccurate if you move the worksheet.

To rearrange the order of the worksheets in your current workbook, you can drag the selected sheets along the row of sheet tabs. To copy the sheets, hold down the Ctrl key and then drag the sheets, releasing the mouse button before you release the Ctrl key.

Adding Your Data with AutoSum

Adding numbers is one of the most common things people want to do with their spreadsheet data. Although more advanced formulas and functions are presented in the next hour, this section shows you how to get quick results with Excel's AutoSum feature.

To apply AutoSum to a range of cells, follow these steps:

1. Activate the cell in which you want to place the sum of the information added together.

2. Click the AutoSum button on the Standard toolbar. Excel tries to guess which data you want to add (see Figure 10.4).

10

FIGURE 10.4

Excel has "guessed" here that the cells above the AutoSum entry are what you want to add.

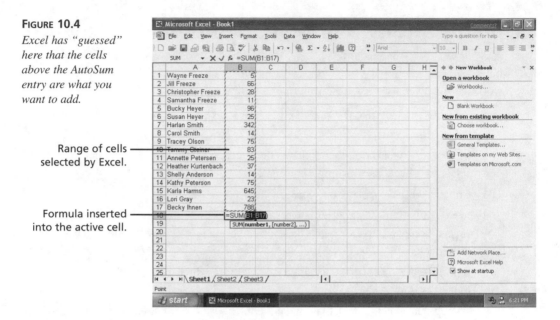

Range of cells
selected by Excel.

Formula inserted
into the active cell.

3. If Excel has selected the correct range of data, press Enter to apply the formula to the active cell. The total of the cells will appear in the active cell.

4. To select a different range to which you want to apply AutoSum, simply select the first cell in the row or column of the desired numbers and drag the mouse to select the rest of the cells you want to add.

5. When the hash marks (sort of like the dashed lines that appear around the edges of a coupon) appear around the desired data range, click the AutoSum button to apply the formula. The total of the numbers you selected appears in the active cell.

Give the cell a name. You might want to label your sum by inserting a title in an adjacent cell. This clarifies the number to people seeing your worksheet for the first time.

Make Your Worksheets Look Good Using AutoFormat

If you are in a hurry but still need to make a good impression, consider using AutoFormat to make your worksheets look their best.

To apply AutoFormat to your worksheet, perform the following steps:

1. Select the range of cells you want to format.

2. Choose Format, Autoformat to display the AutoFormat dialog box (see Figure 10.5).

FIGURE 10.5

Use the AutoFormat dialog box to choose a format for your table and then preview it in the Sample box.

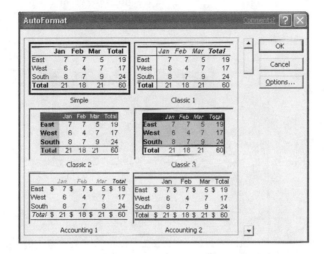

3. Click the Options button to display a list of formatting elements. Insert and delete the check mark next to each element to toggle on and off the various formatting options. You can preview these in the Sample window before applying them to the actual data in your worksheet.

4. When you see a result you like, click OK to accept it

> **Be on the safe side.** Before applying AutoFormat to a range of cells containing formulas and cell references, be sure to save your worksheet so that you can verify AutoFormatting has maintained the integrity of your data.

Supplying Headers or Footers for Your Worksheets

Much like headers and footers add a professional touch and sense of organization to Word documents, they also enhance Excel documents.

Excel 2002 comes with a number of preset headers and footers, which should serve the purpose well. To apply one of these, perform the following steps:

1. Click the worksheet to which you want to apply the headers or footers.

2. Choose View, Header and Footer from the Menu bar.

3. Choose the Header/Footer tab.

4. In the Header or Footer box, click the drop-down arrow and select the header or footer you want (see Figure 10.6).

5. Click OK to apply the header and/or footer.

FIGURE 10.6
Click the drop-down arrow next to the header or footer box to choose a header or footer that most adequately meets your needs.

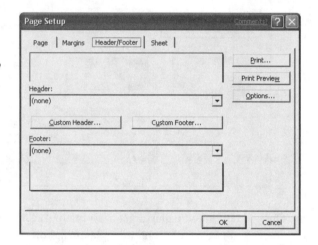

Printing Excel Worksheets

If you are anything like me, you find it easier to review a paper document than a screen full of electrons. This especially is true for spreadsheets. I'm much more at ease marking up a printout of the spreadsheet, which I later can go back and edit as necessary.

To print your own Excel worksheet, perform the following steps:

1. Launch Excel and open the worksheet you want to print.

2. Choose File, Print to display the Print dialog box shown in Figure 10.7.

3. Select the printer to which you want to send the output. In the vast majority of cases where only one printer is installed, Excel will "know" the name of the printer to use.

4. Select the part of the workbook you want to print. The active worksheet means that only the tab currently displayed will print, whereas the entire workbook means everything on each tab of the file.

FIGURE 10.7

The Print dialog box enables you to specify which parts of the worksheet you want to print: the selected text, the entire workbook, or the active sheet.

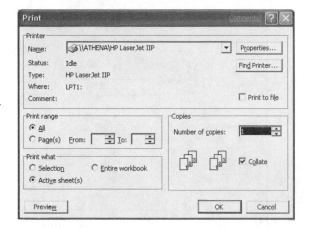

5. Select the number of copies to be printed.

6. Click OK to send the output to the printer.

> **Give me just a little bit....** Printing only part of a worksheet used to be a major hassle, but not with newer versions of Excel. To print a specific section of a worksheet, follow these steps for the best results: Select the area of the worksheet you want to print; then choose File, Print Area, and Set Print Area from the Menu bar to save the selected range. To send the selected output to the printer, choose File, Print and then click OK; press the Print button or press Ctrl+P. Any of these methods will produce a printed copy of the selected cells.
>
> Excel will remember the specified print area until you manually clear it by choosing File, Print Area, Clear Print Area. To confirm that Excel will print what you expect it to, enter Print Preview mode.

Getting What You Want by Using Page Setup Options

Because printing worksheets that actually look good can be a daunting task, you might want to use the Page Setup and Print Preview options in cases where making a good impression is of primary importance.

To work with Excel's Page Setup options, perform the following steps:

1. Choose File, Page Setup to display the Page Setup dialog box shown in Figure 10.8.

2. Select the Page tab to begin setting the options and work your way through all the other tabs (see Figure 10.9).

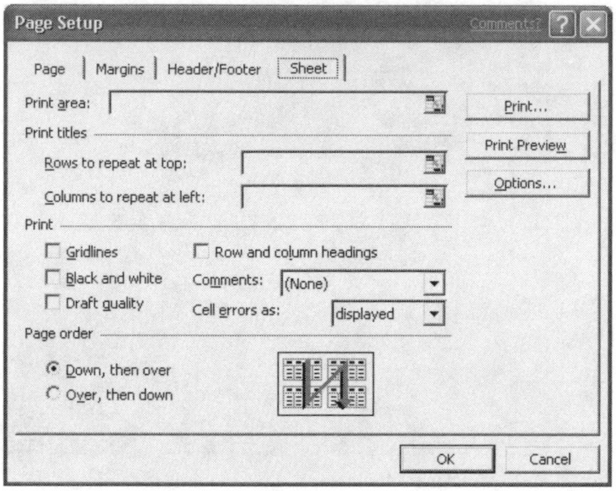

FIGURE 10.8

Use the Sheet tab of the Page Setup dialog box to select the print quality of your output, as well as gridlines, if needed, and row and column headers.

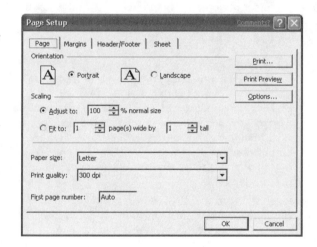

FIGURE 10.9

Be sure to set the page orientation of your document in the Orientation section because many worksheets look better in landscape than in portrait orientation.

3. Some of the options you want to be sure to address are described in the following list:

- On the Page tab, select Portrait or Landscape for your document's orientation. Many worksheets look best in landscape mode.

- Select the Fit to on the Page tab to squeeze your worksheet into as little space as possible. It's similar in concept to Word's Shrink to Fit feature, which tries to fit a few lines of stray text onto one less page of paper.

- Use the Margins tab to place your worksheet in an appealing position. The easiest way to do this is to specify that the worksheet is centered both Horizontally and Vertically.

- Use the Header/Footer tab to apply a header or footer to your output. You can select from a variety of predefined headers and footers, or create your own.

- Use the Sheet tab of the Page Setup dialog box to select the print quality of your output, as well as gridlines, if needed, and row and column headers.

- To print the column headings on each page of a worksheet, go to the Sheet tab and specify that columns repeat on each page. This is a must-have feature for long worksheets.

4. After you set all the desired options, click OK to close the dialog box.

Using Print Preview to Get the Best Results

To see what a document will look like when printed, use Excel's Print Preview feature. This also gives you an opportunity to tweak your document if you see something that isn't quite right. To use Print Preview, perform the following steps:

1. Choose File, Print Preview or click the Print Preview button on the Standard toolbar. The Print Preview window appears (see Figure 10.10).

2. Click the Zoom button to take a closer look or click Setup to go back and tweak some of the options.

3. Click Close to return to Normal view or click Print to begin printing the document as you see it.

FIGURE 10.10

Enter the Print Preview screen to make sure the output meets your needs before sending it to the printer.

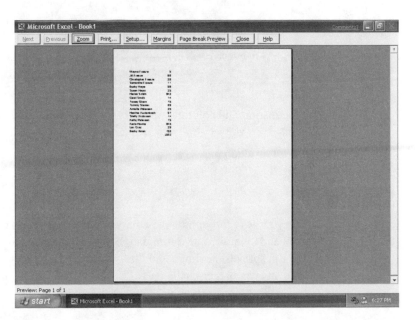

Setting Margins in Print Preview Mode

One of the most common adjustments people want to make to their worksheets before sending them to the printer is to reposition the margins. You can save time by doing this in Print Preview mode, as explained in the following steps:

1. Click the Print Preview screen.

2. Click the Margins button to see indicators that show where your margins are located (see Figure 10.11).

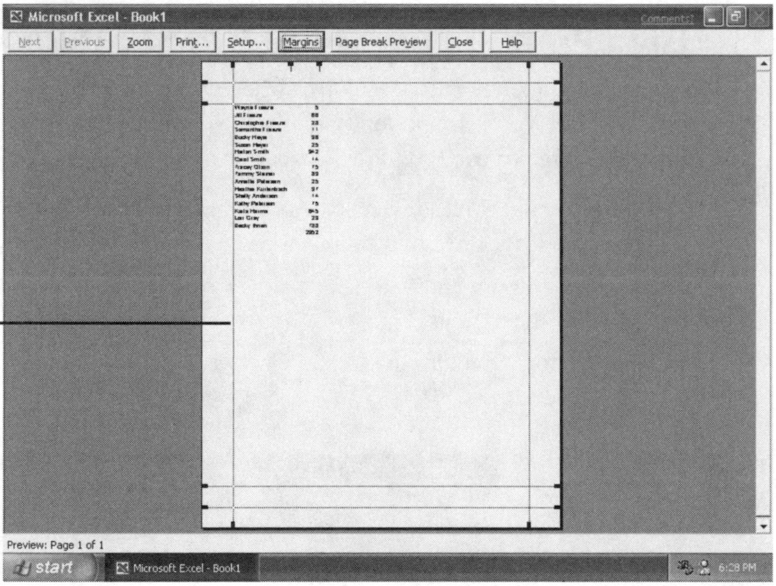

FIGURE 10.11

Click one of the margin lines to drag the worksheet to the position you want.

Margin indicators ———

3. Click the margin and column indicators and drag them to reposition the worksheet on the page.

4. Click Print to send your creation to the printer.

Summary

After working your way through this lesson, you should be pretty comfortable building a basic spreadsheet. Hopefully, any intimidation you might have felt also is gone. With a firm grounding in spreadsheet lingo and the anatomy of the Excel workspace, you are ready to tackle an even bigger challenge.

This bigger challenge comes in the next lesson, Hour 11, where I show you how to create an Excel database. I also introduce you to building charts from your personal database.

Workshop

Now it's time to see just how much you learned in this lesson. I'll give you a short multiple-choice quiz to test what you learned, followed by a suggested activity designed to enhance the skills you acquired during the hour.

Quiz

Select the best answer to the questions from the choices provided and then check your answers in the following section.

10

Questions

1. When it comes to software, which term is *not* unique to spreadsheets?

   a. Cell

   b. Tab

   c. Worksheet

2. Can you move a worksheet from one workbook to another?

   a. Of course, it's a piece of cake!

   b. Workbooks and worksheets are the same thing.

   c. Only if their filenames begin with the same letter.

3. What do you call the feature that helps you squeeze a worksheet into as little space as possible?

   a. The Amazing Ginsu Worksheet Formatter

   b. Honey, I Shrunk the Worksheet!

   c. Fit To

Answers

1. The answer is B. You can find tabs in every Office 2000 application, as well as in Windows itself. Of course, they don't all look the same, but the question addressed the term, not the behavior of the element.

2. The only possible answer is A. The other options couldn't be further from the truth.

3. You chose C? You win! If you chose anything else, you obviously didn't learn anything from the previous silly question like this!

Activity

Launch Excel and enter down the first column the types of monthly household bills you pay, such as gas, electricity, phone, mortgage, and so on.

In the second column, insert some ballpark figures for each type of bill. It doesn't matter whether they are exact. This is just an exercise designed to help you get used to using Excel.

Click the first empty cell underneath the column of numbers and then click the AutoSum button. The total of your monthly bills should appear in the selected cell.

Next, give AutoFormat a whirl to make your budget look nice.

Congratulations! You have created your first spreadsheet! Now it's time to move on to bigger and better things!

Hour 11

When Only a Database Will Do

Do you have a trading card collection or some other type of collection you want to be able to sort or search? Perhaps you are in charge of maintaining the membership list for your daughter's gymnastics team. Then again, you might have a purely business need in mind, such as the capability to track the location of the customers of your small startup company. Whatever the case, you could benefit by creating a database.

A database essentially is a collection of information organized in such a way that you can sort, filter, and analyze it. Many people think they have to use a "real" database program such as Microsoft Access to get true searching and sorting capabilities—not so. In a number of cases, you can successfully create a database in the spreadsheet program that came with your computer. Microsoft's Excel 2002 is especially good at this, as you will see in the pages to come.

In addition to learning how to create an Excel 2002 database, you will be introduced to the following topics in this hour:

- Learn how to create your own special data entry form.
- Discover how to use AutoFit to adjust the size of your columns to fit the largest entry.
- View the data you want by performing searches and filters.
- Analyze your data visually by creating charts.

Planning Your Database

Before creating a database, the first thing you will need to do is to decide what types of information, or fields, you want to maintain for each record or entry. Take an audio CD collection as an example. You might want to keep track of the CD's artist, recording label, title, date released, and perhaps even a list of tracks on the CD.

Going through this process is vitally important to the success and usefulness of your database. After all, you can have megabytes of information stored in a database, but what good is it if you can't learn anything from it? Consider taking the time to plan your database in writing. In addition to listing the types of fields you want to include, approach the task from a second angle, like listing what types of information you want to be able to deduce from the database. Considering the audio CD example, some questions you may ask yourself to determine the necessary fields for a particular artist's database include the following:

- How many of this artist's CDs do I have?
- How can I tell which CD contains which song?
- When did I buy my last CD
- How much have I spent on CDs

At first, it may appear such questions return the exact same results as listing fields you want to track; however, take the time to do the exercise anyway on the off-chance it may reveal new information. For example, in my audio CD example above, I did not originally plan to include the cost of a CD in my data collection, but in looking at my list of questions, the field clearly came into play as one I might want to investigate in the future.

Building a Database in Excel 2002

After you adequately plan your database, you can begin creating it as follows:

1. Launch Excel with a blank workspace.

2. Enter the field names in row 1 (one per cell). These columns and rows of information make up what database programmers refer to as a *table*.

3. If you want these field headers to be visible regardless of where you are in the worksheet, select the row below the field header row and choose Window, Freeze Panes. Now the field headers will always be visible to simplify accurate data entry.

4. Begin filling the table with data, using one row for each CD, doll, trading card, miniature car (or whatever bit of information constitutes a record for your database).

5. Periodically save your database by clicking the Save button on the Standard toolbar.

Once you've followed these steps, you have a worksheet that resembles a database table. You can sort the information, filter it to see only the entries you want, and so on.

Using a Data Form to Enter Excel Database Records

Excel's Data Form feature helps you enter, edit, and find Excel database data. The Data Form is a dialog box that holds text boxes for up to 33 database fields.

To begin using a Data Form, follow these steps:

1. Select the cells containing data within your database. If it does not yet contain data, enter the column headers from which Excel can build the data form.

2. Click Data, Form from the Menu bar. Excel may respond with a dialog box like the one shown in Figure 11.1. If you followed the directions in the previous section, clicking OK will get you the result you want.

3. The preceding action causes the data form shown in Figure 11.2 to open.

FIGURE 11.1

This is your chance to verify which data you want Excel to use in order to build the form.

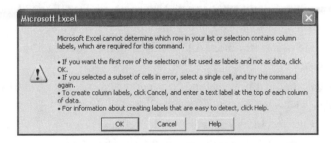

Microsoft Excel

Microsoft Excel cannot determine which row in your list or selection contains column labels, which are required for this command.

- If you want the first row of the selection or list used as labels and not as data, click OK.
- If you selected a subset of cells in error, select a single cell, and try the command again.
- To create column labels, click Cancel, and enter a text label at the top of each column of data.
- For information about creating labels that are easy to detect, click Help.

[OK] [Cancel] [Help]

FIGURE 11.2
A data form like this one can make data entry easier by removing table clutter from your sight.

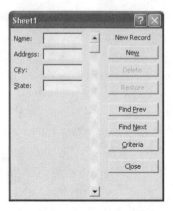

4. To add records, click the New button and then enter the data in the appropriate field. Press Tab to move to the next field or simply click inside the desired text box and begin typing.

5. Choose one of two ways to save the new record:
   - Click the New button to automatically save the current record and enter a new one.
   - Click Close to save your work and close the data form.

Editing Data with the Data Form

Suppose you have created a database filled with contact information for your son's Boy Scout troop, and then a family moves, requiring you to change the address. Make your life easier by performing the following steps using the Data Form to find and edit records.

1. Select a cell inside the database table.

2. Choose Data, Form on the Menu bar to open the Data Form.

3. Click the Criteria button to display an empty Data Form (notice that the word Criteria now appears above the column of buttons).

4. In one or more of the text boxes, type in the criteria for the record you want to locate.

5. Click the Find Prev or Find Next buttons, as necessary, until you locate the record you want.

6. Edit the record by changing the desired text box.

7. If you decide to return to the original record after changing some of the fields, simply choose Remove before saving the record. This restores the entry to its previous state, which is immensely helpful if you accidentally edit the wrong record.

8. To delete the record permanently, click Delete on the Data Form.

9. After you finish making the desired changes, click Close.

10. Save your workbook as usual.

Resizing Cells with AutoFit

Although you have a variety of formatting options available to you in Excel, AutoFit is great for quick cell resizing. AutoFit makes the column width fit perfectly to the contents of the selected cell. In addition, if you select the whole column, it adjusts to fit the longest text entry in the column.

Using AutoFit One Column at a Time

Because rows automatically resize themselves as needed, you will find that you use AutoFit most often to resize columns. To resize a column, perform the following steps:

1. Move the mouse pointer to the border between the column header you want to resize and the next column header to the right. The mouse pointer turns into a vertical line with a double arrow running crossways through it.

2. Double-click this location to resize the column on the left to fit the longest entry.

If using a keyboard is more comfortable to you, try clicking the head letter of the column you want to adjust and then choose Format, Column, AutoFit Selection from the Menu bar. Excel adjusts the column width of the selected text to fit the longest line exactly.

Resizing a Range of Cells with AutoFit

Using AutoFit on a group of columns is almost as easy as applying it to a single column. Just perform the following steps:

1. Click the first column header and drag the mouse pointer through the last column you want to resize.

2. Confirm that the range of columns you want to select is highlighted. This might involve scrolling through the table to verify the fact.

3. Double-click the border between any two of the selected column headers to resize the entire selected area.

Sorting Excel Database Records

Knowing how to sort your database can help you take advantage of even more advanced Excel functions, such as subtotaling a group of records or counting entries that meet specific criteria. To sort your database, perform the following steps:

11

1. Select any cell in the table of the database you want to sort.

2. Choose Data, Sort from the Menu bar to display the Sort dialog box (see Figure 11.3).

FIGURE 11.3

The Sort dialog box enables you to sort up to three database fields in ascending or descending order.

3. Click the Sort By drop-down list box to choose the field by which you want to sort.

4. Select Ascending or Descending to specify the sort order for the selected field.

5. Repeat the process, if necessary, for sorts within sorts by using the Then By boxes. (This is great if you want to sort by a book's format—for example, hardcover—and then within that alphabetically by title.)

6. Click OK to sort the database as specified.

You also can perform a simpler sort if your database meets any of the following criteria:

• The database contains only two column headers/fields.

• The column by which you want to sort comes either first or last in order.

To perform one of the preceding sorts, perform the following steps:

1. Select the column header by which you want to sort your data.

2. Highlight the remainder of the database table.

Help! I can't reach it! If you can't highlight the entire data table after selecting the desired sort column, you should abort the simple sort and perform it using the Sort box, as described in the previous section. Continuing at this point would jumble your records; some of the fields would be sorted, whereas others would remain in their original positions. It is sort of like Humpty Dumpty at that point—you may not be able to put everything back together again!

3. Click the Sort Ascending or Sort Descending button on the Standard toolbar.

4. Be sure to save your newly sorted table before closing or exiting to avoid having to perform the sort again in the future. This especially is useful if you want to maintain an alphabetized table in your database.

Grouping and Subtotaling Your Database

Excel also groups and counts data in your database. This enables you, for example, to count the number of people from each state.

To group and then count selected data in your database, perform the following steps:

1. Select a cell within the database.

2. Sort the database as directed earlier in the hour so that all the records are grouped according to the field you want to group and subtotal. You can group your CDs by artist and then later count the number of CDs you have for each artist, for example.

3. Choose Data, Subtotals from the Menu bar to display the Subtotals dialog box (see Figure 11.4).

FIGURE 11.4

Use the Subtotals dialog box to count or average like data (among other functions).

11

4. In the At Each Change In drop-down list, choose the field by which you want Excel to group your records.

5. In the Use Function drop-down list, specify which function you want to perform on the data.

6. In the Add Subtotal To list, select the same field by which you chose to group your data.

7. Choose OK to subtotal your database.

8. To remove the grouping, choose Data, Subtotals, Remove All. Your database will return to normal.

Using AutoFilter to Find Specific Data

You sometimes might want to extract records that meet specific criteria. For example, if you run a small veterinarian clinic, you may want to send check-up notices to families whose pets are due for vaccinations during a specified month. Maybe you want to print a list of your Beach Boys CDs only. To do either of such tasks, you need to filter your database. To begin filtering records in an Excel database, perform the following steps:

1. Select a cell within the database.

2. Choose Data, Filter, AutoFilter from the Menu bar. A drop-down arrow appears to the right of each column header (see Figure 11.5).

FIGURE 11.5

Drop-down arrow buttons to the right of each column header cell make setting data filters a snap.

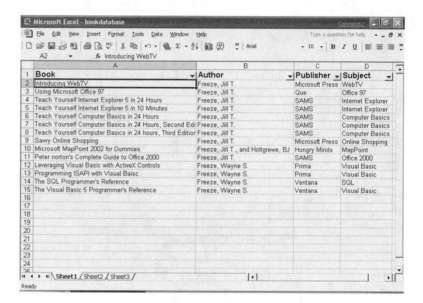

3. Click on the drop-down arrow next to the column you want to filter and then select the desired filter option. You can choose from the following options:

   - You can select only records containing one of the field's listings. For example, you can extract all the records of people who live in South Dakota from the State field.

   - You also can choose only records left blank in the chosen field.

   - By selecting Top 10, you can filter the most common values in the selected field—a quick way to how many CDs you have of a particular artist.

   - Choose All to remove any filters from the selected field.

- By choosing Custom, you can use the Custom AutoFilter dialog box shown in Figure 11.6 to specify multiple criteria for advanced filtering. For example, you could view customers from a particular ZIP code or search for people expressing an interest in your products from a particular state.

FIGURE 11.6

Use the Custom AutoFilter dialog box to select multiple filtering criteria.

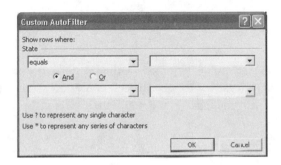

3. You will see only the records in the database that meet the criteria you defined, which you then can edit or print.

4. To remove the filter, choose Data, Filter, AutoFilter, which removes the check mark next to AutoFilter. Your database table will then return to its normal appearance.

11

Calculating Simple Statistics on a Cell Range

Excel makes it easy to perform a simple analysis on a selection of cells. You can apply any of the following functions to a group of selected cells:

- **SUM(range)**: Gives you the total of the selected range
- **AVERAGE(range)**: Calculates the numerical average for the selected range
- **MAX(range) or MIN(range)**: Returns the maximum or minimum value in a range
- **COUNT(range)**: Indicates how many non-zero cells are in the range

To apply these functions to a range of cells, you will need to do the following:

1. Select the cell in which you want to place the result of the calculation.

2. In the Formula Bar, enter an equal sign, =, followed by one of the function names in the preceding bulleted list and then an open parenthesis, (. The result should look like Figure 11.7.

3. Click on the first cell in the desired range. A moving dashed line appears around the cell.

FIGURE **11.7**

In addition to the format of the function shown in the active cell, you will notice that the formula box now carries the function name.

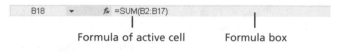

Formula of active cell   Formula box

4. While holding the mouse button down, drag it along to cover the desired range of cells and then release the button. The cell range now should appear in the active cell and on the formula bar. You'll notice that Excel places the closing parentheses for you.

Um, I have a problem here... If you're placing the result of the calculation right below the selected range, be certain you haven't accidentally selected the formula destination cell as well. Doing so will give you a circular reference error, which will result in needing to reselect the cell range to get a valid result.

5. Press Enter to see the result in the active cell.

Applying More Complex Functions

In addition to enabling you to perform basic calculations on a selected range of data, Excel guides you through a number of complex functions using the Formula Palette. To apply a complex formula, perform the followings steps:

1. Select the formula's destination cell.

2. Choose Insert, Function from the Menu bar or click the Function button on the Standard toolbar to display the Insert Function dialog box (see Figure 11.8).

Alternate access. You can access the Function Palette by clicking the Edit Function button on the Formula bar and then clicking the Formula box's drop-down list arrow to see a list of functions. If the function you are looking for doesn't appear on that initial drop-down list, however, you will need to choose More Functions to get to the Paste Function box shown in the preceding figure. The steps presented in the preceding numbered list are merely a shortcut. The alternate method for accessing the Formula Palette

described here is best used to quickly access the palette for the most
recently used function. This eliminates the need to look through the various
categories and function names in the Paste Function box.

FIGURE 11.8

*The Insert Function
dialog box gives you
quick access to the
numerous function cat-
egories and function
names available in
Excel.*

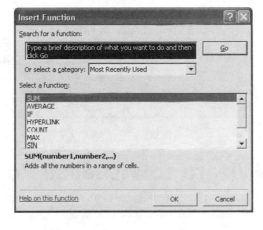

3. Select a category from the Select a category list using the drop-down arrow button
   provided.

4. In the Select a Function box, choose the function you want. If you are not sure
   which one you really want, click one and view its description in the gray area
   below the windows.

5. After you make your selection, click OK.

6. The Function Arguments dialog box opens and displays the arguments (types of
   numbers) you need to enter for the chosen function, along with an explanation of
   the active argument (see Figure 11.9).

7. Enter the appropriate number or cell address for each argument.

Less is better. Do not use formatted numbers as part of your arguments;
instead, use arithmetic expressions. For example, to select 8% as the Rate in
the PMT Formula Palette, enter .08. If 8% is the annual percentage rate,
enter .08/12. Likewise, you should omit commas in large numbers because
commas are used as separators in a formula.

8. After you enter all the arguments, click OK to see the result appear in the selected
   cell.

FIGURE **11.9**

The PMT Formula Palette helps you calculate loan payments even if you can't remember all the formula elements needed to do so.

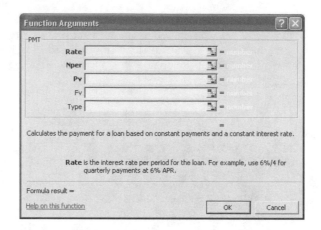

Using ChartWizard to Visualize Your Data

Creating a dynamic, professional-looking chart can speak volumes for your data because it shows, not tells, the reader what's going on. To create a chart in Excel, perform the following steps:

1. Open the worksheet or database table from which you want to build a chart.

2. Select the range of data you want to chart.

3. Click the ChartWizard button on the Standard toolbar to guide you through the process.

4. The first step in using the Chart wizard is to select a chart type. Start with the Standard Types tab. Select a chart type and subtype of interest; preview the result by clicking the Press and Hold to View Sample button.

5. If you don't see anything you like there, try the Custom Types tab shown in Figure 11.10. Based on your data, the selected chart type automatically appears.

6. Accept the data range you want to use by clicking Next.

7. Step 3 of the Chart wizard enables you to set the following options:

   - **Titles Tab**: Enables you to assign to your chart and various parts of it a title, where applicable.

   - **Legend Tab**: Enables you to place a legend by your chart. You can even select the legend's position based on your page's layout.

   - **Data Labels Tab**: Enables you to choose how your data is labeled—by value, percent, name, or a combination thereof.

FIGURE **11.10**
The Custom Types tab in Chart wizard enables you to preview your data in the selected chart's format on-the-fly.

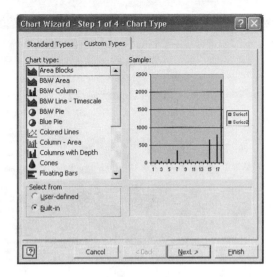

8. Step 4 asks where you want to place your chart—in its own sheet or embedded in the current sheet.

9. Click Finish to place the chart.

Moving and Sizing the Chart or Map

To move or resize your chart, follow these simple steps:

1. Select the chart you want to move or resize by clicking on it. Small, black selection handles appear around the object's parameter (see Figure 11.11).

2. Position the mouse pointer over a handle, at which point it will turn into a double-headed arrow.

3. Click and drag the handle in the desired direction to make the object larger or smaller.

4. To move the object, click inside its boundaries, drag it to a new location, and then drop it into place.

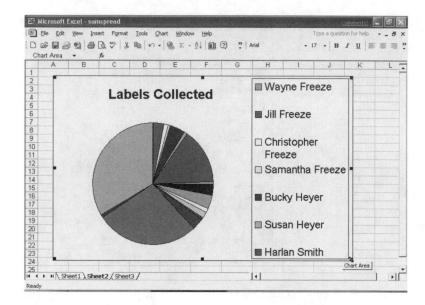

FIGURE 11.11

The chart with which you intend to work is identified clearly.

Summary

I have always found it easier to design a simple database in Excel rather than resort to using overly complicated database software. Now you can do it, too! What's more, you learned how to sort, filter, and perform calculations on your data in addition to charting it.

These two lessons barely scratch the surface of what you can do with Excel 2002. To learn more about the powerful features in Excel 2002, visit your local library or bookstore.

In Hour 12, Connecting to the Internet, we turn our attention to the amazing world of the Internet. You'll learn how to begin embarking on a trek along the information superhighway using Windows XP and the Internet Explorer 6 suite of applications.

Workshop

Now it's time to see just how much you learned in this lesson. I'll give you a short multiple-choice quiz to test what you learned, followed by a suggested activity designed to enhance the skills you acquired during the hour.

Quiz

Select the best answer to the questions from the choices provided and then check your answers in the following section.

Questions

1. Which of the following is *not* a database term?

    a. Table

    b. Record

    c. Chart

2. What is the difference between sorting and filtering your database?

    a. A sort puts items in a specified order, whereas a filter extracts only records that meet a certain criteria.

    b. The two concepts are virtually identical.

    c. Sorts and filters were not covered in this book.

3. How do you resize a chart?

    a. Click inside the chart's area and drag it to size.

    b. Click the chart to select it and then click and drag one of the black handles in the direction you want.

    c. You can't resize them; what you see is what you get.

Answers

1. Although you can create charts from a database, it is not a database term per se; therefore, C was the appropriate answer.

2. A is the only acceptable answer to this question.

3. The correct answer is B. The procedure in answer A simply moves the chart, and C is a false statement.

Activity

Remember that simple budget worksheet you created at the end of the last lesson? Well, now I would like you to open that file and create a simple pie chart from it. Doing this illustrates how much of your monthly budget is dedicated to each type of bill. This is not a complex exercise by any means, but at least you now know how to generate a chart from bits of data.

11

PART III

Logging On to the Internet

Hour

HOUR 12

Connecting to the Internet

Okay, raise your hand if you turned to this chapter in the book first. Aha, caught you! It's understandable though. So many people buy computers to go online because the Internet has so much to offer them. You can do research without schlepping off to the library. You can try items before you buy them. You can correspond with friends for free. You can download software updates the instant they become available. You can bargain hunt. You name it—the Internet can help you with it!

As they say, though, you have to crawl before you can walk. Before you can even get started with life on the Internet, there is a lot you will need to know now. This lesson focuses on the basics like finding an Internet Service Provider (ISP) and how to establish an Internet connection. The next hour shows you how to get and install Internet Explorer 6 and how to make the popular Web browser work for you.

In this hour, you will learn the answers to the following questions, among others:

- I'm not even linked to the Internet; how do I find an ISP?
- Is there anything I should ask a prospective ISP before signing on the dotted line?
- How do I configure Windows XP, Home Edition to establish an Internet connection?

Before you venture online, a lot of work needs to be done:

- You need to find a company to provide your Internet service.
- You'll want to configure Windows XP to be able to dial up that service.
- You need to teach your e-mail program how to find your mail server.
- You need to know Internet etiquette, known as *netiquette*, to study.

Finding an Internet Service Provider

Having all that great new computer gear and software with no Internet connection is like being all dressed up with no place to go. You'll need a connection to the Internet to make it all work.

When you booted your computer for the first time, your desktop probably contained a solitary folder that was littered with icons for AOL, MSN, and others, with each of them vying for your Internet service dollars. So how do you cut through the confusion to decide which one is best for you?

Internet Service Providers and Online Services Explained

Chances are when you booted your new computer, a copy of Internet Explorer was ready and waiting for you. That solves the "How do I surf the net?" part of the equation, but where should you turn to sign up for Internet access? You have basically two choices: the more cost-efficient local Internet service provider or the national services like America Online that provide value added content along with their Internet service. Of course, there are minor variations within the two categories, but those are your primary choices.

What exactly does added content mean? In America Online's case, it means they publish special articles and information for their subscribers to which no one else has access. Maybe a favorite print magazine has agreed to make its content available to America Online subscribers only, or perhaps an investment article was written by a noted financial expert especially for America Online. An ISP, however, just gives you the access, leaving you on your own to find worthwhile content.

Because online services are often plagued by incessant busy signals (See what happens when you get too popular?) and their fees can be somewhat pricey (That added content does costs money!), many people turn to ISPs for their Internet access.

When it comes to ISPs, there are a few different "flavors." You can choose a national provider like MCI or AT&T, a regional provider like EROLS, or a local provider such as DTG, the one I use in rural South Dakota. You will also find a number of cable and satellite TV companies jumping into the Internet business, providing high-speed connections for a price.

There are pros and cons to each of them. If you live in a remote area where calling just about anywhere is long distance, you may need to go with one of the services offered by a telephone company just to get a local dial-up number. If you want dedicated and personal technical support as you get acquainted with your computer and the Internet, you may want to choose a local provider where every single customer's satisfaction is vitally important.

See the section titled "So Where Do I Find a Good One?" later in this lesson for some ideas on how to find the ISP that's right for you.

Assessing Your Needs

Providing Internet service has become such a lucrative and highly competitive business that you are often pelted with opportunities to sign up without even looking for one. You may find an AOL disk in a recent computer magazine, or CompuServe may mail you a disk with a free offer to try them for a month. If you have recently purchased a new computer, much trial software for Internet services was preinstalled on your machine. Your phone bill may even include an offer to jump online with them! You will have no trouble finding a provider, but finding the *right* one is another story.

12

Read the fine print. Offers promising free Internet service for a given amount of time may be tempting, but there could be a catch. Many of them request credit card information, which makes me incredibly nervous. Supposedly, having a credit card number protects the online service if you attempt to use services that levy a fee. However, oftentimes, your account may not be correctly canceled after the free trial is up and you opt *not* to subscribe. That means additional, unexpected charges can be applied to your credit card. So how can you protect yourself? You can start by reading all the restrictions and requirements of the offer before supplying payment information. And more importantly, educate yourself on the proper cancellation procedures before committing to the service. It can save you lots of aggravation in the end.

Before you even begin the big hunt, however, you will need to ask yourself a few questions:

- **How much time will you or your family spend linked to the Internet each month?** Although flat-rate Internet service is common, there are still a few ISPs that limit the amount of access. If you doubt you will spend much time online, you may actually save money by finding an ISP that offers limited access for less money. Of course, as soon as you see just how much the Internet has to offer, you may be finding yourself shopping for unlimited access in no time!

- **How much technical support will you need?** If you are comfortable around computers or have a resident nerd, technical support may not be important, but if you just got your computer, you may welcome all the help you can get. The mere availability of technical support is not enough, however. Even the most lauded technical support isn't worth squat if it ends at 5:00 p.m., just before you get home from work and start to surf!

- **Do you need Internet software?** Many ISPs offer complimentary copies of some of the more popular programs to their customers. If you need it, this may factor into your decision of which ISP to choose because there won't be any software to buy or download. Of course, it should also be noted that Microsoft and Netscape make their Web browsers and e-mail programs available for free download. It can still be a costly proposition in terms of time required to download the material on a standard-speed connection.

- **Where do you live—in a large city or the middle of nowhere?** If you live in a larger city, you will have no shortage of ISP choices. If, on the other hand, it takes a long distance phone call to call the nearest large city, you may have to spend a little more time searching for an ISP with a local dial-up number. Your telephone service provider is a terrific starting point.

- **Do you travel often?** Whether you are an executive frequent flyer or a retired senior with wanderlust, you may find the hundreds of local dial-up numbers offered by the national ISPs valuable if you are always on the go. That way, you can check your e-mail from just about anywhere.

- **How will the Internet be used?** For someone just planning to send and receive e-mail, a standard 56k dial-up connection may suffice. However, if you see yourself eventually downloading computer game demonstrations, music clips, and Web page design goodies, then you may want to jump right in with a higher-speed connection like a cable modem or ISDN or DSL connection through the phone lines.

- **Are you planning to publish your own Web page?** Although many ISPs give you Web space on which to store your Web page with a basic account, you may be able to cut a deal for an account without this benefit if you have no desire to dabble with Web page publishing. Before you reach such a drastic conclusion, you may want to browse Hour 19, *Make Your Own Web Page in an Hour,* to see just how easy publishing your own Web page can be.

Your answers to these questions should give you a good feel for which features are important to you in an ISP. Jot down the things that are necessary and keep the list with you as you do your research.

Now on with the search!

Finding a Good Internet Service Provider

For starters, you can check out the providers who have included access software on your new computer. It doesn't cost anything to take a peek, but before you sign up, just be sure you are clear about cancellation procedures, required methods of cancellation notification, how much notice you need to give, and so on.

Beyond that, the best place to start is to ask friends with Internet service how they feel about their providers. Would they recommend them, or would they switch if they could? Are they plagued with busy signals and system downtime? Do they get help when they need it? Is the ISP responsive when problems do arise?

Simply asking around should give you some strong leads. If it doesn't or if you are the first in your circle of friends to get online, you may want to consult the business section of your local paper (ISPs often advertise there) or make use of that old standby: the Yellow Pages.

Interviewing an Internet Service Provider

After you have a couple of positive recommendations in hand, get your list of desired features in an ISP and start making calls. In the majority of cases, you will find a provider you want to work with from the list of those recommended by your friends, but that doesn't mean you should go into it blindly. After all, your needs may very well be different from theirs.

When you interview an ISP (and yes, I did mean interview), you will want to ask the following questions. Not only will they help clarify whether an ISP offers what you want, but they will also give you some insight into the stability of the provider.

- **Do you have a local dial-up number for my area?** Why pay for toll calls if you don't have to? Besides, you could go broke in a heartbeat!

- **How long have you been in business?** Although it may not seem like a relevant question, it can provide some clues of what the service may be like. A newly

12

established ISP may support the latest and greatest modem speeds and Internet protocols, but there could be some glitches. For instance, user-to-modem ratios may not have stabilized. As a result, you may experience busy signals while the company is growing. Older companies, however, may have had enough time to build a contingency plan should something go wrong (that is, they have replacement modems on site, a backup server, and other emergency management capabilities). However, newer companies may offer more attractive "get-to-know-us" rates that could make the potential risk worth taking. Additionally, these newer, smaller companies may be more willing to please their customers in order to keep them.

- **What kinds of service plans do you offer?** Look for the one that most adequately meets your needs, not some plan with bells and whistles you will probably never use. Just because one ISP offers more than another for the same price doesn't mean it is the best choice for you, especially if you are not likely to use "more." (After all, a single person as the sole Internet user in a household certainly doesn't need seven free e-mail addresses!)

Getting more for less. Some ISPs offer phenomenal rates for long-term contracts. Although these incentives can be a great way to save money with an established provider, use caution when considering them with a new provider. Competition in the ISP industry is fierce; ISPs come and go. I would recommend giving a new ISP a trial period before committing to a long-term contract, especially if you have to pay a lot of money up front.

- **What is your user-to-modem ratio?** The answer to this question is perhaps the best predictor of whether you will experience nonstop busy signals when you want to surf. Optimally, an ISP will have one modem for every five accounts (meaning a 5-to-1 user-to-modem ratio), but many seem to settle on one modem for every eight accounts. Being a subscriber of an 8-to-1 ISP, I can tell you that you will experience some busy signals even at that level. The key here is the smaller the ratio, the better the service is. Be extremely leery of anything higher than one modem for every eight subscribers. (Note that this question is not relevant to high-speed connection inquiries because a high-speed connection means you are essentially online all the time without having to tie up a phone line.

- **Do you have multiple dial-up access numbers?** If so, that reduces the likelihood of getting a busy signal even further.

- **What are your technical support hours?** The answer given here is most critical for those who would like the extra help. As I mentioned earlier, even technical support from Bill Gate's handpicked team of experts is no use if they have all gone home by the time you get a chance to log on.

When you combine the answers to the questions above with your list of desired ISP features, the choice that is best for you should stand out.

So what are you waiting for? Let's get signed up!

Information to Gather from Your New Internet Service Provider

With a little luck, when you sign up for your Internet service, you will get an installation disk that will take care of many of the grungy details of setting up your connection. If an installation disk is not available, however, you may want to have a pen and paper handy to take notes. The ISP will give you more information than you ever wanted to know about the Internet, including many of the items in Table 12.1. You may not need all (or even most) of the information in the table, but you should be aware of the various elements just in case, since every ISP will have its own setup requirements.

Table 12.1 Information to Gather from your Internet/Online Service Provider

Information	Notes
Mail server name	Your e-mail server's domain name, often in the format of `mail.provider.com`
Domain names server (DNS)	Takes the format of a 12-digit IP Address
News server name	The news server's domain name (often `news.provider.com`)
E-mail address	Your e-mail address in the form of `yourname@mail.provider.com` or `yourname@provider.com`
Type of incoming mail server	POP3 or IMAP4
Logon instructions	Information the ISP asks you before allowing you to connect to the service; this usually includes a user identification (userid) and secret password
Dial-up phone number	The number your computer dials to get Internet access; get a second number if you can in case you encounter a busy signal on the first number (again, this is irrelevant for "always-on" Internet like cable modems, ISDN, DSL, and so on)

12

NEW TERM

POP3 and IMAP4. POP3 (Post Office Protocol) is a method of receiving incoming mail that requires you to download mail onto your local machine for viewing unless you explicitly select an option in your mail program to keep it online. It is the most widely used and supported incoming mail protocol in use today. Conversely, Internet Message Access Protocol (IMAP) 4 keeps the mail on the server so you can check it from anywhere without having to download it to your machine. This protocol is less common, but is a fabulous tool for traveling executives and other business people on the go.

They didn't give me an IP Address! If your provider gives you a dynamic IP address (one created on-the-fly), you will not receive this bit of information when you sign up. Your computer will retrieve this information each time you log on.

My addresses don't have the `.com` **after them; what's wrong?** The `.com` was for demonstration purposes only. It is possible that your ISP will issue `.net` addresses instead. These suffixes or extensions are technically known as *domains*, or more specifically, *top-level domains*. They usually signify what kind of entity is providing the information on the given site (that is, `.com` for commercial entities, `.gov` for government entities, `.edu` for educational institutions, and so on).

While signing up for your account, you will also be asked to choose a user name (which makes up the first part of your e-mail address) and a password.

For a user name, many people choose their first initial followed by their surname (for example mine is JFreeze). If this is a leisure account only, consider having a bit of fun with it. Go with celticsfan or catnut or something that fits your personality or interests.

As for your password, make sure that it's something known by very few people, but at the same time something you can easily recall. Pet names and the like are often bad choices from a security standpoint since they're among the first guesses a potential cyber criminal would make. Many believe a combination of letters and numbers is good because it's harder to guess.

Got all that written down? Windows will ask for some of it when you go to set up your Internet connection, and don't worry about what all of that gobbledygook means. All that matters is that you are able to provide the proper information for the New Connection Wizard, which is discussed next.

Setting Up Your Connection Using the Windows XP, Home Edition's New Connection Wizard

To begin working your way through the wizard, grab the list of information you gathered from your ISP, boot up your computer, and follow these steps:

1. Double-click the Connect to the Internet icon on your Windows desktop. If no such icon appears on your desktop, click the Start button and then mouse over the All Programs link. From the resulting menus, choose Accessories, Communications, New Connection Wizard. The New Connection Wizard welcome screen shown in Figure 12.1 opens. Click Next to begin working with the wizard.

FIGURE 12.1

The New Connection Wizard not only helps you configure Internet connections, but it can also help you connect to a small local area network (LAN) as well.

 A little more information, please. If your computer is not fully set up, you may first see a popup window that asks you to supply your location, area code, number to dial for an outside line, and so on. Follow the onscreen prompts to enter the required information.

2. You must then tell the wizard which type of connection you want to create. The first option, Connect to the Internet, is selected by default. Since that's the type of connection you are trying to set up, click Next to continue.

3. You are presented with three ways to connect to the Internet: dialup modem, a broadband (DSL, ISDN, cable modem and the like) connection that requires a user name and password, or a broadband connection that is always on (see Figure 12.2). Most of you will fall into the first category, so select that option and then click Next. The rest of you will need to follow the onscreen prompts to configure your high-speed connection.

FIGURE 12.2

Choose the type of Internet connection that applies to you.

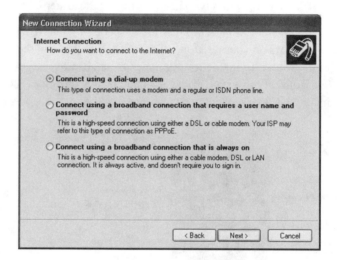

4. Now type in the name of your ISP in the text box provided (see Figure 12.3). The New Connection Wizard will use this information to name the dialup connection you are creating. Click Next To move on.

FIGURE 12.3

The information you enter here will become the name of your dialup connection.

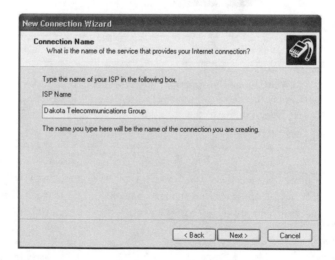

5. The Phone Number to Dial screen (see Figure 12.4) is where you'll type in your ISP's dialup number. Note that in some areas you may need to include a "1", the area code, or both before the dialup number.

   If you're not a hundred percent sure what's needed from your location, you can test the various options by using your household telephone. Dial the ISP-provided phone number, and when you hear the modem squeak and squawk at the other end of the line, you've got the correct phone number. After the number's been properly entered on the provided text box, click Next.

FIGURE 12.4

When you want to connect to the Internet, Windows XP dials the number provided for you.

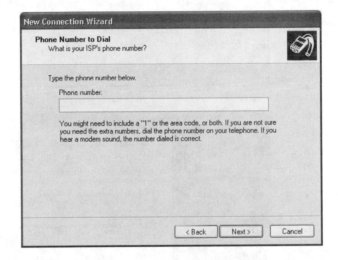

6. Remember that user ID and password you chose when you signed up with your ISP? Now is the time to enter it. The Internet Account Information windows shown in Figure 12.5 asks for your User name and Password. You are even asked to type in your password a second time just to be sure it's correct.

   You are also given three options, which are all selected by default. The first option asks whether you want the current account and password used whenever anyone using the computer logs on; the second asks if you want to make this your default Internet connection, and the third turns on the Internet Connection Firewall for your computer. Depending on your preferences, you may want to leave all three on by default. If so, click the Next button.

7. Ta-da, you did it! The proof is in Figure 12.6. Before you click the Finish button, however, check the option provided to have the wizard create a shortcut to this connection on your desktop. That way you can just double-click the icon when you're ready to link up!

12

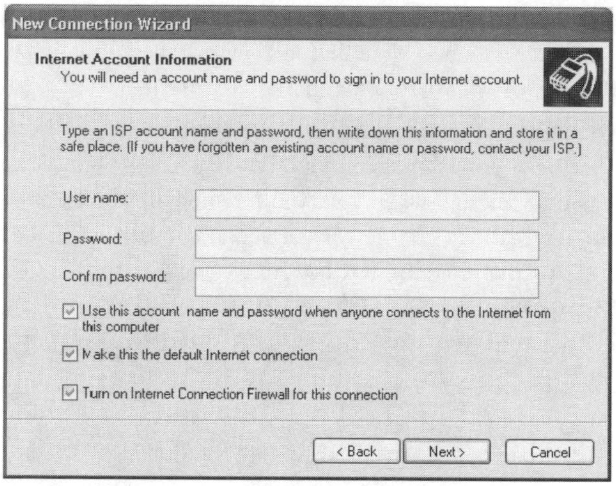

FIGURE 12.5

Your user name and password are requested on the Internet Account Information screen.

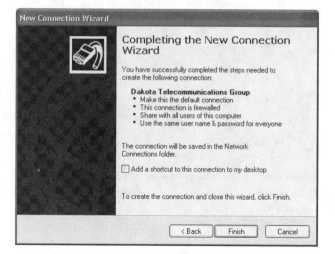

FIGURE 12.6

Click the Finish button to exit the wizard.

Configuring Your E-mail Server

We may as well get all the "administrivia" out of the way at the front end so you can jump right in and have fun in later lessons. With your connection to the Internet set up, you now need to tell Outlook Express (the free e-mail program installed on nearly every new PC) where to find your mail and news servers.

Follow these steps to tell Outlook Express where it needs to go to send and receive your e-mail:

1. Launch Outlook Express by clicking the Start button and choosing Outlook Express from the Start menu. If it doesn't appear on the left side of the menu by default, click Start, All Programs, Outlook Express. When asked whether you want to go online, click No; we don't need an active connection to set up the mail server.

2. At this point you may be asked whether or not you want to make Outlook Express your default e-mail client. Go ahead and say Yes.

3. You will be taken to the Internet Connection Wizard, where you'll enter your Display Name (your name as you want it to appear in the From: field in a recipient's inbox). Type in the desired name and then click Next.

4. You will then be asked to enter your e-mail address. Type it into the text box provided and then click Next.

5. The E-mail Server Names screen shown in Figure 12.7 appears. Use the drop-down box provided to tell the wizard whether you have a POP or an IMAP mail account, and then enter the names of your incoming and outgoing mail servers as provided by your ISP. After the server names a correctly entered, click the Next button.

6. Next, you will need to enter the account name and password. Note that this may be different from your personal user name depending on how many e-mail accounts you requested from your ISP. You can also tell your computer to remember your password by checking the option provided. While it's convenient, it could pose a threat to privacy in that anyone who can get to your computer may be able to read your e-mail. Once the proper information has been entered, click Next.

7. The Internet Connection Wizard congratulates you on your completed setup. As soon as you click the Finish button, you can begin working with e-mail.

12

FIGURE 12.7

The mail server names you received from your ISP should be entered here.

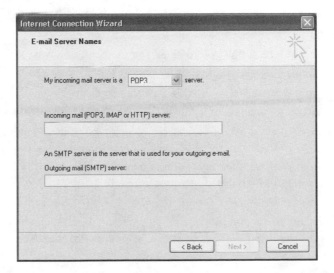

Configuring an E-mail Account from Within Outlook Express

If for some reason you are not prompted to make Outlook Express your default e-mail client (or you simply need to add a new mail server at a later date), you can launch Outlook Express and follow these steps to get up and running:

1. Click the Outlook Express Tools menu and select Accounts. Verify that the Mail tab is the one that is active. The Internet Accounts window appears, as shown in Figure 12.8.

Click here and
select Mail.

FIGURE 12.8

The Add button enables you to choose which type of account with which you want to work.

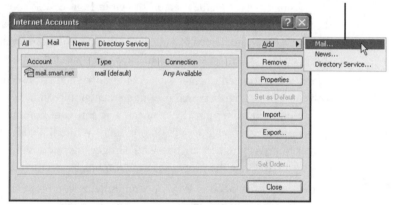

2. Click the Add button and select Mail from the list. The Internet Connection Wizard launches.

3. The first screen asks you to enter your name as you want it to appear in the From field of your outgoing e-mail messages. Type it in and then click Next.

4. Then you are asked to provide the e-mail address assigned to you by your ISP. Click Next when you are finished.

5. The next screen asks you to define which type of incoming mail server you have—POP3 or IMAP. Use the drop-down arrow to make your selection. (If you are not sure of your selection here, don't be afraid to ask your ISP.) You then must type in the names of both the incoming and outgoing mail servers before clicking Next. (Refer back to Figure 12.7 to see what this screen looks like.)

6. Your Internet logon information is requested in this screen—namely your account name/userid and password. After you enter them, click Next to continue.

7. It's time to celebrate; you have entered all the information needed! All you have to do is click the Finish button and then close the Accounts dialog box to begin working with e-mail.

Now Outlook Express will know where to look for incoming mail, and where to route outgoing messages. There is just one last thing to do: set up your news server account.

Setting Up Your News Server

As you will see later in the book, newsgroups can be a terrific resource for asking questions, connecting with people of similar interests, tapping into local online communities, and so on. In order to take advantage of these resources, however, you will need to tell Outlook Express (also a news reader) where to find your ISP's news server.

Just as you had to set up Outlook Express to recognize your mail server, the same holds true for news servers. To do this, launch Outlook Express and follow these simple steps to make your news server available:

1. Click the Outlook Express Tools menu and select Accounts. The Internet Accounts window appears.

2. Click the Add button and select News from the list. The Internet Connection wizard launches.

3. The first screen prompts you to enter your name as you want it to appear in the From field of your outgoing newsgroup posts. The display name you set up for e-mail appears automatically. If you want something different for newsgroups, type it in and then click Next.

4. In the next screen, you are prompted to provide your e-mail address, which will be used in the Reply To line of any news articles you post. Note that if you've set up your mail server already, the correct e-mail address may appear automatically. Click Next.

5. You are asked to supply the name of your news server. You also will be asked whether you need to log on to the news server with a special userid and password. If you check this box, you will be prompted to supply the necessary userid and password. In general, public news servers don't require this extra bit of security. I have mostly seen it used to protect corporate news servers and Microsoft's beta testing community servers.

6. Click Finish to complete the final step. You then will be asked whether you want to download a listing of all the newsgroups available on the news server you defined. Decline for now, since our primary goal is to get everything set up. We will browse through the list of available news groups later.

12

Connecting to the Internet

Now it is time to see if that connection actually works. Follow these simple steps to link up to the Internet:

1. Double-click the dialup icon on your Windows desktop. You will be taken to a Connect [name of your connection] window like the one shown in Figure 12.9.

FIGURE 12.9

The information you asked the wizard to remember is already in place.

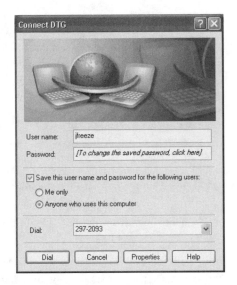

2. The first thing you will need to do is verify that the proper user name and password are supplied. In the second section of the dialog box, you will be asked whether you want the password information you provided to be used by everyone using your machine or just you. (Note that this option is only applicable if you have set up your machine for multiple user accounts as discussed back in Hour 6, Sharing Your PC with Others.) Verify that the phone number supplied in the Dial: text box is the one you intended to use and then click the Dial button.

> **Wanna save some time?** Be sure to check the Save this user name and password to connect check box if you want Windows to remember your user name and password for you. Of course, if privacy is a concern, you may want to think twice about taking this shortcut. If you save the password, anyone who could get to your PC could potentially read your e-mail.

Within seconds, you will be ready to take full advantage of the Internet. As you will see in the next few sections of this book, there is a whole lot out there to enhance your lifestyle, entertain you, educate you, and even help you save money.

Summary

We covered a fair amount of ground in this hour. Not only did you learn about finding the right ISP for you, but also you learned to configure all parts of your dial-up connection and to test it to see that it works.

Before we get into the mechanics of Web surfing and sending e-mail, I would like to present Hour 13, *The Savvy Net Surfer*. In this lesson, you will be brought up to speed on Internet etiquette, safe online shopping, and other tips and tricks designed to make your online experience safe, enjoyable, and fulfilling.

Workshop

Now it's time to see just how much you learned in this lesson. I'll give you a short multiple-choice quiz to test what you learned, followed by a suggested activity designed to enhance the skills you acquired during the hour.

Quiz

Select the best answer to the questions from the choices provided and then check your answers.

Questions

1. What does ISP mean?

   a. Internet service provider

   b. Inside Someone's PC

   c. Impossible Social Practices

2. Which of the following pieces of information will you need from your ISP in order to make a viable connection to the Internet?

   a. The name of your mail server

   b. Your password

   c. The dial-up phone number

   d. All of the above

12

3. What is so great about the New Connection Wizard?

   a. It leads you step-by-step through the process of creating a connection to the Internet, making the process simpler than ever before.

   b. It can understand voice commands.

   c. There is no such thing as a New Connection Wizard!

Answers

1. A wins, hands down.

2. D is the correct answer. You will need all of this information and more to configure your connection to the Internet.

3. B hasn't happened yet. (Notice I said *yet;* I think the capability may come sooner than you think. It is already embedded in Microsoft Office XP.) As for C, well, you obviously didn't follow along with the lesson! That leaves A as the best answer.

Activity

Grab a pencil and paper and prioritize the following ISP requirements from most important to least important:

- Technical support available during the hours I am likely to need it most

- Reasonable monthly rates for connections

- Web space included on which to store a personal Web page

- Unlimited access so I can surf as much as I want

- Local dial-up number from my calling area

- A company that I know is going to be there years from now

- Different pricing schemes so I can save money if I only plan to access the Net a little

- Various modes of payment because not everyone has credit cards and such

- I am willing to commit to a multi-year contract in exchange for better rates

With this list of priorities in hand, start calling any friends and associates who are on the Internet to see who they use. Be sure to ask for both the good and bad so you can match the pros and cons with your own priorities and needs.

After you have chosen a few candidates, give them a call and ask some questions. When you are satisfied with your match, you can proceed with signing up for service.

HOUR 13

The Savvy Net Surfer

Before you become active on the Net, we should take a moment to examine the subtleties of life online. Venturing out on the Information Superhighway without being acquainted with the tips provided in this hour is like driving the crowded streets of New York City without understanding street signs, traffic signals, and other common rules of the road. Someone could get hurt!

Although it is pretty hard to get into trouble simply surfing the Web, no Internet policeman is going to pop out of your monitor and handcuff you if you inadvertently violate one of these rules. But if you plan to work with newsgroups or make a few new e-pals, knowing the rules of the road will give you everything you need to establish a peaceful, online presence. (It can also keep you from looking like a bumbling newbie, which could be useful too!)

In this lesson, I will introduce you to some valuable "rules of the road." In addition, you will also learn about the following in this hour:

- Discover the accepted forms of "netiquette" (or Internet Etiquette).

- Learn about the cryptic emoticons and abbreviations you will find in your e-mail.

- Find out why using a screen name is so important.
- Become a safe online shopper.

What Is Netiquette Anyway?

Well, I have already given you a hint, but here is a better explanation. Back when the Internet was in its infancy, all its users had a common frame of reference. They had to be expert computer scientists or researchers to gain access to the Internet. As the Internet grew, a common language and culture evolved. *Netiquette,* short for *Internet etiquette*, is the result of that growth.

Think of Netiquette as the Internet equivalent to a regional culture or language. Take the United States as an example. My mainstay, Diet Coke, is referred to as *pop* in South Dakota, where I grew up. In Massachusetts where I went to college, *tonic* was often used. In Maryland, where I met my husband, *soda* is the preferred term. This Internet language, along with all the emoticons and abbreviations you will learn about later in the hour, make up a part of the Internet's culture, as do the guidelines found in these pages. Together, they make up what has become known as *Netiquette,* the regional dialect for the Internet.

Trust me; I didn't come up with this lengthy lesson full of guidelines all by myself. In 1995, the Responsible Use of the Network (RUN) Working Group of the Internet Engineering Task Force (IETF) drafted a document (known as *RFC 1855*) highlighting Netiquette guidelines for a variety of users and environments. This document was written as a way to integrate the exploding number of inexperienced new users on the Net as quickly and painlessly as possible.

If you're a glutton for punishment or simply just want to know more about RFC 1855...you can peruse a copy on the Web by surfing over to www.dtcc.edu/cs/rfc1855.html.

I pulled the items most relevant to the average user, translated them to plain English, and added easy-to-understand examples, so what you read here should be both useful and entertaining I hope! For easy reference, I have created top 10 lists of no-nos for each of three categories: e-mail, newsgroups, and mailing lists.

Top 10 E-mail Rules of the Road

E-mail is great for its immediacy, but like writing a letter, it can have its disadvantages. For example, unless you specifically describe your emotions, there is a lot of room for misinterpretation. In addition to pointing out some of these subtleties, the following items illustrate some of the most common mistakes made by people new to the Internet.

If I've said it once, I've said it a thousand times. Please note that many of these common mistakes also apply to newsgroups and mailing lists, but I chose not to repeat them to save space (not to mention to keep you from getting bored!).

Rule One: No Peeking!

Be careful what you write; it may come back to haunt you! The Internet is not a perfect place. As in the real world, it is possible someone may try to sneak a peek at your correspondence. Although the likelihood of that happening is pretty small, this is one of those instances where it is better to be safe than sorry. Use the following rule of thumb: if you would feel uncomfortable putting a message's contents on a postcard and dropping it into a mailbox, then you probably shouldn't e-mail it either.

Rule Two: Knock, Knock

Be sure to verify e-mail addresses before sending a long or personal message the first time. Maybe you are trying to track down an old classmate by the name of Elise Sudbeck. You find an `ESudbeck@webtv.net`, which you are pretty sure is her, but you can't be certain. Drop E. Sudbeck a note mentioning your alma mater and desire to get back in touch and then wait for a response before getting personal. It is sort of the Internet equivalent to knocking on someone's door late at night instead of barging right in! Double-check who is at the other end before making yourself vulnerable.

Rule Three: I'm Sorry, I Thought You Were Someone Else

Many e-mail addresses are made up of a person's first initial followed by their surname (or as much of it as will fit into the allotted space). Take my e-mail address, for example. I use `JFreeze@JustPC.com` for personal e-mail. With my current Internet service provider's eight-character "userid" limit, my name fits. If I was Donna Stephenson, however, I would have a little trouble. DStephen might cause some confusion for people trying to find me, since it could just as easily stand for Dwight Stephens. This might

13

force me to consider other alternatives like DonnaS or even my job title (such as
`adviser@umass.edu`).

NEW TERM

> **Show me your userid, please!** Abbreviated from user identification, *userid* is
> the technical term for the part of your e-mail address that comes before the
> @ sign.

The job title alternative brings us to the next precaution: know exactly who you are e-
mailing. For all you know, `adviser@umass.edu` could be an intake address for students'
questions and is accessed by the entire advising staff, not a personal account. It makes
perfect sense to confirm the situation before sending anything of a personal nature.

Rule Four: DON'T SHOUT!

One of the most common mistakes people new to the Net make is to type an entire message in all capital letters. My friend, Tracy, ventured out to a newsgroup to start a dia-
logue on TV violence. Her keyboard Caps Lock key was pressed, so her messages
appeared in all uppercase. For nearly a week, her Inbox was flooded with reprimands
from self-appointed Net police! Because emotion and voice inflection are not always
identifiable by words alone, capitalization emerged as the notation of choice for shout-
ing. Likewise, the asterisk, *, is used on each side of a word or phrase to denote emphasis just as bold or underlining would do in word processing: "Sheesh, I can't *believe*
anyone would write an entire message in capital letters. WHAT ARE THESE PEOPLE
THINKING?!"

Rule Five: :-)

If you don't know what this symbol means, don't worry. You will hear much more about
smileys and all the other emoticons later in this lesson. For now, it serves as a gentle
reminder to use emoticons to clarify potentially confusing statements. Use them sparingly, however, to avoid diluting their effect. Smileys are like exclamation points; if you
overuse them, you will find a need for double smileys to communicate a higher level of
emotion!

Rule Six: Read All Before You Reply

This rule of thumb probably is more relevant in the workplace than for leisure use of the
Internet, but it is a good one to practice just the same. Before responding to any one e-
mail, check the other messages in your inbox. You may find that a person who has asked
for help or advice in one note has solved his or her problem before you even got online

and may have sent a second note to that regard. Checking multiple messages from the same person before responding to any of them could save you both a lot of time and trouble.

It is also a good idea to scan the header of the message before responding to make sure that you were the primary recipient of the e-mail. You may have simply been copied on a note directed to someone else.

Rule Seven: Sign on the Dotted Line

Along with diligently checking mail headers before responding to a message, you should also watch out for e-mail programs and newsreaders that automatically strip contact information, leaving no return address. Although most modern applications keep this information intact and visible, you will want to sign your name before sending a message out, just in case. This further identifies you as the author of the message or post should the information be unavailable in the header.

Rule Eight: Around the World in 80 Milliseconds

Well, maybe not that fast, but pretty darn quick just the same! Sometimes, it's hard to grasp the true scope of the Internet. It's easy to forget that the person you are e-mailing may be across the world or across town. Given the multicultural nature of the Net, there are a few things you can do to make everyone feel at home, no matter where they live.

- Be patient when waiting for a response to a note sent internationally. The message you sent this morning may get to its destination within minutes, but its recipient in a faraway land may just be crawling into bed due to the time difference. Give it time (24 to 48 hours, depending on the urgency of the message) before resending it or responding in frustration.

- Use caution when including colorful expressions or slang in your e-mail; they might be taken literally by someone who does not speak English as a primary language. He or she may interpret someone's statement about a "redneck" as being someone with short hair who's been out in the sun too long! I'm not poking fun at anyone here; I'm just trying to emphasize the fact that we are all different and may not come from like backgrounds.

- Humor is another of those things that may not translate well, especially sarcasm. Save the humor until you know the recipient well. If you can't resist cracking a joke, however, consider using emoticons or other telltale notations like <grin>, <g>, or ROTFL (which stands for rolling on the floor, laughing) if you are one to laugh at your own jokes. We'll explore these emoticons and other notations in greater details in a few minutes.

13

Rule Nine: I Don't Get It...

My husband will be the first to tell you I get worked up over the stupidest things sometimes, but this is one of my pet peeves: e-mail messages without subject lines. When
scanning incoming mail while online, seeing subject lines gives meaning to the message.
A recipient will want to know whether he or she should drop everything and attend to the
matter or if it can be dealt with at a more convenient time. If it's blank, your recipient
may ignore it for a while. People may even delete it if they are having a bad day! To gain
your recipient's attention (and maybe even preserve their sanity), always use descriptive
yet relevant subject lines on all your messages.

Rule Ten: Don't Believe Everything You Read

You may not realize this, but with many e-mail programs, a user can configure his
or her e-mail address to read anything he or she wants it to read. Remember how you
had to choose a Display Name and an e-mail address for the From: line of your messages
when you were setting up your e-mail? Well, there aren't any computer police standing
over your shoulder making sure you are actually using your own name. Although many
e-mail programs have made the task more difficult to do by blocking the use of invalid
e-mail addresses in the From line, an experienced computer user can still set up such
preferences.

Often, a spoof or forged e-mail address is as blatantly detectable as with
seeu@home.soon. That is obviously someone's attempt at being cute! Businesses that are
mass mailing unsolicited garbage (usually something utterly distasteful like "Babes Here:
Get 'em While They're Hot") will often alter the return e-mail address as described in
the beginning of this rule to avoid an onslaught of angry replies. Luckily, some mail
servers (like mine) will reject bogus e-mail addresses, which cuts down the number of
deceptions somewhat.

Hold it right there! Sending unsolicited e-mail is an offense known as
spamming. In many cases, spammers are denied further access from their
ISP. So, as tempting as it might be to partake in the Internet's free advertising by sending thousands of people e-mail about your hot new product, it
may not be worth the risk.

The moral of the story is if you ever get a piece of e-mail that seems highly out of character for the sender, consider doing the following before responding emotionally:

- Click Reply to see whether the address matches the one you see displayed in your Inbox.

- Don't hide behind an e-mail. If it's a sensitive issue, perhaps it'd be best to discuss it face-to-face instead of depersonalizing the resolution process.

- If the message seems out of character for the recipient, you may want to run a virus check on the message. Many viruses get on a person's machine and spit random messages out to everyone in that person's address book or contact list.

- Send an e-mail note back asking for confirmation of the message.

- Phone the individual to talk it over.

Top 10 Newsgroup Rules of the Road

Newsgroups are wonderful forums. You can exchange thoughts and information with countless people from around the world, pool the wisdom of experts in a variety of fields, and gain the respect of others based on your thoughts and intellect, as opposed to your appearance, race, gender, and so on. You'll discover how to take part in newsgroups in Hour 17, Browsing Online Newsgroups.

To help you make the most of the forums, the following ten pointers examine issues of concern for people new to newsgroups.

 A friendly reminder. Remember to keep the following pointers in mind as you work with newsgroups.

Rule One: Know the Territory

Before posting to a newsgroup or mailing list, read the group for a few weeks to get a feel for its climate. This is perhaps the best way to learn the preferred format of subject lines, which topics actually are discussed in the group, and how participants react to humor. Before posting anything, you should also track down the frequently asked questions (FAQs) for the group to make sure your question isn't already answered there. Some newsgroups periodically post the FAQs, whereas others maintain them on a Web site. The larger, more organized groups do both.

13

Getting the FAQs (pronounced *fax*). To find an index of FAQ Web sites, fire up Internet Explorer; then visit the Internet FAQ Consortium at `http://www.faqs.org/`.

Rule Two: Turn the Other Cheek

If you plan to get involved in some of the newsgroups, be prepared to get flamed. There are millions of people in this world, many of whom may disagree with your opinions or comments. A few people may act on this disagreement by sending you volumes of statistics on why you are wrong. An even smaller group may send you notes like, "Look you dweeb, you are way off-base, here. What a lunatic! Your e-mail account should be revoked!" These are known as *flames*. It is wise to ignore such messages, since letting them know you are riled up could be just the positive reinforcement they need to continue such behavior. If someone has made a valid point, by all means, thank that person if you feel it is appropriate. Now, I trust that my readers won't ever flame anyone, right?

Rule Three: It Is a Small World Out There

Remember that a vast majority of the newsgroups are read by thousands of people worldwide, and one of those people might be your boss or a future boss. For example, if you aspire to be the manager of the Barbie doll section at your local toy store, you probably don't want to post a note on `rec.collecting.dolls`, griping about the store's high prices. Many newsgroups are archived for future reference (not to mention the dozens of search engines that can retrieve posts on demand), so although your words may have disappeared from the news server you use to access your newsgroup, they may still be accessible by other methods.

Be your own detective. Use the Google Groups search engine to see what your friends are saying online or to search for all newsgroup articles mentioning a particular subject. You can access Google Groups by launching Internet Explorer and typing the following in the Address Bar: `http://groups.google.com`. Most other search engines now offer this capability too.

Rule Four: KISS

The acronym for *Keep It Simple, Stupid (KISS)* applies to the Internet too. Unlike television, snail mail, or radio, where the cost of sending the message falls exclusively with the sender, the cost of e-mail or a newsgroup post is absorbed by both the sender and the recipient(s). This cost takes the form of increased time online to download and read the message/post, as well as the extra disk space required to store the note. In some ways, sending e-mail or posting to a newsgroup is like mailing a letter with postage due—the contents better be worth it! Although the cost may not seem like much in the scheme of things, it is hard to buy that the message is unsolicited junk mail.

You may not be able to do much about the people who litter your Inbox or post off-topic ads to your favorite newsgroup (although I have been known to hit Reply and bounce the message back to the sender just to be annoying), but there are ways to cut costs and conserve resources when e-mailing friends and associates or making use of the newsgroups:

- When responding to a message or post, delete any unnecessary text. Keep only enough to give the reader proper context for your comments.

- If you eventually decide to go into business on the Internet, don't send large amounts of unsolicited information to people via e-mail or newsgroups. If you must employ direct e-mail and newsgroups as sales tools, send/post a brief message describing your offerings (in groups where advertising is allowed only) and then ask interested parties to hit Reply to request further details.

> **Know what you are doing.** Before posting any kind of advertising to a newsgroup, make sure it is allowed. One advertising post to a group strictly forbidding advertising could hurt far more than it could help your business. Newsgroups allowing advertising often include the words *marketplace* or *for sale* in their names.

- Avoid posting simple "me, too" follow-ups. It takes up valuable bandwidth and frankly, unless you are a recognized expert on the topic at hand, people couldn't care less whether you agree. If you have additional information to pass along, then naturally, it's okay to do so.

13

> NEW TERM
>
> **Strike up the band(width)!** Bandwidth is a measurement of how much data can move through a channel (such as your modem and computer) at once. Obviously, the shorter the post, the quicker it will download onto your screen. That's why keeping messages short is referred to as *saving bandwidth*.

Rule Five: Get to the Point

When posting an article or comment, cut to the chase. Don't ramble, get on your soap-box, or stray off the subject. Don't waste precious time and resources pointing out others' spelling errors! This, more than anything else, will mark you as an immature newbie, which can in turn ruin your reputation and credibility in the group. People mellow pretty quickly, however, with an apology and a few intellectual insights. After all, we all get carried away from time to time. If we didn't, we wouldn't be human!

Rule Six: The Line Dance

Okay, I admit it; I watch a couple of soap operas on occasion. One newsgroup, `http://rec.arts.tv.soaps.cbs`, discusses my favorite soaps, *As the World Turns* and *The Bold and the Beautiful*, among others. Because the number of shows covered and the volume of posts is so high, a few subject line conventions emerged. Posts concerning my favorite show begin with ATWT, followed by a colon, a space and then the specific subject matter. A sample subject line might read "ATWT: Lily's New Haircut." Each show has its own subject line prefix, and in cases where all the shows are involved (such as posts about Daytime Emmy Award nominees), the word ALL becomes the prefix. Other groups use Q: to denote a question, FS: to mark items for sale, and so on. Reading the group and FAQs before jumping in will help you look like an experienced Netizen (Internet citizen).

Rule Seven: Don't be a Spoilsport!

Technically, this could have been discussed in the preceding section, but it is important enough to give it its own space. When posting a message to a newsgroup that discusses television shows, sporting events, and so on, be careful not to spoil the outcome of the show or event for others. Nothing is worse than scanning the NASCAR newsgroup before watching your videotape of the race only to see someone post: "TERRY LABONTE CLINCHES THE CHAMPIONSHIP TODAY!!!" The race is ruined for you, and you can be sure the poster of the message will get a fair amount of angry e-mail. Of course, the best advice is to avoid the newsgroup altogether until you watch the video-tape, but I know how checking one newsgroup can lead to another, and so on.

If you want to talk about the end of the most recent blockbuster movie or discuss a controversial call by a referee, place the word SPOILER in uppercase in the subject line. Even insert a few blank lines at the beginning of your post for good measure; that way no one can blame you for spoiling their fun, and you can still talk about anything you want.

Rule Eight: Before Clicking Reply

Newsgroups can pose some interesting challenges when it comes to getting information to the right person. If you want to share your wisdom with the original poster by e-mail, you should consider the following before sending the note:

- If the full header is intact, read the article carefully to confirm that the reply-to address matches that of the original author. I can't tell you how many times I have gotten e-mail intended for the originator of a post and because I no longer had access to the original post without a lot of work, I was forced to send the note back to the kind soul offering help/advice. That advice probably never reached its destination. Do yourself (and others) a favor; if originating a post, include a signature with your name/screen name and e-mail address to simplify responding.

- If you are posting a follow-up to the newsgroup, make sure the original author's e-mail address is easy to find so others may respond directly via e-mail if they wish.

- Follow-ups to follow-ups complicate matters even more. In the interest of saving bandwidth, vital header information is often inadvertently edited out. In this case, it is usually best to simply post your contribution rather than risk it not getting to the source. In addition, if you are contributing to a thread that has been around for some time, do your best to keep header information intact.

Rule Nine: Use the Groups to Your Ad-vantage

Everything has its place on the Internet, advertisements included. If you even think about posting ads on some newsgroups, you will practically get run off the Internet with e-mail messages and flames. Other newsgroups such as `http://rec.toys.marketplace` not only welcome ads, but they make up a fundamental part of those groups' charters. Interestingly, it doesn't seem to matter whether you are launching a full-scale business or merely parting with an old collectible gathering dust, the outcome is the same.

To locate groups welcoming ads, search the various newsgroup hierarchies for terms such as *marketplace* or *for sale*. However, just because a group doesn't carry one of these extensions in its name doesn't mean it snubs ads. With `http://rec.toys.cars`, for example, collectors from around the world discuss everything from the paint quality of the latest Matchbox cars to the newest Hot Wheels variations to hit stores. However, ads from fellow collectors also make up a key part of this group's culture. The best way to determine whether ads are accepted in a group is to read the FAQs. If they prove to be elusive, hang around for a while; in a week or two, your answer will be obvious.

13

Beware of scalpers! Scalpers are people who frequent toy stores, snatch up all the good stuff (such as limited edition Hot Wheels cars, *Star Wars* figures, Beanie Babies, and others), and try to sell it on the Internet for outrageous prices. If you participate in a newsgroup regularly, you will most likely make some new friends who can eventually help you build your collection at cost or for trade.

Rule Ten: Giving Thanks

If, after reading the FAQs and monitoring a newsgroup for a while, you would still like to post a question to get reactions/input from the rest of the participants, consider doing the following:

- Thank everyone in advance for his or her help or comments.
- Offer to post a summary of all the recommendations if there is sufficient interest in the subject.
- If there isn't enough interest to justify posting a formal summary, at least offer to e-mail a summary to those expressing an interest in your findings.

Generally, the Internet is a very cooperative, helpful place, and showing appreciation for the help you get can only aid in the long run.

Mysteries of the Net

Earlier, I talked a lot about conserving resources and what you can do to lighten the load; however, there's more to it than making liberal edits and avoiding unnecessary posts. Bandwidth-saving techniques often involve abbreviating words and phrases to save space. In the following sections, I will cover the most common abbreviations, as well as some of the emoticons and expressions used to convey emotion on the Internet. To give you an idea of just how much you will learn, try to decipher the message in Figure 13.1.

Here is the translation of Figure 13.1:

```
Hi! I'm writing about the car you have for sale. Would you be willing to
take a Porsche for trade? My mom really hates the car (sad about what he
wrote) and has been after me to sell it for ages. It is a hot Porsche 944
Turbo S in a limited-edition silver rose metallic color (happy about what
he wrote). I can get her to do 0-60 in 5.5 seconds (the car, not my mom
<grin>), but depending how you drive, your mileage may vary. I hate to
part with it…. Perhaps she'd let me keep it if I gave her a rose (rolling
on the floor laughing)!!!! Anyway, let me know if you are interested.
```

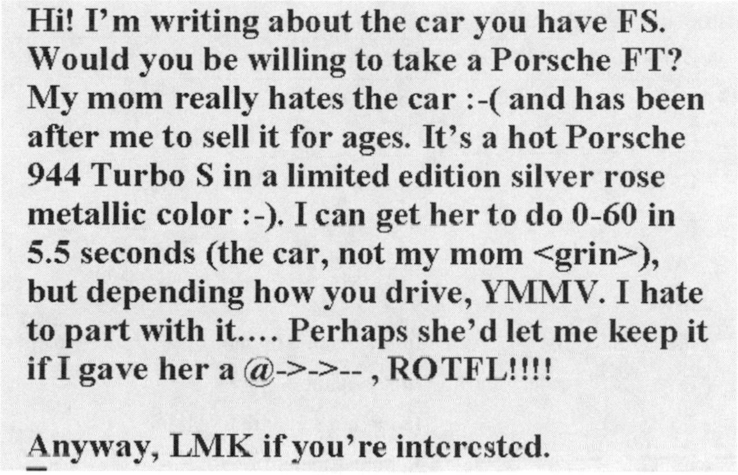

FIGURE 13.1

Messages passed along via the Internet can sometimes look like they are written in an exotic language.

> Hi! I'm writing about the car you have FS. Would you be willing to take a Porsche FT? My mom really hates the car :-(and has been after me to sell it for ages. It's a hot Porsche 944 Turbo S in a limited edition silver rose metallic color :-). I can get her to do 0-60 in 5.5 seconds (the car, not my mom <grin>), but depending how you drive, YMMV. I hate to part with it.... Perhaps she'd let me keep it if I gave her a @->->-- , ROTFL!!!!
>
> Anyway, LMK if you're interested.

Alphabet Soup

Stumped by the title of this section? You won't be for long. As you saw in Figure 13.1, translating e-mail and newsgroup posts can get a little tricky to the untrained eye. If you watch your favorite newsgroup for a few days, you will probably see a post from a frustrated newbie pleading, "Can somebody please tell me what ROTFL means?" Well, here it is—your definitive guide to all the quirky abbreviations you will find lurking in your e-mail or news articles. Well, maybe not *all* (things change so quickly on the Internet, you know), but certainly more than enough to get you rolling. By the time you work your way through the alphabet soup in Table 13.1, Figure 13.1 won't even faze you.

Table 13.1 Common Abbreviations Found on the Net

Acronym	Definition
ADN	Any day now
AFAIK	As far as I know
B4N	Bye for now
BTA	But then again
BTW	By the way
CU	See you
CUL	See you later
EOT	End of thread
FWIW	For what it's worth

continues

Table 13.1 continued

Acronym	Definition
FYI	For your information
G	Grin
GMTA	Great minds think alike
IAC	In any case
IAE	In any event
IC	I see
IMHO	In my humble opinion
IMO	In my opinion
IMNSHO	In my not so humble opinion
INPO	In no particular order
IOW	In other words
JIC	Just in case
LOL	Laughing out loud
OTOH	On the other hand
POV	Point of view
PTB	Powers that be
RE	Regarding
ROTFL	Rolling on the floor laughing
TAFN	That's all for now
TIA	Thanks in advance
TPTB	The powers that be
YMMV	Your mileage may vary

As you can see, most of these abbreviations are derived from common figures of speech. Few need further definition; however, one in particular, YMMV, always seems to baffle newbies when they first hear it. YMMV, which stands for "your mileage may vary," simply means, "This was my experience, but yours may be different." I guess you could say it is one way to cover your rear end online!

These aren't all the abbreviations you will see. If you frequent any of the collectibles/for sale groups, you may see some of the abbreviations shown in Table 13.2.

Table 13.2 Abbreviations Found in For Sale/Marketplace Groups

Acronym	Definition
FS	For sale
FT	For trade
MIB	Mint in box
MIP	Mint in package
NRFB	Never removed from the box
NWOT	New without tag
NWT	New with tag
WTB	Want to buy
WTD	Want to deal
WTT	Want to trade

Furthermore, many narrowly focused groups will abbreviate names of commonly discussed people or topics, such as a TV show's key characters (DD for Daisy Duke from *The Dukes of Hazzard*), star race car drivers (DE for Dale Earnhardt, whom many race fans still miss dearly), or members of the family (MIL for mother-in-law) to create their own shorthand. Rarely does this evolving shorthand need to be explained because the group's readership usually catches on quickly from the context of its use. Unfortunately, the only way to learn these secrets is to watch a particular group for a period. Each group will have its own abbreviations, which is simply part of the culture.

I Second That Emoticon!

If you thought simple punctuation in text was great at capturing emotion in writing (exclamation points to convey excitement or an ellipsis to express an unfinished sentence), then you will really be impressed by punctuation use on the Internet. For example, BTW, :-). BTW is short for "by the way," as you saw in the previous section. The "smile" part of the example is made up of a colon (:), followed by a dash (-) and then a close parenthesis mark ()). If you hold this book in front of you and rotate it clockwise (or merely tilt your head to the left) and read the example again, you will notice that the three punctuation marks actually form a "smiley." Punctuation used online in this manner make up a number of *emoticons,* a word derived from *emotion* and *icon* (see in Table 13.3).

13

Table 13.3 Common Emoticons

This...	Means this...
:-) or :)	I'm smiling or happy about the preceding thought/comment
:-(or :(	I'm frowning or unhappy about the preceding thought/comment
;-) or ;)	I'm winking at you
<:-)	Dumb question
:-*	A kiss

Those are just some of the emoticons. The Net is literally flooded with creative variations of the smiley. Although I would like to give credit where credit is due, it is next to impossible to trace how some of these evolved. Take a look at Table 13.4 to see a few of the more unique ones I have found over time.

Table 13.4 Some More Unusual Emoticons

This...	Means this...
&:-)	From a person with curly hair
:-(=)	From a person with big teeth
C=:-)	From a chef
:-)}<////>	From a guy in a suit and tie (tie design may vary)
@->->...	A rose

These emoticons are most often placed at the end of the sentence or phrase to which it refers to clarify the emotion or intention behind the message.

Sticks and stones. Obviously emoticons are not a substitute for judicious word choice. A scathing or snide remark could still hurt, regardless of how many smileys follow it.

If you would like to learn more about emoticons and their meanings, read the `alt.culture.emoticons` newsgroup.

Express Yourself

As if abbreviations and emoticons aren't enough, there is yet another way to express yourself on the Net. Expressions are words or phrases embedded between greater than and less than signs (< and a >, such as <grin>). Used the same way as emoticons, these expressions are capable of communicating subtle differences in emotion that is hard to capture with an emoticon. Take a basic smiley emoticon that communicates contentment. Changing that :-) to a <grin> adds a playful dimension to the message. Table 13.5 contains some of the more commonly used expressions.

Table 13.5 Popular Expressions You Will Find Online

This...	Means This...
<grin> or <g>	Grin
<big grin> or <G>	Big grin
<blush>	I'm embarrassed by the comment
<snicker>	Playfully making fun of someone
<giggle>	Being silly
<getting on/off my soap box>	About to begin/end a speech about a subject you feel very strongly about
<raising eyebrows>	Disbelief over a matter

It's easy to see how all these elements come together to form a rich culture that, for the most part, doesn't discriminate mainly because it is so diverse. The Internet is a great place to be yourself because you will always find someone else who shares your beliefs and values, and you won't be judged by your wardrobe or waistline.

Some people believe the anonymity of the Internet makes it a cold place; just the opposite is true in my opinion. For all you know, simba@justpc.com (not a real e-mail address) could be a 10-year-old fan of Disney's *The Lion King*, or it could be a famous novel writer hiding behind a screen name. You never know, until that person decides to reveal a clue to his or her identity. Until then, "simba" will be treated with the same respect (or disrespect) other Netizens are treated.

Protecting Your Privacy by Using a Screen Name

In some ways, venturing on to the Information Superhighway is like visiting a big city for the first time; you will want to conduct yourself in such a way as to have a safe and enjoyable time. That is not to say that the Internet is a hotbed of crime, because it isn't. Like anywhere else, however, you will want to take some basic precautions to ensure your safety and privacy.

13

When you set up your e-mail account, you are asked to select a name to use as your e-mail address. In corporate America, e-mail addresses often take the form of a person's first initial followed by their surname. For example, I use `JFreeze@dtgnet.com` for my business account. It gives clients the sense of dealing with a real, legitimate person as opposed to some faceless person at the other end of a modem.

There are times, though, that you would just as soon be a faceless person at the other end of the modem. Using JFreeze, for example, gives advanced computer users plenty of information to begin tracking my physical location. Although the capability to find you gives potential customers or clients a sense of legitimacy and stability, it is not necessarily a desirable thing if you plan on frequenting chat rooms or even newsgroups.

Experienced Internet users wanting to track you down could go to a Web site based on your domain name (JustPC in my example) to see whether such a Web site exists and use it to search for clues to your location. They could plug your name into any number of search engines to draw clues from news articles you may have posted. They could also search a host of online phone books and pair up the entries with clues found elsewhere. The list goes on and on. When it comes right down to it, there are no more clues available to potential "bad guys" on the Internet than there are in the "real" world. Someone could follow you around, paw through your mail, dig through the contents of your trash can, and so on.

The media alone could scare you away by painting the Internet as the equivalent of wandering into the streets of Washington, D.C., alone in the middle of the night. Before you unplug your computer and put it up for sale at a church flea market, however, rest assured that there is plenty you can do to have a positive and safe experience on the Internet. The options are a heck of a lot more effective than anything you could do to protect yourself in the real world as well.

I'm not a pessimist by any means. In fact, it is my belief that crime resulting from using the Internet is far more uncommon than we hear on the news. Most situations can be avoided through the use of common sense and a few tips from someone who has been surfing the Information Superhighway since it was a dirt road!

Be Anyone You Want to Be!

Perhaps the best place to start is by selecting a screen name for yourself. Choose something fun that expresses your personality or a passion of yours. If you are a basketball fan, choose something like `celticfan`. Other options might include `UMassalum`, `cat-lover`, `fluteplayer`, or `NTRPRZ` for a *Star Trek* fan. Use some creativity to come up with alternatives in case your selection is already taken.

Even if you have already selected your e-mail address, think of a good screen name to use for online chats, auction sites, and so on.

Respecting the Rights of Others

If you have chosen a screen name to maintain your privacy, others have probably done the same. As you make more friends online, you will start to correspond with one another by using your real names in e-mail notes.

When encountering other people in online chat rooms, newsgroups, and other public forums, be careful not to reveal their real names. Including their names in a posted news article or in the context of a multiperson chat is a direct violation of their privacy. If it should happen by accident, simply apologize and try to be more careful in the future.

Shopping on the Information Superhighway

Imagine shopping for the holidays without having to do battle over a parking space, or without having to jump out of the path of runaway baby strollers loaded with packages (Where *are* the babies, anyway?)—it is a dream come true, right?

Shopaholic's paradise found! The tips in this lesson only begin to scratch the surface of safe online shopping. If you want to learn more, check out my book, *Savvy Online Shopping*, or visit my Web site at http://www.JustPC.com.

With your newfound link to the Internet, you can be enjoying the holidays this winter without all the blood pressure–raising agony. Bake a fresh batch of sugar cookies while your friends brave the preholiday shopping crowds at the local mall.

Buying from a Buddy: Is It Safe?

After you have spent some time in a hobby newsgroup of choice, you may be tempted to complete your collection (or that of a loved one) with purchases from some of the other newsgroup participants. Unfortunately, this can have mixed results. As you saw earlier in the hour, scalpers often feed off these newsgroups, making it seemingly impossible to acquire that limited edition Christmas ornament without paying hefty secondary market prices.

There are a number of kind souls, however, who will help out a fellow collector without price gouging. I met quite a few of these while frequenting http://rec.toys.cars. So

13

if you decide to make a purchase from someone you met on a newsgroup, follow these tips to improve the odds of having a positive Internet shopping experience:

- Read the newsgroup for a while and watch for any "bad dealer" posts. If you don't see anything on the person from whom you plan to make a purchase and the amount of the purchase is fairly significant, you may want to consider posting a message that asks for anyone else's experience with that person. Be sure to request that responses be e-mailed to you so as not to inadvertently start a flame war if opinions are mixed.

- Read the newsgroup's FAQs to see whether anyone maintains a safe dealer list on a Web page. Many newsgroup veterans will maintain such a page for their fellow collectors. If the FAQs and a few weeks of browsing the newsgroup don't direct you to such a site, post a message asking whether there is such a place you can go for your answers.

- Does the person you are dealing with have a Web page dedicated to her business? If so, she may be more legitimate than her counterpart who is merely posting a few things for sale here and there.

- Does the person or business accept credit cards? If they do, that also signifies permanence and legitimacy.

- Has the person participated in any other group discussions, or has he surfaced only to sell things? A person appearing only to post for sale ads may not necessarily share your love of the hobby; he may just be a scalper in disguise.

Get to the bottom of the matter quickly. Save some time by going to http://groups.google.com (or any other search engine that offers news-group searching capabilities) to search for the person's e-mail address and to see the newsgroup articles he or she has posted over the last month. These should give you valuable clues.

- Know what you are buying. If you aren't buying something MIB (mint in box) or MIP (mint in package), get to know your hobby's grading standards. Die cast cars, for example, are graded C10 for a perfect piece, and the number goes down in specific increments, depending on the type of blemish, its location, and other issues. Many hobbies have specific books that collectors have come to accept as the standard for grading. Consult the FAQs for further details.

Is My Credit Card Number Safe on the Net?

Is your credit card number safe on the Internet? Unfortunately, the answer is "it depends."

> **Here's a number you should NEVER share online.** I don't care who asks you for it, never EVER provide your social security number via e-mail or on a Web form! This single piece of information when linked with your name could open the door to identity theft and other horrible situations. If an entity truly needs that information, you should be able to provide it in another manner.

Many e-commerce sites use something called *secure socket layers (SSL)* to encrypt your entire business transaction, including, most importantly, your credit card number. This protects your personal information from being viewed by unauthorized parties.

> **NEW TERM** **Encryption.** Information is scrambled using a code or password so that others can't read it.

SSL is supported by a number of large Internet storefronts, but many still do not have the resources to implement such technology. In these instances, you will want to find alternative methods for shopping with them, such as sending an order through the mail or calling in your credit card number.

How can you tell if a site supports SSL? Most commercial Web sites make a big thing out of it by mentioning that fact in key data entry locations. Internet Explorer also displays a small icon that shows you whether you are in a secure environment, and some even display a message saying you are about to enter a secure server (see Figure 13.2).

Just because a Web site doesn't support SSL, however, doesn't mean that you have to shop elsewhere. Consider any of the following options:

- Make notes on the products you want to purchase, jot down the company's phone number, and then call and place the order the old fashioned way. Not only do you still avoid the Christmas crowds, but you also save paper and a stamp. If there is a toll-free number, that's even better!

13

FIGURE **13.2**
Internet Explorer displays a padlock when logged on to secure sites. It also displays an S *(for secure) behind the* http:.

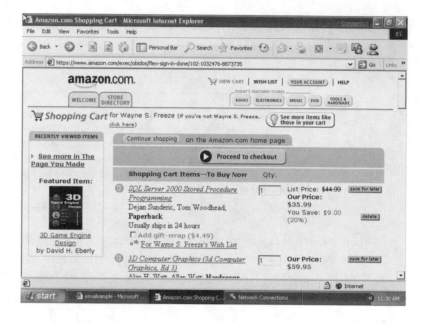

Beware the cordless phone! Boy, and people think the Internet is a security nightmare! Once when I went to put my infant daughter down for a nap, I went to turn on the baby monitor. Instead of hearing her cute little coos and giggles, I got an earful of a neighbor's phone conversation! The monitor picked up the cordless phone transmission! This should make you aware that even more traditional forms of transmission carry significant risks too.

- If you are not a phone person and aren't in a hurry, you can send the order via snail mail. This can save you money in the long run if the company's number is a toll call for you.

- Some merchants are equipped to take your order online and then hold it until you phone in your credit card number.

- Other merchants enable you to set up an account with them so that all you have to do when visiting their site is enter a userid and password, make your selections, and then process your order as normal. Your credit card information and shipping address remain on file with the merchant so that you don't have to rekey and submit it again.

Shopping online offers other benefits too. In many instances, you don't have to pay sales tax on the items ordered. Although postage and handling is charged, you often don't have to spend much to save money overall. If your state sales tax is 5% and you spend $100, you saved $5. Even when a flat-rate shipping charge of $4.95 is added, you still come out ahead, and you don't have to break your back lugging the stuff through a mall full of shoppers!

When It Comes to the Web, All That Glitters Is Not Gold

Remember the days when students had to schlep off to the library to research their term papers? I was one of those students. I pawed through dusty card catalogs, I scanned library shelves for hours trying desperately to find a book that had obviously been improperly shelved, and I spent hours taking copious notes from reference books unable to be checked out. (But no, I didn't have to walk to school in six feet of snow, never missing a day!)

In all seriousness, gathering data from the Internet has simplified the lives of many students. Rather than running out to the library at odd times of the day, students can now use their PCs to research their papers from the comfort of their own homes.

Using computers as a research tool, however, is not for students only. In fact, there are times in our lives when we are all students, regardless of our age or how many years we have spent in the classroom. Consider the following situations:

- You want to invest in a camcorder, but the salespeople at the local electronics stores don't have a clue as to the specifications of each unit and how they differ. Where do you get the information you need? On the Internet, of course. Use manufacturers' Web sites to research the product specifications and suggested retail price and then venture out to the newsgroups to get the reaction of people who have been using the equipment in which you are most interested.

- Have you been transferred to a new area but have no clue how to begin house hunting or searching for the best school for your children? The Internet can give you some solid facts to work with before you travel to the new location and investigate firsthand.

- We don't like to dwell on unpleasant things, but they can happen. Again, the Internet can help you along the way. Whether you or a loved one has been diagnosed with a condition you want to learn more about or if you would like to become involved in an online support group to help you cope with the situation, it is all available on your computer from the privacy of your home. It is no substitute for sound medical advice, but it can help you ask the right questions, make informed decisions, and get the emotional support you need.

13

- Did your granddaughter find a box turtle in the woods out back, but you don't know what to feed it? Maybe she wants to keep it, but you have no idea what kind of home little Tessie the turtle needs. You can find all the answers online and even find forums in which to ask your questions.

These are just a few situations for which the Internet and your new PC can help you research the information you need. The possibilities are virtually endless. We have all heard the old cliché, "Free advice is worth what you pay for it." If that were truly still the case, no one would believe a thing on the Internet. What makes the Internet different? How can we be sure the information we are seeing and basing our decisions on is accurate?

The issue of determining information integrity has grabbed the attention of many prominent scholars, since online content is being cited more and more as a source in written papers. In the following section, I will give you some ways to evaluate the information you find online for its validity, whether you are researching your dissertation or trying to make an informed decision regarding the purchase of a major appliance.

The Importance of Evaluating Online Information

Many people view the Internet as one big encyclopedia full of knowledge, but they lose sight of the fact that entries in real encyclopedias are written by noted experts on the subject. Furthermore, these entries pass through the hands of droves of editors before publication. Although you have experts on the Internet too, you also have a high proportion of people who think they are experts. This requires the information gatherer to work even harder to sort the diamonds from the rocks.

Luckily, researchers and librarians have come up with some criteria to help us evaluate the information we find on the Web. These criteria include a Web site's scope of information, the authority and bias of the data maintained on the site, the accuracy of the information, the timeliness of a site's content, the permanence of the Web site, any value-added features included on the site, and the presentation of the information.

You will explore each of these criteria in detail and then take a look at how to evaluate different types of Web sites (such as sales and marketing Web sites, advocacy Web sites, and personal Web pages) using these criteria.

Scoping Out the Information

The depth and breadth of the information found on a given site depends on the intended purpose and audience of that Web site. Many government sites, for example, archive data for future use, whereas a personal Web page might report on the latest *Star Wars* action figures found in stores and then delete that information later, since it is no longer of value.

To evaluate the scope of a site, look for the following:

- **Stated purpose of the site.** Many Web pages have a stated purpose for their existence. For advocacy or nonprofit organizations, the Web site's purpose may mirror its organizational mission statement or at the minimum, act as an extension of part of its mission. Even personal Web pages may have a stated purpose. Use these statements of purpose for clues to the site's comprehensiveness and potential biases.

- **What they say is covered.** A Web master will often sacrifice overall subject comprehensiveness in order to specialize in a specific area. A gardening club may strive to produce the most comprehensive site on roses out there instead of publishing dribs and drabs on a variety of plants and flowers. If a site chooses to specialize, it is likely that the site will not only attempt to cover the topic in depth, but it will provide links to a number of additional reliable sources specializing in the same topic. These focused sites are often some of the best places to glean lots of information about a given topic.

NEW TERM **Take me to your (Web) Master!** A *web master* is the person who is responsible for coordinating a Web site's content, design, and functionality.

- **Site comprehensiveness.** You can tell a site's breadth and depth of information by scanning its list of topics, site map, or internal links. The volume of information also provides some clues.

It is easy to see how the items in the preceding list work together to give you a good feel for the scope of a Web site's content. You need to know a lot more than the scope of a site's content in order to evaluate it effectively, however.

Determining the Authority and Bias of a Site

One of the best ways to assess the biases of a Web site's content is to look at what is presented and ask, "What does the Web site's owner have to gain from presenting the material as he does?"

Obviously, if a company's Web site says its Zoom910 model of camcorder is the best thing around, you will weigh the statement a lot differently than if a noted and trusted consumer advocacy group's Web site states the same thing. The company has something to gain by touting its product, whereas the consumer advocacy group merely wants to do right by the consumer with no biases.

13

Here are some things you should look for when attempting to evaluate the authority and bias of a Web site:

- **Who provided the information and why?** If a commercial entity (usually sporting a URL ending in .com) produces or even sponsors the Web site, the information is almost guaranteed to be biased in some respect. No profitable company is likely to highlight its shortcomings or product weaknesses online for all to see unless it is legally obligated to do so, as in the case of tobacco products and the mandatory Surgeon General's warning. Web sites maintained by advocacy groups or nonprofit organizations (often with .org extensions) also can be biased, since they exist to right a perceived wrong. As such, they are likely to exaggerate the facts to make a case for their existence. For these reasons, it is important to weigh what is said and put the content into perspective given the potential biases.

- **Is a specific point of view being pushed?** Objective sites will merely communicate the facts without inflicting a point of view on the reader. When evaluating a site for the integrity of its information, you should also be wary of overdramatic use of language, which could signal an exaggeration of the facts.

- **Seeing a stamp of approval.** Web sites that are truly exceptional in content tend to draw a lot of attention. A statement of support from noted experts and organizations in the given field increase the odds of the information being at least reasonably accurate. These stamps of approval can show up in the form of reciprocal links, awards given to the site, and posted quotes or comments from field experts.

NEW TERM	**Reciprocal link.** Two Web sites give links to one another, thus forming a reciprocal link.

After you know where the site's information comes from and have any potential biases fixed in your mind, you are ready to start examining the accuracy of the information itself.

The Pursuit of Accuracy

Unless you know the names of all of the field's experts, you may have a tough time evaluating whether what you are looking at is legitimate or if it is merely a product of a wannabe expert.

To assist you in this quest for accurate information, look for the following in the Web sites you visit:

- **Cited sources.** If a Web site cites the sources of its information and the sources appear to be legitimate, chances are the information is accurate. You could double-check them to be certain, but that would defeat the purpose of providing easily accessible information on the Web.

- **Who came up with this stuff, anyway?** A Web page's author or compiler sometimes will include a link to his or her credentials. At that point, you can decide for yourself whether the person is an expert or even a reliable source.

- **A recognized source of value.** If you are visiting the American Association of Retired Persons (AARP) home page, you will probably respect any sources it links you to, with the assumption that the AARP would be judicious in granting links. Seeing the site in question referenced by a variety of prominent and reliable sources gives the site and the information contained therein more credibility.

Day-Old Data

One of the things that has plagued print media since the beginning is its long turnaround time. The content of printed materials (with the exception of newspapers, of course) often becomes stale before it ever reaches the hands of its desired audience. It is a sad fact of life, yet it is one of the things that makes the Internet so intriguing. Information can be updated within minutes to reflect pivotal news events, changes in the law, or other pertinent information that can change at a moment's notice.

Just because you can quickly update Web content doesn't mean that it is updated often in reality. When a leading toy manufacturer finally made its online presence known, I sent them an e-mail message pleading that they keep their site updated so that it would maintain its value. Unfortunately, like many other large corporations, the information quickly became stale and worthless and was seldom updated. Web pages created by the collectors of this manufacturer's products soon became the freshest, most reliable source of information. It kind of makes you wonder why they even bothered expending the money and effort to get online in the first place!

How do you avoid the pitfalls of day-old data? Here are some things to look for when assessing the freshness of a site's information:

- **Check the "expiration" date.** Many Web pages have a "revised on" date reference somewhere on the page. Depending on the type of content the page provides, the information could be considered old after as little as an hour. Many news sites update themselves as often as every 15 minutes, whereas some sites undergo a scheduled weekly update, which is more than enough. This is one of those instances where your judgment comes into play.

13

- **Revision policy.** In addition to a revised or modified on date, many Web sites also display a policy for updates. Statements such as "This page is updated every 15 minutes," are common. Unfortunately, in many cases, you must simply just wait and see when the information will be updated.

- **Hibernating hyperlinks.** Stumbling onto countless error codes when trying to follow a Web page's links also may be an indicator of a poorly maintained, thus potentially out-of-date, Web page.

Using out-of-date information can have undesirable results in many circumstances. If data appear to be old, you might want to consider looking elsewhere before relying too heavily on such questionable information.

Here Today, Gone Tomorrow!

Whether a site is permanent can tell you a great deal about the information it provides. Finely crafted Web sites produced by college students can disappear after they graduate, or sites that move from server-to-server like cheap antique reproductions at a flea market can be cover-ups for shady activity. It is wise to know what you are dealing with, so consider checking for the following:

- **Now you see it; now you don't.** Whether it's a system upgrade or a new organizational affiliation, Web pages occasionally need to be moved. Look for notices about impending change of location for the Web page. Most reputable Web pages will plan a change of location and prepare users well in advance by placing a notice prominently on the home page. With careful planning, they may register their own domain name, thus making relocation virtually seamless to the user. Sites that suddenly change location without notice should raise a red flag in your mind.

- **The Web page owner's relationship to the host site.** If the Web page belongs to the government or a major corporation, it is probably relatively stable. If, however, the page is maintained by a student using her university Internet account, count on it moving or even disappearing altogether within a few years or maybe even months. That doesn't make them bad sources; it just means you had better grab the information you want while you still can.

- **Transitory information.** There are some cases where the site's information may be of temporary value. Consider a politician's election page or a page dedicated to the aftermath of a tragedy like an earthquake or plane crash. After these sites have served their purpose, they most likely will not continue to be updated and may even disappear after a certain amount of time. If you need information from a site like this, it is best to get it when you see it, just in case it disappears.

Time is of the essence anywhere, especially on the Internet, where the number of Web sites grows by some staggering number each month. Unless you see signs that a Web site archives its data for future access, it is best to get the information while you can.

Value-Added Site Features

Some Web sites include value-added features such as sections moderated by an expert, search engines, navigational help, and other items. Because of the time and effort that went into designing and creating them, these sites are likely to be around much longer than their typical counterparts.

Beauty's in the Eye of the Beholder

We have all seen flashy Web pages with little content to back up the special effects, but there are some presentation and design elements that contribute to the professionalism and legitimacy of a Web site. These include intuitive site organization targeted to the specific audience, appropriate use of graphics and other multimedia features, and navigational links back to the home page or site map of the site. Use of these elements implies a planned, stable Web site that you can return to with confidence.

Questioning Your Sources

Given all these factors, how can you possibly evaluate a site's worthiness as a resource? Just use the following questions as a guide. The more questions to which you answer *yes*, the higher is the quality of the source.

1. Is it clear who is sponsoring the Web site?

2. Is there a way to verify the legitimacy of the company/organization/individual (a phone number or street address, not just an e-mail address)?

> **Check it out!** Because it can be hard to verify the legitimacy of an individual, it is wise to use extreme caution when relying on a personal home page as a source of information. For best results, try to find the source of the claim or statistic to verify the information.

13

3. Is the page relatively free of typos and grammatical errors? Although these may not seem like important considerations, they communicate a lack of quality control, which means other information may go unverified.

4. Are the sources of factual information cited so that you can double-check the page's claim with the original source?

5. Is any advertising on the page clearly set apart from informational content?

6. Is there a date posted on the page indicating when the content was last updated?

7. Has the page been completed, as opposed to being under constant construction?

8. Is the information advertising free?

9. Are the biases of the company/organization/individual clear?

10. Can you tell when the Web page first appeared on the Internet?

Web sites are not substitutes for good, sound research, but they can be a vital source of timely information and lead to more obscure resources. By using the preceding questions as a guide, you should have a better feel for which Web sites are potential gold mines for information.

Summary

Whew, that was some hour! I know it was long, but since it was mostly reading instead of steps you had to follow, I figured it could still be completed in an hour. In this hour, you learned all about the culture of the Internet, how to make safe transactions, and how to evaluate the integrity of the information you see online.

Now that you are adequately trained for full-contact Internet activity, it's time to move on to the nuts and bolts of working with the Internet. We will start in the next hour by getting you acquainted with your Web browser, Internet Explorer 6.

Workshop

Now it's time to see just how much you learned in this lesson. I'll give you a short multiple-choice quiz to test what you learned, followed by a suggested activity designed to enhance the skills you acquired during the hour.

Quiz

Select the best answer to the questions from the choices provided and then check your answers in the following section.

Questions

1. Which of the following is *not* acceptable Internet etiquette?

    a. If your response to a post is of interest only to the original poster, e-mail it to them directly instead of posting it on the group.

    b. Before contributing to a newsgroup, read the FAQs to be sure your question isn't addressed there.

    c. When starting a new business, gather as many e-mail addresses as you can from relevant newsgroups and e-mail them all your offerings.

2. What do :-) and :-(mean?

    a. I'm happy about what I wrote/I'm sad about what I wrote.

    b. These marks mean nothing on the Internet or anywhere else.

    c. Hey, you don't put punctuation marks together in that order!

3. When it comes to information found on the Internet...

    a. You can't believe a word you read.

    b. You should evaluate what you read to help determine the integrity of the information.

    c. Accept everything you see as the gospel truth; no lies or tall tales are allowed on the Net!

Answers

1. If you engage in the behavior described in C you may get run off the Internet faster than you can bat an eye!

2. A is the appropriate answer here. If you chose anything else, you have obviously been snoozing through the lesson!

3. Neither A nor C true, so B is the correct answer. You can find information ranging from heavily researched facts to bold-faced lies.

Activity

Now that you are familiar with many of the abbreviations, emoticons, and expressions found on the Internet, you are ready for this little exercise.

Grab a pen and paper, and try composing a note using as many of the items you learned about during the hour as you can (shoot for including ten). Remember, you have emoticons, abbreviations, and a whole huge assortment of goodies to choose from.

13

HOUR 14

Navigating the Information Superhighway

The vast majority of first-time computer owners finally decide to take the plunge because they want to get on the Internet. How do I know? Because rebates from Internet service providers have popped up everywhere, making PCs more affordable than ever. Combine that with the fact that the Internet is just plain fun, and new computers start flying off the shelves at an astonishing rate.

In this hour, I will bring you up to speed on using Internet Explorer, the Web browser created by Microsoft. After this lesson, you will be cruising the Information Superhighway like you have been there all your life!

Here are some other topics you have to look forward to this hour:

- Familiarize yourself with the many ways you can visit a Web site.
- Discover how to save a Web page to your Favorites list.

- Learn how to search the Web using Internet Explorer 6's new Search Assistant.
- Find out how the AutoComplete feature can save you time.

The Web Surfing Primer

Before I jump into the nitty-gritty of using the Web browser itself, I would like to introduce you to some of the basic Web concepts.

When you are sitting in front of your television watching Monday Night Football or your afternoon soap, take special note of the commercials. Even more than toll-free numbers, you will hear things like, "Come visit us online at `http://www.DietCoke.com`." This is proof positive that the Web is not only mainstream, but it is here to stay.

The www stuff is called a *Web address,* or *URL*. To continue on with the Diet Coke example, if you enter `http://www.DietCoke.com` into Internet Explorer, you will soon be visiting the official Web site of Diet Coke. The first page you see typically is referred to as the *home page*. On this page, you usually will see some text with graphics; some of this text may appear in a different color or at the very least, underlined. This unique text is referred to as a *link*, a fundamental concept of the Web.

> **Hidden links.** In an attempt to make sites more aesthetically appealing, Web page designers often will make "invisible" links. In other words, the plain text and link text look identical. So how can you tell where the links are that will take you elsewhere? Simply run your mouse pointer over the page. An arrow-shaped pointer indicates basic text. A pointing finger means your mouse is on a link you can click to be taken to another Web page.

When you click a link, you are transported to another page on the current Web site or even to an entirely different site. This interconnection of links is how the Web gets its name.

So there you have it—an oversimplification of Web concepts. But hey, we all know you would rather be surfing than reading technobabble, right?

Seeing the Sites

With Internet Explorer 6, there are more ways to jump to a Web site than you can possibly imagine (see Figure 14.1). The methods include any of the following:

- Type the URL into the Address Bar and then press Enter (or click the Go button at the right end of the Address Bar).

- Click the Favorites menu item and select a site from the drop-down menu of previously saved favorites (of course you won't find much here if you haven't saved any pages yet).

- Use the Favorites button to open a Favorites window on the left side of the browsing area. You can now hop from Favorite to Favorite without having to reopen menus.

- The drop-down arrow button to the right of the Address Bar opens a list of recently visited URLs. Just double-click one to pay a visit.

- The History button takes you back in time to sites you have visited over the past three weeks. More on how to work with this later in the hour.

- After you browse several pages in the current Internet Explorer 6 session, you can click the drop-down arrow next to the Back button to jump to up to nine of the most recently visited sites.

FIGURE 14.1
Move to a Web page in any of these ways.

***I took my best shot at callouts, please OK

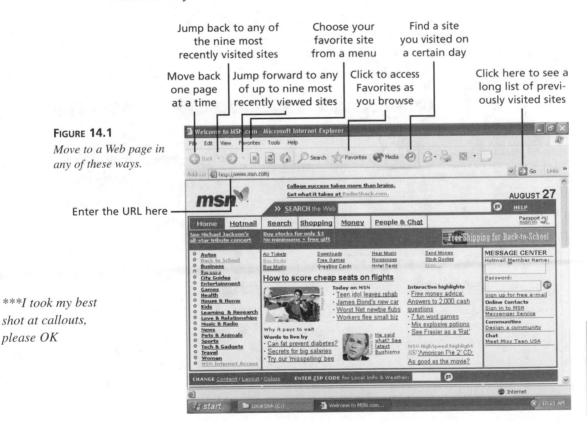

- Click the Back button to browse back through recently visited Web pages one at a time.

- If you have used the Back button to return to other pages, you can use the drop-down arrow next to the Forward button to skip ahead to any of the up to nine pages you visited in the current session.

Revisiting History with the History Button

Have you ever read something that you wanted to go back and find at a later date only to discover you can't remember where you read it? Maybe you are searching for a new gymnastics club for your daughter. You see one you kind of like, but you decide to keep looking for something better. A couple of days later, you decide to get more information from that first club you sort of liked, but you didn't save the Web page as a Favorite. What do you do now?

Thanks to the History button, there is hope. If you can remember the approximate date on which you visited the site, you stand a fair shot of finding it again. Just click the History button, click the link that best corresponds to the suspected date, and then glance through the list of sites until you locate a URL that looks familiar (see Figure 14.2). It may take a couple of tries, but you will find it eventually.

FIGURE 14.2

By default, you can isolate any day over the past week or any week over the past three.

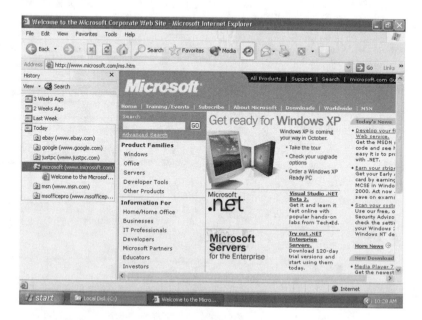

If don't have time for a leisurely stroll down memory lane, then you can use the View drop-down arrow in the upper left corner of the History pane. Just click it and point to any of the following special views to help find that mystery page:

- By Date
- By Site
- By Most Visited
- By Order Visited Today

You can also search the History links by clicking the History pane's Search button. If you type in a word or words, Internet Explorer 6 will go back in time and attempt to retrieve that lost gymnastics club.

Getting out of History mode is a snap; just click the History button on the Standard toolbar a second time or click the x in the upper right corner of the History frame. Your Internet Explorer 6 viewing area returns to its full size.

Working with Favorite Web Sites

After you find a Web page worth revisiting, you will want to file it in an easy-to-find location by right-clicking the page while it is onscreen and selecting Save Add to Favorite from the menu that appears.

Internet Explorer gives you wonderful Favorites management capabilities, as you will see in the next few sections. It has even made it possible for you to exchange your Favorites lists with others and browse Web sites offline!

Organizing Your Favorites

Optimally, you will have a good folder structure in place before you save any pages to your Favorites list; however, reality says a few are bound to sneak in there before you take the time to map everything out. That's okay; the Favorites list is fairly easy to manage after the fact as well.

There are multiple steps involved in organizing your Favorites, as you will see:

1. With Internet Explorer up and running, click the Favorites menu item and then choose Organize Favorites. The Organize Favorites dialog box pictured in Figure 14.3 opens.

14

FIGURE 14.3

The Organize Favorites dialog box makes it quick and easy to keep your favorite Web sites in order.

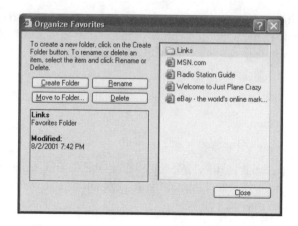

2. The first thing you will need to do is create some folders in which to store your favorite Web sites. Try to place your Favorites into specific categories such as Cats, Quilting, Places To Go, Dreamcast Games, Job Hunting, and so on. Also keep in mind that you can nest folders; for example, underneath the Places To Go folder, you may have subfolders for Museums, Fairs, and Vacation Spots. When you have some good folder names in mind, click the Create Folder button. To create a nested subfolder, just click the folder under which you want to place the new folder and then click Create Folder.

3. A new folder appears at the bottom of the screen (or in the location you specified, if it is a nested folder). Its blue highlights prompt you to enter a name for it. Type in the chosen name and then press Enter. The folder has been created.

4. Repeat the process until all of your favorite Web pages have a logical home.

5. Now comes the fun part: moving the pages you previously saved as Favorites to their new homes. Click on the first link in your list of Favorites.

6. Click the Move to Folder button to display the Browse for Folder dialog box as shown in Figure 14.4.

7. Click on the folder to which you want to move the selected page and then click OK.

8. The selected item now will appear in its new folder. Repeat the process of selecting a link and moving it until all of the links have a home.

9. To see which pages are located within a folder, click on the folder once. The page titles will appear underneath their specified folder. Click the folder again to "hide" the pages.

10. When everything is in its place, click the Close button to leave the dialog box.

FIGURE 14.4

This box displays each of the new folders you created. Of course, it will look pretty sparse at first.

Just droppin' in.... If you have a short Favorite list, it may be easier to just drag and drop the links into their new folders. To do this, access the Organize Favorites dialog box (click Favorites, Organize Favorites from the menu bar), click the name of the link you want to move, and drag it up to the desired folder. The mouse button can then be released to drop the link into the folder.

Now you have a neat and tidy list of Favorites that is easy to navigate and share with others, as you will see a little later in this lesson.

Sharing Your Favorite Sites with Others

The capability to share Web sites and Favorites lists with others in a variety of ways is one of the most useful enhancements to recent revisions of Internet Explorer. For the first time, you can effortlessly swap links with users of the other main Web browser (Netscape) and e-mail Favorites folders of links to others sharing your interests. It even makes toting favorite links from work to home or vice versa a breeze.

With Internet Explorer, there are several ways to share your favorite Web sites with family, friends, and associates. They include the following:

- E-mailing a link to the Web page
- Sending the entire Web page
- Exporting your entire Favorites list
- Exporting a single folder full of goodies

- Sending the page as an HTML file attachment
- Importing Favorites sent to you by others (or transferring your Favorites from work to your home machine or vice versa)

We cover many of these operations in detail in the sections that follow.

E-mailing a Link to a Web Page

Follow these steps to send someone a link to one of your favorite sites:

1. While you are browsing the page you want to share, click the File menu item and then point to Send, Link by E-mail. Internet Explorer launches Outlook Express (or whatever e-mail program you've chosen to use for your default) to assist with the task. The subject line will be filled in with the title of the page, and the link will already be printed as part of the message.

> **Say what you are thinking.** Go ahead and add any text you want to the message (you will learn how to do this in the next lesson, but it is not terribly difficult if you want to give it a shot now). Now the recipient knows why you thought the link may be of interest to him or her.

2. Type in the e-mail address you want (or use the Address Book as described in Hour 16, Sending and Receiving E-mail) and then click Send. The recipient will receive an e-mail containing your message, along with the link you chose to send.

3. To visit the resource, all the recipient needs to do is click the link provided; it's as simple as that!

E-mailing the Entire Web Page

Use these steps to send the entire Web page to a recipient. Before going to all the trouble, you will want to make sure the recipient has the capability to read HTML-formatted mail.

NEW TERM

> **HTM what?** HTML stands for *hypertext markup language*, the special programming language that makes a Web page look similar to any visitor whether they are using a PC, Mac, or WebTV.

To send the page to someone else, follow these steps:

1. Browse to the Web page you want to send.
2. Click the File menu item and then choose Send, Page by E-mail.
3. Internet Explorer will launch Outlook Express and give you an opportunity to fill in the recipient's e-mail address and any additional text.
4. When everything is ready to go, click Send. Output similar to a standard e-mail message with images embedded in it will be sent to the recipient's e-mail account. Note that the recipient may need to maximize his or her e-mail screen to see the page in its full glory.

Exporting Your Favorites List

What if you change jobs and want to take your list of favorite professional-related Web sites with you? Suppose that you are getting a new computer and are handing your old one down to the kids. Wouldn't it be great if you could take your Favorites list with you? Follow these quick steps to get the job done:

1. From within Internet Explorer, click File and then point to Import and Export. The Import/Export Wizard in Figure 14.5 appears. Click Next to begin.

FIGURE 14.5

The Import/Export Wizard is your starting point for exchanging Favorites.

2. Choose Export Favorites from the list of possible actions and then click Next.
3. You will now need to choose the folder you want to export. Just click it and then click Next. Please note that you can only export one folder at a time. If you click

14

the top-level Favorites folder, all folders will be exported. Otherwise, you can only take one folder at a time—no picking and choosing.

3. The Export Favorites Destination screen gives you two options: to export your Internet Explorer 6 Favorites to another Web browser on your system (like Netscape) or to save it to a file location by clicking the Browse button. After you locate the spot, give the file a descriptive, easy-to-remember name such as Shopping or Cat Favs. Internet Explorer automatically will save it as an HTML file with an .htm file extension. After you make your selection, click Next.

> **Where should I put it?** If you plan to take the file to work, you may want to cut a disk containing the file, which will mean using the A: drive. If you are connected to a LAN or similar network, consider saving the file to one of the shared directories for easy retrieval. If you plan to e-mail the file to yourself or somebody else, just tuck it away in an easy-to-remember spot on your C: drive so that you can easily attach it to an e-mail note.

4. The wizard displays a message saying that you have successfully completed the Import/Export Wizard. All you need to do is click Finish to complete the process. A small dialog box appears saying that the export was successful. Click OK to close the wizard.

Importing Those Favorite Links

Now it's time to get those imported Favorites where they belong—back on a computer! Follow these steps to import Favorites into another copy of Internet Explorer:

1. On Internet Explorer's File menu, select Import and Export. The Import/Export Wizard launches. Click Next to begin the process.

2. You will now need to select Import Favorites from the list of actions provided and then click Next.

3. Browse to the location in which the Favorites list was saved. It may be your A: drive if you transported the list via disk, or a saved e-mail attachment if you mailed it to yourself. Note that an e-mail attachment must be saved to your hard drive before you will be able to import it.

4. When you find the file, double-click it and then click the Next button.

5. At this point, you may specify a folder under which to nest the imported favorites by clicking on it; otherwise, its own folder will be created. Click Next to proceed.

6. A message appears that says you are about to complete the wizard. Click Finish to make it official. A small dialog box appears stating the import was executed. Click OK to acknowledge the dialog box and dismiss the wizard.

What about Netscape? As mentioned, these HTML files can be imported into Netscape too, but you will need to consult the procedures in the help files of the target version of Netscape for the most up-to-date, step-by-step directions.

Dealing Specifically with E-mailed Sharing

To perform the export/import via e-mail, there are some things you will need to know. First, the export is performed exactly as previously described. To send it via e-mail, you will need to launch Outlook Express, begin composing a new message, and then click the paper clip icon and browse to the desired HTML file to attach it to the message.

If you are on the receiving end of a Favorites list passed on by e-mail, you will have to save the file attachment somewhere on your computer before you can perform the import as described previously.

Searching the Web Using Internet Explorer's Search Companion

Searching for material on the Internet can be frustrating, especially when your boss needs to know the answer to a question quickly and you have no idea where to begin your search for the answer. If you have spent any time at all working with search engines, you have undoubtedly noticed the difference between them. The same search string entered into multiple engines can produce wildly unpredictable results.

Coming attractions. Without a little guidance, it can be next to impossible to find anything on the Net. That is why the goal of the next lesson is to help you find what you are looking for online. Stay tuned!

14

Although Internet Explorer can't decide for you which search engine is best, it can call your preferred search engine into action. Follow these steps to work with the Search Companion:

1. With Internet Explorer and an active connection to the Internet running, click the Search button on the Standard button bar. The Search Companion pane on the left side of the screen, as shown in Figure 14.6, appears.

FIGURE 14.6

The Search Companion pane enables you to search while you surf.

2. Type the word or phrase you want to search in the text box provided and then click the Search button.

3. A series of options designed to help you target your search appear in the Search Companion pane while some preliminary results appear in the main Internet Explorer viewing area (see Figure 14.7).

4. Click the links of interest to view them. And remember, you can use Internet Explorer's Back and Forward buttons to move between screens.

FIGURE **14.7**
When the question, "What books has Jill Freeze written?" was entered, the Search Assistant returned the screen in this figure.

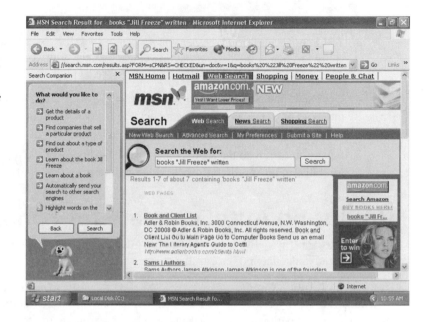

Finding Things on a Web Page

Some Web documents can ramble on forever, which is why you will want to know how to perform a search within a specified Web page. Just follow these steps to perform a search on the current Web page:

1. With the page you want to search displayed in Internet Explorer, click the Edit menu item and then click on Find (on this page). The dialog box shown in Figure 14.8 appears.

A shortcut. Rather than using the menu commands, you can press Ctrl+F to display the Find dialog box.

FIGURE **14.8**
Internet Explorer's Find dialog box helps you get where you want to go on a Web page quickly.

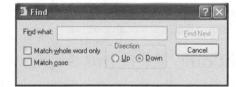

14

2. Type in the word or phrase you want to find on the current page.

3. Tell Internet Explorer whether you want it to look for a whole word match or simply to match the case of the text you entered. Just place a check mark in the appropriate box(es).

4. Click the Find Next button to send Internet Explorer after the next occurrence of the word or phrase. You can even click the Up or Down button to tell Internet Explorer which way to search. (By the way, Down is the default search direction.)

5. After you complete the search, click the Close button at the top right side of the Find dialog box or click Cancel. Either will remove the box from the screen.

Introducing AutoComplete for Forms

If you have ever used the Internet Explorer Address Bar to work with Web sites, then you have already encountered a form-like element—that is, a text box complete with drop-down arrows ready for you to insert the text of your choice.

You will routinely come across forms on Web pages you visit, whether it is a search form at your favorite online bookseller or a basic search engine form. The first time you enter text into a form, Internet Explorer will ask you whether you want the Web browser to "remember" your entry. Known as *AutoComplete for Forms,* this feature, when enabled, will recall entries typed into a given form by displaying a drop-down box of selections much like you see with the new AutoComplete for Web Addresses. To accept a suggestion on a future visit to the same form, merely double-click it and then click the necessary button to start the search.

Although the feature is tremendously helpful for repeated searches at the same location on the same topic, it also can be a potential invasion of privacy. Suppose that you are trying to research your company's competition, look into a personal medical condition, or track down an elusive Pokemon toy for your son's birthday. If people use the computer after you did, they could see what you had been searching for. Of course, they would have to be visiting the exact same sites as you did, but if you work with common search engines, it is a distinct possibility.

In response to this potential concern, Internet Explorer gives you the opportunity to enable, disable, and clear this AutoComplete feature.

Modifying AutoComplete Forms Settings

To change the way AutoComplete works on your computer, follow these steps:

1. On the Internet Explorer Tools menu, choose Internet Options.

2. Click the Content tab to open it. In the Personal Information section of the screen, you will need to click the AutoComplete button. The AutoComplete Settings dialog box appears (see Figure 14.9).

FIGURE 14.9

The AutoComplete Settings dialog box is where you can really take control over this powerful feature.

3. Check or uncheck the Forms item as desired to turn the AutoComplete Forms feature on or off.

4. If you want to leave AutoComplete for Forms enabled but want to clear your entries, click Clear Forms.

Hold it right there! Clicking Clear Forms will delete everyone who uses the computer's AutoComplete for Forms entries. A better strategy for protecting your privacy may be to turn off the feature when you begin using Internet Explorer and then turn it back on before leaving the application.

5. After you finish adjusting the settings, click OK. You will need to click OK to close the Options dialog box and continue working in Internet Explorer.

This works for Web sites too. You can use the preceding strategies for protecting your privacy with regard to the Web sites you have visited by disabling AutoComplete for Web Addresses while you are working. Remember, turning off AutoComplete for Forms protects your privacy on one level, but other users of your machine could accidentally stumble onto the sites you visited by accessing the History entries or by seeing them in the Address Bar drop-down list.

14

Summary

In this hour, you were taken on a whirlwind tour of Internet Explorer. Although it wasn't even close to scratching the surface of all of the neat things it can do, it gives you more than enough to get started. You know the basic terminology, how to get from one Web page to another, how to work with Favorites, and even how to search the Web for a site of interest.

The next lesson will be another jam-packed hour, as I show you how to find the proverbial needle in the haystack of Internet sites.

Workshop

Now it's time to see just how much you learned in this lesson. I'll give you a short multiple-choice quiz to test what you learned, followed by a suggested activity designed to enhance the skills you acquired during the hour.

Quiz

Select the best answer to the questions from the choices provided and then check your answers in the following section.

Questions

1. What does the History button do?

    a. Enables you to search or browse through an assortment of Web sites you visited during the past three weeks.

    b. It launches a special Web page dedicated to American History.

    c. It is a special search engine that will fetch historical information on any date you give it. It is a joint project between Microsoft and the Associated Press.

2. What do you call the Web sites you save and put on a special Internet Explorer list so that you can revisit them with ease?

    a. My Sites

    b. The Best of the Net

    c. Favorites

3. Can the AutoComplete feature "remember" Web addresses and information you type in to forms?

    a. Yes, as long as the feature is enabled.

    b. No, AutoComplete only remembers your name.

    c. There is no such thing as AutoComplete; this was a trick question!

Answers

1. If you chose A, you are correct. Although the other choices may have been fun, they are not what the History button does in this application.

2. Okay, those who did *not* say C, go back and reread the lesson!

3. A is the correct choice. AutoComplete can be a tremendously helpful feature after you get comfortable working with it.

Activity

Here is another listing exercise for you. Take a moment to think about all your interests, whether professional or personal. Now make a list of ten possible Favorites folder names. Ten may sound like a lot, but it isn't when you factor in all aspects of your life, including things you have always wanted to learn about or do but never had the time.

Feel free to list your answers here or on a separate sheet of paper.

    1. _____

    2. _____

    3. _____

    4. _____

    5. _____

    6. _____

    7. _____

    8. _____

    9. _____

    10. _____

14

Hour 15

Finding Things Online

With millions of Web pages and more than 10,000 newsgroups out there, it is a wonder anyone finds anything at all! Sure there is something for everyone, but finding that "something" can take a whole lot of time and energy unless you know where and how to look.

In this hour, I will show you how to find just about anything on the Internet, answering the following questions:

- What are search engines?
- When should I consider using a subject index instead of a search engine?
- Are there any tips you can provide for the types of words and phrases I should use in a search?
- What exactly can I search on the Internet—just Web sites?

Where's the Good Stuff?

You can uncover the good stuff on your travels through the Information Superhighway in a number of ways. Some of the most common include but are not limited to the following:

- **Start Here.** From the Microsoft Internet Start page (or from whatever page you are currently browsing), you click your way through a maze of links that take you to some great hidden information.

- **Follow that sign!** Some of the more frequently visited sites on the Net sell advertising in the form of colorful, rectangular banner advertisements. These ads often feature "come-on" lines to get you to click on the rectangle and be transported to their site. Occasionally, the click is worth your while, but you never know until you try.

- **A friend of a friend of a friend....** A buddy of yours may surf onto a really cool site and give you its address to check out. This can be one of the best sources of good information. This method can also be extended to include the reference of Web sites in a newsgroup you trust.

- **I saw it on the tube.** With the increasing number of corporations and organizations online, you often see references to Web page addresses on the television news and commercials, as well as in a variety of printed media. Although that's by no means a testament to its quality, you can often access a wealth of information about a favorite product this way.

- **The old guessing game.** Say, for instance, you are interested in buying a new Toyota 4-Runner but you want to learn more about its specs. Rather than query a search engine for Toyota 4-Runner, you may decide to guess its URL and type www.toyota.com into Internet Explorer's Address Bar. You will be surprised how often the old guessing game actually works!

- **From Web sites you can trust.** If you are into auto racing, you would probably put more confidence in a site recommended by perhaps NASCAR itself than by one listed on Billy Bob's Racin' Archives. It's not to say that sites listed at Billy Bob's are bad, but it is human nature to place more confidence in a known entity.

- **Subject indexes.** Sometimes you are just in the mood to surf on a certain subject matter. One of the best ways to start such an adventure is to use a subject index. We will discuss these more thoroughly later in the hour.

- **Searching for clues.** A well-thought out search using an appropriate search engine can be incredibly fruitful when it comes to honing in on something very specific. We will cover search engines in great detail later in the hour.

Many of the methods described above are pretty self-explanatory, but the last two, subject indices and search engines, are worth exploring in detail. They may seem like simple concepts on the surface, but there are some subtleties that can help maximize your results while minimizing your expenditure of time.

Staying On-Topic: The Value of Subject Indices

Have you ever finished a tasty meal with the feeling you would love to have something sweet, only you weren't sure what you wanted? Experiencing the Internet can be kind of the same way. Your pulse quickens as the modem crackles into activity. You check your e-mail and then set out to do some free surfing (that is, non–task-oriented surfing).

You have been thinking about getting a new puppy, but aren't sure what kind. You have heard great things about Golden Retrievers, but aren't sure you want a dog that big. This sort of unfocused wandering is a perfect candidate for using a subject index.

What Is a Subject Index?

A subject index is basically a site that sorts Web sites into a variety of broad subject areas like entertainment, sports, computers, shopping, and so on. Those primary subject areas are then sorted into smaller subject areas. For instance, sports may be broken down into categories like basketball, water sports, gymnastics, and motor sports. Finally, motor sports may contain categories like NASCAR, drag racing, and so on (see Figure 15.1 for a diagram).

FIGURE 15.1

Subject indices are organized in a hierarchical manner, making it relatively simple to find what you are looking for.

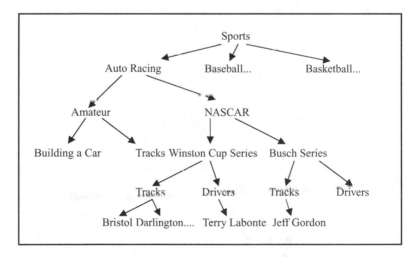

This structure makes it easy for you to find topics of general interest, while making it convenient to drill down to more specific material as you desire.

Since humans most commonly generate subject indices, you often stand a better chance of finding good content faster. Why? Because information goes where it should be placed, not where some mathematical formula says it should go. (This will make more sense as you read about search engines and how they work.)

The premiere subject index, Yahoo!, started the subject index rage and even spawned books and magazines dedicated to Web surfing. To follow in Yahoo!'s successful foot-steps, many search engines have created their own subject indices in addition to their searching capabilities. These subject indices usually contain links to sources positively reviewed by the host site's personnel and in some cases are based on surveys completed by the users.

There must be some misunderstanding. Please don't misunderstand what I'm saying here about Yahoo!. Although it was primarily a subject index in its infancy, it has evolved to so much more today—a rich tool for searching the newswires and other valuable sources of information.

Where Are Subject Indices?

Check these sites when you want to go surfing but aren't exactly sure what you are look-ing for. You will find gobs of good sites each time you log on no, matter what you are in the mood for!

- Yahoo! (http://www.yahoo.com)
- Nerdworld (http://www.nerdworld.com)
- About.com at (http://www.about.com)
- Excite Channels at (http://www.excite.com)
- GoTo.com (http://www.goto.com)
- Lycos (http://wwwlycos.com)

Drilling Down Through Yahoo!'s Subject Index

Point your Web browser to http://www.yahoo.com and follow these steps to see just how simple it is to hone in on very specific information using a subject index:

1. Click Recreation and Sports.
2. Choose Hobbies.
3. Click Collecting.
4. Choose Toys. (Did you notice airsickness bags and aluminum foil balls on the list of choices? Some people....)

5. Pick Stuffed Toys.

6. Select Beanie Babies.

See how quickly you were able to find something very specific? And best of all, you didn't have to plow through tens of thousands of links like you would with a search engine.

The Least You Need to Know About Search Engines

The term *search engine* may conjure up images of squeaky, dusty old machinery lurching into action in some isolated warehouse, but in reality, they are simple to use and quite innovative.

Search engines are tools you can use to search Web pages, newsgroups, and other things. They follow every link they can find, indexing every word along the way. This is what makes them so valuable. With a well-placed query, you can snatch an illusive piece of information in a heartbeat. Several types of search engines are discussed in the following sections.

Just the Basics

Calling these search engines basic is a bit of an understatement. They can often search the Web, newsgroups, sound files, and even the newswires in some cases. What's more, you can usually report the results in a variety of formats depending on your specific needs. Structured queries are getting easier to submit by the day with drop-down boxes, which enable you to determine whether the search should be run on the words you type as a phrase only, on one word or the other, on both words in the same document, and so on.

> **Search engines with a brain? Believe it!** It's true; many search engines actually have built-in intelligence now. For example, if you search on "Vikings" during football season, matches relevant to the Minnesota Vikings football team will surface to the top. At any other time of the year, you may find more about the Norwegian Vikings. Pretty neat, but the success rate with these can vary widely.

Since the ways that search engines accept data can vary, I strongly urge you to read their individual search instructions. The time you spend doing that will pay for itself many times over.

15

You are not out of your league. Many search engines offer advanced search options. In the vast majority of cases, it only means you can specify more fields to which the search can comply. The bottom line is that if you are looking for something very specific, advanced search options may single-handedly save you from having to weed through hundreds of useless, unrelated Web sites. Go for it!

So where can you find some of these robust search engines? Check some of these out:

- **Google (`http://www.google.com`).** According to the Search Engine Showdown (`http://searchengineshowdown.com`), Google has indexed a whopping 625 million Web pages that it will search for you with amazing speed. This makes it currently the largest search engine available.

- **FAST Web Search (`http://www.alltheweb.com`).** This search engine claims to be the largest, but according to Showdown, it comes in just behind it with 539 pages included in its database. Still, that's not bad by a long shot!

- **MSN Search (`http://search.msn.com`).** MSN Search's claim to fame is that it will not return links to adult content. For example, entering the word "sex" will return zero links. You are, however, presented with a link to a specialized adult content search engine. (However, I won't divulge what it is here.)

- **Altavista (`http://www.altavista.com`).** With an estimated 423 million sites indexed, this engine is no slouch either. Altavista has some Advanced search options you will also want to explore, such as an option to search on pages from a specified country only.

- **Northern Light (`http://www.northernlight.com`).** This highly rated search engine also boasts access to special collections of full-length articles (for a fee) from a variety of credible sources.

- **Lycos (`http://www.lycos.com`).** One of the earliest search engines, this site houses all kinds of fun stuff to browse. Be sure to check out their Advanced Search Options and Parental Controls for expanded search capabilities.

This list is by no means exhaustive, but it's more than enough to give you a taste of the individual search engines on the Internet.

When a Half Billion Pages Just Isn't Enough, Try a Meta-Search

If you want to kill several birds with one stone, you may want to consider using a meta-search engine. These powerful beasts can search and return results from multiple search engines at the same time. That's right; you need to enter only one query! Of course, you lose some of the functionality found in some search engines' advanced features, so there are trade-offs.

In some cases you can select which search engines are part of the meta-search, whereas others operate with a set of defaults. Typically, the meta-search engine grinds through each search engine until a certain amount of time elapses. It may get through all of the search engines, or it may barely make it through one. A lot depends on how much time the meta-search gives itself and how bogged down the Net is at the time of your search.

The way these meta-search engines return results varies widely, so I have provided information on a few of the more common meta-search sites.

- **Debriefing (`http://www.debriefing.com`).** This engine searches AOL, HotBot, Excite, Altavista, MSN, Fast Web Search, and Yahoo! For starters, Debriefing's results are ranked in order of how many times a page appeared on search engine top ten results lists. For example, if you searched Debriefing for calico cats, the results displayed would reflect the links that most often appeared on various search engines' top ten lists. The more search engines rank a site in their top ten list, the higher it is placed in the Debriefing results list. You can increase or decrease the amount of time Debriefing gives itself to perform the search using the Advanced options.

- **DigiSearch (`http://www.digiway.com/digisearch`).** Pick any of the 18 search engines available in which to perform your search. You can also specify how much time is spent on the search. Although the results from each search engine are presented separately, DigiSearch does give you the ability to search newsgroups and assorted directories.

- **Dogpile (`http://www.dogpile.com`).** Dogpile does produce, well, a pile of results. Unlike the others, however, it gives you the ability to search the newswires—the very thing that got me started on this tool in the first place. Although the results seem to be achieved quickly, they are not combined, which means the same link could easily come up under each engine.

Again, this is just a small sampling of what is available out there. If used to their fullest potential, meta-searches can be an invaluable tool!

Searching for a Search Engine

Have you ever had a boss who was so into meetings, he or she would plan a meeting to plan another meeting? Well, the concept of searching for a search engine must appear nearly as ridiculous!

However, with new, more specialized search engines appearing on the scene daily, the ability to search for a search engine is not so off-base. A great place to start is C|Net's site (`http://www.search.com`). This well-organized site is your gateway to more than 800 search engines, ranging from the old standards like Excite to recipe databases.

Tips for Refining Your Search Criteria

Search engines are awesome tools, but if not used wisely, they can be tremendously overwhelming. Knowing how much information to include and how best to include it can go a long way toward helping you find what you really want quickly and efficiently.

Some of these points may seem like common sense as you read them now, but trust me, they aren't necessarily the first things that pop into your head when you need to find information quickly.

- Place as many appropriate words as you can think of in the search field. The more focused you make the search, the less work you will have weeding out the results. For example, if you typed "gymnastics club" into the search field, you would get hundreds or even thousands of links from a variety of clubs across the country. If, on the other hand, you use the words "Wheaton, Maryland Gymnastics Club," you are more likely to locate the specific gym you wanted.

- In searches with multiple words, be sure to define the following: if the words should be treated as an exact phrase, if both words must just exist in the same document, or if a page with one or the other word alone is acceptable. Try to come up with exact phrase searches whenever possible. These seem to provide the most relevant results with minimal sifting through inappropriate links needed. Most search engines ask you to place phrase searches in double quotes ("[phrase]") if they don't provide a drop-down box enabling you to select such an option.

- One of my favorite tips is combining strategies. For example, suppose you are trying to find out if a local bookstore is on the Web. First, you may want to perform an exact phrase search on the word *bookstore*. Don't panic; you will get more results than you can imagine! Now place a check in a "Search these pages only" check box. You will find this on most of the major search engines these days. Now change the search parameters from "Exact phrase" to "All words" and type in the city and state. Fire off the search. Within a few seconds, you will have a manageable list of results that should meet your criteria.

> **Look before you leap.** Before going through this multistep process, be sure to explore the advanced search capabilities of the engine you plan to work with. They may just have a way to tag each word with an "and" or "or." I have seen some implementations of this, however, that are far harder to use than the two-step method I described above. I just wanted you to know you have options!

15

- Choose your weapon wisely. If you are searching for something exotic, the more Web pages you can search, the better. On the other hand, you may do better searching for something exotic on one of the many focused search engines. For instance, searching for a Bourbon Chicken recipe on HotBot could take an eternity, but performing the same search on Search.com's team of 13 recipe search engines will provide accurate results in a heartbeat.

- If your search isn't real focused, you may want to consider browsing a subject index. As you scan the available topics, something may jump out at you and grab your attention.

- You can find a lot of timely information on the Net, but it may mean turning to newswire and newsgroup searches. Why? Because the freshness of data found on Web search engines is variable at best. The data can range from being a day old to a month or more, which does you absolutely no good when you need to learn about a current event or recent development.

- Try different mainstream search engines to get a feel for their styles, biases, reporting capabilities, and ease of use. Just because the biggies all have indexed more than a half billion documents doesn't mean they will return identical results. You will eventually grow to rely on one engine for a certain type of search and on others for different circumstances. It does take some time to determine which works best for which topic.

With all these tips on hand, you should have everything you need to conduct a fruitful search for information on the Web's search engines.

Conducting Product Research Online

Are you in the market for a camcorder? How about a refrigerator or new car? Maybe you want to find out just how good that hot new video game is. The Internet can help you with all that and more.

By doing a little research, you can help ensure that your purchase is not only the best one for you, but that you get the highest quality for the least amount of money. Who doesn't love a good bargain, right?

Which One Is Best for Me?

You often approach a major purchase with a firm idea of what you want. Maybe your buddy loves his Dodge Durango, so you have decided that's the way to go for your next car. Maybe all the magazines say a certain model of digital camera is the only way to go. It's great when you have leads like that to begin your search, but what if you are starting from scratch and are open to all kinds of possibilities?

Lurking all over the Web are tools called *decision guides*. They ask you a series of questions and, based on your answers, return a list of suggestions.

Guidance Abounds Here!

Whether you are looking for guidance in finding a food processor, a family pet, a laser printer, or cheese, you will love browsing the Active Buyers Guides (`http://www.activebuyersguides.com`).

Pointers for selecting air purifiers, teas, beer, mixed drinks, national park vacations, and DVD players are just a few of the decision guides represented here.

Considering a Home Theater?

Okay, so you need to replace that puny 20-inch color television. Should you look into digital TV? Will a projection TV work in your environment? Homestore.com offers plenty of Home Theater help at
`http://www.homestore.com/HomeTech/Living/Decision`.

In addition to providing help in selecting a TV, it will help you decide between satellite and cable, if you are ready to invest in digital TV, or whether building a home theater is right for you.

Need New Wheels?

Trying to figure out what car would suit you best, given your family size and driving habits? Perhaps the folks at Kelly Blue Book (http://www.kbb.com) can help.

In their Tools*Tips*Advice section, you will see a link to their decision guides. You can search by criteria to have the decision guide provide selections based on current models, or you can perform a side-by-side comparison of new versus used models.

What Do Others Think?

Once you have settled on a specific model, it's wise to dig a bit deeper and see what others have to say about it. One way is to browse relevant newsgroups to see what people are saying. Are a lot of people who use a certain brand of computer complaining about overheating and system failures? Are certain models frequently recommended to newbies hanging out on the group?

That method, although extremely useful, can take a fair amount of time to produce results. If time is of the essence, consider browsing some product reviews. Table 15.1 gives you some leads to the more useful ones you will find on the Net.

Table 15.1 Sites for Online Product Reviews

Item	Place	Web Address
Books	Amazon	`http://www.amazon.com`
Books	Barnes & Noble	`http://www.barnesandnoble.com`
Computer games	GameSpot	`http://www.gamespot.com`
Computer goods	ClNet	`http://cnet.com`
General	Consumer Reports	`http://www.consumerreports.com`
General	Consumer Review	`http://www.consumerreview.com`
General	Consumer Search	`http://www.consumersearch.com`
General	Epinions	`http://www.epinions.com`
General	RateItAll	`http://www.rateitall.com`
Video games	VideoGames	`http://www.videogames.com`

Prices That Can't Be Beat

Now that you have decided what you want, it's time to find it for the best price possible. I think I could be a multimillionaire and still love a good bargain!

One of the cool things about researching a purchase online is that you can compare prices at hundreds of outlets without wearing out your shoes, burning up gas, and dealing with shopping mall frustrations.

Table 15.2 lists some of the places you can visit to do a bit of comparison shopping. (However, make sure you factor in shipping charges as you shop.) Now, onto the goodies you have been waiting for....

15

Table 15.2 Sites for Online Comparison Shopping

Item	Place	Web Address
Auctions (online)	AuctionWatch	http://www.auctionwatch.com
Automobiles (new)	CarsDirect	http://www.carsdirect.com
Automobiles (new and used)	Cars	http://www.cars.com
Books	AllBookstores	http://www.allbookstores.com
Computer gear	PriceWatch	http://www.pricewatch.com
General	DealTime	http://www.dealtime.com
General	MySimon	http://www.mysimon.com
General	PriceGrabber	http://www.pricegrabber.com
Vitamins/prescription medications	DestinationRX	http://www.destinationrx.com

The tools in Table 15.2 help you compare prices for online merchants, but what if you want (or need) to buy locally? Check out SalesHound (http://www.SalesHound.com). You can search local sale prices online to help you get the best deal in a hurry.

Facts by the Fistful

Whew, talk about information overload! Want to skim through the *CIA World Factbook,* the *Guinness Book of Records,* or the *Information, Please Almanac*? Need to track down a phone number, e-mail address, or ZIP code? Want to surf over to an online magazine or newspaper? Are you hoping to do some research for a report you need to write?

Just about every credible online source you can think of can be found by visiting Refdesk (http://www.refdesk.com). Dictionaries, *Roget's Thesaurus, Bartlett's Book of Quotations*…the list is endless! You will even find links to oodles of phone books and e-mail directories to help you track down that long lost roommate from college.

I have been following this site for years, and it just keeps getting better. Plenty of material is here—so much that you can easily find yourself sidetracked when paying a visit. You will just have to build in some extra time for leisure surfing!

Summary

The Internet is an amazing source of information. From tracking down that old college roommate to getting caught up on the latest news from your hometown, it's all available to you on the Internet!

The tools of your research trade include a host of subject indices and general purpose search engines. In addition, you will find some hybrid tools, including meta-search engines, all-in-one search pages, and pages upon pages of specialized search engines.

I also introduced you to some wonderful research and comparison shopping sites. Why, this lesson alone could pay for the book!

In the next hour, we are going to explore the world of sending and receiving e-mail using Outlook Express.

Workshop

Now it's time to see just how much you learned in this lesson. I'll give you a short multiple-choice quiz to test what you learned, followed by a suggested activity designed to enhance the skills you acquired during the hour.

Quiz

Select the best answer to the questions from the choices provided and then check your answers.

Questions

1. When would a search with a subject index come in handy?

    a. When you are looking for general information, but have nothing overly specific in mind

    b. When you are looking for information on a subject you would study at school like English, math, science, and so on

    c. When you can't find the information you want anywhere else

2. Which of the following is considered a meta-search engine?

    a. Yahoo!

    b. Switchboard

    c. Dogpile

3. Which of the following tools will help you find the best prices online?

    a. DealTime

    b. Bucks and Bytes

    c. Dealirious

Answers

1. A is the correct answer. Subject indices are a wonderful place to begin unfocused quests for information because you can begin with a broad topic and drill your way down to something more specific.

2. C, Dogpile, is the meta-search engine since it allows you to search multiple search engines with a single query. Yahoo! is a searchable subject index, and Switchboard is one of the many sites that can help you find people.

3. A is right, although all the information you will find online could easily make you "dealirious"!

Activity

For a fun experiment, go to `http://www.dogpile.com`. Perform a Web search on your full name (e.g., Jill Freeze). See anything interesting? Are different items returned in each search engine? Did your name draw a blank? If you have an unusual name, your search may not have generated any results. You are not off the hook. Try the assignment inserting someone else's name instead (e.g., a spouse, friend, child, or business).

HOUR 16

Sending and
Receiving E-mail

Once you use e-mail, you won't be able to imagine living without it. It is
quick; there is no waiting for a letter to get from one coast to another, and it
only takes minutes instead of days! It is also convenient; you can interact
with the person on the other when the timing works for you. Finally, it is
cheap; in most cases, you can send as many e-mails as you want for one regular monthly rate. Try doing that with a standard telephone!

In this lesson, you will learn the basics of sending and receiving e-mail with
Outlook Express, Microsoft's free e-mail program. More specifically, we
will look at the following:

- How do I send or receive an e-mail attachment?
- What does that red exclamation point to the left of a message header
  mean?
- How do I add people's information to my Contacts List?
- Can I make my messages fancy?

The Anatomy of the Outlook Express Workspace

The first step in getting to know an application is to familiarize yourself with its workspace. What are the various screen elements called? What kinds of things will you see there? These are all critical bits of information you will need to make the most of this book, along with Microsoft's Help files.

Figure 16.1 illustrates a sample Outlook Express 6 screen. I have included callouts to assist in identifying vital elements.

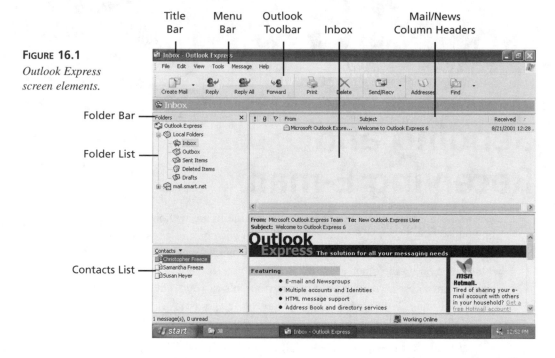

FIGURE 16.1
Outlook Express screen elements.

The title bar, menu bar, and Outlook toolbar (or button bar) are nearly identical to ones you will find in other Windows applications. The title bar presents the name of the application, along with the currently selected element, and the menu and button bars are tweaked slightly to include functions needed for Outlook Express's messaging capabilities. Table 16.1 describes elements unique to Outlook Express and how they function.

Now that you have your bearings, let's zoom in on the toolbar buttons you will use in Outlook Express (see Figure 16.2).

Table 16.1 Unique Outlook Express Elements

Element	Function
Folder Bar	Displays the name of the currently selected folder
Folder List	Holds the folders you have defined in Outlook Express, including ones for your mail and news server
Inbox	Lists all messages contained in the currently selected folder
Contacts List	If you have a small list of contacts like I do, then you can see nearly every entry in the contacts list pane
Mail/News Column Headers	Labels each of the displayed elements in the currently selected folder

FIGURE 16.2

Use the Outlook Express toolbar to get the job done quickly.

They are, from left to right, as follows:

- **Create Mail.** Press this button to start composing a new e-mail message or to post an article in a newsgroup.

- **New Message Drop-down Arrow.** Click this button to compose a new message with one of the pieces of stationery supplied with Outlook Express.

- **Reply.** By pressing this button with a message selected or displayed, you send a reply to that message to the author only, not everyone else who may have received the message.

- **Reply All.** Use this button with the desired message displayed or selected to respond to everyone who originally received the message.

> **You never know who may be listening.** Use extreme caution when pressing Reply All. E-mail addresses may often contain few clues indicating who is actually going to receive a message. For example, your boss's personal e-mail address, unbeknownst to you, may be something like CelticFan@JustPC.com. You wouldn't want anything incriminating to get into his or her hands, so unless you are absolutely sure who will be reading the message, I would suggest you stick with the Reply button.

- **Forward.** Want to share an e-mail message with someone else? Select it and then press the Forward Message button.

- **Print.** Click this button to send a copy of the currently selected message to your default printer.

- **Delete.** Use this button to delete the currently selected message. Note that the message will just be crossed out and tagged until you deliberately purge it if you have an IMAP mail server.

- **Send and Receive.** This button opens up a status window that reports the status of tasks currently being handled by Outlook Express. It also reports any errors it encounters.

- **Addresses.** Press the Addresses button if you want to look up, add, or edit a contact in your Address Book.

- **Find.** Clicking this button opens a dialog box from which you can search for an e-mail message on your computer.

- **Find Drop-down Arrow.** Not only can you search for messages from the resulting menu, but you can also look for people in your Contacts List and find text in the current e-mail message.

As you can imagine, there are countless ways to go about doing things in Outlook Express. For example, you can begin composing a new message using any of about a dozen methods ranging from accessing the menu item to double-clicking the chosen recipient's contact icon in the contacts pane.

Throughout this lesson, I will present just one way to complete a given task—that is, the way that I believe to be the simplest and most intuitive. That doesn't mean it is the only way (or even the best way), by any means. (We all have different learning styles and preferences, after all.)

Look at it this way: the less time I spend presenting multiple ways to accomplish a task, the more goodies I can cram into the 400 pages I'm allowed!

Composing an E-Mail Message

In order for your e-mail message to reach its destination, you will need to have the recipient's e-mail address. This address is commonly expressed as `username@adomain.com`. Any address not conforming to the proper format will result in the message being returned to the sender.

NEW TERM | **Domain**. This is the name given to a site that is an officially registered provider of information on the Internet. Domain names are usually made up of two or more elements separated by periods. Some examples are `www.msn.com`, `www.umass.edu`, or `www.justpc.com`.

Sending a Message to One Recipient

To send a message to another person on the Internet, follow these simple steps:

1. With Outlook Express running, press the Create Mail button. A New Message window like the one shown in Figure 16.3 appears.

FIGURE 16.3

The New Message screen is where it all begins, whether you are sending a note to one person or many people.

16

2. The insertion point blinks in the To: field, prompting you to enter the desired e-mail address. Type in the address, verifying that it conforms to the standard e-mail address format.

3. Next, click the Subject: line area and enter a descriptive title for the message.

> **Not to change the subject or anything, but....** Try to make the subject lines of your messages as succinct as possible while making sure the true essence of the message is spelled out. How can you tell if you have accomplished this? Ask yourself the following: Will the recipient be able to assess the urgency of the contents based on the subject line? Will he or she likely know to what you are referring in the subject line? An affirmative answer to either of these means you are off to a good start!

4. Click inside the main pane of the New Message window, which is where you will write the body of your message.

5. When you have finished typing your message, press the Send button to send it on its way.

> **How fast is fast?** If you don't believe e-mail is a fast method of communica-
> tion, try the following little experiment. Compose a new message and place
> the following address in the To: line: Netwriter@JustPC.com. Type "Basics
> 3 Test" in the Subject line and then press Send. Wait a few seconds and then
> press the F5 key to refresh your Inbox. You should see a response almost
> instantly from the Netwriter autoreply that I have set up (barring a major
> Internet traffic jam).
>
> Can you believe it? A message traveled to my mail server in Maryland and
> back to you that quickly. I don't care if you live across the street or halfway
> around the globe; that's pretty amazing!

Sending a Message to Multiple Recipients

You can send a message to multiple people in a variety of ways, and each method means
something slightly different.

You can include multiple e-mail addresses in the To: line; just separate them with a
comma (,) or semicolon (;). This method is best used in instances where every addressee
is a targeted recipient of the message. For example, if you manage a group of people,
you may want to notify all of them when you will be out of the office on vacation. In this
case, each person is the intended recipient of the message.

You may also use the CC: line for multiple recipients. This differs from the method
described above in that addressees defined on the CC: line are not expected to take action
on the message. If, for example, you need to send an important note to a client, you may
want to send your boss a copy of the note for his records. This is the perfect time to use
the CC: line. You can also include multiple addresses on the CC: line simply by separat-
ing them with a comma or semicolon.

Finally, the BCC: (blind carbon copy) line makes addresses in this line invisible to the
primary recipient of the message. You may want to use BCC: when e-mailing a staff
member about a potential disciplinary action so that your boss has a copy for her information. This may help you down the road if the situation turns ugly.

Creating the Message Body

You may think there is little more to composing a message than just plain typing, but you
are only half right. Yes, it can be that simple, but you can do so much more with formatting messages in Outlook Express. You can generate a bulleted list, use flashy stationery,
or add a unique signature.

It all begins with Outlook Express's counterpart to the standard toolbar (see Figure 16.4). If you have used any other Microsoft applications (see our crash course on Microsoft Word and Excel earlier in the book), you will undoubtedly recognize some of the buttons and their functions. You should note that you may need to enlarge the window to full screen size in order to see all of the buttons. The buttons are as follows from left to right:

FIGURE 16.4

These buttons handle your basic message manipulation.

16

- **Send**. Press this button when you have finished writing your message to send it on its way.
- **Cut**. Want to move a block of text somewhere else in your message? Just select it by using your mouse and then pressing the Cut button. The text will disappear and be held in a virtual clipboard until you paste it in the desired location.
- **Copy**. Select text you want to have repeated elsewhere in the message or in another message and then press the Copy button. The text will remain in its original location, as well as in the clipboard, for later use.
- **Paste**. Use this button to place text stored in your clipboard in the desired position.
- **Undo**. If you need to undo the last formatting change you made, use this button. It also works for deleting text but is slower than using other methods like the Backspace button, the Delete button, or highlighting the desired text and press Delete.
- **Check Names**. Can you only remember part of an e-mail address? After you have typed in the portion you know, press the Check Names button. Outlook Express will search your Address Book for a match. If it finds more than one, it will list them all so you can pick the one you want.
- **Spelling.** This handy tool will help keep misspelled words out of your e-mail for good.
- **Attach File**. Click here to begin the process of attaching a file to your e-mail message.
- **Set Priority**. If you need to draw attention to a message, this is the way to do it. Press this button to cycle through your options, which include Normal (default), High, and Low priority (see Figure 16.5).
- **Set Priority Drop-down Arrow**. You may also set a message's priority by clicking on the Set Priority Arrow and dragging the mouse pointer to the desired priority level.

FIGURE 16.5

The icon shown here tells you at what priority level the current message is set.

This icon signifies —
urgency.

- **Digital Signature**. This button lets you associate a digital signature with your message so the person at the other end can verify that it is from you.

- **Encrypt Message**. Press this button to scramble outgoing messages as an extra safety precaution.

- **Offline.** Clicking this button lets you compose messages without being connected to the Internet. You can prepare them offline and send them later when you are able to be online.

The toolbar immediately above the composition window gives you all kinds of tools to help you format your message and make it look nice. Since you were brought up-to-speed on word processing formatting earlier in the book, we will skip it in this lesson because Outlook Express behaves just like Word and Excel in that regard. Rest assured that the normal suspects are present, such as bolding, underlining, indenting, and font color.

All e-mail programs are not created equal. Just because you put color in your message doesn't mean the person receiving it will be able to see it. If the recipient is using Outlook Express or another HTML-compliant e-mail client, then all should be well. If her program isn't HTML compliant (meaning it cannot read text like a Web page would produce), the text may simply take on its normal black appearance. If neither of you is sure how your programs will handle the situation, send a short note describing what you have done with the text, and ask the recipient to describe what she sees.

Attaching a File to Your Message

Now that your message is all ready to go, you may have an occasion to attach a file to the message. Perhaps it is a Word file with a favorite recipe or a recently scanned photo of your new home. There are countless reasons why you may want to attach a file to your message, and that is definitely an easy thing to do! Just follow these steps:

1. With the message displayed onscreen, simply click the paper clip button on the message's toolbar. You will see a dialog box nearly identical to the typical Open or Save dialog box.

2. Click your way through the directories until you see the file you want to attach.

3. When you have found the file, click it to select it and then press Attach. You will see a new line under the Subject line of your message called Attach that displays the filename and size.

Assessing What You Have in Your Inbox

After you have sent a few pieces of e-mail, you are bound to get some messages back.

When you log onto your Internet service provider (ISP)and launch Outlook Express, the mail you have received appears in the Message List box, or Inbox. Several items are displayed by default for each piece of mail (see Figure 16.6); they include the following:

FIGURE 16.6

Use this information to determine what a message is about before you open it.

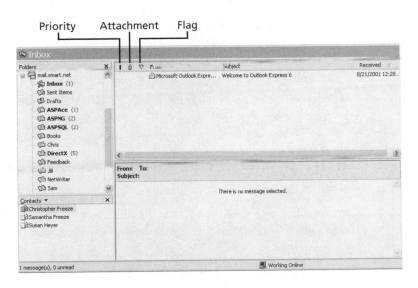

- **Priority**. The first column is the Priority column. Look here to see which messages are high and low-level priorities. If a message carries a high-priority level, a red exclamation point appears. If it is low level, a black down arrow will appear. Finally, if this column is blank, it means the message carries the normal default priority level.

- **Attachment.** This column displays a paper clip icon to tell you whether a file attachment is present in a given message.

- **Flag**. Click inside this column to flag a message for future action. A little red flag icon appears to remind you need to revisit the message.

- **From**. This column displays the name or e-mail address of the person or company sending the e-mail message.

> **Who?** Can't see the full name of a message's sender? Just run your mouse over the line in question. A screen tip—like box displaying the full content of the line appears. This trick works for long subject lines too.
>
> Or if you routinely have this problem, you can lengthen the From or Subject columns by clicking the border between the column button you want to resize and the column button to the immediate right, and then dragging the mouse to the left or right as needed.

- **Subject**. Hopefully this column provides a vivid description of the message's content so you know where to place it in your personal priority list. Of course, the subject title's accuracy relies entirely on the sender, so you will need to judge it accordingly.

- **Received**. This bit of information tells you when the given message appeared in your mailbox.

Reading a Message

Now comes the fun part—getting to read the goodies in your Inbox.

When you click on a message's header, its contents will appear in the Preview pane. (You saw the Microsoft test message in the Preview Pane back in Figure 16.7.)

If you want to work with a larger copy of the message, double-click it. When you are finished reading, click the Close button (the red X in the upper right corner of the window) to close the message window.

New messages will appear in boldface type with a closed envelope icon. After you have read a message, the envelope icon will appear to be opened.

Not impressed, huh? Try this: click on a column header like Received. All the messages will be sorted in order of receipt with the oldest first. Click it again, and Outlook Express will sort the list in the reverse order. You can sort any of the columns using this method.

Checking for New Messages

By default, Outlook Express will check for new e-mail messages every half-hour. You can ask it to refresh on demand by pressing the F5 key or the Send and Receive button, or you can adjust the time that elapses between automatic refreshes.

To adjust the time, follow these steps:

1. Click Tools and then select Options.

2. Go to the General tab and look about halfway down the list. The section of the box is called Send/Receive Messages (see Figure 16.7).

3. Next to the Check for new messages every ___ minutes option, you will see a spin box containing the number 30. Use the buttons to adjust the number up or down as desired.

FIGURE 16.7

Use the arrow buttons to define the amount of time you want to pass between checks for new e-mail.

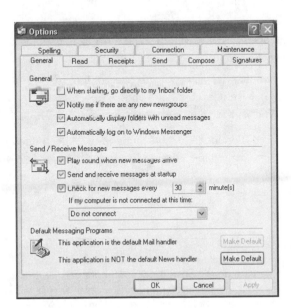

Are you sure? It is very tempting to program frequent e-mail checks. After all, no one likes to miss anything, right? Well, there is a distinct downside to frequent Inbox refreshes. First, it places an increased load on your ISP's mail server which may already be trying to service more people than it can be expected to handle. Second, the frequent checks can slow down other online activities. For instance, Web pages may load slower, Real Audio transmissions may experience static, and so on. Just give it careful thought before settling on a real low number.

4. When you are satisfied with the number, click Apply to apply the change.

5. Press OK to save the change and close the dialog box.

Reading File Attachments

When you double-click a message to read its contents, there are three ways you can tell if the message contains an attached file (actually four, if you count the obnoxiously long download times of messages with long attachments):

- If the Attach column appears on your message list display, you will see a paper clip icon on the line of messages containing an attachment.

- If a file attachment is present, a paper clip icon will appear at the top right corner of the message's preview window. You must have double-clicked the message in order to see this.

- After you double-click a message to open it, look for the Attach: line underneath the Subject line. In it, you will see an icon representing the file type of the attachment, and you will see the size of the file.

To open the attached file, double-click its icon in the Attach line of the message. Outlook Express will automatically launch the application that created the file (usually Word or an image-browsing program installed on your machine) if it is installed on your machine. If it is not, Outlook Express will give you some choices of installed applications to choose from.

Put on the brakes! If the attached file contains an .exe, .vbs, or .com file extension, do not open it until you have verified the sender of the file. Opening such a file can unleash a harmful virus if the source is not trustworthy. And even if it appears to be a Word or Excel file, it's probably a good idea to run it through a virus scan just to be safe.

Taking Action on a Message

Once you receive a message, there are a variety of actions you can take on them, ranging from deleting them to replying to them to saving them. In the following sections, you will see just how simple it is to perform each action.

Deleting a Message

As time goes on, you will get more junk mail than you know what to do with. That's why you should know every possible way to delete a message.

When you glance at your message list, you can tell right away that some items are junk mail because you won't recognize the From address, or the subject line will read something like "Make $10,000 in a week!" To delete these, all you have to do is click on the message to mark it and then press the Delete button. The message will disappear (or it may be marked for deletion for those using the more obscure IMAP mail servers).

It won't let me delete! If the messages in your Inbox are stored on your mail server, you will need to be connected to the server to process the deletions.

Mastering multiple deletions. You can save tremendous amounts of time and keystrokes by deleting multiple messages at once. To delete messages scattered throughout the message list, click each message while holding down the Ctrl key and then press Delete. To delete a group of contiguous messages, click on the top one, press the Shift key, and then click on the bottom one. All messages in between the two points should be highlighted. Press Delete to mark them all.

Then there are the messages that need further examination before you can delete them. Maybe the subject line seems intriguing, but turns out not to interest you. Maybe a Web site sends a weekly electronic newsletter that you read and then promptly delete.

In these cases, you will most likely double click the message to read it and then press the Delete button on the message's toolbar.

Uh-oh, I made a mistake! You may not be able to bring a message back once it has been purged from your system, but you can undo a deletion mark (IMAP servers only) before purging your system. Just right-click on the message you marked by accident and select Undelete from the shortcut menu.

POP3 mail servers also have one last rescue opportunity—the Deleted Items folder. By default, deleted messages will be kept there until you explicitly delete them.

Forwarding a Message

What if your brother sends you a great joke, and you want to share it with a buddy? This is the perfect time to learn how to forward a message. The procedure is so easy, in fact, it doesn't even require a lengthy step-by-step walk-through.

Double-click on the message to open it if it isn't open already. Next, press the Forward Message button. A window similar to the New Message window will appear, only this window will include the entire text of the forwarded message.

All you need to do to send the message on its way is fill in the To: line using any of the methods described in the previous hour and then press the Send button. Before pressing Send, however, feel free to enter a personal message above the forwarded message.

Protect your sources. When you forward a message, the header information of the person who sent you the message is automatically included as well. If this is an important business associate or client, you may want to delete the header information to protect their privacy.

Replying to a Message

Replying to a message works similar to forwarding a message as described above. You press either Reply or Reply All, add your message, and then press Send. Since you are responding to a message you have received, there is no need to fill in the To: line; Outlook Express does it for you.

There are some important subtleties you should understand before making use of this feature, however. Earlier, you learned how to e-mail multiple people using a variety of methods (multiple names on the To: line, CC: entries, and so on). When you reply to a note that has gone to multiple people, it is important that you realize Reply to All will send your response to everyone who received the original message, including "invisible" people on the BCC: line. As a result, you may want to get in the habit of using Reply exclusively unless you absolutely don't mind whether the entire world hears what you have to say in your response.

Saving a Message

No matter how much you try to avoid it, there may be some messages you won't have the heart to part with, especially that cute joke your nephew sent you. At work, you may find keeping a log of messages almost mandatory. IMAP mail server users, keep in mind that the messages will remain in your Inbox until you delete them, so your Inbox may become unmanageable sooner or later as a result of the sheer volume of messages. Furthermore, if you leave large numbers of messages on your mail server, you may "max out" your allocated disk space with your ISP before you even realize it, which can lead to additional fees and other expenses.

Saving a message may seem like a pretty basic task, and it is, once you have Outlook Express all set up for it. Before you can tuck those valuable messages away though, you will need to create some folders in which to store them.

Follow these steps to create a folder for saved messages, move the message to its new location, and delete it from the Inbox:

1. Find a message you want to save and think about what type of folder you would put it in if it were a physical piece of paper to be stored in a manila folder. It may be something like The Sudbeck Project, Humor, Recipes, Dissertation Notes, and so on.

2. Click on Local Folders near the top of your All Folders list pane to highlight it.

3. Click File and then choose Folder, New. The Create Folder dialog box shown in Figure 16.8 appears.

FIGURE 16.8

This is where you will name each storage container for your messages.

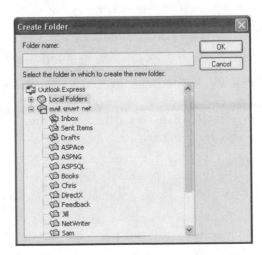

16

4. Enter the name of the new folder and then press OK. The new folder appears in alphabetical order in the Folder list pane.

5. Next, click on the message you want to move to the new folder and hold the mouse button down while dragging the message to its new location.

6. Once there, release the mouse button to drop the message into the folder. Outlook Express will automatically delete (or mark the message as deleted for IMAP users) in your Inbox.

7. Repeat the steps above as many times as needed until your filing system is all set up.

8. Attention IMAP users: when you are finished moving everything, remember to clean up your Inbox by clicking Edit and selecting Purge deleted messages.

Once you have created all of the folders you need, saving messages will be a snap. Just click and drag (or drag and drop) the message to its new location.

Adding Information to Your Address Book

What good is having a versatile tool like the address book when it doesn't hold any information? Exactly! So grab all those scraps of paper and business cards and head over to the computer.

> **Let me get that for you....** By default, Outlook Express puts the e-mail address of anyone you reply into your Contact List. You can go in later and add his or her full name, home address, and other information of interest.

To begin filling your book with all kinds of useful tidbits, follow these steps:

1. With Outlook Express up and running, press the Addresses button on the Standard Toolbar. A window displaying a list of previously defined contacts appears. If this is the first time you pressed the Address Book button (or you have never sent a reply to anyone via e-mail), the fields may be empty.

2. Press the New button at the top of the page and select New Contact. A window like the one shown in Figure 16.9 appears.

   In the Name tab, you will have the opportunity to enter the following information:

   • **Name**: This includes separate fields for first, middle, and last name. The field Display is for the name as it will appear on your Contacts List (automatically taken from the three name fields) and an optional Nickname field in which you can place the person's screen name or nickname.

FIGURE 16.9

The Name tab asks for basic information about the contact.

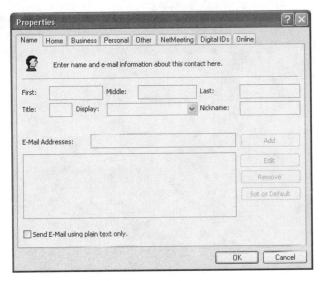

•**E-mail addresses**: Type in the contact's e-mail address and then press the Add button. This first address will automatically be declared the person's default e-mail address. You can add additional e-mail addresses by typing them in and pressing the Add button.

Ask first. Don't just assume a contact would prefer you e-mail them at work (unless of course the contact is exclusively work related). Some companies have very strict policies about personal mail passing through their system. Be sure to ask contacts with multiple e-mail addresses where they would prefer to receive mail from you.

3. Enter all known information about the contact on this first tab, including a nickname if you have one you would like to use.

4. Click on the Home tab to insert personal information about the contact, including the address of their personal home page if they have one (see Figure 16.10).

   The Home tab gives you places to insert the following information:

   - Street Address
   - City
   - State/Province
   - Zip Code
   - County

   - Phone
   - Fax
   - Cellular Phone Number
   - Personal Web Page Address

FIGURE **16.10**

The Home tab lets you keep track of a contact's home address, phone number, and so on.

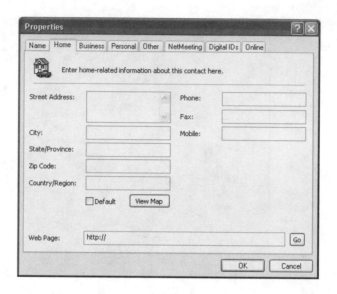

5. To enter information about the person's place of employment, click the Business tab. You will have spots to enter the person's job title, department in which he or she work, Fax number, pager number, and so on (see Figure 16.11).

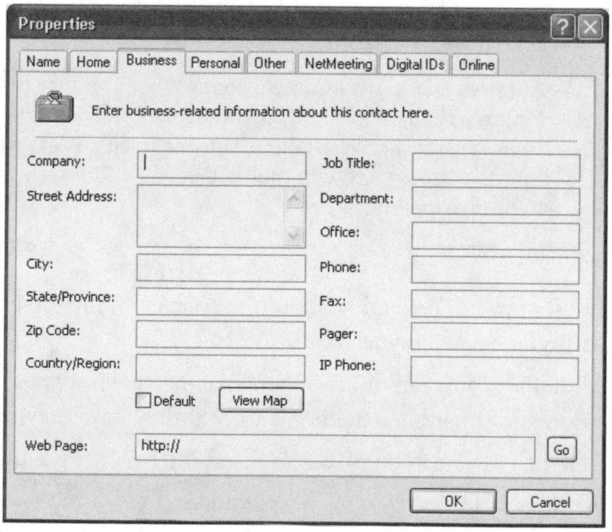

FIGURE **16.11**

The information contained in the Business tab makes it easy to find friends and family at work.

The Business tab lets you keep track of the following:

- Company
- Street Address
- City
- State/Province
- ZIP Code
- County
- Job Title

- Department
- Office
- Phone
- Fax
- Pager
- Business Web Page Address

6. Click on the Personal tab to track additional information about a contact like their birthday, spouse's/children's names, gender, and so on.

7. When you have finished entering all of the data you can find, press OK. The contact information will be saved in your Address Book. The defined name will also appear conveniently on Outlook Express's Contacts List pane.

Composing a New Message Using Address Book Information

If you hate having to memorize (let alone type) lengthy e-mail addresses, you will love using your Outlook Express Address Book. There are multiple ways to retrieve a contact's e-mail address from your Address Book when composing a new message.

To launch a new message box with a single recipient's e-mail address already included, double-click on the desired person's contact icon in the Contacts List pane. If your needs are a bit more complex, do any of the following:

- Press the Create Mail button as usual and then click on the contact icon in the To: line to launch the Select Recipients dialog box shown in Figure 16.12. If you already have the primary recipient's address in place, click the contact icon in the CC: line and proceed according to the steps that follow.

- With the New Message Window displayed, click Tools, Select Recipients from the menu bar. This opens the dialog box shown in Figure 16.12 as well. To move a contact into a certain message header section, click the person's name and then click the button corresponding to the header in which you want his/her name and address placed.

- Begin typing the person's real name in the To: line or the CC: line. Outlook Express will use AutoComplete to "guess" the desired contact's name. If the name that appears looks like it matches the one you have in mind, press Enter to accept it.

FIGURE 16.12

The Select Recipients dialog box makes it easy to put the contacts you want in the place you want them.

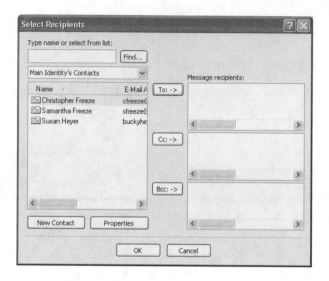

Editing a Contact's Information

People are constantly moving or changing jobs. As a result, you will want to know how to change the data contained in your Address Book. It is really quite simple, as you will see in the steps below:

1. With Outlook Express running (no Internet connection needed), press the Address Book button.

2. Use the scroll bars to move to the desired contact. If you have a huge list, you can type the person's name into the Type Name box. As you type each letter, Outlook Express will highlight the closest match.

3. Once you have found the entry you need to modify, double-click it. The familiar Properties dialog box corresponding to the selected contact will open. The first thing you'll see is a summary screen on which no changes can be made. You'll have to open the tab you need to modify before attempting to make any changes.

4. To edit an element, just click inside its text box and make the necessary changes. Don't forget to visit each of the tabs that may be affected by the change(s).

5. When all the necessary changes have been made, press OK to save them.

Variation on a theme. Changing an e-mail address is a bit more tricky. To delete it, click it to select it and then press the Remove button. To change default e-mail addresses, click the address you want to make the default and then press the Set as Default button. To add an address, type it into the text box provided and then press the Add button.

Summary

This lesson presented the basics of using e-mail in Outlook Express. You learned how to send and receive messages, as well as work with your address book

In the next hour, I'm going to show you how to use Outlook Express as a news reader.

Workshop

Now it is time to see just how much you learned in this lesson. I'll give you a short multiple-choice quiz to test what you learned, followed by a suggested activity designed to enhance the skills you acquired during the hour.

Quiz

Select the best answer to the questions from the choices provided and then check your answers.

Questions

1. What does a paperclip icon next to a message header mean?

    a. There is a virus attached to the message.

    b. The message contains important information about a discount for purchasing massive quantities of paperclips.

    c. A file is attached to the message in question.

2. What does BCC mean?

    a. Other recipients can't see that the message was sent to the address you placed in this field.

    b. Burn the Carbon Copy.

    c. Uh, don't you mean CC:?

3. Does Outlook Express add e-mail addresses to your Contacts List by default?

   a. No way!

   b. Yep, but only e-mail addresses to which you send a reply to a message.

   c. Outlook Express can't do anything on its own <sigh>!

Answers

1. And the winner is…C!

2. A. It is just your little secret….

3. If you read the lesson carefully, you would know that B was the proper answer to this quiz question.

Activity

It's time to go on a scavenger hunt. Wander through your house, dig through your desk or purse, check all your pockets and junk drawers…. What are we after? Addresses, phone numbers, and e-mail addresses scrawled on bits of paper, napkins, matchbook covers, and bill envelopes of course!

Find as much of this data as you can, and get it into your address book. And plug in the birthdays while you're at it. Not only will this activity help eliminate clutter, but it'll help you locate the information you need more quickly.

Hour 17

Browsing Online Newsgroups

If you feel comfortable sending and receiving e-mail with Outlook Express, you will catch on to news reading in no time! Although the function bears a striking resemblance to using e-mail, you will want to become intimately familiar with a few concepts and special features.

In this hour, you will learn all about reading newsgroups with Outlook Express. We will address the answers to the following questions, among others:

- With tens of thousands of newsgroups out there, how in the world do I find the ones of interest to me?
- When should I reply to the author of a message as opposed to posting a response to the group?
- I see the word thread mentioned a lot on newsgroups; what does it mean?
- How do I send a copy of an interesting post to a friend?

How Do I Find the Good Stuff?

Although it's true that flashier Web-based discussion groups have garnered more attention than their text-based Usenet counterparts, there is still a lot of information available.

Since each person has a unique set of interests, our definitions of "the good stuff" often vary. Therefore, I will show you how to find groups matching your interests instead of pointing you to specific newsgroups.

With all the ways to find a good newsgroup, here are a few of the more reliable ones:

- **Word of mouth.** You seldom go wrong with newsgroups recommended to you by friends and associates. People like me who have been cruising the Information Superhighway since it was a dirt footpath tend to know which groups generate great dialog, as opposed to spam-infested groups containing endless flame wars on off-topic subjects. (How's that for a nice image?)

NEW TERM
Flame war. Generally, a flame war consists of a group of off-topic, libelous messages that attack a poster's views or even something as simple as his or her spelling errors. (Makes you glad you have got that Outlook Express spell-checker, huh?)

- **Found it on the Web.** While researching a certain subject, you may wander across a Web site proven to be a wealth of information. Sites specializing in specific topics will often point you to useful newsgroups. These are usually excellent leads to follow.

- **Search me!** Surf over to Google Groups at `http://www.groups.google.com` and perform a search on a topic of interest. The search results will reveal which groups discuss your favorite topic. Why is this potentially more useful than Outlook Express's newsgroup search function? Newsgroup discussion topics aren't always covered in the name of the newsgroup. For example, if you ask Outlook Express to find newsgroups with a specific toy or collectible in their name, you may not get any hits. A newsgroup article search on Google Groups, however, points you in the direction of a newsgroup that may discuss your item of interest.

- **Browse the list.** If you have eyes with great stamina, you may want to simply browse through the list of newsgroups available on your news server. To access this, launch Outlook Express and then click on the name of your news server. (You remember setting up the news server back in Hour 12, Connecting to the Internet, right?) A screen like the one shown in Figure 17.1 will appear, listing each newsgroup your Internet service provider (or the owner of the configured news server) subscribes to. Simply use the scroll bar to move your way through the list. And don't say I didn't warn you it'd be a lengthy proposition!

- **Search the list.** Outlook Express lets you perform a search on the list of available newsgroups. To perform one, simply enter the desired term in the Display news-groups that contain: text box. A list of newsgroups like the one shown in Figure 17.2 will be returned.

FIGURE 17.1

Use the scroll bars to browse the list to see what catches your fancy.

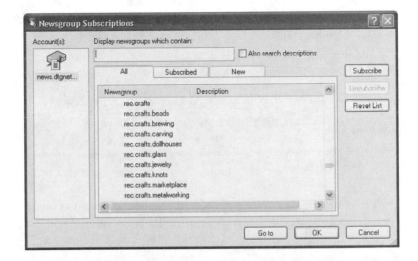

FIGURE 17.2

A newsgroup search should narrow the field of possibilities consid-erably.

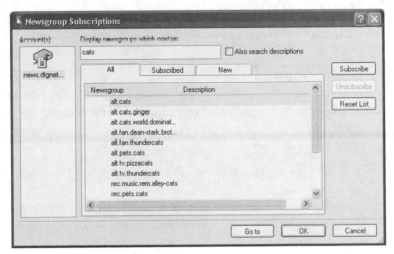

Subscribing to a Newsgroup

The simplest way to subscribe to a newsgroup depends on how you are viewing the group in question. If you are browsing through or have searched the All list, subscribing is as simple as double-clicking the group's name.

If, on the other hand, you have decided to browse through the group (click the name of the group and then click the Go To button), you will be subscribed to the group by default. Should you not like what you see, you can easily unsubscribe by right-clicking the group's name on the File List and then choosing Unsubscribe from the shortcut menu (see Figure 17.3).

FIGURE 17.3

While browsing a newsgroups, unsubscribing (or subscribing) is a mere shortcut menu away.

From that moment on, the newsgroup you just subscribed to will appear on the File List in alphabetical order under the name of the news server.

Before Jumping In...

Before you jump into a newsgroup discussion, you should do a few things. Doing these things will ensure that you have the most positive newsgroup experience possible.

First, you will want to observe the group for a while. Are the participants understanding or judgmental? What abbreviations does the group tend to use? Are there any special header codes you should use? (For example, one newsgroup dedicated to CBS soap operas asks that you use ATWT before the titles of posts relating to *As the World Turns,* BB before posts pertaining to *The Bold and the Beautiful,* and so on.)

You will also want to check out the Frequently Asked Questions (FAQs) before posting a question to make sure that the topic isn't covered there first. Some groups post FAQs periodically, whereas others host them on a Web site. Keep an eye out for a mention of them. If you don't get any leads after a week of lurking, post a request for a point in the right direction.

It is also wise to spend time observing the general tone of a group. Are they almost hyperintense about their subject, or do they seem to maintain a good sense of humor? In time, you will become a pro at sensing a newsgroup's climate.

Finally, get acquainted with the group's charter or purpose. Posting an item for sale in a group whose sole purpose is to debate modern philosophical issues is a big no-no. There are plenty of newsgroups set aside for such purposes, so it is really not worth getting chased out of a newsgroup over.

Reading a Newsgroup

You don't have to subscribe to a newsgroup in order to read it, as I demonstrated earlier. However, typically you will be subscribed to a newsgroup when you go to read it. Either way, the basic principles are the same.

1. Launch Outlook Express with a live connection to the Internet.

2. Scroll down your File List until you see the name of the newsgroup you want to read. If you cannot see the group on the list and a plus sign appears next to the name of the news server, you will need to click the plus sign to expand the folders underneath the news server.

3. Click the newsgroup's name to begin reading. By default, messages are presented in the order they were posted, with the newest being shown first. A plus sign next to the message means the message is part of a thread (ongoing topic of discussion) and that there are responses to it that you can see by clicking the plus sign (see Figure 17.4 for an example of an expanded thread).

4. To begin reading a message, all you have to do is double-click it. The article appears in a window similar to the one shown in Figure 17.5. Remember, if a plus sign appears next to a message, that means there are additional messages underneath it.

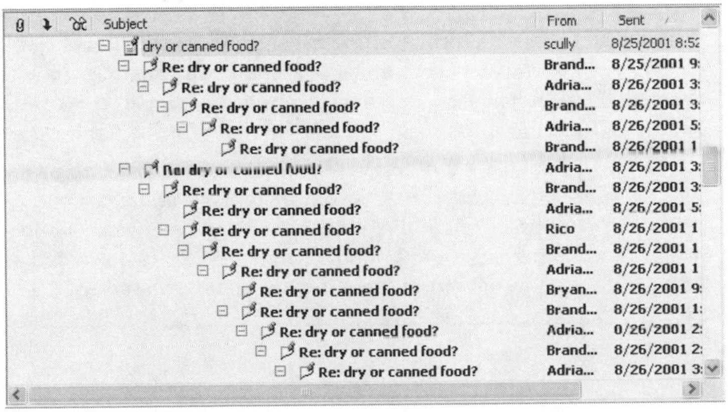

FIGURE 17.4

If you think these threads are getting complicated, you ain't seen nothin' yet!

FIGURE 17.5

The message window is totally resizable by clicking on the edges and pulling the window out.

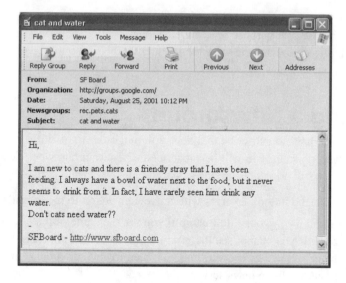

5. From within a message, there are multiple actions you may take on an article, as shown below:

- **Reply Group**. This button launches a Reply message window with the newsgroup's address already in place. Note that messages composed in this manner will be posted to the newsgroup for the entire world to see, as evidenced by the presence of the Newsgroup line item instead of the To line. You continue composing the message just as you would a regular e-mail message.

Netiquette notes. Before you respond to the group as a whole, make sure what you have to say has value or interest to more people than just the original poster of the message to whom you are responding. Posting simply "me too" or "I agree" messages are generally frowned on unless you are a noted expert on the subject. If the primary purpose of your note is to show the author your support, then opt for the Reply button instead.

Also, be sure to include enough of the message you are responding to so that readers have a context for your remarks. Otherwise, if it isn't relevant, edit it out in the interest of saving bandwidth. Saving bandwidth basically decreases the amount of time needed to download a message and conserves the amount of space it takes up on mail servers.

- **Reply.** Pressing this button routes your message directly to the author of the post to which you are responding. In fact, Outlook Express even inserts the author's e-mail address and the subject line he or she used, prefixed with a RE: for you. This is the best way to relate a relevant personal experience, show your support, or share an off-the-wall fact that may not be of general interest.

- **Forward**. If you want to send a newsgroup article to a friend or colleague via e-mail, or even send a copy to yourself for safe keeping, press the Forward button, type in the person's e-mail address (or double-click the To: icon to use an entry from your Address Book), add any notes you want to include, and then press Send.

- **Print.** Press this button to send the message to your default printer. Outlook Express will use its default print settings, which should be fine in the majority of cases. However, if you want to have more control over your output, you will want to click File and choose Print to access the Print dialog box.

- **Previous**. Press this button to view the message that came before the one currently being displayed.

- **Next**. To move to the next message in the list, press this button.

- **Addresses.** Click this button to access your Outlook Express address book.

Posting Your Own Message to a Newsgroup

If, after much observation and research, you have decided to go ahead and post your question or comments to a newsgroup, follow these simple steps.

1. Click on the folder of the newsgroup to which you would like to post your message.

2. Press the New Post button on the Outlook Express toolbar. A standard New Message box opens with the name of the selected newsgroup already completed.

3. Want to cross-post to more than one newsgroup? If so, complete these steps to select additional newsgroups:

   - With the New Message window displayed, click Tools and choose Select Newsgroups, or press the Newsgroups icon in the Newsgroups line of the message. A dialog box like the one shown in Figure 17.6 appears.

   - Click on a newsgroup you would like to add to the list, and then press the Add button to place them in the list.

17

FIGURE 17.6

Adding additional newsgroups to the distribution list is a snap.

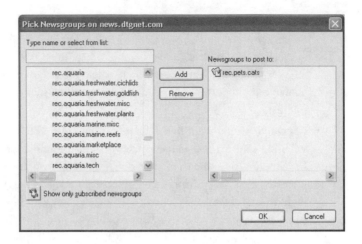

Open up a world of possibilities. By default, only the groups you are subscribed to appear in your list of choices. To view all possible groups, press the Show only subscribed newsgroups toggle button.

• When your list is complete, press the OK button. All of the groups you added to the list will be entered into the Newsgroups line.

Cross-posting caution. Use extreme caution when posting the same message to multiple newsgroups. Posting off-topic messages to lots of newsgroups at the same time is considered spamming, which can land you in a whole lot of hot water with your Internet service provider (ISP), not to mention guarantee that you will receive tons of angry e-mails. It is best to cross-post when you are sure your message is acceptable and relevant to each newsgroup's charter, and when you think each group might have a slightly different "take" on your question or comment.

4. Type in the text of your message as you would do with an e-mail message, and don't forget to check your spelling!

5. When the message meets with your approval, press the Send button. Outlook Express will display a dialog box saying that your message is about to be sent to the newsgroup server and that it may not show up immediately in your display.

6. Press OK to close the message box and continue working in Outlook Express.

Canceling an Article You Posted

Suppose that you put a collectible up for sale in one of the newsgroups that allows such posts, and you sell the item within a day. Canceling the post not only reduces the load on news servers across the Internet, but it gives people one less article to browse. It also keeps you from having to send a million, "I'm sorry, but I have already sold it" e-mails.

Before you begin, there is something else I should clarify. You can only cancel articles you have submitted and not posts from others that may be offensive or off-topic.

To recall an article you posted to a newsgroup, do the following:

1. Launch Outlook Express with a live connection to the Internet.
2. Open the newsgroup in which you posted the article by clicking its name on your Folders List.
3. Find your article and then right-click over it to open a shortcut menu.
4. Select Cancel from the menu. A message box appears to let you know the cancellation is in progress.

> **It takes time.** Please note that this will not instantly remove your article from news servers across the world; this will take some time. You should also be aware that canceling a post will not remove it from the computers that may have already downloaded it with other messages from the same newsgroup.

5. Press OK to let Outlook Express know that you agree to the terms of the cancellation.

Finding a Newsgroup Message

If you thought trying to dig up an old e-mail message was a nightmare, finding the messages that interest you the most in a newsgroup that generates hundreds of posts a day can be even more challenging. Outlook Express gives you a great way to sift through the lots of material—the Find Messages tool.

Follow these steps to locate a message in a newsgroup:

1. With Outlook Express open and connected to the Internet, click Edit and select Find, Message. The Find Messages dialog box pictured in Figure 17.7 appears.
2. Fill in the field(s) you want Outlook Express to search: From, Subject, or Body.

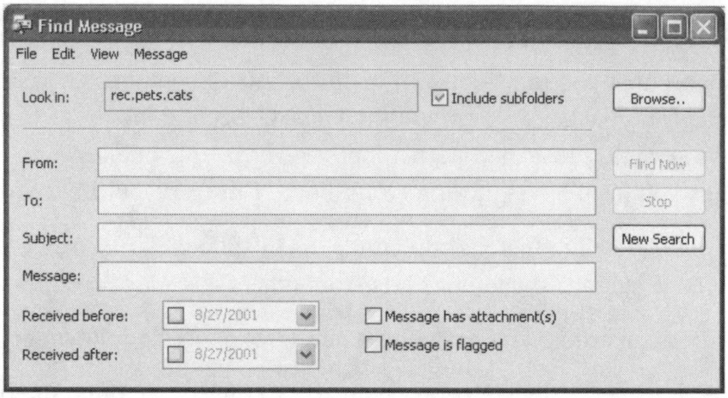

FIGURE 17.7

Fill in as many details as you can to get the most applicable posts returned.

Find Message

File   Edit   View   Message

Look in: rec.pets.cats   ☑ Include subfolders   Browse..

From: Find Now

To: Stop

Subject: New Search

Message:

Received before: ☐ 8/27/2001 ▾   ☐ Message has attachment(s)

Received after: ☐ 8/27/2001 ▾   ☐ Message is flagged

3. In the lower section of the dialog box, choose Received Before or Received After the date specified by clicking the desired check box. If you want to use a date other than the one currently displayed, press the drop-down arrow to open a calendar from which you can choose an alternate date (see Figure 17.8).

FIGURE 17.8

Double-click the date to insert it in the date box.

4. Press the Find Now button. The results will be displayed at the bottom of the Find Messages window as shown in Figure 17.9.

5. Press the Close button (the X in the upper-right corner of the window) to resume working in Outlook Express.

Viewing Replies to Your Post

If you are like most people, you want to see the replies to your posts as quickly as possible. In the past, you had to sift through the newsgroup to find it. Now there is an easier way. By simply changing your view of a newsgroup's messages, you can see replies to your posts in a heartbeat. Here's how you do it:

1. After establishing a connection to the Internet, open the newsgroup in which you posted the message by clicking its name in the file list.

2. On the View menu, select Current View and then Show Replies to my Messages.

FIGURE 17.9

You can sort the results by clicking the column headers just as you can with e-mail or general newsgroup browsing.

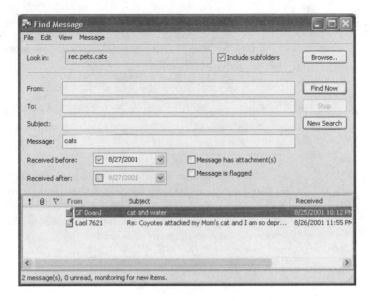

3. A message window like the one you typically see will appear, only this window will display your messages alone. Click the plus sign to view all the headers of the posts nested under yours.

4. To return to the All Messages view, go to the View menu and select Current View, Show Replies to My Messages again to restore the view to its previous state.

Conserving the Space Consumed by Newsgroup Messages

You can do a number of things to decrease how many posts you must wade through and the amount of disk space these messages take up. In the sections that follow, I will introduce you to a number of these options.

Marking Messages as Read and Viewing Only New Posts

One of the more basic ways to trim down the message list for a newsgroup involves marking messages as read and then changing the current view to reflect only new messages. This will make skimming the messages much more efficient and will undoubtedly free up disk space on your machine. Once you have gone through these steps for each newsgroup, you will be set for the long run, since you will always have fewer messages to deal with.

To mark messages as read and change the current view, follow these steps:

1. Connect to the Internet and launch Outlook Express as you would if you were going to read the newsgroups online.

2. Click the name of the first group you would like to browse.

3. Begin reading the messages of interest. Note that Outlook Express automatically marks messages previewed for five seconds or longer as read.

Tweaking the number. If you feel the five-second speed doesn't quite work for you, you can adjust it by opening the Tools menu and then selecting Options and choosing the Read tab as shown here. In the Mark message read after displaying for second(s) line, use the arrow buttons to nudge the amount of time up or down as desired.

4. When you have finished going through the entire group, open the Edit menu and select Mark All Read.

KISS. This stands for *keep it simple and save* (a variation on the old theme). If there are messages you may want to see again, save them. That way, you won't have to return to All Messages view and wind your way through thousands of messages.

5. Next, you will want to change your current view so that Outlook Express will display only unread messages. Click View and then select Current View, Hide Read or Ignored Messages. A lot fewer messages appear. In fact, the display may remain empty until you refresh it by pressing F5.

> **Restoring the view.** If you want to see all current messages again, regardless of whether they have been read, open the View menu and then select Current View, Show All Messages.

Remove Old News Messages

Outlook Express currently stores news messages up to five days old on your machine for quick retrieval. If you feel newsgroup articles are taking up far too much space on your system, you may want to reduce the number of days worth of messages that are stored locally.

To do this, open the Tools menu, select Options, and then click the Maintenance tab as shown here in Figure 17.10.

In the Delete news messages ___ days after being downloaded line, use the arrow buttons to reduce the number of days allowed.

FIGURE 17.10

The Maintenance tab is where you will specify the allowed age of news articles stored locally.

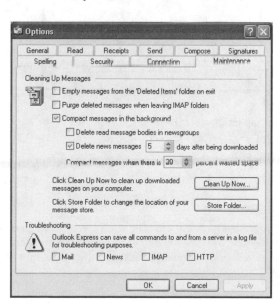

17

Compact Stored Messages

You know how trash compactors can compress the bulk of waste? Well, you can do the same with stored newsgroup messages to lessen the space they take up on your hard drive. Just follow these simple steps to optimize newsgroup message storage:

1. Find the newsgroup in the file list you would like to compact first.

2. Right-click on its name and select Properties from the resulting shortcut menu.

3. Choose the Local File tab as shown in Figure 17.11. Look at the amount of wasted disk space!

FIGURE 17.11

The newsgroup shown here has wasted only a tiny amount of my hard drive space, but wasted space can add up quickly when you subscribe to several newsgroups.

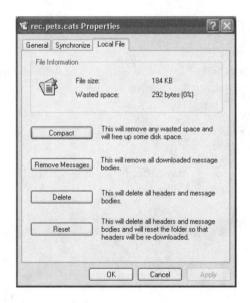

4. Press the Compact button. Outlook Express will go to work to reduce that percentage of wasted disk space to zero.

5. Repeat the steps above to clean up each newsgroup for which you have messages stored on your machine.

You always have options. The Local File tab also gives you the opportunity to remove the message bodies to save space (the Remove Messages button) or to delete the complete messages (the Delete button).

Summary

This hour presented a quick overview of reading and posting messages to newsgroups. Although the reading and posting functions are very similar to what you will find in Outlook Express e-mail, some major differences arise when it comes to offline newsreading.

Thanks to Microsoft, you can now read entire newsgroups offline, or just selected posts. The flexibility is at an all-time high. If you need to conserve time online, you will definitely be able to make some headway here!

The next hour, Downloading Goodies from the Internet, I show you where to find neat graphics for your personal Web page, how to locate fun software demos and shareware, and even give you the details about how to worked with compressed files (also known as ZIP files).

17

Workshop

Now it's time to see just how much you learned in this lesson. I'll give you a short multiple-choice quiz to test what you learned, followed by a suggested activity designed to enhance the skills you acquired during the hour.

Quiz

Select the best answer to the questions from the choices provided and then check your answers.

Questions

1. Which of the following numbers is closest to the number of newsgroups out there?
   a. 150,000
   b. 25,000
   c. 1,500

2. In general, is it a good idea to post a message simply declaring your agreement with the poster of a message?
   a. No; you should only do it if you are a recognized authority on the subject.
   b. Sure; people who hang out in newsgroups love keeping mental tallies of how many people agree versus how many people disagree with them.
   c. Yes; the more messages, the merrier!

3. Is there a way to find the messages you are looking for?

    a. Nope; you are on your own!

    b. Yes, and it's called using your eyes to scrutinize each message out there!

    c. Yes; it is a special Find tool similar to the one used for locating e-mail messages.

Answers

1. B is the correct answer, and the number literally keeps growing by the day!

2. A; B and C aren't even close to true for the most part, unless someone is specifically taking a vote on a certain matter.

3. C; Come on, surely you had to know the other two were wrong!

Activity

Here is a fun assignment for you. Use any or all of the methods presented in this hour to find newsgroups of potential interest to you. Find at least three to which you would subscribe. Once you are subscribed, prepare the groups for offline viewing. Try both complete message downloads and "pick and choose" on demand. Run the download and give offline newsreading a test drive.

Does it work for you?

Do you feel like offline browsing would save you time online in the long run, or does offline browsing somehow feel a little awkward to you?

Which method do you prefer, downloading the whole thing up front, or picking and choosing the messages you would like to see?

HOUR 18

Downloading Goodies from the Internet

Want to download a computer game demonstration for your son to try before you shell out $40 for it? Has your daughter been begging you to download a Britney Spears desktop theme for her? Are you hoping to build your own Web page but need some backgrounds, buttons, and other things to spruce it up?

This hour shows you how to use Internet Explorer 6 to accomplish all of these things safely and with minimal hassle. In addition, you will learn the answers to the following questions, among others:

- Can you point me to some comprehensive collections of graphics for my diverse range of interests?
- Why would I want to save the Web Page Complete?
- How do I save just a single graphic on a page?
- What are these .zip files I keep seeing, and how do I open them?
- I have downloaded this great new shareware game, now how do I go about playing it?

Finding Free Stuff for Your Web Pages

Since I am going to show you how to whip up your own Web page in the next lesson, let's go scouring the Web for cool Web page design elements first.

More Web sites are dedicated to providing free Web graphics and sound files than you can imagine. I will give you some good leads a bit later in the section, but there are a few things you need to know about these free graphics and sound files before you start saving every cool thing in sight.

First, you should know that most graphic and sound sites have some requirements for use. They vary widely from merely requesting a reciprocal link to their site to charging a fee for use on commercial sites. In general, you can expect to see the following restrictions, although you should always read the published guidelines for use for the specifics.

- You may use as many elements as you want on a personal Web page as long as you give credit to the source. Some places are satisfied with a text credit and link, whereas others prefer you to include a link to their site using their graphic logo button. You will find directions for doing this on the graphic host's Web site.

- If you plan to use the graphics for a commercial site, be prepared to either seek permission in writing or pay a small usage fee. Not all sites have these restrictions, but they are fairly common and are not unreasonable.

- Over time, many people have scoured the Net for great graphics, uploaded them onto a single site, and claimed them as their own. If you have ever entertained the thought of creating your own page of themed graphics for people to download, you may want to skip it unless you have your own original artwork to publish or you have obtained permission from the creator of the graphics you plan to include.

Don't let these restrictions overwhelm you; they are there to protect people's property and to discourage wrongful use more than anything else. A lot of great artwork is out there, whether it's a hand-painted floral background image or a college student's thoughtful interpretation of current hit he played and made available as a MIDI (sound) file.

Where do you begin looking for some of these goodies? Table 18.1 lists some good sites you will want to check out for graphics, and Table 18.2 gives you some starting points for locating sound files.

Arrrgh! Be prepared for virtual spitballs! If you go surfing for graphics on your own, be prepared to get pelted with virtual spitballs. They are not real spitballs of course, but they are equally as annoying. As you browse around, minding your own business, you might suddenly be assaulted by a barrage of pop-up advertising windows. They will come at you faster than you can duck (or close them). One graphics site popped up no fewer than ten windows at me! Needless to say, that site didn't make this book!

Table 18.1 Graphics Sites Worth Checking Out

Site Name	URL
About.com	`http://webclipart.about.com`
Free Graphics	`http://www.freegraphics.com`
#1 Free Clipart	`http://www.1clipart.com`
Google Image Search	`http://images.google.com`

Table 18.2 Sound Files Worth Investigating

Site Name	URL
The MIDI Farm	`http://www.midifarm.com`
MIDI Explorer	`http://www.musicrobot.com`
CPR's MIDI Archives	`http://www.cprmidi.web.id`

18

Gimme more; I gotta have more! Many of the more popular search engines let you search for specific types of files in their advanced search section. Check there for even more leads.

When You Find Something You Want to Use

If you are like many people, you are probably a bit wary of downloading graphics and sound files from the Internet. That is understandable, due to all the computer virus horror stories floating around. However, you will be happy to learn that you cannot catch a computer virus by downloading an image or sound file. Viruses are most commonly found in program files, in VB Script code tucked into e-mail messages, and in even more rare instances, inside Microsoft Word documents containing harmful macros.

So now that I have put your mind at ease regarding viruses, let's go through the steps to execute in order to save a sound file or image.

Saving a File for Future Use

To save a file on your computer for later use on a Web page, do the following:

1. Using Internet Explorer 6, open the Web page containing the image or sound file you want to save.

2. Right-click over the link to the image or sound file (or over the image itself); then select Save Picture As (for images) or Save Target As (for sound files) from the shortcut menu.

3. The usual Save As dialog appears, with the appropriate file extension already selected (see Figure 18.1). By default, Windows XP will suggest the My Pictures directory when the Save Picture As option is chosen, but you can always opt out of that location. All you have to do is click to a logical folder in which to store all your Web stuff and then give the file a more descriptive name if necessary to help you figure out what it is down the road.

FIGURE 18.1

Internet Explorer 6 figures out the format of each file and automatically saves it as such.

4. Once the file has a good home and has been appropriately named, click the Save button. The file will be saved on your hard drive for use later. It's that simple!

Saving the Whole Enchilada at One Time

If you see numerous graphics on a single page that you want to save and are running short on time (and perhaps even patience) to save each one separately, you will love this Internet Explorer 6 option. On graphic sites that display all the objects in a subject category on one page, you can now save the entire page in HTML format and extract what you want later. It may not be the perfect solution, but there are times it can beat saving ten items one at a time.

Just follow these steps to save an entire Web page for use later:

1. Open the page you want to save in Internet Explorer. Keep in mind that graphic sites often have several layers of pages, so you will want to be sure the page that pictures all of the images you want is what is being displayed. A link to them will do no good in this instance.

2. On the File menu, select Save As. The usual Save As dialog box appears.

3. Click your way to the folder in which you want to store the page.

Put it in a safe place. Have you ever put something in a "safe" place only to forget where it is? Even though a page seems a whole lot different than the images you have been saving, I suggest that you keep them in the same directory. That way there is no question where you put what when you go to design that killer Web page!

4. In the Save as Type box, use the drop-down arrow if necessary to choose the Web Page, complete option.

5. Click the Save button to move the page to its new location on your computer. It will be right where you put it when you go to find it.

What about sound files? You might be wondering if you can do the same thing for a group of sound files. Unfortunately, it is just not possible. The theory behind saving the Web page complete is to save everything it takes to display the chosen page locally without linking up to the Internet. Obviously a Web page cannot be playing a dozen songs simultaneously. If the Web page plays a single tune by default when you visit it, then yes, that file will be saved along with the page, but no others will be available. You will have to save the songs the hard way (one by one) or hope the Web page designer makes .zip files available. (See the next section for more on .zip files.)

To extract elements of the saved page later on, open it in Internet Explorer and then pull out the desired images as you did above. To put them on your Web page, read about that in the next hour.

18

Locating Shareware or Game Demos Worth Downloading

If you work around others who use their computers for both work and pleasure, you will no doubt be standing at the copier one day when you hear two people talking about this incredibly addictive new shareware puzzle game. Your ears may perk up, and you may even ask them where they found the cool game.

This is how much of the best shareware gets its publicity—through word of mouth, where the download URL (Web address) is passed from one person to another. The following are ways you may stumble onto things worth checking out:

- Visit a site like C|Net (`http://www.cnet.com`) or ZDNet (`http://www.zdnet.com`) to see about its hot downloads. These reputable sites will often point you to some incredible stuff.

- Many well-known software companies will post partially playable demos of upcoming titles on their Web sites for free download. You will hear about these in magazine articles or by simply wandering by the site for a game that you already play often.

- Browse major shareware archives or search engines like Shareware.Com (`http://www.shareware.cnet.com`) to see what downloads are most popular and to surf for titles that may be of potential interest or use to you.

- It is also possible that you will literally just stumble onto something while surfing or searching the Net for something entirely different. For example, you just performed a search on Golden Retriever puppies. You may wander onto a site on which someone has posted a puppy screensaver or a bunch of cool Clip Art you can use on your Web page.

Dealing with Downloadable Programs

Now that you have some leads to free software and demos, you are ready to begin downloading some goodies. Follow these steps to begin working with downloads:

1. Using Internet Explorer 6, navigate to the Web page containing the link to the file you want to download.
2. Click on the link to the file you want to download. The File Download dialog box shown in Figure 18.2 opens.
3. Next, you must tell Internet Explorer whether you want to Run the program from its current location or Save it to disk on your machine.

FIGURE 18.2

The File Download dialog box gives you a choice of what to do with the selected file.

Know what you are downloading. Some of the more graphic-intensive programs are huge and can take what may seem like an eternity to download. In general, you can expect to download between 12 and 18 megabytes (1,024k/megabyte) in an hour with a 56K connection to the Internet. However, note that this amount can dip as low as 8 to 10 meg per hour during high traffic times. Plan your downloads accordingly, since you will need to tie up the phone line the entire time.

Decisions, decisions.... If you are downloading a sound file and you want to hear it before saving it to disk, choose Run from current location. It won't take up valuable space on your machine if it turns out to be something you don't want to save. If it is a program you want to download now but check out later, save it to disk. Otherwise, it may be automatically purged when Internet Explorer cleans up its temporary files, and you won't be able to find it again.

18

Walk before you run. Don't be deceived by the words "Run from current location." Running a program on your machine still presents potential virus threats. Be prepared.

4. After you have made your choice, click OK. If you chose to save the file to disk, a Save As dialog box appears. Click to the directory in which you would like to store the program and then hit the Save button.

5. When the download has been successfully started, you will see a download status screen like the one shown in Figure 18.3. It will display the file name and size and then attempt to estimate how much time the download will take.

FIGURE 18.3

The status bar gives you an indication of how much progress has been made.

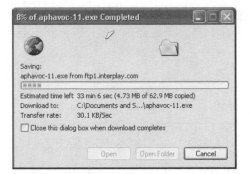

Take a closer look. Usually, the page you accessed for the download will tell you whether you are downloading an .exe file or a .zip file. If it doesn't, you can see the file type in the status box. You will want to know this information so you can choose the appropriate way to handle the file later on.

5. Should you need to abort the download for whatever reason, just press the Cancel button and the status box will disappear.

6. When the download has been completed, Internet Explorer will display a message saying that the download is complete. Click the Close button to dismiss the message box.

Now that the file is on your machine, what do you do with it? Since downloadable programs essentially come in two types of files, .exe files (executable files) or .zip files (zipped or compressed files), you will need to take different actions to install or use different programs. See the applicable section below for details.

Working with Zipped or Compressed Files

The more you go digging for treasures on the Internet, the more likely you are to come across files that have been zipped or compressed. So what in the world does this mean? Zipping files is a way of compressing them so that they take up less space and are downloaded in a shorter amount of time. You will most often see the .zip file extension used with shareware and other large applications, but it is now more commonly used for packaging images or songs from similar categories for quick, easy retrieval.

Once upon a time, you needed a program called *WinZip* on your machine to decompress such files for you. Now, Windows XP is quite capable of doing that all by itself.

After a .zip file is on your machine, you can expect to follow these steps to begin installing or running the new program:

1. Click the green Windows Start button and then point to All Programs, Accessories, Windows Explorer. When Windows Explorer is fully launched, put all your navigation skills to work to click to the file you downloaded (see Figure 18.4).

FIGURE 18.4

Notice something different about the folder in the lower right corner of this screenshot?

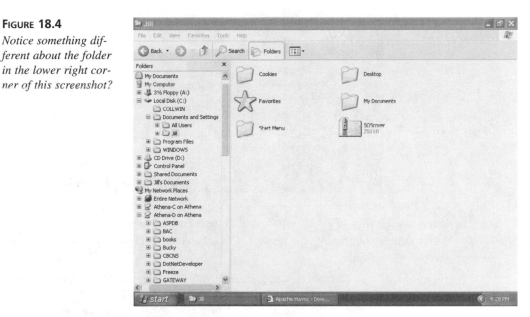

2. Double-click the icon for the compressed file. Icons for the files packaged in the compressed file you just downloaded appear onscreen. Typically, you will see an executable file for the program itself and a readme file that highlights all the details. Figure 18.5 shows you the contents of a sample compressed file I downloaded.

3. Double-click the readme file to view any special instructions. Windows Notepad launches, displaying the contents of the selected readme file. When you are finished reading the file, click Notepad's Close button to shut the Notepad window.

4. Next, double-click the program icon. Windows XP may issue a Compressed Folders Warning. If the program and readme files are the only ones in the compressed folder, go ahead and click the Run button. It's okay in this situation, since there clearly weren't any other supporting files included in the package.

5. If there are files in addition to the program and readme files, you will need to extract the files to a new location. To do this, simply click the Extract All button on the Compressed Folders Warning box.

FIGURE 18.5

Opening a compressed file is like opening a surprise package—you won't know what you are getting until you open it!

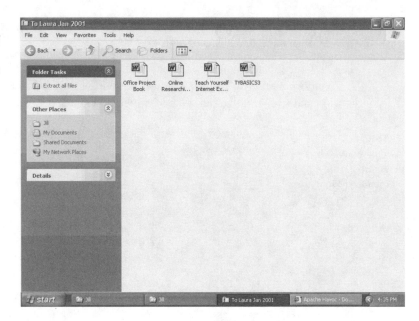

6. Windows XP launches the Compressed Folders Extraction Wizard shown in Figure 18.6 to guide you through the process. Click Next to begin working your way through the wizard.

7. Using the Browse button, click to a location in which you would like to place the files and then click the Extract button.

8. You will be taken back to the Select a Destination screen shown in Figure 18.7. Click Next to move on.

FIGURE 18.6

Once again, a friendly wizard is there to guide you.

FIGURE 18.7

The path of the directory you browsed to now appears in the text box provided.

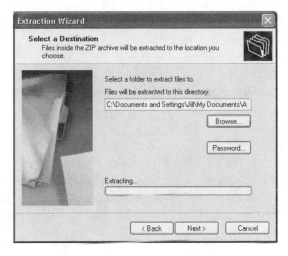

9. A window appears saying the extraction is complete. Place a check mark next to the Show extracted files option and then click Finish.

10. Icons for the extracted files appear onscreen in Windows Explorer. Simply double-click the program icon and follow the onscreen prompts to install and then run the newly downloaded program.

Working with an Executable File

In many ways, dealing with an .exe file is simpler because it involves fewer steps, but there is a drawback in that you may not have program descriptions or a readme file immediately available for your use. In addition, .exe files generally take a much longer to download.

To run your newly downloaded executable file, do the following:

1. Click the Start button on the Windows taskbar and then select the Run menu item. The Run dialog box in Figure 18.8 appears.

FIGURE **18.8**

Windows may attempt to guess which program you want to run as it did here.

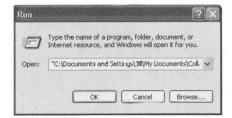

2. If the name of the program you want to run appears, simply click OK. If it doesn't appear, click the Browse button, click your way to the desired program, and then double-click it. Its name will then appear in the Open box. Just press OK to continue.

3. You will either be greeted by some kind of setup wizard that will ask you specific questions about your system, or the program will open, ready for use.

Summary

I bet you never thought finding and downloading goodies on the Internet was so simple! Since you went to all the trouble to locate some fun graphics and music, it's only fair that we let you strut your stuff.

In the next lesson, you will learn how to build your very own Web page. We can't cover everything there is to know in a single hour, but you will at least be able to produce a piece of the Web you can call your own.

Workshop

Now it's time to see just how much you learned in this lesson. I'll give you a short multiple-choice quiz to test what you learned, followed by a suggested activity designed to enhance the skills you acquired during the hour.

Quiz

Select the best answer to the questions from the choices provided and then check your answers.

Questions

1. Which of the following Web sites is where you can find music files?

    a. MIDIBarn

    b. MIDIFarm

    c. Moosic.com

2. When it comes to using graphics you find on the Web for commercial use, which of the following statements is most accurate?

    a. Hey baby, take anything you want!

    b. You toucha my graphics, I breaka your face!

    c. E-mail the graphics owner/designer to negotiate terms.

3. What does Windows XP do with compressed or zipped files?

    a. It gives you a wizard to extract them into a useable form.

    b. It chews them up and spits them out.

    c. You need to download a special utility to open these types of files, since Windows can't deal with them.

Answers

1. In this lesson, you were introduced to B, the MIDIFarm.

2. The correct answer is C; come on, you didn't really believe the other two choices, did you?

3. A; C was true not so very long ago, but Windows has come a long way, baby.

Activity

Make a list of all your hobbies and interests. Which one would make a great theme for a Web page? Is there a song that fits the mood you are trying to create?

Go on a virtual scavenger hunt online to see just how many icons, Web page backgrounds, and sound images you can find that fit the bill. (I highly recommend that you actually do this exercise and not skip it. If you don't, you may have a rather uninteresting Web page at the end of the next lesson!

18

Hour 19

Make Your Own Web Page in an Hour

Web pages are amazing. You can use them to share photos and news with friends and family, display your wares or tout your business, and even champion a cause.

A few years ago, building Web pages was a daunting task for nerds only. Not anymore! In this lesson, you will find out how to whip one up in an hour or less. You will also uncover the answers to the following questions:

- What program should I use to create a Web page?
- Can I make a site with frames like I have seen on the Net?
- Is it possible to build a Web site with a theme rather than going in and setting the background, text, and link colors manually?
- How do I add sound to my Web page?
- Now how do I get all of this published to the Web?

Before you dive in and start constructing a Web site, it's important that you do a little planning. Do you want a single page full of pictures for the relatives to browse or an intricate site where each major topic has its own page?

Consider making an outline of the topics or information you want to cover; this will help make your best option a bit more obvious to you.

There is also a lot to consider with regard to the aesthetics of your site. Does it need to be flashy and fun, or is it intended to be functional more than anything else?

Some general design tips to consider include the following:

- If you plan to have a lot of content, try to split it up into multiple logical pages. This reduces download time for your visitors and makes finding items of interest a bit easier.

- Use graphics judiciously. If it adds meaning to the page, go ahead and add it; otherwise consider skipping it for the sake of a quicker download time.

- Avoid "busy" backgrounds. That bright swirly, rainbow design you downloaded may look neat now, but with text over the top of it, visitors may be in for a major headache.

- Music can be a mood enhancer or a download hog—you decide! A pleasing tune can make a visitor's stay even nicer, but few things can turn a person off more than a poor quality sound file looping dissonantly in the background. If it doesn't augment the experience of visiting the site, then it may be wise to scrap it and save the download time for graphics.

- Use a little color sense. Obviously, a pink background works for a Barbie doll lover's Web page but not for that belonging to an auto repair shop. A well-chosen color really can affect a visitor's response to your site.

Choosing Your Web Authoring Tool

There are tons of programs out there that can be used to design a Web page. Microsoft FrontPage 2002, at around $150, helps users at any level produce a high-quality product. You can then have a number of multipurpose programs that can help you build a Web page out of an existing document. For example, Microsoft Publisher and Microsoft Word guide users through the Web page design process, whether you are converting a document already produced in that application or you need to start from scratch.

For this lesson, we are actually going to use Word 2002's Web Page Wizard. It's easy to use; it gives quick, professional-looking results; and most people already have Word installed on their machines, which means it's also free.

In addition to designing the basic site, I will show you how to customize it with images, sounds, and all the goodies you could ever want for a first Web page.

We are only scratching the surface here. Whatever you do, please don't expect this to be an all-encompassing introduction to Web page design. There is only so much we can do in an hour. You will have a respectable and functional Web site in the end, but we are only seeing the tip of the iceberg of what can be done. If the topic interests you to the point where you would like to investigate it in greater detail, you should definitely visit your local bookstore. Entire books (thick ones at that) have been written on Web site design. It is a complex but fascinating topic.

Using Word 2002's Web Page Wizard

With your Web site plan and design ideas tucked firmly in your head, it's time to dive into the Web Page Wizard.

For the sake of this exercise, let's make a personal Web page. You should have the hang of it by the time you are ready to venture out and do something a bit more ambitious.

To begin working with the wizard, launch Word 2002 and then proceed as follows:

1. If the New Document task pane appears on the right side of your screen, click the General Templates link under the New from Template section of the pane. (To open this pane, simply click File, New and then click the link described above.) The Templates dialog box opens.

2. Access the Web Pages tab and double-click the Web Page Wizard icon shown in Figure 19.1.

19

FIGURE 19.1
Wizard icons look different than template icons.

The Web Page ——
Wizard icon

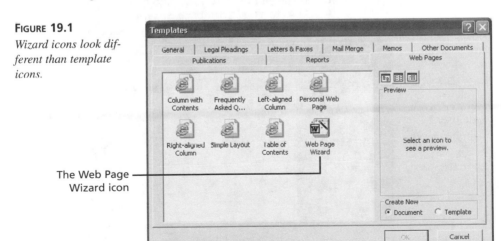

3. The Web Page Wizard opens, displaying a description of what it helps you accomplish. Click the Next button to begin working with the wizard.

4. The first thing you are asked to do is name the Web site and then choose a location in which to store it (see Figure 19.2). Simply type the desired information into the text boxes provided, or in the case of the file storage location, use the Browse button to click to the location you want. Click Next to move to the next step.

FIGURE **19.2**

On the left side of the wizard window, you will see just how many steps you have left to complete.

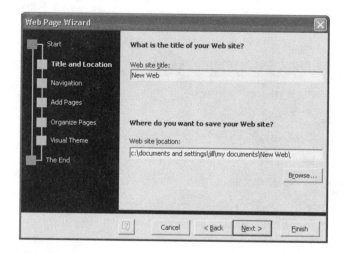

5. Next, you will need to choose the type of navigation you want for your site. Choices include Vertical frame, Horizontal frame, and Separate page. Click the button for your chosen option, as shown in Figure 19.3, and then click Next.

FIGURE **19.3**

The wizard shows you what each choice will look like on your Web site.

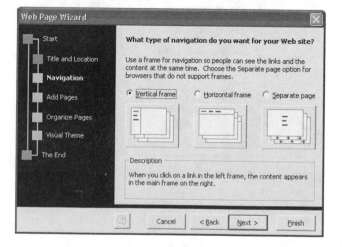

6. The Add pages to your Web site screen comes next. For this exercise, we won't need to add any, but keep it in mind for future projects because I'm sure it will come in handy! Not only can you add pages, but you can remove them and move them as well. Click Next to move on.

> **Now *that's* cool!** When you go to add a Web page down the road, check out the Add Template Page button. Word has a bunch of prefabricated pages all ready to go, including ones suited for frequently asked questions and other common layouts.

7. Next, you are asked to organize the navigation links to your Web pages. Simply click a page name, followed by the Move Up or Move Down button to shift things around. You can also rename a page on this screen by clicking a page name and then clicking the Rename button in the bottom right corner of the page. When the pages have all been named, click Next.

8. Now it's time for the fun stuff: selecting the visual theme for your site. You can choose to add a theme (the default) or keep the background of your pages white. Leave the default option selected and then click the Browse Themes button. The Theme dialog box shown in Figure 19.4 opens.

FIGURE 19.4

The Citrus Punch theme is shown here

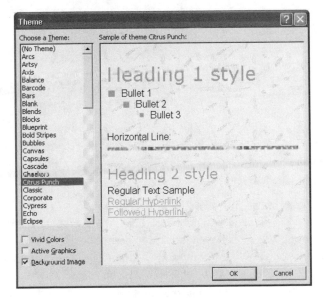

19

9. In the Theme dialog box, you can preview the choices available by clicking a name of interest. You will see samples of the background, text, link colors, bullet shapes, and so on. When you have found one you like, click the OK button.

10. When bumped back to the Web Page Wizard, the name of the theme you chose should appear in the Add a Visual Theme box. Click Next.

11. The Web Page Wizard now has all the information it needs to build your page. Click the Finish button to put the wizard to work building your new Web site.

Adding Text to Your Web Site

The first page of your Web site (based on the Personal Web Page template) contains a number of headings customized for personal information. If you look closely, you will see sections that say "Type some text." Triple-click them to highlight the whole phrase; then type in the information warranted by the section's title.

Uh, I wouldn't do that if I were you. When working with a template-based Web page, don't attempt to edit the hyperlink text (the underlined text). Doing so will result in the hyperlink disappearing and your new text appearing as plain text only. I will show you how to add your own hyperlinks later on in this lesson.

You can use all of the Word tools available to color, size, and align text within the template.

Including a Hyperlink on a Web Page

As you already know from your Web browsing and such, a hyperlink is a bit of text (often underlined) that, when clicked on, transports you to another Web page. What you may not necessarily know is that a hyperlink can be an e-mail address, too. When you click a mailto hyperlink, a new preaddressed message window from your default e-mail program is launched, ready for you to type in a message and click Send.

When it comes to building any kind of hyperlink, Word is pretty smart. Typing `http://www.whateverdomain.com` or `mailme@whateverdomain.com` is enough for Word to do the job; it produces the underlined hyperlink text and leads the viewer directly to the specified source. What if you want to turn a word or phrase into a hyperlink instead? Perhaps you want visitors to be able to click your name to e-mail you instead of simply showing them the raw e-mail address. No problem; just follow these quick steps to get the job done:

1. With the Web page you want to edit displayed, click the spot in which you want to place the hyperlink.

2. Next, click the Insert Hyperlink button on Word's Standard toolbar. If it's not visible because of the way your toolbars are set up, simply click Insert, Hyperlink on the Menu bar. This launches the Insert Hyperlink dialog box shown in Figure 19.5.

FIGURE 19.5

Name the hyperlink and enter its address in this dialog box.

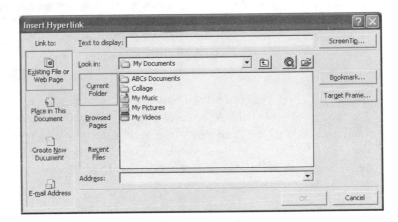

3. In the Text to Display box near the top of the dialog box, enter your name, the title of the Web site, or whatever it is you want your viewer to see onscreen as a hyperlink.

No need to reinvent the wheel. If the text you would like to convert to a hyperlink already appears in the document, simply select it, right-click over it, and choose Hyperlink from the shortcut menu to access the Insert Hyperlink dialog box shown back in Figure 19.5.

4. Near the bottom of the dialog box is a place to type in the hyperlink's address. This is where you will enter the Web site URL. If you want to link to an e-mail address, click the E-Mail Address button on the lower left corner of the dialog box. Type the address you want to link to along with a subject line for the messages generated from the hyperlink. After you have verified that the information you provided is correct, click the OK button. The hyperlink you defined now appears as defined on your Web page.

19

> **Savvy shortcut.** Does the Web page you want to link to have a long, awkward URL? If you recently visited the page, click the Existing File or Web Page button and then click the Browsed Pages button. A list of recently viewed Web pages appears. Just click a link to select it.
>
> If it is saved as a Favorite but you haven't visited it lately, surf over to Internet Explorer; then highlight its address in the Address Bar, right-click, and choose Copy from the shortcut menu. Next, go back to Word's Insert Hyperlink box, click inside the Address box, right-click, and choose Paste from the list. No retyping needed.

Images on a Web page can also be turned into hyperlinks. For example, on your family Web page you could publish photos of each member and set it up so that visitors are taken to a certain family member's Web page when they click that person's picture. To do this, select the image, right-click it to reveal the shortcut menu, and then choose Hyperlink from the list. You will be taken to an Insert Hyperlink dialog box similar to the one you saw earlier.

Adjusting the Background of Your Web Page

Whether you have used the wizard to create your Web site or have done it from scratch using a blank Word document as your starting point, you can do a lot to change the look and feel of your page.

Changing the Background to a Solid Color

Tired of a flashy background? Want to change the color of the page altogether? Consider a solid-color background. In order to make the switch, you will need to click inside the Web page and then choose Format, Background from the Menu bar. You are presented with a basic palette of colors from which to choose (see Figure 19.6). Just click a color swatch box to select it, and you are good to go.

Of course, if none of the swatches meet with your approval, you can choose the More Colors option rather than clicking one of the boxes. This brings up the Standard tab of the Colors dialog box as shown in Figure 19.7. In this tab, you can select from an even larger number of colors by clicking the desired spot. Still want more? Try the Custom tab where you can use all kinds of buttons and levers to select one of thousands of possibilities. After you have made your choice, click the OK button.

FIGURE 19.6
40 preselected color choices await you.

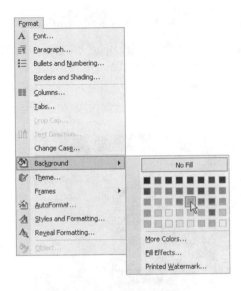

FIGURE 19.7
You will find literally every color of the rainbow and then some on these two tabs.

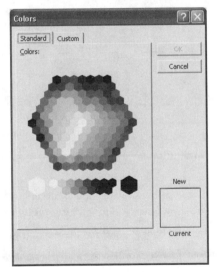

19

Using an Image for a Background

I wouldn't recommend using a photo of your family pet as a Web page background because it can be difficult to see text over several colors. Special, more subdued backgrounds downloaded from the Internet make great images on which to place text.

To apply one of these images, you will need to do the following:

1. With the Web page you want to modify open, click Format, Background, Fill Effects. This launches the Fill Effects dialog box.

2. Open the Picture tab of the Fill Effects dialog box. A sample of the currently selected image (if applicable) is displayed as shown in Figure 19.8.

FIGURE 19.8

Although a special photo may be cute, it probably doesn't belong in the role of Web page background.

3. Click the Select Picture button to access your hard drive in search of an image you would like to use.

4. When you have found the image you want to use, double-click it. It will now appear in the Picture tab's preview window along with its file name.

5. To designate the image as the background for the current page, click OK. The Fill Effects dialog disappears, leaving the Web page with its new background.

Oh my, what have I done? Word tiles the image you select just like you are tiling a floor. The only difference here is that with an actual photo, you could end up with a busy, cluttered mess on your hands. If the results aren't what you expect, don't panic! Press Ctrl+Z, and the slate will be cleared for you to start over again.

Including an Image on Your Page

If you just want to include a picture of your kids, family pet, or car on your Web page, all you need to do is insert an image. You will be amazed at how quickly this can be done.

Click the mouse pointer to select the location for the image and then click Insert, Picture, From File to open the Insert Picture dialog box. Navigate your way to the desired image; then double-click its name when you find it. The dialog box closes with your image set in its new position.

Adding Background Music to Your Page

Remember that mood music mentioned previously? Well, here is where you can add it. Before I show you how, though, there are some things you should know. First, sound files must be applied to each Web page on your site; Word cannot play your sound file sitewide. Second, remember to choose your tune wisely. Music takes visitors extra time to download, so make it worth their while.

Here is how to add music to your Web page:

1. Open the Web page to which you would like to add a music file or sound clip.
2. Right-click over any of the toolbars to open the shortcut menu and then click the Web Tools item. A floating Web Tools toolbar like the one shown in Figure 19.9 appears.
3. Click the Sound button (the left button on the bottom row) to open the Background Sound dialog box shown in Figure 19.10.

19

FIGURE 19.9

Access some of the funky, more advanced Word Web development tools using this toolbar.

— Sound button

FIGURE 19.10

Choose the sound file you want to use; then tell Word how many times you want it played.

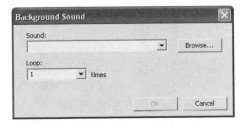

4. Next, click the Browse button to work your way to the desired sound file on your hard drive. Once you find it, double-click it; the filename will then appear in the Sound box.

5. To select how many times you want the sound file played, use the drop-down arrow button, choose a number between 1 and 5, or have the file played over and over again (infinite).

At the risk of stating the obvious.... Looping a song may not be a bad idea if you expect visitors to linger on the page, but looping a voice-recorded welcome message that keeps repeating itself could get more than a little annoying. Choose your option wisely.

6. Once both options have been set, click OK to dismiss the dialog and continue working with the Web page.

Doing It My Way

Templates and wizards are helpful for setting up just about anything, but creating a Web site may not be the best time to use them. You can build your Web page from scratch starting with a blank Word document and saving it as a Web page by clicking File, Save as Web Page.

Just make sure that the home page of your site carries the name "index." Most commercial Web servers require this to map your site from the location they give you for storing the Web pages and related files.

Where Do I Go from Here?

You have a complete Web page or maybe even an entire site; how do you publish it to the Web?

Here is where I can point you in the right direction, but then I must step back. Internet service providers (ISPs) and Web hosting services often have different requirements and methods for uploading a Web page/site. If I lead you one way and it is not the best way, I may do more harm than good. However, I do have a few suggestions to get started.

First, pay a visit to your ISP or Web host's Web page. These companies usually post step-by-step directions for publishing a Web page to their servers online. If they don't, then a call to their customer support line may be in order. If you do end up consulting a human for the task, make sure that you find out the exact URL visitors will have to enter in order to view your site. (Online instructions should include that information.)

Announcing Your New Web Page

What good is a Web page without people to view it? To announce your new little spot on the Web, surf over to your Web site using Internet Explorer; then click File, Send, Link by E-mail. An Outlook Express New Message window appears with a link to your Web page already entered in the body of the note. Just address the message by using your Address Book or by typing in the addresses manually, add a few words explaining the link you have included in the message, and then hit Send.

Within minutes, your friends and family will learn all about your new Web page!

Summary

Designing a Web page/site can be a blast with all the right tools. In this lesson, you learned how to put Microsoft Word to the task. Although it can do the job, Web page design isn't the application's forte, but for around $150, applications such as FrontPage 2002, NetObjects Fusion MX, Macromedia Dreamweaver 4.0, and HoTMetaL Pro 6.0 increase ease of use and add functionality.

At least we accomplished our goal: getting a page up on the Web. If this is something you would like to do more of, plenty of cool tools and books are available to help make the project a bit easier.

This lesson completes the Internet section of the book. Our attention now turns to multimedia. The first lesson shows you how to select add-ons for your PC, such as digital cameras, scanners, DVD drives, and others.

Workshop

Now it's time to see just how much you learned in this lesson. I'll give you a short multiple-choice quiz to test what you learned, followed by a suggested activity designed to enhance the skills you acquired during the hour.

Quiz

Select the best answer to the questions from the choices provided and then check your answers.

Questions

1. What tool can help you design a Web page/site?

   a. NewsPage

   b. BackPage

   c. FrontPage

2. Which of the following is good Web design advice?

   a. Use graphics and sound files carefully, since they take a lot of time to download.

   b. Record yourself saying, "Welcome to my home page," and set it to play over and over again (the infinite loop option).

   c. Take a picture of yourself in a bright Hawaiian shirt (or muumuu) and use it for your Web page background.

3. How do you go about publishing the page or site to the Web?

   a. Dial 1-800-ON-MY-WEB.

   b. You will need to consult your ISP either online or via telephone since many have different procedures.

   c. Use the Zip-to-Web Wizard.

Answers

1. C is the correct answer; the others don't even exist, at least when it comes to computer software!

2. A; the second two options could induce headaches and frustration among your visitors, causing them to avoid your site forever.

3. B; only your ISP can give you the most successful solution.

Activity

Let's start simple for your first Web page. First, pull out a piece of paper and list your hobbies and interests. Can all these items be combined on one page, or do you really need to build a Web site, where each interest item gets its own page?

With that decided, launch the Web Page Wizard and preview the available themes. Do any of them match your personality or interests?

Once the wizard is done building your site, enter all the applicable hyperlinks to Web sites devoted to your interests. Also figure out where you may want to include the pictures you will scan or take with your digital camera in lesson 23, Digitally Yours: Working with Electronic Images.

How does the page look? Perhaps you would like to experiment with text fonts or color.

When you are satisfied with it, save it and click File, Web Page Preview. Does it look as good as it did before?

Congratulations! You just built your first Web page! I can promise you, the more often you tinker with it, the easier and better looking it will be!

19

PART IV
The Multimedia PC

Hour

HOUR 20

Spiffing Up the Ol' System

Your computer may have been perfect for you whenever you bought it, but so much can change. Maybe you have decided to pursue digital photography, or perhaps you have gotten hooked on computer games that require a bit more RAM than what is on your machine. If you have a flair for crafting, you may want a better quality color printer to produce iron-on transfer shirts, memory quilts, and other things.

The bottom line is there is a fair chance you will eventually want to do a few things to spiff up your old system and make it more suitable for your favorite activities.

In this lesson, I will present a few of those possibilities including the following:

- How much RAM do I need, and why do I need so much?
- What if I want to watch DVDs on my PC?
- Are there any keyboard shortcuts I should know?

- I am having trouble seeing my mouse pointer; can you help me?
- What kind of printer should I get?

All About RAM

Memory, or more specifically, random access memory (RAM), is used to hold programs and data you are running on your machine. If you want to run more programs or work on larger data at the same time (bigger Microsoft Word or Excel documents), you will need more memory to perform such tasks. Computer games are also notorious memory hogs. Even having four or five open Internet Explorer windows consumes more memory than only one or two windows. In some ways, ample RAM can enhance the performance of your computer even more than a faster central processing unit (CPU) chip would.

Memory modules come in several different formats. The most popular format today is known as SDRAM. SDRAM comes in two varieties, PC-100 and PC-133. They come in various sizes ranging from 64MB to 256MB. The exact format of memory you have depends on your computer's make and model. For this, you will need to consult the documentation that came with your computer.

Dealing with the mysteries of memory. Before you go to purchase more memory to upgrade your system, you need two bits of information from your PC's documentation or manufacturer: how many slots for memory are currently occupied on your motherboard and how many are available for expansion? Because you don't want to throw any parts away unless absolutely necessary, this information will be vital in the purchasing decisions you make. For example, if you have little RAM now with only two slots for expansion, you will want to buy the largest memory module you can afford. That will enable the PC to grow with you, helping you run the most current applications of the day. If you have a moderate amount of memory, a couple of smaller modules may be enough to keep your system running smoothly.

Do not touch! Until you know what you are doing, you should not open your system console yourself in search of this information. Not only are the parts inside fragile, but also in some cases, a sticker over the edge of the console's opening cracks when the console is opened, rendering your warranty null and void. Now, if you call the manufacturer and are talked through opening the console, that is a different story since their step-by-step guidance may not only solve your problem quickly, but they may make a note in your customer record that keeps the warranty intact.

You should also be aware that memory prices fluctuate. Before making a purchase, I suggest monitoring the prices for a few weeks. A dollar a megabyte was once considered cheap, but in recent times, prices have fallen to under $20 for 128 MB of RAM!

What are your software needs? What about the software you hope to install in the future? All software packaging displays minimum system requirements, including CPU speed, RAM, and operating system. Make sure that your system exceeds that minimum RAM amount. If it only meets that amount, you may end up frustrated with your machine's performance. Minimums are just that—minimums. It's good to build in wiggle room, and when memory prices are reasonable, you can always upgrade.

Types of CD Drives

Look through the advertisements for new computers, and you will see several types of CD drives: CD-ROMs, DVD-ROMs, and CD-RWs.

How did we get this much variety? When the stereo industry wanted to improve the quality of music, it moved to a digital format. They released albums on compact discs, or CDs as they are now called. Because the compact disc stored a series of bits and bytes, it was only natural that the computer industry adopted the same physical medium, which it dubbed a CD-ROM, for compact disc, read-only memory.

A CD-ROM has approximately 650MB of information on a single disk. You cannot write to a CD-ROM. The contents of a CD-ROM are fixed when the CD-ROM is manufactured. This was ideal for software companies who distributed their applications on a CD-ROM instead of 20 or more floppies. It actually saved companies money, since the cost to make a single CD-ROM was about the same as to write several floppy disks.

Game producers could now build bigger and more complex games with better graphics. Encyclopedia publishers could now load information onto a CD-ROM, making them easier to use and allowing the addition of sound files, videos, and other graphics.

Computers can also read and play music CDs in a standard CD-ROM drive. In fact, I'm always playing music CDs on my computer while I write!

The video industry then saw the advantage of CD-ROMs and developed digital video disc (DVD) technology to allow it to distribute videos on a plastic disc rather than on videocassette. However, videos occupy much more space than sound, so the video industry increased the capacity of a DVD disk to about 5GB. Amazingly, this was done with a disc the same size as original compact discs, making it necessary to have components that could play both music CDs and video DVDs.

The computer industry is presently jumping on the DVD drive bandwagon. Many high-end computers now come equipped with DVD drives. Most DVD-ROM drives will also

20

read CD-ROMs. Just as CD-ROM drives can play CDs with music, most DVD-ROM drives play DVD movies.

Although not much software is available in DVD-ROM format today, that is expected to change in the near future. Eventually, perhaps in another few years, DVD-ROMs will replace CD-ROMs in computers entirely, just as CD-ROMs have pretty much replaced floppies.

For an exciting look into the cutting-edge present and near future, consider this possibility: DVD-writable drives. Although they first surfaced in mid-2001, they are still too expensive for the average consumer to adopt.

Other Disk Drives You May Encounter

People need disk drives to store data. (We talked about this a bit a few hours ago when we explored backing up your data.) Some popular types are the Zip, CD-R, CD-RW, and DVD-RW drives.

Zip drives use disks that hold about 100MB to 250MB of data. They are designed to be a floppy disk supplement or replacement, but they never really quite caught on with mainstream users. Laptop owners often use Zip drives to back up their hard drives and to archive data for future use. Other individuals who need to exchange files that won't fit on a floppy disk also use them. Zip drives are declining in popularity as CD-R and CD-RW rise in popularity. The increased popularity of CD-R and CD-RW is due in part to their economy, both in terms of money and data storage space, which beat Zip drives hands down.

CD-R (recordable) and CD-RW (rewritable) drives are specialized forms of CD-ROM drives that allow you to write data to the disc. A CD-R allows you to write data to the physical disc only one time. After data has been written to a disc, it cannot be rewritten. A CD that is written by a CD-R drive can be read by any CD-ROM drive or even the CD player in your stereo at home.

A CD-RW, however, allows you to create CDs that can be written, erased, and written on again. As with a CD-R disk, a CD-RW can be read by any computer with a CD, CD-R, or CD-RW drive. Most writable CD drives included with new computers are CD-RWs, which are capable of recording both types of disks.

Video Cards: Making Your Display Behave

A video card translates the bits and bytes inside a computer's memory into a signal that can be displayed on a video monitor. About five years ago, that was about all a video card needed to do. Today, video card manufacturers like ATI Technologies, nVidia, and GeForce build video cards that perform many different functions.

Extra software is included to decode DVD videos in hardware, thus freeing your CPU to do other tasks. Also, some video cards now include a television tuner that will let you watch and even record your favorite TV shows on your computer. Some even include special outlets and hookups that will let you record directly from a video camera to your PC so that you can capture pictures and movies without additional hardware!

> **Look before you leap.** A "hot" video card can really make an ordinary machine extraordinary, but many budget computers have economical all-in-one video/sound cards, which means it may be impossible to plug a high-end video card into the machine. Check your documentation before shopping for a new video card.

One of the biggest influences in the video card industry has been the computer gaming industry. As computer game developers develop new games, they tend to push the hardware right to its limits. Video card manufacturers realized that they could improve the performance of computer games by adding special hardware support inside the video card for performing functions the game developers used to write into the software. Shifting functions to the video card did two things: the special video hardware was able to perform those functions much faster than the software could, and by moving the functions outside the CPU, it made available more CPU cycles to enhance and drive other aspects of the game.

For machines able to outfit a new video card, such a purchase may very well breathe new life into a once modest PC.

Sound Cards and Speakers: Do You Hear What I Hear?

A sound card is obviously used to generate sounds, but what may not be so apparent is the fact that internally, there are two different types of sounds. First, there are sound files that contain the complete sound you hear. These are known as *.wav* (pronounced wave) files. Other sound files are known as *MIDI* sound files. These files contain a series of music notes and voices that are played back through virtual musical instruments in the sound card. Also, if you like to listen to music you can download .mp3 music files from the Internet and play them on your computer through your sound card and speakers.

In addition to these files, your computer also has the capability to play regular music CDs. Simply pop one in the CD-ROM drive and Windows will recognize that it contains music and will automatically begin to play it.

Just like your stereo needs speakers to play sound, so does your sound card. Depending on how you use your computer, you may want inexpensive speakers or really good speakers. In general, if you want to play games, music, or DVD movies on your computer, a good set of speakers will be worth the investment. After all, a good subwoofer will work wonders for those explosion scenes in the movie *Top Gun!* If quality music is a priority, don't expect the economy speakers furnished with that budget desktop or average laptop to produce anything of real quality with its onboard speakers; you may even want to add a good set of speakers to your outfit. Some PC manufacturers even provide speaker/sound options on their PCs that not only include good speakers and a subwoofer, but also provide surround sound capabilities complete with two extra speakers!

Upgrading speakers may not be worth the cost and potential installation headaches, but it is certainly worth keeping in mind for your next PC.

The Key to Keyboards

Keyboards and mice are the primary way a user interacts with his or her computer. Keyboards come standard with most computers these days. The primary difference between one keyboard and another is how they feel. Some have a softer touch, whereas others have a firmer touch. There are exceptions, however. Microsoft has developed a "natural" keyboard that is designed to be ergonomically better for long hours at the keyboard. Other manufacturers have made colorful keyboards with pictures on the keys so that even the youngest user can be a part of the computer age.

However, very few people end up upgrading a keyboard; they simply adapt to whatever comes with their new system.

Your Keyboard: The Simplest Way to Talk to Your PC

If the display monitor is the primary way your computer communicates with you, the keyboard is the primary way to communicate with the computer. To make it easier to use your computer, Windows allows you to control the speed of the keyboard repeat function and the rate at which the cursor blinks.

Keyboard Settings: How Slow Can You Go?

To change the keyboard's settings, click Start and then choose Control Panel. Next, click the Printers and Other Hardware link and then choose the Keyboard option to display the Keyboard properties dialog box shown in Figure 20.1.

Some of us are faster typists than others. I certainly wouldn't hold any speed records, which is why I keep the repeat speed slow. Given the way I linger over the keys, most of my work would end up looking like thisssss if I didn't change the speed.

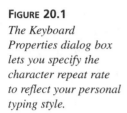

FIGURE 20.1

The Keyboard Properties dialog box lets you specify the character repeat rate to reflect your personal typing style.

To change the repeat speed on your computer, do this:

1. Move the Repeat delay slider from Long to Short to set how long you must hold the key before the repeat function starts. I keep mine on the second from the slowest slot.

2. Move the Repeat rate from Slow to Fast, as desired, to set how quickly the characters will be repeated.

3. Click in the text box below both sliders and press a key to see if you are comfortable with the repeat rate.

4. To save your changes click OK. To abandon your changes, click the Cancel button.

Keyboard Shortcuts You Shouldn't Live Without

Did you know that you don't always need a mouse to use Windows? You can enter a sequence of keystrokes that accomplishes what a mouse can. In cases such as resizing a window, keyboard shortcuts can be rather complicated, but using the keyboard may be faster than using a mouse when multiple steps or menus are involved.

Here is a list of some of my favorite keyboard shortcuts:

- **Getting help:** Press the F1 key. If there is help available, it will automatically be displayed, and the help you get is based on the context in which you are working. For example, if you are writing a letter in Microsoft Word and press F1, you will get the Microsoft Word help files, not some generic computer help file.

20

- **Closing the currently active window:** Press the Alt+F4 keys. This is the equivalent of pressing the Close button on the title bar or choosing File, Exit.
- **Undo change:** Press the Ctrl+Z keys. This is an easy way to get out of tight fixes.
- **Copy selected information:** Press the Ctrl+C keys. This will copy the selected information from the current window onto the Clipboard.
- **Paste information from the Clipboard:** Press the Ctrl+V keys. This will paste whatever is on the Clipboard into the current window.
- **Selecting menu items:** Press the Alt key by itself to transfer the focus to the menu bar. Then you can use the left and right arrow keys to select the main menu option and then press the down arrow key to select the submenu you want. Then press the Enter key to choose the menu item you want to execute or press the Esc key to move back one level. If you press the Esc key enough times, you will eventually reach the same place you were before you pressed the Alt key. This is definitely not very intuitive, but it certainly proves you can do Windows with a keyboard!
- **Using the Windows key:** That funny key with the Windows logo located between the Ctrl and Alt keys does the same thing as clicking on the Start button on the taskbar. From there you can use your arrow keys to select the menu item you want to execute and then press the Enter key to start it.

Of Mice and Menus

Unlike keyboards, there are a wide variety of pointing devices available for your computer. They come in different sizes and shapes, and some (like Microsoft's IntelliMouse) have special features such as a wheel that you can spin to scroll the information onscreen. Infrared mice, known as *optical mice*, do away with the finicky mouse balls in favor of a more high-tech solution; some are even wireless!

A good mouse is worth its weight in gold though. It is more comfortable (fewer hand/finger cramps), and the level of frustration with a good optical mouse is significantly lower.

Finally, some mice are really not mice at all. They can be more accurately referred to as pointing devices. Many laptops have touch pads on which you move your finger to control the pointer, whereas trackballs look a whole lot like upside-down mice in that you roll a ball that looks like what is normally under your mouse with your fingers to navigate the screen.

Moving with Mice

As you saw in our Solitaire game experiment earlier in the book, a mouse makes your computer easier to use, at least for some people. Although every function in Windows can be performed with a keyboard, many tasks are made easier with a mouse. (Just try to resize an application window with your keyboard.) A mouse is an indispensable tool for using Windows, one you won't want to do without.

However, using a mouse isn't always a pleasant experience for everyone. For example, if you want to use a mouse with your left hand, the left mouse button falls under your middle finger and not your index finger, which is uncomfortable for many people.

Likewise, you may want to adjust the double-click speed and how fast your mouse will respond to your movements by using the Mouse Properties window. To display this window, click Start and then click Control Panel. Next, click the Printers and Other Hardware link and then the Mouse link.

Left-Handed Mice

Although mice are generally preconfigured for use by the average right-handed person, the buttons can easily be swapped on the mouse by using the Mouse Properties dialog box (see Figure 20.2).

FIGURE 20.2

Make your mouse a lefty if necessary by using the Mouse Properties dialog box.

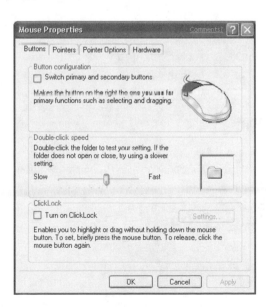

20

To change the mouse button's configuration, do the following:

1. Open the Mouse Properties dialog box by clicking Start, Control Panel, and then clicking the following links: Printers and Other Hardware, Mouse.

2. On the Buttons tab, click the Switch Primary and secondary buttons check box and then click OK to change the setting. Remember, if you configure the mouse for left-handed use, you will need to click the right mouse button instead of the left to do this!

Clicking Speed

Does Windows think you clicked twice on an icon, instead of registering a double-click? There is a difference. Does Windows register two clicks as a single double-click? Then you may be interested in tweaking the double-click speed. This is done on the Buttons tab of the Mouse Properties dialog box (see Figure 20.2).

To change the amount of time between clicks for a double-click, follow these steps:

1. Open the Mouse Properties dialog box from the Control Panel, as shown in preceding sections.

2. On the Buttons tab, move the slider in the Double-Click Speed section toward Fast to decrease the time between clicks for a double-click or to Slow to increase the time.

3. Then move your mouse to the test area and try clicking twice. If Windows thinks you double-clicked, the folder will open or close. If you didn't double-click fast enough, the folder won't change positions.

4. Click the OK button to accept your changes.

Rolling the Mice

You can adjust how much the cursor on your screen will move for a given mouse movement on the Pointer Options tab of the Mouse Properties window (see Figure 20.3). You can also adjust the speed of mouse motion until you are comfortable with it.

Changing Mouse Properties

To change the mouse properties, follow these steps:

1. Open the Mouse Properties window from the Control Panel and select the Pointer Options tab.

2. In the Motion frame, move the slider toward Fast to increase the distance the mouse pointer will travel on the screen for a given mouse movement, or toward Slow to decrease the distance.

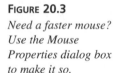

FIGURE 20.3

Need a faster mouse? Use the Mouse Properties dialog box to make it so.

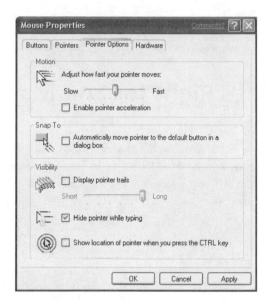

3. Click the OK button to dismiss the dialog.
4. To restore the original settings, move the slider halfway between Slow and Fast.

Mouse Tracks (Trailing Pointers)

If you have difficulty trying to find your mouse pointer, you may want to set a pointer trail. A pointer trail is a series of pointer icons displayed along the path you move the mouse pointer. When you stop moving the mouse, the pointer trail disappears.

Makin' tracks. Pointer trails are very useful if you have an older laptop computer with a passive matrix display. When you move the mouse quickly with this type of display, the mouse pointer isn't always visible. The pointer trail makes it easier to find the mouse pointer and track its movement on screen.

20

To enable pointer trails, do the following:

1. Open the Mouse Properties window from the Control Panel, and select the Pointer Options tab.
2. In the Visibility section, check the Display pointer trails checkbox.
3. You can adjust the length of the pointer trail by moving the slider between Short and Long.

4. If you are not happy with the setting, uncheck the Display pointer trails check box.

5. Click OK to save your changes and close the Properties window.

Printers: What's Right for You May Not Be Right for Me!

Choosing a printer may seem like a simple task, but that couldn't be farther from the truth. In fact, the decision was a whole lot easier 10 years ago when laser printers were as outrageously priced as color printers, leaving dot matrix and inkjet printers the only affordable option for most personal use.

Today's market offers two types of printers to basic users: color inkjet printers and monochrome laser printers. Although other types of printers are available, the price is not always right for most users.

A more in-depth look will help you see why the selection process has gotten more complex.

Color Inkjet Printers

Color inkjet printers differ from one another mostly in terms of print speed. A few high-end color inkjet printers have a finer print resolution, which make printed photos look a little crisper. They may also have the capability to print on multiple types of material like transparencies, T-shirt transfers, paper-backed fabric, and so on. Other than these differentiating features, most color inkjet printers are nearly identical.

Inkjet printers work by spraying tiny ink bubbles on the paper from a print head as it moves across the paper. After each pass, the paper moves forward a little bit, and the print head passes back in the other direction.

Printing an average sheet of paper can take anywhere from 10 seconds to several minutes, depending on what is being printed (that is, the graphic intensity of the output). Text always prints faster than graphics. A page with a couple of lines of text will print very fast, whereas a full-page picture will take what seems like an eternity.

Inkjet cartridges may print anywhere from 200 to 500 pages or more before they need to be replaced. Some printers use a single ink cartridge, which entails different colors (to produce combinations of colors) plus black. One of the downsides to a color inkjet printer is when you run out of ink for one color, you have to replace the entire cartridge. Unfortunately, that often leaves you with inaccurately colored documents.

The vast majority of color printers available today include a second black cartridge (in addition to the color cartridge) inside the printer that will automatically be used for printing black text. That way, if you run out of one ink color (except for black of course), you can still print out text-based documents in black ink.

Replacement cartridges for color printers can get pricey, so before you purchase a printer, you may want to browse cartridge replacement prices to make sure you are getting the most for your money.

If it sounds too good to be true, then it probably is. You will find lots of cheap generic cartridges or cartridge refill kits out there, but using a non–brand name cartridge in your printer may make the warranty null and void. Read the printer's documentation carefully before making such a purchase.

Laser Printers

Laser printers are a bit more expensive than inkjet printers, but they are generally faster and produce much higher-quality text output. This is rapidly changing, however, as inkjet quality improves, and the cost of building laser printers decreases. Three hundred dollars would buy you a top-of-the-line inkjet or a laser printer, so the decision boils down to whether or not you need color output, and how important printing speed is to you. It should also be noted that no matter how quickly inkjet output dries, there's always still a chance for smearing the output which could be problematic for small/home business users.

When it comes to toner cartridges, inkjets and lasers are again pretty competitive. You should note, however, that the real expense with lasers may be in replacing the drum—not a frequent expense, but one you should be aware of nonetheless.

Selecting the printer that is best for you is not a simple proposition; a number of factors enter into the equation, including the following:

- We would all like to have the latest and greatest printer out there, but like it or not, price is often a limiting factor.
- Do you anticipate most of your text output to be for professional-looking documents or will your printer be primarily for family use?
- Are you planning to use multiple printers? For example, I use an old Hewlett-Packard laser printer for work-related documents and a new Hewlett-Packard color inkjet for producing personalized greeting cards, photo transfers for making memory quilts and T-shirts, and reasonably good prints of pictures (both photos and children's artwork) for the grandparents.
- Will you be running multiple copies of most output or will single copies be the norm?
- How important are a good warranty and technical support to you?

20

After you have answered the above, you are ready to begin some serious printer shopping. First, look at your budget; the issue of cost goes far beyond the initial investment. You have to factor in other things like the price of replacement cartridges and whether you need to buy special paper for the printer. (Some lower-end printers may cost less, but you have to buy special inkjet paper for them, which may offset the initial purchase savings in the long run).

> **The brand may make a difference.** Don't assume that all printers using the same technology cost the same to operate. Get to know the cost of supplies for various brands of printers too. Watch out for the economy cartridges that cost less than their "regular" counterparts but hold less ink. Whatever you do, make sure you are comparing apples to apples.

Also consider intended use. Although it is true that color printer output costs more than monochrome printer output, the price difference may be quickly made up, for example, by creating your own greeting cards instead of shelling out two bucks apiece in the local card shop. If quality printed output is key to a new home business you may be launching, a laser printer may be well worth the investment. Even if you want to produce spot-color brochures, you can still do so with a laser printer by purchasing special preprinted paper from an office supply store or mail-order specialty paper store. These good-quality papers give you professional color output without needing to compromise print quality.

Now that the price and type of printer you need is fixed in your mind, you can focus your attention on the easy part: selecting a brand. Doing this requires you to compare warranties and the availability of technical support between brands. With the increasing competition among printer manufacturers, purchasing incentives like rebates should also be explored.

Consider also a brand's reliability and length of time manufacturing printers. Hewlett-Packard printers are pretty hard to beat from a reliability and warranty standpoint, but they may cost more than their Lexmark, Epson, and Canon rivals. Ask your friends what brands have given them positive experiences and also consider surfing newsgroups and Web sites to gather data.

> **Get the latest scoop from the experts.** One place you may want to surf when considering a new printer is ZDNet at http://www.zdnet.com. They publish reviews of all kinds of hardware, often pitting one brand against another.

If you have considered all the questions posed here, your choice should be pretty clear. Now you can start shopping for the best price, and if you read earlier lessons in this book, you should be able to save a fair amount of money.

Adding a Printer to Your System

With the advent of plug-and-play technology, hooking up a printer to your PC is a piece of cake. Of course, because there are potentially two ports (parallel or USB) to which a printer can be connected, you will want to consult your printer's documentation to discover exactly where you should plug in the device. You will also want to check the printer's box before leaving the store to make sure you have the appropriate printer cable. Few things are worse than getting a new toy home and finding you can't even play with it because you are missing a crucial part!

After the printer is plugged in, you will need to define the printer within Windows. To do so, simply follow these steps:

1. Open the Control Panel, click the Printers and Other Hardware link and then click the Add a Printer link.

> **Printers...unplugged.** If you installed the printer (plugged it in) with the computer off, Windows recognized the addition on startup and helps you get everything ready for action.

2. The Add Printer Wizard shown in Figure 20.4 appears. Click Next to begin working your way through the wizard.

FIGURE 20.4

The Add Printer Wizard is designed to make installing and configuring a printer easier than ever.

20

3. Next, you will be prompted to specify whether the printer is a local printer (attached directly to your machine), or a network printer (attached to another machine on your home computer network). Typically, Local Printer will be the appropriate answer. Click Next to continue.

4. The Wizard attempts to find the printer connected to your machine. If it was unsuccessful, you will have to add it manually. Click Next to begin doing so.

5. You will then need to define to which port the printer is connected. Windows XP gives you a bit of help there. Click Next when the proper port has been selected.

6. You can click the name of your printer's manufacturer and model in the respective windows, as shown in Figure 20.5. If you don't see your model listed (or you received an installation disk with your printer), click the Have Disk button.

FIGURE 20.5

You have literally dozens of manufacturers and models from which to choose.

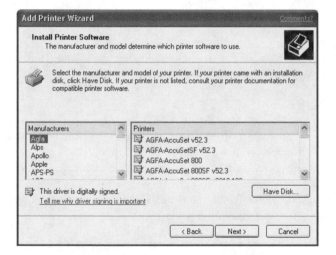

7. If you click the Have Disk button, you will see a dialog box prompting you for the disk. Insert the disk, click your way to the installation files you were provided, and then click OK. Click Next to move on to the next screen in the wizard.

8. Since the steps from here on out vary depending on your personal situation, just follow the onscreen prompts until you reach the end of the wizard.

9. Click the Finish button to complete and close the Add Printer Wizard.

There are some other peripherals I want to tell you about too, like helping you choose a scanner or digital camera in Hour 23, *Digitally Yours: Working with Electronic Images*. I will also introduce you to some cool computer game gizmos in Appendix A: Optimizing Game Performance.

Summary

In this hour, I presented many of the improvements you can make to a PC in order to bring it back to life or put it on the cutting edge of performance. Hopefully, you have a better grasp of why various enhancements work and which options are best for you, given your particular wants, needs, and desires. Some discussions, like the selection of scanners and digital cameras as well as choosing joysticks and other gaming devices, will come later in the book.

Next up, get ready for some fun. I will show you how to use Windows Media Player to listen to tunes on your PC, watch movies, and even burn your own music CDs.

Workshop

Now it's time to see just how much you learned in this lesson. I'll give you a short multiple-choice quiz to test what you learned, followed by a suggested activity designed to enhance the skills you acquired during the hour.

Quiz

Select the best answer to the questions from the choices provided and then check your answers.

Questions

1. What does RAM stand for?

    a. Randomly amazing miracles

    b. Redundant ambiguous machine

    c. Random access memory

2. What do you call an upside-down mouse?

    a. A little confused

    b. A mouse in trouble because a cat has batted him around a bit

    c. A trackball

3. Which of the following is *not* a type of printer?

    a. Laser

    b. Inkjet

    c. CD-R

20

Answers

1. C; The others may only *seem* true at times....

2. C; Trackball is the right answer.

3. C; Hah, three C answers in a row! Did I confuse you?

Exercise

Write down three things you wish your computer performed better. Now skim back through the pages in this lesson. Did you find any potential solutions to your problems?

HOUR 21

Getting Sights and Sounds on Your Computer

Did you know that in addition to being a lean, mean Internet surfing machine, a word processor, a spreadsheet compiler, and a computer game playing device, your PC has the potential to become a compact disc (CD) player, radio tuner, sound recorder, digital video disc (DVD) player, and television too?

Okay, maybe you have heard about some of the possibilities, but a few may surprise you, especially when you learn how little it takes to get up and running.

In this hour, I will show you how to turn your PC into an amazing collection of sights and sounds. We will answer the following questions to name a few:

- Can I tell my computer which CD tracks to play?
- How can I make my own music CDs for parties or commuting in my car?

- What kinds of audio streams will I find on the Internet?
- How do I control a DVD movie?

In the past, Windows included a collection of utilities to perform various multimedia functions. It included a special CD player, a media player that handled Internet audio, a third party video viewer, and more. Now, nearly everything is handled by Windows Media Player. That means a whole lot less stuff to learn about your PC before putting it work!

The Computers Are Alive, with the Sound of Music!

Playing audio CDs using Windows Media Player is a real treat. Much like with stereo components, you can program Windows Media Player to play only the tracks you want, to repeat the current disc until you stop it, or to play selected tracks at random (often known as *shuffling*).

Let's begin with the basics though: playing an audio CD. When you insert an audio CD into your computer's CD-ROM drive, the Windows Media Player typically launches on its own. If it doesn't, you can call it into action by clicking the Start button on the Windows taskbar and then choosing All Programs, Accessories, Entertainment, Windows Media Player.

The CD begins to play automatically while the Windows Media Player attempts to download CD information from the Internet. If an active Internet connection is available, the names of the artist, album, and individual tracks will appear in the Windows Media Player Window. If no connection is found, the text will be filled in with generic information like Unknown Artist, Unknown Album, and Track 1.

 Later, 'gator. If you dial up to the Internet after the CD has started playing, you can tell the Windows Media Player to go out and download album information. To do this, click the CD Audio button on the left side of the Windows Media Player window and then click the Get Name button. Within seconds, full album information will be downloaded for you.

You can control the CD by using the buttons on the Windows Media Player panel, as shown in Figure 21.1.

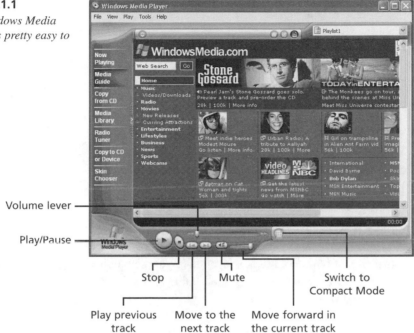

FIGURE 21.1

The Windows Media Player is pretty easy to control.

Volume lever

Play/Pause

Stop   Mute   Switch to
Compact Mode

Play previous   Move to the   Move forward in
track   next track   the current track

Um, don't you think something's missing here? Observant readers may notice I didn't point out Move backwards in the current track button. That is because such movement is disabled in audio CDs.

Although most of the buttons pictured in Figure 21.1 are self-explanatory, a few could benefit from more detailed coverage. For example, if a CD is playing, the big round Play button becomes a Pause button. Likewise, when the CD is stopped, the big round button becomes a Play button.

The Volume button is essentially a slider lever. Click it and drag it to the right to make the music louder or drag it to the left to make it softer. Also fairly new to the Windows Media Player is the Mute button, which silences the music the instant you click it.

You will also notice a big window full of all kinds of colorful animations. When not displaying videos, this window produces all kinds of funky visualizations for your viewing pleasure. This visualization window can be customized, too, but I'm sure you would rather learn how to burn music CDs, play DVD movies, find radio stations and police scanners on the Internet and other cool stuff like that than fiddle with the look of your Windows Media Player.

21

Setting CD Playback Options

By default, the CD Player will play the current disc once through and then stop. However, a number of additional playback options are available to you, too, all of which can be set with little more than a couple of mouse clicks.

To set them, click the Play menu on the Windows Media Player with the desired CD playing and then click either of the following options. Note that clicking the selected option a second time will remove the check mark, thus deselecting the chosen option.

- **Shuffle**—Instructs the Windows Media Player to play tracks on the selected disc at random. This option is a great way to refresh the predictability of an overplayed CD!
- **Repeat**—Click this playback option to have Windows Media player repeat the selected CD until you tell it to stop.

More Facts About the CD in the Hot Seat

If you poke around Windows Media Player a bit, you will discover a lot of interesting tidbits about the CD currently being played. Table 21.1 shows you what bits of information you will find where.

Table 21.1 Gathering Information About the CD

To Discover This...	...Look Here
Artist's name	In Now Playing mode, the top line of text above the visualization window. This data also appears in the Copy from CD window.
Song title	Look just below the artist's name. This information also appears in the Copy from CD window.
List of songs on album	On the right side of the windows is a pane reserved for the list of songs on the currently playing CD. This data also appears in the Copy from CD window.
Length of each song in minutes	Immediately to the right of each song is its length expressed in minutes and seconds. This information also appears in the Copy from CD window.
Copy status	In the Copy from CD window, you can learn whether a CD has been copied to your Media Library (the place where all your personally copied music files are stored), in the process of being copied, or in the copy queue.
Genre	Windows Media Player assigns a music style to the CDs it can identify. This information is in the Copy from CD window.
Style	The music style of the CD also appears in the Copy from CD section.

To Discover This...	...Look Here
Artist biography	From the Copy from CD window, click the Album Details button. A picture of the CDs cover and list of tracks appears along with a link to an artist biography. This information is not available for all artists, however.
Album review	Click the Album Details link to locate links to any available album reviews.

Selecting CD Tracks to Play

Do you own CDs containing only two or three tracks you like because you have to take the good music along with the bad? We all do, I'm sure! Then there are those intense cases of song obsession where you swear you could listen to the same song over and over again for hours on end.

Well, Windows Media Player has a simple solution for you. By disabling unwanted tracks, you can play only the songs on the CD you want to hear. You will, of course, need to do this while the CD is playing. Using the default Now Playing view shown in Figure 21.1, right-click the songs you don't want to hear; then choose Disable Selected Tracks from the shortcut menu. The songs you disabled are grayed out, leaving the ones you want to hear with their usual bright print. Believe it or not, Windows Media Player remembers this information regardless of how many times you remove the CD, play others, and then return to it!

To enable the songs again, simply right-click them and choose Enable Selected Tracks from the shortcut menu.

Burning Music CDs

If you have a recordable CD drive, then you have the makings of your own personal recording studio. If you like Herb Alpert, Madonna, The Dixie Chicks, Jessica Simpson, Donna Summer, ZZ Top, and John Tesh, you can have them all on one CD (as scary as that may sound). It's your call!

Hey baby, wanna buy a Rolex? Obviously, these CDs should be created for personal use and not sold for commercial use. Reproducing music for resale without permission is a blatant violation of copyright laws. It should also be noted that borrowing a friend's CD to make a copy is also a copyright violation. That's true whether you want to copy the whole CD or a single song.

21

Three major steps are involved in burning your own CDs. First, you must record the music to the Media Library on your hard drive. This makes duplication quicker, simpler, and more flexible in terms of track choice. Second, you will need to create a playlist for the CD, which basically tells the Windows Media Player which songs you want on the CD. The actual burning of the CD is your last step.

Copying Music Files to Your Media Library

Copying files to your Media Library is not only the first step required to burn a music CD, but it also enables you to play favorite tunes directly from your hard drive. Fragile CDs can stay nice and safe in their jewel cases, and people who travel with laptops, personal PCs, or other portable devices can now "take with them" dozens of CDs from their home music libraries!

You will need to follow these steps in order to copy music from your audio CDs to your Media Library:

1. Put the CD you want to record in your CD-ROM drive and give Windows Media Player enough time to download album information. This makes it easier for you to decide which tracks you want to record versus those you want to leave behind.

2. Next, access the CD Audio window by clicking the Copy from CD button on the left side of the screen. As shown in Figure 21.2, this window displays all pertinent information about the album in your CD-ROM drive.

FIGURE **21.2**

It is easy to be selective about the songs you copy.

3. By default, all tracks of a CD are selected for reproduction. You can remove specific songs by clicking inside their check box to remove the check mark. Only songs with a check mark will be copied to your Media Library.

4. To begin copying the files, click the round, red Copy Music button. The Copy Status column will keep you apprised of the job's progress.

Are you a copycat? Various music labels are experimenting with copy protection methods that would prohibit the duplication of a commercial CD. Most of these technologies are still in the testing stage, but there may come a day when they're commonplace.

You can even listen to the CD while the job is running. Simply click the Play button to play the CD. Your computer will continue copying the specified files in the background.

Building a Playlist from Files in Your Media Library

My CD collection is filled with albums containing only one or two songs I actually like. What a waste! I have a stack of Various Artists compilation albums that is higher than I care to admit! If only I could get them on just one album to enjoy on a regular basis….

Creating a playlist is the answer to many people's wishes. You can select only the songs you want and burn a CD or maintain on your hard drive that simple list alone. You can create a party mix for a shindig in your home, or you can compile a playlist of your favorite songs of all time and listen to them repeatedly while working at your computer or using your portable music device. However, to be included in a playlist, a song must first be copied to the Media Library, as directed in the previous section.

Getting spaced out. Copying a single song much less an entire CD can take tens of megabytes of disk space if done using the MP3 sound file format. With Windows Media Player's Audio 8 format, you can get the quality of MP3 for around a third of the disk space.

By default, Windows Media Player copies your files at near CD quality. (You can bump up the quality by clicking Tools, Options, opening the Copy Music tab, and moving the Copy music at this quality lever to the right.) With this default file size, an average music CD will take up 28 megabytes of disk space. The highest quality files take a whopping 86 megabytes of storage.

Given the large size of most disk drives these days, you may not encounter any problems with storing your files, but you should be aware of the sound file sizes just the same.

21

To build your own Windows Media Player playlist, follow these steps:

1. Click the Media Library button down the left side of the screen. This takes you to the Media Library window shown in Figure 21.3.

FIGURE 21.3

The Media Library is where you will create playlists and organize your media collection.

2. Next, click the New playlist button at the left end of the Media Library button bar. Windows Media Player asks you to name the playlist you are about to define.

3. Type in a name that accurately describes the list and then click OK. Your new playlist will be added to the My Playlists collection on the left side of the window.

4. Now you will need to add songs to the playlist. In the left pane of the Medial Library window, you will see a list of all the CDs you have stored in your library. Under the Album section, click the name of a CD containing a track you want to include in the playlist. The album's track listing appears in the right half of the window.

> **A different light.** The contents of your Media Library can also be viewed by artist or genre if you prefer. Just click the plus (+) sign next to the preferred method of organization to see the contents displayed in the chosen manner.

5. Click the name of a track you want to include and then hit the Add to Playlist button. Remember, you can select multiple tracks by holding down the Ctrl key while you click.

Easy does it! Keep in mind a CD can only hold 74 minutes of music, and you probably want to come in a bit under that to make sure you get a good, complete copy.

6. Keep adding sound files until all the songs you want have been added. If the playlist is going to be accessed on your PC only, then the playlist can be as long as you want. If it is destined for a CD or portable device, then you may want to be a bit more judicious in your selections, since not all of it is likely to fit.

Making Your Own CD

Now that you have invested all that time and energy into making a good playlist, it is time to turn it into an audio CD.

Start by verifying that your recordable CD drive is properly connected to your computer. Then make sure you have a blank CD in the drive that's ready to record.

The two kinds of blank CDs. In Hour 4, *Choosing Your Backup Media*, I introduced you to both recordable (CD-R) and rewritable (CD-RW) CDs. You may want to revisit that lesson to refresh your memory before purchasing blank CDs.

Just follow these steps to make a CD:

1. Launch Windows Media Player and access the Media Library.

2. Once there, click the name of the playlist you want to record on the blank CD.

3. Now click the Copy to CD or Device button on the left side of the Windows Media Player. The tracks on the chosen playlist appear onscreen with checkboxes next to each one.

No Copy to CD option? This feature may not have been installed with Windows Media Player. You can either get your CD containing Windows Media Player and install the add-in from there, or you can download it from the Web using Windows Media's Help, Check for Player Upgrades command.

21

4. Make sure that the tracks you want to include in your CD or device are checked, and then click the little red Record button in the upper right corner of the Media Player window.

Where do you want to put it? If your device (writable CD drive or portable music device) is not always connected to your computer, Windows Media Player may prompt you to connect it and then hit the F5 key.

Music and Videos on the Web

One great thing about Windows Media Player is that it is equipped to handle just about any kind of audio or video it finds on the Net. Simply click the sound or video link, and Windows Media Player fires up with its familiar, easy-to-use controls. As you surf the Net, you will find you can use Windows Media Player to watch movie trailers, see video game footage, or listen to sound clips of a soon-to-be released single.

Go ahead, give it a test drive. Launch Windows Media Player with a live connection to the Internet and then click the Media Guide button. From there, you can jump to Movies, Music, Business, Webcams, or Sports, to name just a few topics. Try one video and an audio clip. It is just like playing a regular CD, isn't it?

Tuning into the Radio Online

You want to try something really interesting like go browsing for radio stations around the world? Seriously, from peppy contemporary music stations in Denmark to rap from Chicago, it is all out there. Listen to local news from Jamaica or hear a top-rated morning show from the East Coast.

Now what? I won't bore you with all the politics, but to make a long story short, radio advertisers and their respective talent protested the broadcasting of their ads online by "regular" radio stations, so many stations have disabled their live audio streams for the time being. Others have found creative workarounds. I just thought you should be prepared to hit a few roadblocks as you search for your favorite radio station online.

To learn more about this dispute and one company's solution, point your Web browser to: http://www.internetnews.com/IAR/article/0,,12_786891,00.html.

Although you can access radio stations from a variety of points across the Net, the best place to start is Windows Media Player's Radio Tuner. Just launch Windows Media Player, click the Radio Tuner button on the left side of the screen, and you are at your starting point, as shown in Figure 21.4.

FIGURE 21.4

Get a jumpstart to your favorite radio stations or just ones you listened to most recently.

You will see links to several featured stations on the left side of the window, along with links for types of music in the upper right section. If nothing strikes you there, click the Find More Stations link. From there, you can search by ZIP code or tune in to some editors' choice stations by clicking their links.

Really though, who knows the postal code for an elusive city across the world (or for that matter if there even is a postal code)? What you really need is the Advanced Search (click the Use Advanced Search link underneath the ZIP code text box). The Advanced Search lets you look for stations based on genre, language, country, state, link speed, band (AM, FM, or Internet only, not Genesis or Cheap Trick), or a keyword of your choice.

Once you have performed your search, the results appear in the right half of the screen. Simply click the link of interest and choose Play to hear the radio station's broadcast (see Figure 21.5).

In addition to playing a station whose link you clicked, you can also click the Add to My Stations link to add it to your My Stations list, which will make it easier to find the next time around, or Visit Website (to learn more about the selected station).

21

FIGURE 21.5

When you click the link of an interesting station, you are faced with three choices.

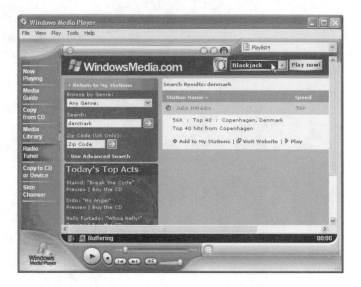

Eavesdrop on the police. You will also find police scanners, fire dispatchers, and air traffic controllers online. To listen in on one of 27 major metropolitan area police scanners, surf to `http://www.apbnews.com`. Windows Medial Player is all you need to begin listening.

For the Record

With a microphone and Windows XP, Home Edition, you can record the voices of friends and family for use in e-mail and on Web pages. The quality isn't professional caliber, but hey, it doesn't cost much, so who can complain?

To begin working with the Windows Sound Recorder, click the Start button on the Windows taskbar and then select All Programs, Accessories, Entertainment, Sound Recorder. The Sound Recorder window shown in Figure 21.6 appears.

Next, verify that your microphone is properly connected to the back of your PC. If it is, you should be able to click the Record button and begin recording instantly. No more hitting Play *and* Record to set the recorder in motion! Use the other buttons just as you would those on any tape recorder you have used in the past.

To save your recording, go to the Sound Recorder's menu bar and click File, Save on; give the file a meaningful name; and then click the Save button. You will now be able to access the file from any software application that enables you to insert or embed .wav files.

FIGURE 21.6

This recorder is even easier to use than the cassette recorders of yesteryear.

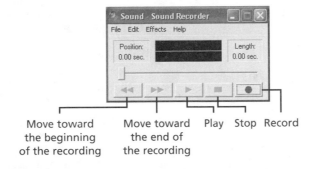

Move toward the beginning of the recording

Move toward the end of the recording

Play   Stop   Record

So big! Although you can only record 60 seconds worth of audio, you should know that the files are huge! It will take what seems like an eternity to mail, open, or download them onto a Web page, so use them sparingly.

What Is DVD Anyway?

I remember the day DVD was introduced as if it was only yesterday. Popular electronics stores carried only a couple of models of DVD players, and you could count the number of videos available in this format on both hands.

Now it looks as though DVD is here to stay. You can find DVD players in a variety of price ranges and forms, now that the Sony PlayStation 2 includes DVD capability. Video discs can be found by the binful at those wholesale clubs/membership warehouses.

DVD is the next generation of optical disc storage. Not only can DVDs hold more data and run faster than other optical storage devices, but they can also hold video, sound, and computer data. Furthermore, DVD broadcasts at twice the resolution of VHS videos and Dolby sound. Some of the technology's biggest supporters believe DVD may eventually replace audio CDs, videocassettes, laser discs, CD-ROMS, and perhaps even game cartridges. In fact, the technology has gained the support of major electronics companies, computer software manufacturers, and a near majority of movie and music studios. It certainly looks like DVD is here to stay!

It is important, however, to understand the difference between DVD and DVD-ROM players. A DVD player refers to the video players you connect to TVs. These players play only video discs like those you rent at your local video store. DVD-ROM players, on the other hand, can be found in newly manufactured computers. DVD-ROM drives not only read video discs, but they also can read audio and data CDs.

21

Even if your computer didn't come with a DVD-ROM drive, you can always upgrade later by either swapping out your old CD-ROM for a DVD-ROM or adding the DVD-ROM to your machine as an additional drive.

I Want My DVD!

You can do lots of things to maximize the value of the DVD-ROM drive you choose. Here are some important considerations:

- **Your current processor speed.** If the computer into which you wish to put a DVD drive has anything slower than a 133MHz Pentium processor, DVD performance may suffer.

- **The availability of titles you want to view.** Although there aren't many computer software titles that take full advantage of DVD technology yet, remember that a DVD-ROM can play DVD movies and any audio CD. Also, if you are not convinced that there are many DVD videos out yet either, surf over to the DVD Review at http://www.dvdreview.com and take a look around; that should change your mind in a hurry!

- **Durability.** Do you have children who repeatedly watch the same movie? I know my kids are like that, often wearing out a poor VHS tape within weeks. At least DVDs are more durable, and they don't disintegrate over time like videotapes do. However, you do have to consider potential smudging and scratching of the DVD's delicate surface.

- **The best in DVD.** To get the most out of DVD video, try to get a setup that includes a hardware decoder board. This essentially maximizes DVD performance while minimizing the strain on your computer's processor. Obviously, it is more technical than that, but this gives you more than enough information to make the best purchasing decision.

Don't try this at home! If you are new to computing, I strongly urge you *not* to try installing a DVD-ROM setup on your own. PC components can be fragile, and the insides of your machine can be confusing. It can even be dangerous if you don't know exactly what you are doing. If you must install such a setup, either do it at the time you purchase your machine, pay to have it done by a professional later, or even better, find a buddy who knows computers to do it in return for soda and a pizza.

- **Hardware versus software decoding.** If your computer is slower than a 300MHz Pentium II, it is a good idea to invest the extra money into a hardware decoding board. Faster processors, however, may be able to handle the demands.

- **The rest of the setup.** To get the most pleasure out of DVD videos, you may want a 17-inch monitor or larger; good multimedia speakers, complete with subwoofers; and a high-quality sound card. You can get by with less than this, but these three items comprise the optimum setup for DVD video enjoyment.

Playing a DVD Movie

Okay, this is so simple, I'm almost embarrassed to write about it because I will sound like I'm repeating myself! To play a DVD using Windows Media Player, put the DVD in the DVD drive and wait for Windows Media Player to launch itself and start the movie.

The button you used to skim forward through a CD's current track is the counterpart to a VCR's fast forward button. Likewise, the Next track/Previous track buttons move you backward or forward through chapters on the DVD movie.

A chapter? Aren't we talking computers, not books? DVD-formatted movies are divided up into bookmarked scenes called *chapters*. They help you navigate to particular points within a movie.

The one DVD-centered command you will most likely want to know is how to run the movie the whole size of the screen, since many DVD videos display in letterbox format (to look more like you are "at the movies.") To do this, click View, Full Screen. The movie-viewing window expands to cover the entire monitor surface.

Summary

Playing sights and sounds on your computer were the focus for this lesson. You saw how similar it is to use your PC to play an audio CD, the radio, and a DVD movie. You also learned how to record sound bites, and you even walked through the process of burning your own CD. Not bad for an hour!

While we are on the topic of sights and sounds, let's take a look at instant messaging in the next hour. It is the new technology/tool that lets you find friends who are online at the same time you are and chat with them in real time.

21

Workshop

Now it's time to see just how much you learned in this lesson. I'll give you a short multiple-choice quiz to test what you learned, followed by a suggested activity designed to enhance the skills you acquired during the hour.

Quiz

Select the best answer to the questions from the choices provided and then check your answers.

Questions

1. Which of the following do you have to do before you can burn your own CD?

    a. Copy the sound files to your Media Library.

    b. Send $5 to each of the artists whose music you plan to record.

    c. Sing to your PC to get it accustomed to hearing music.

2. What is the recording tool described in this lesson a part of?

    a. Office XP

    b. MSN Motormouth Kit

    c. Windows XP

3. What does DVD stand for?

    a. Droopy Vinyl Disc

    b. Digital Video Disc

    c. Dormant Vinyl Disc

Answers

1. Wow, we can sure tell *this* lesson was written late at night! A is the correct answer.

2. I can see A, but B? Nope—it's C!

3. B is the correct answer. (I just couldn't resist poking fun at records, the long-lost cousins of audio CDs.)

Activity

Pop a bag of fresh buttery popcorn, grab a soda, and surf over to http://www.dvdreview.com. Your mission there is to find at least three movies that would appeal to each member of your household. Browse the upcoming release lists or search through the film vault to find your favorites.

HOUR **22**

The Instant Messaging Primer

We all know snail mail can take days to reach the intended recipient, and heaven help you if they snail mail back! It could be two weeks before you get the answer to your questions.

You could call the person, but will they be home when you are free to talk? If they are home, can you afford the lengthy conversation that is likely to follow?

With e-mail, at least the message gets there quickly, but you have no idea if someone is at the other end of the line to read it.

Instant messaging takes the timeliness lacking in snail mail, the expense related to phone calls, and the element of the unknown in e-mail and tosses it out for something far more immediate—instant messaging. The following are a few points of interest in this lesson on instant messaging:

- What is instant messaging, and how does it differ from e-mail?
- What do I need to get started with instant messaging?
- How do I find my buddy online?
- Can I control who can send me an instant message?

Have you ever sent someone an e-mail message only to find a response in your Inbox moments later because the recipient was online at the very same time? Techies would say you were "real-timing it" at that point, since your message arrived and was responded to almost immediately.

Now imagine kicking it up a notch—that is, turbo charging e-mail, if you will. With instant messaging, not only does your message reach its destination ASAP, but you can also tell whether your recipient is online. You can even control when others "see" you online or not.

There is more than one flavor of instant messaging service. We are looking at Windows Messenger because it comes with Windows XP, but it should be noted that there are other services out there like the one offered by America Online (AOL). Not all messaging services can interact with one another, so you may find yourself changing or adding another messaging service depending on what your friends and family use.

What Is Instant Messaging?

Since instant messages appear to be a unique combination of e-mails and online chats, let's take a closer look at how they differ from each of these. Once you understand that, you will know exactly how one medium is different from another, and which one is best used when.

When it comes to instant messages versus e-mails, there are three differences you need to keep in mind:

- Instant messages are delivered in real-time, whereas e-mail messages are collected for you to view at your convenience.
- Unlike e-mail, instant messages are temporary in nature. The words you see onscreen during an instant message conversation disappear the instant the message window is closed, unless you specifically opt to save the conversation. E-mail messages remain in your Inbox or on your computer until you delete them.
- E-mail is basically text only with the potential to add pictures or a sound clip. With Windows Messenger, you can use your PC to call someone's phone or to place a PC-to-PC call.

Instant messages bear a bit more resemblance to online chats; however, there are some significant differences between the two where privacy is concerned.

Windows Messenger is a bit more personalized than the average chat room because you have full control over who can participate in a conversation. It is also more private than a chat room. When you go to set up a chat room, the entire world could know about the conversation, since it is most likely publicized on the host community index page or someplace like that. With a Windows Messenger conversation, only you and your contact(s) know the conversation is even taking place.

You should also know that anyone can use Windows Messenger no matter what Internet service provider they use as long as they have Windows Messenger installed and configured on their computer. It's also worth noting that any friends or family you may have using WebTV will be able to chat with you using this service.

Configuring Windows Messenger

Before you can begin chatting in real-time, you will need to acquire a .net Passport and set up Windows Messenger on your computer. (Windows Messenger is typically installed with Windows XP.)

Where can I find Windows Messenger Service? If you don't see it on your Start menus, then you will need to find your Windows XP installation disk and install if from there.

Follow these steps to get your .net Passport and set yourself up for Windows Messenger:

1. To launch the application, click the Start button and then point to More Programs, Windows Messenger. You will see a Windows Messenger Window with a single text link in the center..

2. Click the Click here to sign in link. The .NET Passport Wizard shown in Figure 22.1 appears.

I'm not going out of the country; why do I need a passport? Rather than have an assortment of user names and passwords for various Internet sites, a .NET Passport gives you a single sign-in and password identity. This eliminates multiple passwords, which can become hard to remember over time.

You can also add a Wallet to your account, which will store credit card and shipping information remotely so you can shop securely and efficiently—no more filling out zillions of forms everywhere you shop! It should be noted, however, that Microsoft Wallet isn't supported at every online merchant. You may want to check whether or not your favorite sites support it before you go to all the trouble to set it up.

FIGURE 22.1

The .net Passport Wizard Welcome screen tells you a little about the passport's capabilities.

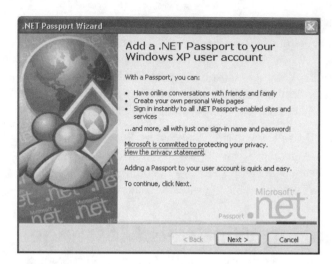

3. Click the Next button to begin working your way through the rest of the setup wizard.

4. The first screen asks you if you have an e-mail address. Let's assume that your answer is Yes since you've been working your way through this book. Click the Yes option and then click Next.

5. Type your e-mail address in the text box provided and click Next to continue.

6. Next, you are asked to enter a password. This password must be at least six characters long, and it may contain letters (upper- or lowercase), numbers, and standard symbols. You'll need to type it a second time to verify that it's correct and then click Next.

7. To keep your passport safe, you'll be given the opportunity to define a secret question. Use the drop-down box provided to select the question and then type in the correct answer. Should you forget your passport password, you will need to provide the answer to this question in order for the password to be revealed. Click the Next button to move on.

8. For additional security, the wizard asks you to provide details about where you live. Drop-down boxes are provided for Country/region and State, but you'll have to type in the ZIP code. This information will be requested in addition to the answer of your secret question in order to release the passport password. Click Next.

9. At this point, you may opt to simplify registration at Passport-enabled Web sites by sharing your e-mail address or other passport information. The choice is yours. Just click the desired option (if any) and then click Next.

10. If you chose to keep your e-mail address/registration information to yourself, you'll see a screen that says you're done setting up your .NET Passport. Click the Finish button.

Adding Contacts to Your Windows Messenger List

After you finish setting up Windows Messenger, you will see a window like the one shown in Figure 22.2. This is the Windows Messenger window you will see each time you launch/log into the program.

FIGURE 22.2

Hmmm... it looks pretty quiet around here without some contacts!

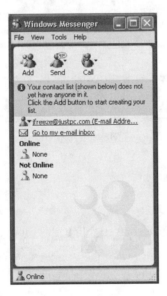

The first thing you will notice is a message in a shaded area saying your contact list is empty. An instant messaging service is no good without someone to interact with, so let's add some contacts to that list!

When Contact E-mail Address Information Is Known

Since the process is a little different, depending on whether not you know the person's e-mail address, I have divided the steps into two separate sections. If you know the address/sign-in names of the contacts, you can add them to your list by following these steps:

1. Click the Add button at the far-left end of the Windows Messenger button bar. You will see the Add a Contact dialog box shown in Figure 22.3.

FIGURE 22.3

You are given two ways to add a contact to the list.

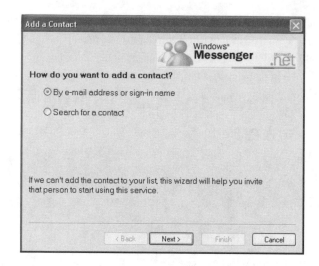

2. Verify that the By e-mail address or sign-in name option is selected and click Next.

3. Type in the address or signing name and click Next.

4. You receive a message saying that the person was successfully added to your contact list. If they aren't using Windows Messenger, Microsoft will send them a note inviting them to do so.

5. Click Finish to close the dialog box.

Searching for a Contact

If you need to track down a prospective contact, follow this set of steps:

1. Click the Add button at the far-left end of the Windows Messenger button bar. You will see the Add a Contact dialog box shown in Figure 22.3.

2. Select the Search for a Contact option by clicking its button and then click Next.

3. You will then be presented with a search window like the one shown in Figure 22.4. Add as much information as possible to help narrow the search. Using the Search for this person at drop-down box, you can have Windows Messenger search the Hotmail Member Directory or the address book on your computer. Select the appropriate database and then click Next.

4. You will receive a message stating whether it could find the contact. If it can, that person will be added to your contact list. If it found multiple matches to your search, you'll be prompted to select one. If it can't find a match at all, you can click the Back button to redefine your search.

FIGURE 22.4

The more information you provide, the easier it will be to find the desired contact.

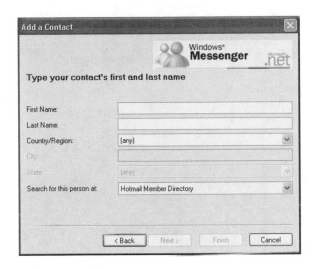

22

Sending an Instant Message

Now that you have somebody to contact, let's try sending an instant message. Just follow these easy steps, and you will be chatting in no time!

1. Launch Windows Messenger as described earlier in the lesson. Your defined contacts will either be listed as Online or Not Online.

2. Double-click the name of an Online contact with whom you wish to speak. You will see a dialog box dedicated to that instant messaging session, as seen in Figure 22.5. The dialog's title bar will say something like "Jill-Instant Message" where Jill is the name of your selected contact.

3. Near the bottom of the Instant Message window you will see a large, blank text box with a Send button next to it. Click inside that text box to activate it, type in your message, and then press Enter (or click the Send button if you prefer). Your message appears on your contact's screen instantly, awaiting his or her response. When he or she responds to you, the new message appears under yours, automatically scrolling the screen up as necessary in order to display the full message.

> **Hey, where'd you go?** If at any time during the instant messaging session your contact becomes unavailable, you will see a message to that effect in a blue message bar at the top of the chat window.

4. Keep repeating step 3 through the entire conversation. When you are done with the chat, simply close the dialog box using the Close (X) button.

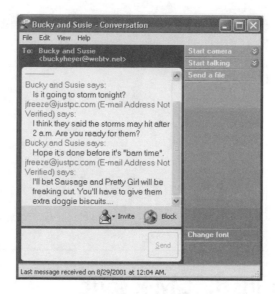

FIGURE 22.5

Soon your Instant Message screen will be as filled with chatter as this one is!

Temporarily Changing Your Windows Messenger Availability

You should be aware of a few other basic instant messaging functions. For example, you should know that just closing Windows Messenger windows does *not* log you off the instant messaging server. In fact, you don't even need Windows Messenger windows open at all in order for the application to run; it can do everything from its cozy little spot next to the clock on your Windows taskbar.

To keep others from bugging you, you will either have to get off the Internet or put out a virtual Do Not Disturb sign.

Changing the way you appear to others online is a breeze. In the main Windows Messenger window, you will see an arrow button next to your contact icon. Click it and choose from any of the following options: Online, Busy, Be Right Back, Away, On the Phone, Out to Lunch, or Appear Offline. The first option lets everyone know you are out there, and the last one sends a clear "nobody's home" signal. All the others leave a prospective contact with the impression you could be available again at any moment.

Perking Up Your Instant Messages

Looking at plain text all day can get boring, so why not add a little pizzazz to your instant messages? You can do this in one of two ways: by changing the text font you use or adding emoticons to express emotion through icons.

Changing the Instant Message Type Font

Like your handwriting, the font you use for instant messaging can be a reflection on your personality. To modify it, click Tools, Options from the Windows Messenger Menu bar. Open the Personal tab and then click the Edit Font button on the lower right side of the dialog box. The Change My Message Font dialog box shown in Figure 22.6 opens.

FIGURE 22.6

Change a font, italicize it, enlarge it, make it red; whatever your pleasure, you can find it here.

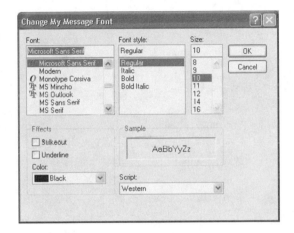

Using the scroll bars available, browse the list of possibilities. Click it to see a preview in the Sample box. Change as many attributes as you want: style, size, color, and so on. When you like what you see in the Sample box, click OK to apply your modifications.

Expressing Yourself with Emoticons

You remember emoticons from a few hours back, right? Those are the smiley faces made of punctuation marks and other keys? Well, Windows Messenger takes emoticons to a whole new level. Here, they are colored and shaped like the real thing rather than a skill-fully placed set of punctuation marks.

Table 22.1 presents the emoticons supported by Windows Messenger. Use this table to type your own emoticons in a message, or to interpret ones sent to you by a contact. To enter one in an outgoing instant message, simply type words into the text box as usual, followed by a space and then the keystrokes presented in the table.

Big or little, it doesn't matter. As you look at Table 22.1, you should note that the letters can be upper- or lowercase. I just presented them in upper-case for clarity's sake.

Table 22.1 Emoticons supported by Windows Messenger

Icon for Emoticon	Description	Key Sequence
	Smiley	:-) or :)
	Open-mouthed smiley	:-D or :D or :-> or :>
	Smiley says	:-O or :O
	Smiley with tongue out	:-P or :p
	Winking smiley	;-) or ;)
	Sad smiley	:-(or :(or :-< or :<
	Crooked smiley	:-S or :S
	Stern smiley	:-I or :I
	Thumbs up	(Y)
	Thumbs down	(N)
	Red heart	(L)
	Broken heart	(U)
	Red lips	(K)
	Gift with a bow	(G)
	Red rose	(F)
	Girl	(X)
	Boy	(Z)
	Camera	(P)

22

Icon for Emoticon	Description	Key Sequence
	Beer mug	(B)
	Martini glass	(D)
	Telephone receiver	(T)
	Cat face	(@)
	Coffee cup	(C)
	Light bulb	(I)
	Hot sun	(H)
	Sleeping half-moon	(S)
	Star	(*)
	Musical eighth note	(8)
	E-mail	(E)
	Windows Messenger icon	(M)
	Vampire bat	:-[or :[

Tell me you didn't mean that! The ability to display emoticons is an option that needs to be set in Windows Messenger. If it is not enabled, the result could leave the person at the receiving end of the emoticon under the impression that he or she is receiving expletives! If you see something that looks questionable in an instant message, consult Table 22.1 before reacting to make sure it isn't an innocent mistake. You can save yourself some potential trouble ahead of time by clicking Tools, Options and then selecting the Show graphics (emoticons) in instant messages option if it isn't already enabled.

Changing Your Display Name

When you configured Windows Messenger access, you had to submit your e-mail address. Unless you tell Windows Messenger otherwise, it's this e-mail address others will see onscreen. To change that e-mail address into a display name, start by opening Windows Messenger; clicking Tools, Options; opening the Personal tab and then clicking inside the My Display Name text box and entering the desired screen name. Click OK to apply it.

Restricting Instant Messaging Accessibility

Is there a way to make instant messaging capabilities available to specific contacts only? You bet! Windows Messenger gives you full control over who can see you are online and who can send you instant messages. That way, you can take advantage of the immediacy of instant messaging without getting an endless stream of unwanted interruptions.

To define who can and can't communicate with you via instant message, you will need to do the following:

1. With Windows Messenger running, click Tools, Options from the Menu bar. This opens the Personal tab of the Options dialog box.

2. Open the Privacy tab to see a dialog box like the one shown in Figure 22.7.

FIGURE 22.7

This user has cut everyone but one contact off from instant messaging contact.

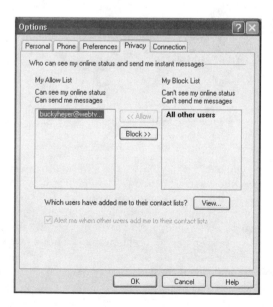

3. By default, everyone is on your Allow list, but that can be easily changed. Click the name of the contact you want to block from access and then click the Block button. That places the selected contact on your Blocked List. You can always go in and change it again, but until then, that person (or persons) is prohibited from sending you instant messages. They can still reach you by using traditional e-mail, however.

4. Keep moving contacts from one column to another until you are satisfied with the lists and then click OK to apply them and dismiss the dialog box.

There are two more things I would like to point out about the Privacy tab. The first is a View button that, when clicked, displays the name of everyone who has added you to their contact list. It is important to remember that you may not have added all these people to *your* contact list. You may want to consider doing just that so you can enable or disable their access to you on demand.

The second item of interest is a little check box that basically says, "Alert me whenever someone adds me to their contact list." I keep this item checked all the time. It may seem unimportant to do this, but having this information is a powerful tool in managing your instant messaging accessibility and privacy.

Operational Options

As I mentioned earlier, Windows Messenger pretty much runs in the background until you specifically log on or off. You can change the way the program runs, however, by using the Preferences tab of the Options dialog box. To do this, click Tools, Options; then open the Preferences tab.

These options are controlled by a set of six check boxes as shown in Figure 22.8. They are all enabled by default; however, they can be easily disabled by clicking the check box to remove the check mark.

The options available in the Preferences tab include the following:

- **Run this program when Windows starts.** By default, Windows Messenger will launch when you boot Windows. Deselect this option to force a manual launch of the application.

- **Allow this program to run in the background.** Leaving the option as it is enables you to do other things on your computer while waiting for incoming instant messages.

- **Show me as "Away" when I'm inactive for ___ minutes.** Unless you tell it otherwise, Windows Messenger will convert your status to "Away" after 20 minutes of inactivity.

- **Display alerts near the taskbar when contacts come online.** This option gives you a visual cue when a defined contact logs on to Windows Messenger.

- **Display alert near the taskbar when an instant message is received.** Another good option to keep enabled, this one lets you know that a new message was received, regardless of whether you are in another program.

- **Play sound when contacts sign in or send a message.** By default, a musical chord plays when this event occurs. Although I like using the audio option at home because it grabs my attention better than a visual cue, it may not be welcomed in a work setting where the sound may bother others.

FIGURE 22.8

The Preferences tab allows you to adjust Windows Messenger to run the way you want it.

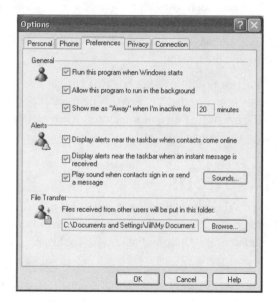

Hearing Voices

In some situations, hearing voices is a bad thing, but that is not the case with Windows Messenger. With the right equipment, you can call anybody around the world. Windows Messenger gives you two ways to conduct a voice conversation with your PC: a PC-to-telephone call or a PC-to-PC call.

It used to be that Internet-initiated phone calls were free, but not anymore, at least for PC-to-telephone calls. Windows Messenger taps into Net2Phone to provide PC-to-telephone service. I have found in testing this service that the sound quality is less than optimal, especially since users are now charged for the service. When such calls could be made for free, tolerating a little line noise seemed fine. However, given the charge for the service, I have decided to focus on PC-to-PC calls in this lesson. The sound quality may not be the greatest, either, but you can't beat the price!

Do You Have What You Need?

In order to place a call from your computer to another PC, you will need a few things in addition to your Windows Messenger account. These items include the following:

- A full duplex sound card or USB port
- A set of speakers and microphone or a headset that plugs into the available USB port
- A modem with an active Internet connection with a minimum speed of 28.8K

If you have everything you need to take advantage of voice communication, then you are ready to begin the setup work.

Working Your Way Through the Audio Tuning Wizard

The only real setup needed in order to conduct computer-to-computer voice conversations involves plugging in your microphone and working your way through the Audio Tuning Wizard. This wizard helps ensure that your microphone and speakers are up to the task of communicating by voice.

Before you begin running the wizard, however, there are some general guidelines regarding microphone use you will want to know. These include the following suggestions:

- Close any other programs running on your computer that play sound.
- Verify that the microphone and speakers are properly plugged in and turned on.
- Keep the microphone reasonably close to your mouth when speaking. Three to five inches away is optimal for most types of microphones.
- To avoid hearing echoes or feedback, keep your microphone pointed away from the speakers. If you hear either type of interference, click the Cancel button, reposition your microphone and then try again.

With these guidelines in mind, you can start working your way through the Audio Tuning Wizard by doing the following:

1. Launch Windows Messenger and then click Tools, Audio and Video Tuning Wizard. You will be greeted by a window that basically reiterates the guidelines presented above. Click Next to continue with the wizard.
2. The first order of business involves setting speaker volume. After you have verified that your speakers are properly connected, click the Test button shown in Figure 22.9. You will hear a test sound play on your computer. You can make it softer or louder by clicking and dragging the Speaker Volume lever left or right, respectively.

FIGURE 22.9
*Choose from 11
speaker volume levels.*

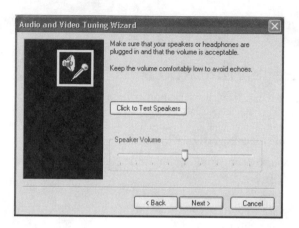

3. When the volume meets with your approval, click the Stop button and click Next to continue.

4. You are then asked to read some words into the microphone to verify its sound level and volume. If the sound level indicator turns yellow while you speak, you are in business. If not, keep moving the microphone and adjusting the volume using the lever provided until it does.

5. Once you have gotten a good microphone sample, click Next. Congratulations, you have completed the wizard and are now ready to begin talking over the Internet via voice!

Calling Another Computer

Okay, now you are ready to place your first call. In the Windows Messenger window, click on the name of a person you want to contact. (Remember, he or she must have speakers and a microphone properly configured in order for this to work.) Next, click the Call arrow button and choose Computer. The contact will be invited to accept your call. If that person doesn't accept the invitation, it may simply be because he or she is not set up to deal with it.

Take turns speaking just as you would over the telephone, only this time you won't have the hefty bill to show for it!

Summary

There are so many ways to communicate with others using your PC. In this hour, we looked at the immensely popular instant messaging technology using Windows Messenger. You learned how to get it up and running and how to engage in a real-time text or voice chat.

Now that you can send e-mail, chat with, and listen to your friends and family using your computer, it is only fitting that I show you how to share photos and other images with them. That is the focus in our next lesson.

Workshop

Now it's time to see just how much you learned in this lesson. I'll give you a short multiple-choice quiz to test what you learned, followed by a suggested activity designed to enhance the skills you acquired during the hour.

Quiz

Select the best answer to the questions from the choices provided and then check your answers.

Questions

1. What do you call the list of people you can contact with Windows Messenger?
    - a. Buddies
    - b. Contacts
    - c. Messengees

2. Can you block someone from being able to send you instant messages?
    - a. Yes
    - b. No
    - c. Uh, what was the question again?

3. Which of the following is NOT needed to conduct an Internet-based voice call?
    - a. DVD drive
    - b. Microphone
    - c. Speakers

Answers

1. B is the correct answer. A is wrong, and there is no such word as C!
2. If you said A, you have the correct answer.
3. A is the correct answer. DVD drives have nothing to do with instant messaging whatsoever, and speakers as a choice was in there just to make it a bit of a trick question!

Activity

In this lesson, you learned two ways to search for potential contacts who are already signed up to use the Windows Messenger.

Try at least five names of people you know in the search tool. If you come up empty, consider e-mailing some of your buddies to get them on the instant messaging band-wagon. It is a whole lot of fun and reasonably priced, too!

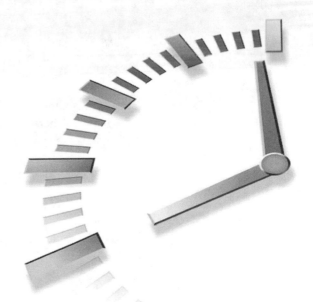

HOUR 23

Digitally Yours: Working with Electronic Images

Never run out of film again. Always take the perfect picture. Turn normal studio pictures into works of art. Share photographs with friends and family around the globe for free. Welcome to the world of electronic imaging!

Whether you are scanning old photos or taking pictures with a digital camera, you will be amazed at what awaits you in the field of digital imaging.

In this lesson, we will experiment with the following topics:

- What is the difference between one scanner and another?
- How do I choose the best digital camera to meet my needs?
- How do I organize my photos using the My Pictures folder?
- How do I view my photos as a filmstrip or slideshow?
- Can I burn a CD of photos to share?
- What is the best way to print my photos or publish them to the Web?

Before you can start working with images, you need to have a device that can get them on the computer for you. There are two primary choices in that department: scanners, which take a picture of paper photos for storage on the PC, and digital cameras, which let you take pictures with virtual film for storage on the computer.

> **The third option.** Digital video cameras are becoming increasingly popular and less expensive too, so if you plan to make movies, this may be the best option for you. More about that in Hour 24, *Star in Your Own Movie or Music Video.* In general, however, I find them a bit too bulky for simple picture taking.

Since not many people get these devices up front, I have taken a great deal of time in this lesson explaining the ins and outs of purchasing each type of device.

Selecting a scanner is pretty straightforward, but a digital camera is another story entirely. There are so many different features to consider, and you can spend anywhere from $50 for a "toy" model to more than $1000 for a high-end model.

In the following sections, I will introduce you to the various features of each; then you can decide what best fits your personal wants and needs.

Selecting a Scanner

Like computers, scanners come in all shapes, sizes, and price points. Choosing the right one for you involves a lot more thought than simply choosing a brand within your budget. Scanners are available for around $100, but many may not be capable of doing what you want at the level of quality you desire. You do often get what you pay for.

In the following sections, I will show you all the things you can do with a scanner. This is critical information for selecting the right scanner. I will also show you how a scanner works, and give you the scoop on which features are worth the extra money and which ones may be unnecessary.

What Scanners Can Do for You

Scanners are one of those peripherals that are equally useful for work and play. A scanner can convert a paper document into a word processing document, produce high-quality images for a corporate Web page, or even scan the merchandise you sell at online auctions. You can also scan old photos to preserve them for the long term and maybe even touch them up a bit). You can put your children's pictures on special transfer media for creating personalized T-shirts and memory quilts. You can also put current photos on special-theme CDs for long-term storage or sharing.

Whether your needs are personal or professional, it is easy to see how a scanner could come in very handy!

How Do Scanners Work?

If you ask me, scanners seem to work like magic! In reality, they work by moving a row of silicon cells from the top to the bottom of the scanner's bed. These cells basically bounce light off of and through the object on the scanner bed. The results are then translated into color waves that eventually become the photo-realistic image you see onscreen.

Which Scanner Is Right for Me?

Because the scanning needs of the average user are fairly basic, I'm going to oversimplify the decision-making process a bit. In the fall of 1997, I bought a scanner for around $100, which was incredibly cheap at the time. I have to say that the results have always been more than acceptable for my needs. The same holds true today; why pay hundreds of dollars for a scanner when one for well under $100 does the trick? If you eventually become a professional graphic artist or Web page designer, then you can go out and pay the big bucks; but for now, your money would be better spent on a less expensive scanner. That way, you can afford to pick up some good photo editing software if you don't receive any with the scanner.

If you do have the money and hope to enlarge and print out photos on your color inkjet printer, here are some things to look for when shopping for a scanner. With scanners, there are fewer features to consider and compare than you may think. First, check the number of levels of color a scanner can replicate. This information is often expressed in bits, and the general rule of thumb is the bigger, the better. The more bits at which a scanner operates, the more authentic are the coloring and details of the image. However, as you may also expect, there are always exceptions to this rule. Some manufacturers soup up their scanners to deliver better performance than their counterparts with the same specifications. In any case, the minimum quality you should consider is 24 bits.

Another specification, or spec, is the scanner's optical resolution. Although 600 dpi is best for reproducing fine art, line drawings, and detailed photos, 300 dpi is sufficient for the needs of many.

Dabbling with DPI.... DPI actually stands for dots per inch. The more dots per inch, the tinier the dots are that make up an image. And the tinier the dots are, the better the image quality since small dots (technically called pixels) can form neatly rounded edges or sharp corners more effectively than their larger counterparts.

You will also see mention of parallel and USB scanners. You will need your hardware and software specs to determine whether you need a parallel or USB scanner. Parallel scanners can work with just about any current PC no matter what version of Windows you are running. Some parallel scanners will even let you pass through to your printer, but make sure the printer you have will be happy with the scanner you are considering, or neither may work properly.

USB scanners are much faster than parallel scanners, but they require Windows 98 or newer operating systems plus a special USB port on your machine. Check your system specs carefully before making a final decision, or at least make sure you can exchange the scanner if there is a problem.

I could throw in a ton more technobabble about how a scanner works and how the various features can be interpreted, but unless you are doing high-quality scanning for a living, just about any scanner will do.

The World of Digital Cameras

Do you have dozens of rolls of exposed film lying around just waiting to be developed? Are you tired of spending $15 for film and developing of 24 exposures, only to find three or four of them acceptable and even fewer that are actually good? Have you ever wished you could keep only the good pictures and just throw out the bad? Now you can, thanks to digital cameras!

Choosing a Digital Camera

Choosing a digital camera is a bit more complicated than selecting a scanner. When it comes to selecting a good one, there is lots to consider, and in this case, the average user *will* be able to see the difference.

The price of digital cameras varies widely, ranging from $50 (for low-resolution models marketed at youth) to several thousand for professional models. Let me help you decide which features are worth paying for and which may not be worth your investment.

In the following sections, I examine all the major considerations and provide guidelines you can follow to make your decision.

Price Does Matter

Unfortunately, price is still a dominating factor for most of us. Although you can get inexpensive digital cameras, be leery of them. They are a great and economical way to teach children basic photography skills, but you can't rely on them for photo-realistic output in all lighting conditions.

Expect to pay $300 or more for a digital camera that truly rivals 35mm quality. Although that may seem like a lot of money, just think of how much you will save over time on film and film processing! There are intangible benefits to a good digital camera—you can take pictures whenever you want without having to worry about the cost or wait involved with developing them. Think about it; how many times have you shot up the end of a roll of film on useless stuff just to get to the prized pictures you shot somewhere in the middle of the roll?

Higher Resolution: An Investment Worth Making

Regardless, don't settle for a camera with anything less than 640×480 resolution. Even then, don't expect crystal-clear results.

When you scan an image or shoot a digital picture, the result needs to be enlarged to be of any real use. If it weren't enlarged, you would have a tiny image about the size of a postage stamp. The downside to this, however, is that when you make a low-resolution image bigger, it can become grainy or pixilated. That means the resulting image will not be sharp to the eye.

Given that, take a look at Table 23.1 to see a list of image resolutions and their corresponding results.

Table 23.1 Camera Resolutions and Image Production Results

Image Resolution	Product
640×480	Produces a 3 1/2×5 printout at best
1024×768 (1 megapixel)	Produces an acceptable 5×7 photo quality image
1280×1024 (1.3 megapixels)	Produces prints up to 8×10 in size
1.6 megapixels and up	The higher the resolution, the greater the image detail and the bigger the high-quality image produced

Also keep in mind that even if you don't anticipate generating large images, the higher resolution may also enhance the quality of smaller images, and it will certainly give you higher-quality results on the Web.

CMOS Versus CCD

I won't get too technical on you here, but this is a spec worth knowing a little bit about. CMOS and CCD describe the types of light sensors in the digital camera. Although CMOS sensors generally cost less and have a longer battery life than their CCD counterparts, CCD cameras are more responsive to various lighting conditions. Thus it is possible that a higher resolution CMOS camera may actually generate inferior results when compared with a slightly lower resolution CCD camera.

Printed Output Versus Online Output

If you plan to use a digitized image on a Web page, you can generally get by with a lower resolution. However, if you are hoping to print your own photos from digital camera output, you will want to go with the highest digital camera resolution you can afford, as well as the best color printer you can get your hands on.

> **You may not get what you pay for.** Where printers are concerned, paying more doesn't necessarily give you better print quality. Many times the higher price tag can be attributed to increased printing speed or commercial-rated durability. Take your time and choose widely, using the tips from Hour 20, *Spiffing Up the Ol' System.*

Give Me Light!

Digital cameras in any price range will shoot reasonably good pictures in sunlight, but if you hope to make use of the camera inside, having a flash is a must. Some fancier models even have red-eye reduction, which is a plus when photographing people.

The good news is that although you won't find flash capabilities on the least expensive models, it is becoming a standard feature on higher-end models.

Putting Things Into Focus

Focus features are similar to those found on traditional 35mm cameras. With fixed focus, one size fits all, so-to-speak. Autofocus automatically focuses on a specific object or person, although the subject's surroundings often become somewhat fuzzy. Manual focus with f-stops and various other settings, enables you to tweak your view, like with professional 35mm cameras.

In general, the low-end digital cameras use fixed focus because it is the most reasonably priced option. Autofocus is available on midpriced cameras because it offers some artistic freedom without the headaches of knowing about f-stops and other complex features. Available to professional photographers are the $1,000-plus cameras that give them the freedom and quality to which they have grown accustomed.

As always, these general rules of thumb are subject to exceptions and change. As more technical features become less expensive to incorporate, you will start seeing them on lower-priced models because all the manufacturers will be competing heavily for your business.

More Power to You!

Digital cameras can eat batteries almost as quickly as I can put away a plate of fresh, hot, and gooey chocolate chip cookies, especially a camera with a liquid crystal display (LCD) and flash capability.

Although lithium batteries provide the longest life, they can often be so pricey that they offset any savings you may see by switching from a standard camera to a digital camera. I have read that Rayovac's rechargeable alkaline batteries typically last longer than NiCads and may actually save you money in the long run, but your mileage may vary. To complicate matters further, prices of batteries and other power sources are constantly fluctuating, so what may be true as I write this may no longer be true when you read this!

Finally, if you often take pictures indoors and have access to an electrical outlet, you may want to buy the manufacturer's optional A/C adapter to save energy.

To extend your battery life even further.... Use the A/C adapter when downloading images to your PC. That way, you can shoot the photos without being tied down by the device's power cord in the nearest electrical outlet, and you won't burn up batteries while performing maintenance tasks.

Zooming In on the Subject

Fixed focus cameras may do just fine for shooting scenery or group pictures of your son's swim team, but you will be much happier with a model that gives you at least a 2x zoom. That way, you can tighten the shot to capture a special moment or a silly smile.

However, when it comes to zoom lenses, read the fine print. You will want to be sure you are getting optical zoom instead of digital zoom. The optical zoom resets the resolution of the image you zoom in on to the highest level possible, whereas digital zoom merely crops the image without considering the resolution. This makes digitally zoomed images appear grainier than their optical counterparts.

Even if you don't read the fine print, the price and zoom factor should be a dead giveaway. Cameras touting noticeably higher zoom factors than the norm are most likely employing digital zooms. Likewise, if the price is obviously lower than an equivalent camera, that may be a clue that this is digital and not optical technology.

Getting Connected

At the time of this writing, there are two primary ways a digital camera can be connected to your PC for image download. The oldest and slowest way is by plugging the digital camera into your computer's serial port. This former standard is quickly being replaced by USB, a method that transfers data many times faster than a serial port.

Get fired up! As you begin researching digital camera specifications, you may see references to FireWire support. Apple Macintosh heavily supports this high-speed connection, but it hasn't really caught on in the world of IBM compatibles. Intel is hard at work developing an even faster successor to USB, known as *USB 2.0*. You should see more of this over the next few years.

Before you buy a digital camera, check your PC's documentation to make sure that it can even support USB. Although many do, there are still some budget models that may not. As they say, "Better safe than sorry!"

Buying Your Virtual Film

Like traditional cameras need film to store images, digital cameras need SmartCards, floppy disks, or other specialized media. The average camera comes with 4 to 8 megabytes (MB) of storage, but you can purchase media that will hold as much as 90MB or more before you need to dump it onto your computer.

On the road again. If you plan to take the camera on your family vacation to Disney World, I strongly suggest that you take a laptop computer with you if you have one. This enables you to start each day with clean storage media, and it radically reduces the odds of inadvertently erasing cherished memories. Alternatively, you can invest in a high-capacity storage device for your camera, if picture storage away from home becomes a priority. For example, I can purchase various sizes of memory sticks for my Sony CyberShot camera. This means for a modest investment, I can leave the laptop at home and store pictures on these little chewing gum-sized sticks instead. Check the storage media your camera uses (floppy disks, CDs, memory sticks, smart cards, etc.) and browse the market for a high capacity alternative you can afford.

Some storage media can fit right into your computer's floppy drive with a special adapter, whereas others, like Sony's Mavica, store images on a standard PC floppy disk making it a breeze to use. Although the Mavica has won many over with its standardized storage media, you can only fit up to five high-resolution images on a single floppy. That can be bothersome, especially when all your spare floppies fly out of your pockets while on a roller coaster ride during your theme park vacation!

Having It All!

The majority of cameras, except for the extreme low-end models, come with an LCD that gives you a glance at the picture you just took—a great way to kill, on the spot, those shots that aren't perfect.

Unfortunately, these tiny displays are huge battery hogs. Make sure you get a camera with an optical viewfinder and an LCD so that you can save your batteries for what really counts—more pictures!

Some argue that LCDs give you more authentic "what-you-see-is-what-you-get" results when it comes to composing a picture, but although that may be true, remember that we are dealing with computerized images here. With a photo editing program, you can get exactly what you want regardless of actually ended up inside the camera.

You Oughta Be in Pictures!

Although you can e-mail your images to family and friends, post them on a Web site, or print them out on your color printer, how do you share images with noncomputer users?

Some digital cameras come with a TV-OUT outlet that lets you connect the camera to any TV from which you can either give your slide show manually or program the camera to cycle through the images one-by-one. Of course, this implies that the images are still on your camera's storage media, which may not be practical.

Speak to Me!

Many digital cameras give you the opportunity to record 30-second sound bytes for each picture. Although this is a wonderful way to preserve that special Mother's Day program in which your son performed or that speech your sister gave at a local rally, it does soak up precious space on your storage media. You decide if sound is important to you or not. Also, just because your camera supports sound doesn't mean you have to use it; it can be turned off and on, giving you the opportunity to take advantage of the feature on demand.

Still Versus Video

You can also get digital camcorders from which you can create movies and still shots using the software provided. With digital camcorders, the storage media is the tape on which you record the video, so there is no pricey storage media to purchase.

If you decide to go with a digital camcorder, expect to pay between $800 and $1,000. Also, if you travel a lot, you will want to factor in the camcorder's bulkier shell, which could be a real pain to lug around.

Your Scanner or Digital Camera and Windows XP

My how things change—and this time for the better. Windows XP is so smart about detecting new hardware, you could install it with your eyes closed!

First, you will need to consult your PC and scanner or digital camera documentation to make sure you are plugging everything into the proper spot, Once you are all connected, turn on the device.

After a few fleeting moments of disk drive activity, Windows XP announces the presence of new hardware via a text balloon over the right end of the Windows taskbar. Seconds later, a dialog box similar to the one in Figure 23.1 appears.

The digital camera or scanner is literally all set up, ready to go to work for you.

FIGURE 23.1

Because Windows sees my Sony CyberShot camera as a removable disk drive, the dialog box's title bar reads "Sony MemoryStick (E:)." Your title bar will most likely say something different.

From Digital Camera to...

You may have also noticed in Figure 23.1 that several digital camera operations are available to you without having to scour the Start menu for them. They are as follows:

- **Copy pictures to a folder on my computer using Scanner and Camera Wizard**. This moves the pictures from your digital camera to your computer.

- **View a slideshow of the images using Windows Picture and Fax Viewer**. This lets you quickly browse the contents of your digital camera without having to move the pictures to a hard drive.

- **Print the pictures using Photo printing Wizard**. This enables you to immediately print selected photos on a printer to share with others.

- **Open folder to view files using Windows Explorer**. This allows you to see images already stored on your computer.

- **Take no action.** This closes the dialog box and leaves the images in place on your camera.

Acquiring Pictures with the Scanner and Camera Wizard

23

To move images from your digital camera to your computer's hard drive, you will have the help of the Windows XP Scanner and Camera Wizard.

You can transfer the pictures by following the set of steps below:

1. Plug the camera into your Windows XP computer and turn it on. In seconds, you will see the dialog box shown back in Figure 23.1.

2. Click the Copy pictures to a folder on my computer option and then click the OK button. This launches the Scanner and Camera Wizard Welcome Screen.

3. Click the Next button to begin importing the images onto your hard drive. The wizard displays a dialog box displaying a preview of all photos on your digital camera's storage media (see Figure 23.2).

FIGURE 23.2

The wizard makes it easy for you to decide which images to keep and which to toss out.

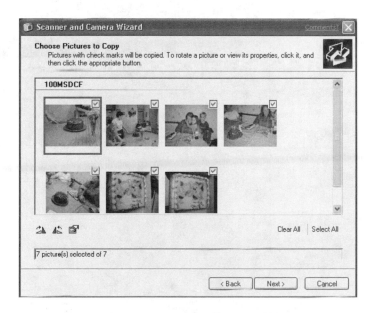

4. By default, all images will be moved to the hard drive. However, you can easily eliminate certain pictures by clicking the green check mark in the upper right corner of the unwanted image. Once the images you want are marked for big move, click Next.

> **All or nothing.** If you only want to keep one or two out of the set, you may want to click the Clear All button on the lower right part of the dialog box. This deselects all the images, meaning you will only have to click the handful you want to move/keep.

5. The Select a Picture Name and Destination dialog box shown in Figure 23.3 opens, presenting you with four important decisions to make. First, you will need to pick a name for the selected set of pictures. The more descriptive it is, the easier your life will be down the road. Disney 2002 for your summer vacation or Samantha 7 for your daughter's 7th birthday are good options. Type the chosen name into Step 1 of the dialog box. Each of the pictures in the set will reside in that directory with a unique number to identify it.

6. Next, you will be asked to name the folder in which you would like to store the images. By default, the folder will be given the name you selected in the previous step, and it will appear in the My Pictures hierarchy. I strongly recommend you leave it there so that all your images are in one central location.

FIGURE 23.3

This is where you will tell the wizard how you want your pictures stored.

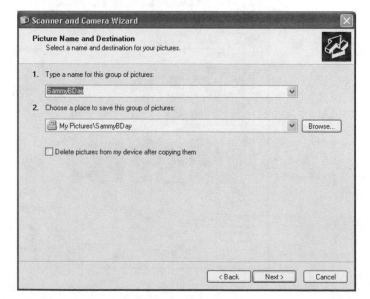

7. Finally, by checking the box at the bottom of the dialog box, you can instruct the wizard to delete the images from your camera once they have been moved to your computer. They will stay on your camera by default, so if you want to eliminate the step of manually deleting them from the camera, go ahead and check the box. Click Next to proceed.

8. The wizard relocates each image to your hard drive one-by-one, as you can see in Figure 23.4. When the job is finished, the wizard reports the successful transfer of your pictures to the hard drive and presents some additional options for actions you can take on the images. You can opt to publish the photos to a Web site, order prints from a photo printing Web site, or do nothing more with them (the default). Click the Next button to continue.

23

FIGURE 23.4

The Scanner and Camera Wizard gives you an ongoing status report of the file transfers.

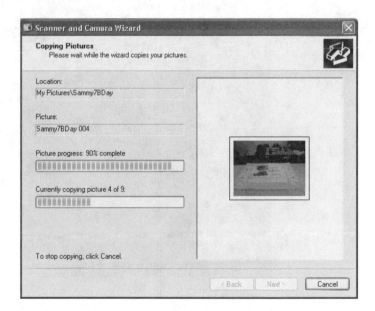

9. The wizard reports how many pictures were copied to your hard drive and presents a link you can click to view them. Click Finish to exit the wizard. When the wizard closes, the relocated pictures appear onscreen in the newly defined My Pictures directory. I will show you how to work with them later in the hour in a section called Managing Your Images from the My Pictures Folder.

Viewing a Slideshow of the Images on Your Camera

This is a wonderful way to browse images on your camera, especially when you are away from your own computer. If you have a friend or relative with a Windows XP machine and the proper cables, you can share the photos right there on the spot. Just plug in the camera, turn it on, and follow these steps to conduct a slideshow:

1. Plug the camera into the proper cable, turn it on, click the View a slideshow of the images option, and then click OK. After a few moments, a slideshow loads (see Figure 23.5).

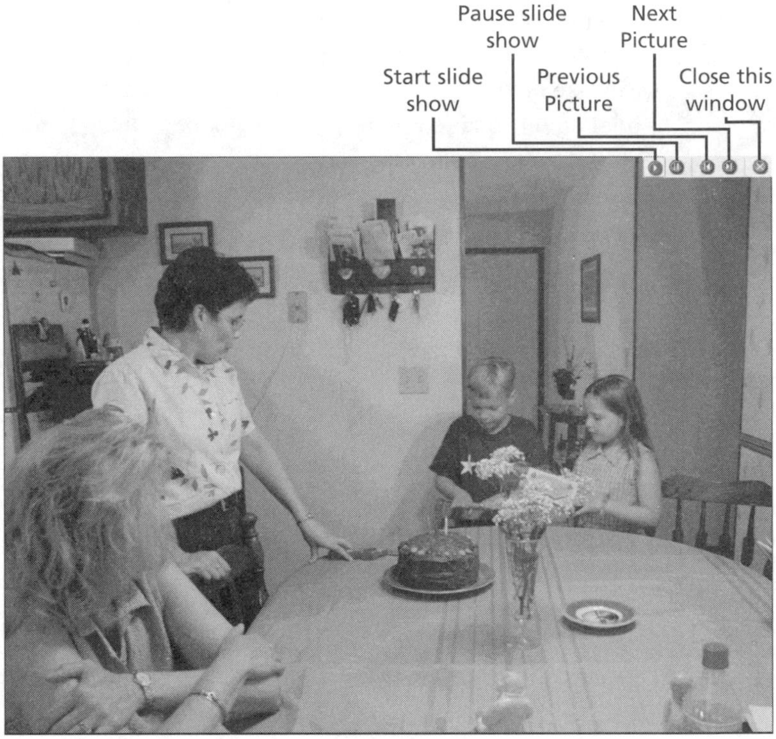

FIGURE 23.5

A set of five buttons in the upper right corner of the screen let you control the slideshow with a single mouse click.

2. The slideshow commences with each photo being displayed for a few seconds. If for some reason it doesn't start on its own (or if you need to restart the slideshow after pausing it), simply click the first button, the green Start slideshow button.

3. To pause the slideshow, click the second button. The current image stays onscreen until you restart the slideshow or move to another image.

4. The next two buttons let you move through the pictures one-by-one. The first button takes you backward, and the second takes you forward.

5. To close the slideshow, click the red Close button at the right end of the button bar.

Printing the Images Residing on Your Camera

Windows XP makes it easy to print images directly from your digital camera. Simply plug the camera into your computer, turn it on, and then follow these steps:

1. To get started, click the Print the pictures option, and then click OK. This launches the Photo Printing Wizard. Click Next to begin working with the wizard.

2. Previews of the photos residing on your digital camera appear inside the wizard's dialog box. (It is nearly identical to the dialog box shown back in Figure 23.2.) By default, all will be printed, but you can pick and choose the ones you want by clicking their check marks to toggle them on and off. When you are happy with your selection, click Next.

3. The next step requires you to define the printer you want to use. If there is only one printer connected to your computer, you are all set. Otherwise, use the drop-down arrow box to choose the one you want to use.

4. If you merely want a plain paper copy if the picture in normal quality, you can click Next to move on. Otherwise, click the Printing Preferences button. From there, you can choose paper type, print quality, and so on. The placement of these options will vary depending on the type of printer you are using. With the desired printer options set, click OK to dismiss the dialog box and then Next to continue with the wizard.

5. Now it's time to choose the layout of your prints (see Figure 23.6). You can print out a single large image, a sheet of 3 1/2×5-inch prints, wallet prints, and so on.

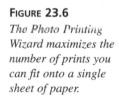

FIGURE 23.6

The Photo Printing Wizard maximizes the number of prints you can fit onto a single sheet of paper.

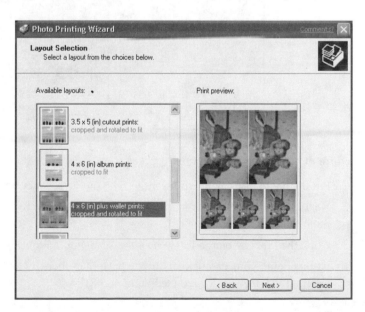

In fact, they do look much like those professional photo sheets from photographers. Click the layout/size you want and then click Next.

6. The Photo Printing Wizard sends the job to your printer, and within minutes, you have a set of photos just like you ordered.

Opening the Folder to View Files

This option takes you directly to the files on your camera using the My Pictures folder interface. See the section entitled, Managing Your Images from the My Pictures Folder, for a detailed explanation of how to work with this interface.

Scanning Images into Word

When you plug in your scanner and turn it on, Windows XP attempts to auto-detect it (determine what is the make, model, and manufacturer). After it determines the type of scanner, it launches a Word insert picture window like the one shown in Figure 23.7.

FIGURE 23.7
Your scanner is now ready to pull an image into Word.

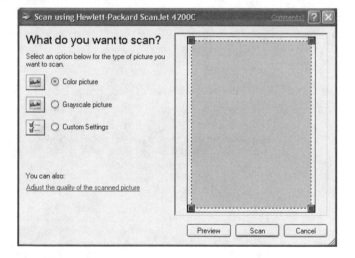

Perform the following steps to run the scan:

1. Put the photo or drawing you want to scan on the scanner bed and close the lid.

2. Next, tell Word whether it is a color or grayscale image by clicking the applicable radio button.

3. Click the Preview button to see how the scan would look.

4. At this point, you can click any of the hash mark borders and drag them in or out to crop the image as desired (see Figure 23.8).

FIGURE 23.8

Take as much or as little of a picture as you want by clicking and dragging its borders.

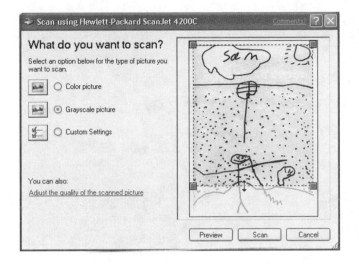

5. Are you happy with what you see? Click the Scan button. The full size image appears in your Word document in seconds.

6. When you save the Word document, the scanned image will be saved as part of a Word file. If you want to be able to save the scan as a .jpg image file for use on the Web, read on to the next section.

Redefining Scanner Defaults

Scanning an image directly into Word is certainly convenient, but what if you want to put it on the Web, print it out, or modify it using a picture editing tool? Being able to save it as an image file would be helpful.

By resetting the scanner's properties, you can tell it to call the Scanner and Camera Wizard into action instead of Word. To do this, hook up your scanner to your PC, turn it on, and then follow these steps:

1. Click the Start button on the Windows taskbar and then choose Control Panel. From there, click the Printers and Other Hardware link, followed by the Scanners and Cameras link.

2. Right-click over the scanner's icon and choose Properties from the shortcut menu.

3. Open the Events tab seen in Figure 23.9. In the Action section, use the Start this program drop-down box to select the Scanner and Camera Wizard as your new default.

FIGURE 23.9
Choose the program you want to fire automatically or have Windows XP ask you each time the scanner is started.

4. If you can't decide which program you would use most often, choose the Prompt for which program to run option. Now you are prepared for anything.

5. Click the OK button to save the new default settings.

Safely Removing the Hardware from Your Computer

Although Windows XP can recover successfully from less-than-optimal system shutdowns, it is always good to take the time to properly shut down the system. The same holds true for unplugging your scanner or digital camera from your computer.

To safely remove the hardware from your system, double-click the Safely remove hardware icon shown at the right end of the taskbar in Figure 23.10 and then click the single menu item that appears to confirm it.

FIGURE 23.10
A single menu item leaves you no doubt about what needs to be selected.

Create taskbar with
single menu item

Managing Your Images from the My Pictures Folder

Whether you want to e-mail a photo to a friend, compress images for inclusion on a photo CD, or publish a directory of photos to the Web, this is the perfect starting point. To get there, click the Start button on the Windows taskbar and then select the My Pictures link.

Setting Up the My Pictures Slide Show

Once inside My Pictures, you can set up a custom slideshow by clicking the pictures or folders to include in the show and then clicking the View as a slideshow link.

If zero or one image is selected, the entire directory will be included in the slide show. If two or more photos are selected, only the selected photos will be included in the show.

Don't forget your shortcuts for selecting multiple files. Either hold down the Ctrl key while clicking random files, or to grab several files in a row, click the first files, press the Shift key and while holding it down, click the last file you want to include.

E-mailing Photos to Friends and Family

I love e-mailing pictures to friends and family. When my kids receive a gift from someone, I take their picture with it and e-mail it to the gift-giver along with a thank-you note. When something special happens, I snap a shot and e-mail it to their grandparents halfway across the country.

I love the immediacy of digital photography, and although these cameras may cost more up front than their film counterparts, the purchase pays for itself many times over by eliminating film and developing costs.

To send a photo via e-mail, you will need to follow these steps:

1. From the My Pictures directory, click the picture you want to share and then click the E-mail this file link in the File and Folder Tasks section of the task pane.
2. Windows XP displays a Send Pictures via E-Mail dialog box saying it can "Make all my pictures smaller" so that it not only downloads quicker from the Internet or it can also fit it on the recipient's screen. You can also choose to "Keep the original sizes," which may increase download time and make it harder for the recipient to view. Click the Make all my pictures smaller option shown in Figure 23.11.

23

FIGURE 23.11

An optimized message travels the Internet faster than the original.

3. Once the file is compressed, an Outlook Express New Message screen opens, bearing the name of the image file as the note's subject line. The image file is also already attached to the message, so before sending it on, just address it and add a personal note to the body of the message.

4. Click the Send button to send the message and attached image on its way.

Creating a Photo CD

There is no real mystery to burning a photo CD. In fact, if you review Hours 3 and 4, *Getting Organized with Windows* and *Health Care for PCs,* you will find everything you need to know right there. Literally, all you have to do is select the files and then copy them to their new location. A piece of cake!

Ordering Photo Prints from the Internet

Just because you don't have a photo quality color printer doesn't mean you can't have printouts of your digital images.

Microsoft has forged a partnership with a company that can generate printed output for you and then send it to you via snail mail.

To take advantage of this service, enter the My Pictures directory, select the images you want to have printed, and then click the Order pictures online link. You will need to follow these steps in order to complete the process:

1. The above actions launch the Microsoft Online Print Ordering Wizard. Click the Next button to begin working your way through the wizard.

2. All the images you selected are displayed onscreen, giving you another chance to pick and choose the photos you want printed. Make your selections and then click Next.

3. Microsoft gives you multiple photo printing companies to choose from. Click one and then click Next.

4. Since the steps required at the providers will vary, simply follow the onscreen prompts to select and order your photos.

Publishing Photos to the Web

Here again Microsoft employs a wizard to make the task easier. To publish photos to the Web, visit the My Pictures directory, select the files you want to publish to the Web, and then click the Publish the selected items to the Web link. This launches the Web Publishing Wizard. Click Next to continue.

You are given a second chance to select the images you want included on your Web page. Make your choices and then click Next. Microsoft gives you a few choices for the location of the upload: some online storage services and any other network location you specify.

Again, since the steps needed for each of the selections may vary widely, you will need to follow the prompts onscreen for best results.

Additional Information Worth Noting

If you look closely at the My Pictures task pane, you will see many familiar commands. From within My Pictures, it is possible to move, copy, and delete your image files with ease. Simply select the files you want and then click the applicable link.

Viewing Your Virtual Filmstrip

The default thumbnail view of the My pictures directory makes it a snap to find what you are looking for, but there is an even better option: viewing the images as a filmstrip (see Figure 23.12).

To move to this view, click View, Filmstrip on the Menu bar When you click a photo in the filmstrip at the bottom of the screen, it appears in the large viewing window. Using the buttons provided, you can do the following from left to right:

- **Previous Image (Left)**. This button puts the photo immediately to the left of the currently viewed photo in the primary viewing area.
- **Next Image (Right)**. To look at the next picture to the right of the currently selected image, click this button.
- **Rotate clockwise**. This button can be used to turn an image taken sideways into its proper position.
- **Rotate counterclockwise**. This button can also be used to reposition an image.

FIGURE **23.12**
Filmstrips make it fun and easy to browse through your photos.

Summary

This lesson only scratches the surface of digital imaging, but hopefully, it gave you enough information to get up and running. After reading this, you should have a better idea of what to look for in a digital camera or scanner. You should also be prepared to do some basic image browsing, sharing, and printing.

In the next lesson, we make the leap from static images to moving images. You are going to learn how to use Windows XP's Movie Maker to produce your own movies or star in your own music videos!

Workshop

Now it's time to see just how much you learned in this lesson. I'll give you a short multiple-choice quiz to test what you learned, followed by a suggested activity designed to enhance the skills you acquired during the hour.

Quiz

Select the best answer to the questions from the choices provided, and then check your answers.

Questions

1. What is a megapixel?

   a. A fat pixel

   b. Uh, don't you mean gigapixel?

   c. A unit of measurement for digital camera resolution.

2. When you plug your digital camera into your Windows XP computer, what happens?

   a. The operating system automatically detects most cameras, meaning there is no installation necessary.

   b. You must insert the camera's CD at the same time to ensure smooth installation.

   c. The camera takes your picture.

3. Which of the following programs opens by default when you attempt to scan your first image?

   a. Outlook Express

   b. Microsoft Word

   c. Adobe Photoshop

Answers

1. C is the only acceptable answer here.

2. A; Windows XP is pretty smart as far as installing hardware goes.

3. Although B, Microsoft Word, does open by default, in this lesson, I showed you how to change this.

Activity

Since the world of digital cameras changes so often, surf on over to ZDNet (http://www.zdnet.com) and skim through the newest digital camera reviews. Not only is this a great way to get the lowdown on cutting edge features, but it can also keep you up-to-date on the street prices of various digital camera models.

Hour 24

Star in Your Own Movie or Music Video

Even if you don't dream of being an award-winning director or star on the big screen itself, you can have a lot of fun playing around with the Windows Movie Maker.

Not only can you transfer home videos to your PC, but once they are there, you can also do so much with them. In this lesson, I introduce you to the Windows Movie Maker. We will experiment with some of the more commonly used features and attempt to answer the following questions among others:

- What do I need to get started with the Windows Movie Maker?
- Can I hook up my old video camera and VCR to the computer?
- Can I watch videos residing on my camera/camcorder on my PC?
- Are there things I can do to maximize the quality of my videos and sound recordings?
- How do I cut the length of a video clip?
- Can I make smooth transitions from one clip to another?

Have you ever taken some video footage with your camcorder and wished you could e-mail it to someone? With Windows Movie Maker, you can!

You can e-mail video or publish it to the Web, and the viewer just needs Windows Media Player in order to watch it.

The Bare Minimum

Aside from cutting-edge game playing, video production can be one of the most demanding tasks for your computer. Just because your computer meets the minimum requirements for running Windows XP doesn't necessarily mean it will be amenable when working with videos.

Here is a quick rundown of necessary items to get started as an amateur movie maker with Windows XP Movie Maker:

- A 300 MHz Pentium II class or faster machine. "Or faster" is the key phrase here. The faster the machine, the better your performance is.

> **Do you have a digital camcorder at your disposal?** If you have invested in a fancy digital camcorder, you will see even better results than those working with "regular" camcorders or VCRs. However, improved performance comes with a cost. You will need a 600 MHz system at bare minimum plus 128 MB of RAM (memory). Again, the further you go beyond those specs, the better is your capability.

- According to Microsoft, you will also need at least 64 MB of RAM, but I am not sure I would even try it with less than 128 MB of RAM. I mean you can try it, of course, but the results may be less than optimal.

- You will also need a minimum of 2 GB of free disk space to get started. You will need plenty more if you intend to make or save a lot of movies. Of course, disk space is cheap these days, so you can always add on if necessary (see Hour 20, *Spiffing Up the Ol' System,* for more information on adding memory).

- An audio capture device like a microphone will come in handy for recording voice narratives for your movies.

- Of course, you will also need a video capture device like a camcorder, digital camera with video capabilities, or something similar. You can use the high-end digital video camcorders, or you can use an older analog camcorder or VCR.

- For true digital video captures from a digital video device, you will need an IEEE 1394 DV capture card to hook the device to your computer. Likewise, you will need a special video adapter or capture card for your analog device. Consult your computer and camcorder documentation, as well as the ZDNet (http://www.zdnet.com) Web site for guidelines for making the best choice under your particular circumstances.

Planning for a Great Video

The right hardware goes a long way in making a great video, but a little planning never hurts either. You can do a lot to boost the quality of your movie before you even pick up the camera. Obviously, you can't plan spontaneous videos, but if you are out to make one, then you may find some of these tips helpful.

Keep the Background in the Background

One thing that makes a video sluggish is something called a *low framerate*. As you know, videos are made up of lots of pictures "pasted" together. When the pictures are very similar from one frame to another, the computer has to do very little work to refresh the screen and move to the next frame, thus speeding up the framerate.

If, on the other hand, you do a lot of panning (moving from one side to the other) across a wide area or shoot with a "busy" or moving background, then video performance is bound to suffer.

The solution? Choose solid or static backgrounds whenever possible. If that isn't possible, try focusing the camera on your primary subject by bringing him or her closer to the lens or using a telephoto lens to zoom in on him or her. This reduces the depth of field, making the background fuzzy and less distracting.

Light Up Your Life

It goes without saying that your video subject should appear in adequate lighting conditions. What kind of lighting is best? Soft, diffuse, and most importantly consistent lighting will give you the best results. Harsh lighting like direct sunlight may cause shadows or silhouettes to appear instead of your subject.

It may be worth taking some sample shots before you go into production to maximize your results and minimize the time commitment of the subjects.

It's What You Wear That Counts

Believe it or not, the clothes your video subject wears can dramatically affect the quality of your video. Bright colors can "bleed" onto the subject's face and other surroundings, and stripes can cause distracting moiré patterns (video artifacts that make the lines look like they are crawling or moving onscreen).

24

The best advice is to stick with something that closely resembles your subject's coloring yet stands out from the background.

Presenting Windows Movie Maker

Okay, just a little bit longer before we get to the good stuff…. Before you begin working with Movie Maker, it is a good idea to know your way around its workspace. Figure 24.1 illustrates the parts of the Movie Maker screen.

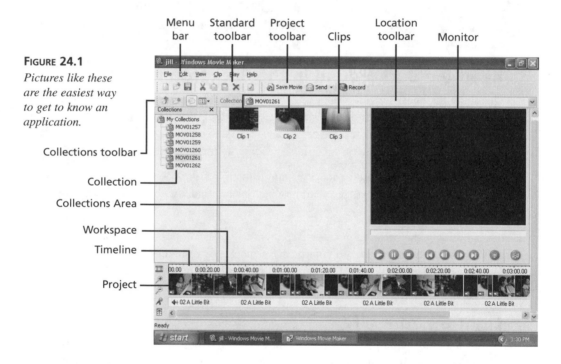

FIGURE 24.1
Pictures like these are the easiest way to get to know an application.

Here is a bit more detail about each element so that you will know your way around when we get rolling:

- **Menu bar/toolbars.** These elements perform similar functions to their counterparts in other Windows applications. You can open and save files, change views, and gain single-click access to unique Movie Maker tasks. You can also move, show, and hide Movie Maker toolbars like other toolbars you have worked with previously.

- **Collections Area.** In the left pane, you will see a list of the video collections and files you are working with in the current project. In the right pane, you will see shortcuts to clips contained within the selected file or movie in your collection. Movie Maker automatically creates a new clip whenever the entire makeup of the frame changes suddenly.

- **Monitor.** Drag a clip into the monitor to view it or play a whole project by clicking Play, Play Entire Storyboard/Timeline. Use the buttons underneath to control video play much like you did in Media Player. The seek bar above the buttons lets you know how much of the clip or movie has been viewed or has yet to be viewed.

- **Workspace.** This is the proper term for the strip of workspace near the bottom of the window. This is where you will drag all your clips to make a movie. You can view your project in two ways: Storyboard or Timeline (as shown in Figure 24.1).

Getting Video for the Movie

Although Movie Maker lets you record video while being hooked up to the computer, we only have an hour here, so let's assume you have video somewhere you want to work with during this lesson. Maybe it is currently on a videocassette, in your camcorder, or on your digital camera with video clip capabilities. Regardless, you will have to do the following to make the movie (or movies) and their associated clips available for use in Movie Maker:

1. With your video device securely attached to your PC, copy the files to your hard drive. If your device is perceived as an added disk drive, as with my Sony CyberShot digital camera, then you can use Windows Explorer, as described in the Relocating Files on Your Machine section in Hour 3. Otherwise, you may need to use the software that came with your video device, or the capture adapter or card (in the case of older analog devices). Your mission here is simply to get the content onto your PC's hard drive. For simplicity sake, you may want to put the files in the My Videos folder.

2. Next, you will need to import the files into Movie Maker. With Movie Maker up and running (click the Start button, then point to All Programs, Accessories, and click Windows Movie Maker), click File, Import from the Menu bar. A Select File to Import dialog box opens. You will immediately notice it looks a lot like any standard Open or Save As dialog box.

3. Click your way to the file you want to import and then double-click its name when you find it. Movie Maker takes a few moments to scan the file and create clips as needed (see Figure 24.2).

4. The selected file then appears by name in the My Collections window. You can view any clips Movie Maker generated by clicking the file's name. Images representing the resulting clips appear in the right Collections Area pane.

24

FIGURE 24.2
Pictures like these are the easiest way to get to know an application.

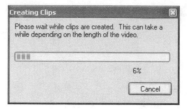

The movie and clips are now available for use in your current project. Repeat the steps above until all the video images you want to use can be viewed in the Collections area.

Pasting Clips Together

You can view the movie files as they exist on your hard drive, but you could have a whole lot of fun pasting clips together to make a real movie.

To get started, click View, Storyboard on the Menu bar. The Movie Maker workspace view now resembles a film where each clip you place eventually becomes an image on that film. This is the best way to see which clips are where in the movie you are piecing together.

Now, to move a clip into the project, click the applicable filename, click the image of the clip you want in the Collections area, and then drag it into the desired position on the Storyboard (the filmstrip-looking thingy). Don't forget: you can certainly use a clip more than once if you want.

> **I don't get it.** By default, Movie Maker divides a movie file into clips when the majority of the video's background changes in a single frame. This can be helpful for longer videos, but for shorter ones, it can be a real pain. To disable this feature, click View, Options on the Menu bar, and then clear the Automatically create clips option. Clicking OK dismisses the dialog.

If the file you want to use in your project is a single clip, simply click its filename in the My Collections pane and drag it onto the desired position on the Storyboard.

Trimming the Clips

You can shorten a clip by using Movie Maker's Timeline view. This is a great way to cut unwanted parts out of your clips. You should also know that any changes made to the clips are saved in the project files. The source files are not modified in any way, so enjoy!

To trim your clips, follow these steps:

1. First, you will need to click View, Timeline to change the workspace view.

2. Next, click the clip you want to shorten. You will see that the clip's image is outlined in blue, its duration on the project timeline is shaded, and two gray trim handles appear at either end of the clip's timeline (see Figure 24.3).

Trim Handles

FIGURE 24.3
Trim your clips as desired using the trim handles.

3. To begin trimming, run your mouse over one of the trim handles until it becomes an east/west double-headed arrow. (Obviously, you will click the left handle to trim from the front of the clip or the right handle to trim from the end of the clip.) This ensures that you are in the right position to grab the trim handle. To make the trim, click and drag the handle in the desired direction and then release it in place. You can use the elapsed time as a guide or keep an eye on the monitor that displays the frames you are dealing with as you drag the trim handle.

> **Double-check your work.** To verify that the clip meets with your approval, click the Play button in the Monitor. Only the selected clip will play.

Repeat as necessary to get all your clips to the desired length.

Rearranging the Clips

As you work with the project, you may discover that you want to move a clip from one spot to another. That is what makes working with a computer so great—you can move it with ease.

To relocate a clip, you will first need to enter Storyboard view by clicking View, Storyboard. Next, click the image of the clip you want to move and drag it across the filmstrip. See the dark line that moves as you drag the clip? This is where the click will be placed when you release the mouse button.

Adding Cross-Fade Transitions

Isn't it neat how real movies fade out of one scene and gradually fade into another? Well, you can do that, too. Movie Maker gives you the ability to fade out of and into adjoining clips by entering the Trimline view and then clicking and dragging the second clip so it over laps the first clip.

You can overlap the two clips as much as you want, but keep in mind that the audio tracks will be overlapped as well, potentially making it confusing and just plain noisy if it is not done effectively.

After the desired transitions are in place, click Play, Play Entire Storyboard/Timeline to view the whole sequence of clips in the monitor.

Saving Your Work

The two kinds of saves you will need to perform in Movie Maker are Save Project and Save Movie.

Remember how I said a project held links to your video files? Well, saving a project means that the files you have chosen to work with for the current project will stay intact as will the edits you have made to them (trims, fades, and so on). When you click File, Save Project, you will have the opportunity to save these elements so you can go back and work with them at any point.

Saving a Movie, however, splices all your work together to create a final product. When you click File, Save Movie, you will see a dialog box similar to the one shown in Figure 24.4.

FIGURE 24.4

You can add a title or description to your video.

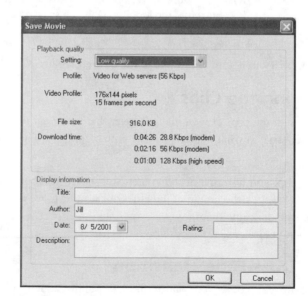

At the top of the dialog box, you will see a drop-down box from which you can choose the quality of your movie. You can choose a low-quality version for play on a Web server or a high-quality version for playing on your PC. The estimated download times at various Internet connection speeds appear halfway down the dialog box.

You will notice that Movie Maker filled in the author and date for you, but you can also title the movie, describe it, or give it a rating.

When you are finished filling out the box, click OK. You will be taken to a standard Save As–like dialog box where you will give the movie a filename. Movie Maker will attempt to provide one for you, which you can keep or type in an appropriate one, and then click the Save button. Movie Maker displays a status box like the one in Figure 24.5 to let you know your movie is indeed being made.

FIGURE 24.5

It may take a while to pull everything together, but soon you will be able to enjoy the fruits of your labor.

 Good things come to those who wait. The higher the quality of video you are making, the longer it will take Movie Maker to pull it all together.

When the job is done, Movie Maker asks you if you want to watch the movie you just made. Click Yes or No as desired. If you click Yes, Windows Media Play opens and plays the movie.

Creating a Soundtrack for Your Movie

As they say in nearly every infomercial, "But wait, there's more!" You can add a special soundtrack to your movie, too. Maybe you want to narrate your son's Little League game or make a music video of your daughter dancing to the latest Britney Spears track. Perhaps you want to create an anniversary movie for a special couple containing wedding video footage with "their song" playing as the soundtrack. The possibilities are almost endless.

Movie Maker makes it a piece of cake to do any of these things.

Recording a Narrative

If you have a microphone that connects to your PC, you are in business. The good news is just about any microphone will do, since computers have a standard-size mic jack.

To begin recording a voice narrative track for your movie, just follow these steps:

1. Launch Movie Maker with your work in progress and plug in your microphone.
2. Enter Timeline view by clicking View, Timeline.
3. To the left end of the Timeline workspace, you will see a tiny button with a microphone on it. Click it to open the Record Narration Track dialog box shown in Figure 24.6.

FIGURE 24.6

You can monitor the elapsed time of your recording on this dialog box.

4. You should see the words "Mic Volume" next to the Line: item. If those words don't appear, you will need to click the Change button and select Mic Volume from the Input Line drop-down box; then click OK.

> **Make it good!** In Hour 21, *Getting Sights and Sounds on Your Computer,* I presented some tips for making sound recordings on your computer. Now might be a great time to review them.

5. When you are ready to begin recording, click the Mute Video Soundtrack option and then click the Record button. You will see the elapsed counter works its way up, and the video plays on the Movie Maker monitor so you can see what you are narrating.
6. To end the recording, click the Stop button. You will be prompted to give the recording a filename and to save it. Do as instructed and then click Save. The narrative will appear in the Collections area with its own special sound icon.

7. Move the narrative to your project's soundtrack by clicking and dragging the narrative's icon into the Soundtrack workspace (the thin white area just beneath the images on the project's Timeline.

8. You can tweak the balance of sound by clicking the Set Audio Levels button, which resides just below the microphone button. Just click and drag the lever button toward more audio or more video sound as desired and then click the Close (X) button.

Remember to save your project. At this point, you can even save the movie as described above if you are happy with it.

Adding Tunes to Your Movie

Believe it or not, adding music to your video is even easier. Just record the song as you would in Windows Media Player (flip back to Hour 21 if you need a quick refresher) and then in Movie Maker, click File, Import. Navigate to the sound file you want and then double-click its name or icon.

The file and sound icon appear in the Collections area. To add it to your movie, click and drag it down to the Soundtrack bar (the thin white bar just below the Timeline images). Remember to set the audio levels by clicking the bottom button on the left side of the Timeline. Click and drag the lever to favor video audio or your chosen audio soundtrack. Save your project; then save the actual movie when you like what you see.

Summary

Working with images, sounds, and movies on your PC can be a tremendous amount of fun. It is also a great way to preserve videos that might otherwise fade or wear out over time. Imagine a CD of your wedding video, and in time, we will even be able to record our own DVDs. Again, here, we could only scratch the surface with this nifty tool, but it gives you enough to get started.

Sadly, this concludes our tour through computer basics. You should be armed with everything you need in order to fully enjoy your new PC. Please drop me a line to say hello and tell me what you thought about the book (JFreeze@JustPC.com). Do you like the de-emphasis of hardware in favor of fun things like instant messaging, digital photography, and other aspects, or would you rather learn about how a PC works? Please let us know what you liked or didn't like so we can make the best book possible. Your opinions DO count!

Unlike many authors, I take the time to answer every e-mail message personally. It may take me a while if I'm in the heat of another book, but each one eventually gets attention. After all, if it weren't for my readers, I wouldn't be doing this at all! :-)

Take care and happy computing!

24

Workshop

Now it's time to see just how much you learned in this lesson. I'll give you a short multiple-choice quiz to test what you learned, followed by a suggested activity designed to enhance the skills you acquired during the hour.

Quiz

Select the best answer to the questions from the choices provided and then check your answers.

Questions

1. What should your video subject wear for best results?

    a. A solid color that stands out from the background but is not so bright that it causes color bleeding.

    b. A thin, striped turquoise and fuchsia shirt that is guaranteed not to get lost in the background.

    c. Wear something similar in color and pattern to the background so that people see your face and not your clothes.

2. How are clips trimmed in Movie Maker?

    a. You can't trim them. What you see is what you get!

    b. Enter Timeline view and then click and drag the trim handles.

    c. You have to trim the clips in Media Play, not Movie Maker.

3. What do you call the clip transition Movie Maker uses?

    a. Now You See It, Now You Don't.

    b. Cross-Fade.

    c. Fade to Black.

Answers

1. A offers the best results. The others will either give you a headache or cause your video device to combust while trying to focus.

2. The best way to get the job done is B.

3. B and C were the only logical choices here. B was the correct answer, however.

Activity

There is a lot more to Movie Maker than we could cover in an hour. Glance through the Movie Maker help files to see what else you can do with this fun tool!

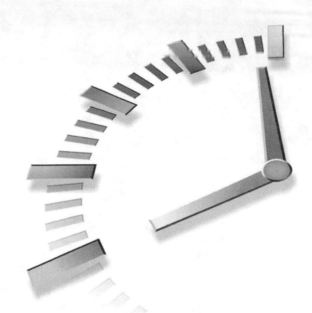

PART V
Appendixes

Appendix

APPENDIX A

Optimizing Game Performance

Think of this as a bonus chapter of sorts. After all, who among us hasn't wanted to lengthen the 24-hour day at one point or another?

In this bonus lesson, you will learn about various gadgets, controllers, joysticks, and other add-ons you can buy to make your computer gaming experience more fun and sometimes even more authentic. I will also show you how to take advantage of Windows XP, Home Edition's Compatibility Mode, which helps games designed for previous versions of Windows run more smoothly.

Let the Fun Begin: Joysticks and Other Game Controllers

People buying computers for the first time will often mention many different reasons why they want one. Balancing the checkbook and organizing recipes usually top the list, as if you really need to rationalize this important decision!

After the computer is home, however, it ends up being used for two main purposes: surfin' the Internet and playing computer games. Even if the computer was purchased to help educate the kids, game playing becomes one of its biggest uses.

Although some games are easily played with a mouse and keyboard, most of them benefit from having a specialized gaming control such as a joystick or gamepad. It helps to make playing the game more realistic and accurate over using a keyboard and mouse.

Not every game needs a joystick. The Sims, Black & White, and many other games need only your keyboard and mouse for effective game play.

The Joy of Joysticks

The classic game control is the joystick. Joysticks have been used with personal computers since the 1970s. They allow you to provide accurate input to the computer in two dimensions.

Computer joysticks are modeled after the flight controls of a fighter aircraft and often include triggers, buttons, and switches that allow you to perform many different functions. Joysticks are mostly used in flight simulator games such as Microsoft's Flight Simulator 2002 or in a variety of driving games to make steering a bit easier. Racing games even have steering wheels, as you will see later in this bonus lesson, but they can be a lot more expensive than your average joystick.

In a combat flying game, you don't want to spend your time hunting for keys on your keyboard to unleash a weapon; you may get shot down while searching for the radar key on your keyboard! The buttons on the joystick allow you to perform some of the most commonly used functions in your aircraft, without looking for the correct keys on your keyboard.

Come on over to my 'pad! Joysticks can be used in other games like many of the first-person combat games, but you may want to use a gamepad instead. Driving games such as Midtown Madness 2 and NASCAR Heat also support joysticks, although you may find a steering wheel more enjoyable.

The Force (Feedback) Be With You!

The latest trend in joysticks is to include force feedback to help you feel what is happening in the game. It builds on the concept of the rumble packs used for game consoles like the Nintendo 64 or the Sony Playstation 2, but provides a much more realistic experience. When you are flying a plane that is getting pelted, you can "feel" the bullets hit you. When you try to enter a loop, you will feel the joystick fighting you every step of the way.

The biggest downside to a force feedback joystick is the cost. Most force feedback joysticks (or at least the nice ones worth owning) cost close to $100. Less expensive ones are available, but they can produce an unimpressive watered-down effect. If you are a hard-core gamer with lots of flying games, you may want to invest in the best force feedback joystick out there. However, if you have only one flight simulation game in your huge collection of games, the expense may not be worth it.

Force feedback joysticks also make playing first-person air combat games, such as Microsoft Combat Flight Simulator 2, much more authentic and enjoyable because you can feel the bullets hitting your plane as you get shot. You may also feel your hand jerking back as you pull the trigger on your own gun. Okay, obviously getting shot isn't enjoyable in the literal sense, but force feedback effects can increase the thrill factor for gamers.

Who needs the distraction? Although force feedback joysticks provide a more realistic experience, they also can be distracting. You may not want to use one when your goal is to win. This is especially true if you compete against other players online. As with a lot of things, however, it is all a matter of personal preference.

Flight Controllers, Flight Yokes, and Rudder Pedals

A flight controller is a device that allows you to control the throttle of your airplane. In addition, flight controllers also have a number of switches and buttons. These switches and buttons allow you to perform a number of different functions such as switching from one weapon to another, raising and lowering flaps and landing gear, and switching radar modes. The switches and buttons on a flight controller complement the switches and buttons on a joystick, so you focus on what is happening in a game rather than searching for keys on your keyboard.

If your main interest is flying commercial jets or general aviation aircraft, you may want to consider a flight yoke. A flight yoke is similar to a steering wheel, but in addition to turning left or right, it also moves in and out. Most commercial aircrafts use yokes instead of joystick-like controls, making your virtual flying experience a bit more authentic. Even some real combat aircraft, such as the P-38 Lightning, use yokes instead of sticks. As far as your game is concerned though, a joystick and a flight yoke are identical, so which one you prefer to use is really up to you.

To complete your flight experience, a set of rudder pedals is absolutely necessary. Although you can control your virtual airplane with just a joystick or flight yoke, a real airplane also uses a set of rudder pedals, since an airplane moves in three dimensions instead of two. When you don't have a set of rudder pedals, most flight games will automatically control the rudder for you. Although this is fine in most situations, you do lose a little bit of the realism without them.

They are a must! Rudder pedals are critical for any serious flight simulators that use piston powered airplanes, especially the air combat games.

Get Real with Steering Wheels

If you think you can beat Jeff Gordon in a NASCAR race, you gotta get a steering wheel! A steering wheel makes your driving game much easier to play (and win). Using the keyboard makes for choppy control, and a joystick doesn't quite "handle" like a steering wheel.

A steering wheel includes a gearshift for you to control your driving gears. Sometimes a steering wheel package comes with a gas and brake pedal combination to make the game play more realistically. Also, some steering wheels include force feedback to make your driving experience even more realistic. You can feel those bumpy roads, fight the car while making a sharp turn on gravel roads, hustle to bring a car back under control after a major crash, and so on.

For the more unreal drive. Many people find gamepads easier to use on some driving games, especially the games that don't try to provide a realistic driving experience. They offer a bit more subtle control than a keyboard alone, and they provide control that nearly mimics game consoles like Sony's Playstation 2.

Gamepads: Turning Your PC into a Nintendo

Gamepads, as mentioned earlier, are similar to the controls you find on a Nintendo 64 or Sony Playstation 2. They are full of buttons and pads that allow you to choose multiple directions for game movement. These buttons make it easier to play sports games such as FIFA 2002. They can also be used with many other types of games.

Before You Buy

Choosing a game controller is a highly personal matter. There are many different models from which to choose. If possible, try out the controller in the store before you purchase one. While you are trying it out, you should consider the following things:

- See how the controller feels in your hand. Is it comfortable to hold? If you are left-handed, is the joystick optimized for a right-handed person? It may be uncomfortable then.

- Does the joystick base stay flat when you move the joystick to the extreme limits? In most combat flying games, you will find yourself moving from one extreme to another. A wide, heavy base is in order here.

- Decide if the buttons and switches are easy to reach and use. Try to reach buttons and switches without looking at them, because when you are playing your game, you will be watching the screen and not your game controller.

- If you are buying a flight control system, make sure that it is compatible with your joystick. Generally, you are going to want to buy the flight control system from the same company that made your joystick.

- When buying rudder pedals or automobile pedals, are the pedals so close together that they are difficult to use? Likewise, are the pedals so far apart that they don't fit easily under your desk or table where your computer rests?

- Make sure that the controller is compatible with your system. Obviously, if you don't have a universal serial bus (USB) port on your machine, don't get a USB game controller. Such ports are pretty common now with printers, scanners, and digital cameras all making use of these special outlets. You'll need to check your PC's documentation to see just how many you have available. For example, if you only have one port which is being used by your printer, you may not want to be connecting and disconnecting the printer every time you play a joystick-enabled game.

- Does the joystick support the game you want to play? Although a simple joystick is supported by nearly all games, the same may not be true of your new force feed-back joystick. Nothing is worse than paying a lot of money for a gizmo you can't use.

- Does DirectX support your new game controller? As more and more games come to rely on DirectX support, this is an increasingly important issue. You don't want to invest in an older, less expensive game controller today, only to replace it in a year or two because DirectX, a technology on which most of today's hottest games rely doesn't support it.

A

Adding a New Game Controller to Your Machine

The two types of game controllers you can connect to a PC are port controllers and USB devices. Game port controllers have a long 15-pin socket for plugging into your PC's game port, and USB devices plug into any available USB port on your machine.

As a rule, USB devices tend to offer a bit better performance than their game port counterparts. However, the biggest appeal is the fact that although many computers have only one game port, newer PCs have multiple USB plugs, thus making it easier to have multiple devices hooked to your PC at once.

With USB devices more prevalent these days, let's take a look at how to install a USB device. You can simply plug the device securely into your computer. Windows XP, Home Edition works to automatically identify the device for you. Ah, the wonders of plug-and-play devices!

Is There a Problem with Your Device?

If the device is not automatically detected or doesn't perform as expected, Windows XP's Hardware Troubleshooter may be just what the doctor ordered.

To access the troubleshooter, click the Start button and then click the following links in this order: Help and Support, Fixing a Problem, Hardware and system device problems, Hardware Troubleshooter.

The troubleshooter appears on the right side of the screen. You will see a series of questions to help pinpoint the problem. Answer each one by clicking the appropriate answer button and then click the Next button to continue.

Follow the onscreen directions to resolve the problem.

Solving Game Problems

Few things are as frustrating as installing a cool game and finding it doesn't work. Of course, there are literally dozens of reasons the game may not be working. The problem could be as simple as adjusting your monitor's resolution or as complex as requiring you to download and install a newer version of DirectX. You may even have to run the program under the Windows XP Compatibility Mode.

The first step in resolving the problem, of course, is to properly diagnose it. Windows XP has a special troubleshooter to help you get your games up and running—the Games and Multimedia Troubleshooter.

To begin using it, click the Start button and then click the following links: Help and Support, Fixing a problem, Game, Sound, and Video Problems and on the right side of the screen, Games and Multimedia Troubleshooter.

Once again, the troubleshooter will lead you through a series of questions to help you hone in on the problem. Once the problem has been isolated, you will be given directions on how to resolve it. Just follow the onscreen prompts.

Introducing the Program Compatibility Wizard

Microsoft has gone to great lengths to make sure the most popular computer games run correctly under Windows XP, but some older programs designed for previous editions of Windows could fall through the cracks.

If you happen to run across a rare game that doesn't work properly under Windows XP, you can run the program in something referred to as Compatibility Mode. While running in Compatibility Mode, your PC emulates the environment of previous versions of Windows, thus enabling older games to run as designed.

To run the Compatibility Wizard, follow these steps:

1. Click the Start button and then click Help and Support, Find Compatible Hardware and Software for Windows XP; then in the See Also section of the navigation pane, click the Program Compatibility Wizard link.

2. The first screen of the wizard simply explains the purpose of the wizard. Click Next to move to the first step in the wizard.

3. You will need to tell the wizard how you want it to locate the program in question: from a list of programs installed on your machine, from the game CD, or by manually navigating to the program file. Click Next when you have chosen the desired option.

4. Since the steps you follow from here will vary greatly, simply follow the onscreen prompts. When you find the setting that works best, Windows XP will save it and then launch the program every time using those special settings.

With all these tips and tricks handy, you should have a fulfilling gaming experience on your PC whether you picked up the hottest new simulation game on the market, or you've taken a fancy to older PC classic title like the original SimCity, the first Duke Nukem, and so on!

A

APPENDIX B

So You Want to Purchase a Computer?

Many of the people who read this book will have already purchased a PC, but just in case you are still in the research phase, the following are some things to consider before you make the big investment:

- **Know what you want to do with the machine**. What is your primary reason for purchasing a PC? Are you looking for a high-powered gaming platform? Do you want to surf the Web? Will you be bringing work home from the office?

  If the latest and greatest games are what you want, sink your money into the best machine you can afford. Games are constantly on the cutting edge of bigger technology, so you will want as much room to grow as you can possibly get. An upgraded video card may make a noticeable difference for flight simulators, racing games, and so on. Of course, you will also want a full multimedia setup and plenty of RAM. You can never have too much RAM! In fact, you may want to sit at a sweet 256k for a Windows XP system, especially if you will be sharing the machine with someone else.

For the Net surfers among us, investigate the high-speed Internet connection possibilities in your area before making a purchase. If, for example, you have cable modem service available at an affordable rate, you may very well want to consider getting that instead of a more traditional Internet connection. This means that the standard modem that comes with machines is virtually useless to you, so you may want to swap it out for more RAM, since you will most likely get the cable modem from the service provider. Again, a multimedia setup is a plus, but there is no real need for a fancy video card for the Net.

If work is prompting you to make the purchase, then the software bundled with the PC may sway you one way or another. Obviously, if your company uses Microsoft Office XP, you will probably want to choose a machine that comes with Office XP (or at the very least, Microsoft Word 2002 with the inclusion of Excel 2002 even better). No matter what the advertised retail value of a software bundle is, it has no real value for you if you can't make use of it.

- **When it comes to monitors, try before you buy**. It's tempting to go after the largest monitor on the market, but not only is that an expensive option, but it may also not be the best one for you.

When it comes to monitors, there is a lot to consider. First is the price. Upgrading to that big, fancy flat panel monitor may cost you hundreds more, and the sheer size of some of these monsters is nothing to take "lightly." You can't set these huge 22-inch anvils on just any old desk! They need a large, well-supported, commercial-rated surface. Most importantly, the viewing quality/area gained by the increased monitor size may be a lot less than you think. For example, I tested various screen resolutions on 17-, 19-, and 21-inch monitors at a local store before ordering my newest PC. I opted for the 19-inch display. There was noticeable improvement over the 17-inch, and it was $600 less than the 21-inch. The 21-inch monitor just didn't offer $600 more in value in my opinion, but your experience may differ. I strongly suggest you try out some monitors before making a final decision.

- **Read the fine print**. Offering a $99 (or even free) PC with a three-year Internet service commitment has become quite the marketing ploy lately. Although it may look like a great deal on the surface, you may not get what you are expecting.

Before you take advantage of such a deal, get answers to the following questions: (1) How much is the Internet service per month? Around $20-$25 is standard for a basic personal account these days. If it is more than that, beware. (2) Are the fees paid monthly, or as one lump sum up front? (3) What happens if you break your contract? Perhaps you may move within the three years, or maybe the constant inability to connect to the Net because of busy signals frustrates you. At any rate, you should know your rights and any potential penalties.

- **When a deal isn't a deal**. Many electronic superstores offer PC packages complete with scanner and color printer. Although these are both fun accessories, they may not be the models you want. These bonuses tend to be entry-level equipment, which may be fine in a number of cases, but if you have dreams of printing photos or making t-shirt transfers on that new color printer, you may want something better. Do some price checking of the individual components as well, because you may find the package deal isn't the financial bargain manufacturers make it out to be.

- **The desktop versus laptop dilemma.** Unless you are on the road a lot and need to take your computer with you, a desktop will give you much more machine for your money. Additionally, laptops lag behind desktops in terms of speed of processors, so if you really need speed and performance (and computer game fanatics often do), a laptop may not cut it. However, if you live in a small space, a laptop may suit you quite well, since it doesn't take up much space. Just bear in mind that while the price of laptops has dropped dramatically, it's still only moderately competitive with its desktop counterpart.

- **Know the warranty and availability of technical support**. When you buy your first computer, sometimes it helps you feel at ease to know that it has a good warranty. Get the longest parts warranty you can find when choosing where to make your purchase. Also make sure the manufacturer's technical support is available to you during the hours you use your new PC most. If it isn't, it is of no value to you.

  As for those add-on warranties you see, they can be terrific values or awesome rip-offs. Considering a monitor's replacement cost, paying $70 to only protect it for three years is not the value that you can find on warranties for your whole system. The $19.95 I paid to protect my daughter's desktop system from Sam's Club for three years was a real bargain.

- **If you can only afford to upgrade one thing**. Put your money into more RAM. That will give you the most noticeable difference performance-wise. Bumping up your PC's processor speed a notch or two may not return an improvement you can see for anyone but the power user or cutting-edge game guru. Extra RAM will come in handy no matter what the task.

B

APPENDIX C

Getting Your New Computer Ready for Action

After you get your new PC home, there are some things you should consider doing to maximize both the life of your computer, and your comfort at the keyboard.

- **Save it!** Computers generally come packed in large boxes with lots of padding, whether you mail order the PC or simply pick it up at your local wholesale club. Although these boxes are indeed cumbersome to store, there may come a time when you may appreciate having the original packaging around. Suppose that your monitor dies and you need to send it back to the manufacturer for replacement or repair. Finding a box big and sturdy enough to do the job may be harder than you ever anticipated. What if you need to move cross-country? You certainly wouldn't want to put your computer onto a moving van unprotected! Instead of throwing the boxes away, consider storing something in them along with the packing material. That way, you have an extra place to stash your clutter, but you are still ready to pack your PC up safely if need be.

- **Chill out or do some warm-ups!** If your PC was shipped or hauled home during times of colder temperatures, you should give the console and monitor time to adapt to the temperature in your home before turning it on. A vast majority of central processing unit (CPU) failures happen when a machine is turned on. Equipment that experiences extreme changes in temperature is especially prone to malfunction, so give it a little time. Even as little as two hours can make all the difference in the world.

- **Get some support!** Before unpacking your PC, double-check the stability of the surface on which you plan to set it up. If it is a heavy folding table (such as a banquet table), make sure that the braces are locked in place. If it is a desk, look underneath the desktop to help you find the sturdiest place for the monitor. Putting a huge monitor on a fragile, unsupported desk return could spell big trouble for both the desk and the PC, not to mention your feet and knees if they're underneath it at the time of the big collapse!

- **Look at the big picture**. This is something you may even want to do before you get the new PC. Go to the desk/table on which you plan to put the computer to do a lighting check. What you are trying to determine is whether direct sunlight will hit the computer's screen. Checking the lighting at various times of the day is ideal, but it is most important that you check it at the time you think you will be using the PC the most. Direct sunlight hitting your monitor can make it impossible to see the screen, so it is better that you discover any problems before you hook everything up.

- **Check with the powers that be**. Take a look around your work area and make sure that you have an adequate power supply. Try to have dedicated outlets for your PC instead of sharing the outlets with your hair dryer, VCR, and other small appliances. Overloading your home's wiring can result in blown fuses or electrical fires.

- **Suppress the surge!** Invest in one of those surge protectors for your new PC. That way, you can plug the monitor, the console, and the printer all into one power supply that you can control with a single switch. If you can, find a surge protector with a built-in phone line outlet so that you can protect your equipment from all angles. Whatever you do, make sure you are getting a rated surge protector. A simple power strip will do no good in an electrical storm. You can get a plain old power strip for as little as $2 or $3, but a good surge protector goes for $30 or more. This is one item on which you may want to splurge. If you have a TV tuner card in your PC that will be connected to a cable cord, you will want to make sure it is run through a surge protector, too. Basically, any line from the outside going into your computer should be attached to a surge protector to reduce potential damage to your equipment.

- **Room to grow**. Something else to consider when setting up your workspace is storage. You will need to have a safe place to put all your software disks, a place where they will be free from dust and close at hand while you work. You will also want to have a special place for printer paper, spare ink cartridges, and computer books like this one. The documentation, receipts, and warranty slips that came with your machine should also be stored in a safe location.

- **Bottom's up!** If you intend to spend large amounts of time at your computer, a good office chair is worth its weight in gold. Not only does it keep your backside from falling asleep, but a good one will also support your back as you work. You can also adjust it to a comfortable height to reduce the likelihood of eye and wrist strain.

- **Ringing in your ears**. You will want to make sure a phone line outlet is close to your workspace. You will need it for your modem if you decide to connect to the Internet over the phone line. However, even if you don't intend to connect to the online world, having a phone that reaches your computer will be invaluable if you ever need to call technical support with a problem. With phone in hand, you can be prepared when they try to walk you through the diagnosis or solution to the problem.

> **Going cordless?** You may want to keep your cordless phone base/recharger away from your hard drive, since it can potentially wreak havoc with it. It is not a common problem but one you should be aware of nonetheless.

- **The old-fashioned way**. There are certainly a lot of high-tech ways to remind you to do something. You could get Outlook 2002 and begin using the calendar and alarm functions, or you could do it the old-fashioned way with sticky notes and a pen. I can guarantee that as soon as you get off the Internet, you will think of three things you meant to check out; it happens to me all the time! With a sticky note pad, you can write it down as soon as you think about it and then slap the note to the edge of your monitor. Now the information is there when you need it!

C

INDEX